DOUGLAS
PROPLINERS
DC-1–DC-7

DOUGLAS PROPLINERS
DC-1–DC-7

ARTHUR PEARCY

Airlife
England

Dedication

This volume is dedicated to my good friend, and the friend of many, Harry Gann, ex-Manager, Aircraft Information, with the Douglas Aircraft Company, Long Beach, California, who over several decades has served faithfully historians, the airline fraternity and many many more, with photos and information from the company archives which he maintains. His knowledge of the history of the company is second to none, his patience never ending and his search for the unknown fantastic. Without his steadfast help, this author alone could not adequately have completed any of the books connected with the company. Harry operated as a one man band, and is himself a tireless and keen aviation buff; he is also a keen photographer and has a unique record of flying with the famous 'Blue Angels' team over the years. He is a past President of the American Aviation Historical Society (AAHS) and a member of the Board of Directors of the Douglas Historical Foundation; he organises the two-weekly flights of the Douglas DC-2 airliner maintained by the Foundation on lease. Harry had been employed at Long Beach for nearly forty years, served in the US Army in Europe during the Second World War, being wounded, and hospitalised in the United Kingdom before returning home to the USA. He resides in Bahama Lane, Huntington Beach, with his wife Dee. One son is in the USAF, flying at least one tour as pilot on the McDonnell Douglas KC-10 tanker aircraft, a successful product of his father's company at Long Beach. In 1992 Harry retired from the company, but is still involved deeply in aviation history and photography.

Copyright © 1995 by Arthur Pearcy

First published in the UK in 1995
by Airlife Publishing Ltd

British Cataloguing in Publication Data
A catalogue record for this book
is available from the British Library

ISBN 1 85310 261 X

Printed in Singapore by Kyodo Printing Co. (S'pore) Pte Ltd.

Airlife Publishing Ltd.
101 Longden Road, Shrewsbury SY3 9EB, England

Contents

Foreword

by Sir Peter Masefield

IN ALL the annals of world air transport, one historic series of seven individual types of piston-engined aircraft stands out above all others. Those seven dominated the field and led the way forwards into the jet transport era.

For a quarter of a century – between May 1931 and October 1958 – Douglas Commercial aircraft (the first of the DCs) together comprised more than 60 per cent of the world's airline fleets. With them, for the first time, air transport began to make profits at fares which the public could afford.

In peace and in war the Magnificent Seven (DC-1 to DC-7) crossed the oceans and, reliably and economically, changed air transport from sparsely-used, short-haul operations to worldwide business, available to everyone.

In Arthur Pearcy, these historic seven aircraft have found a chronicler worthy of their attainments – an Englishman who brings a proper perspective to bear upon a great American contribution to world communications. This book is, indeed, further evidence of that 'special relationship' which has made Anglo-American co-operation, in every aspect of aviation, such a feature of more than eighty years of aeronautical progress.

I warmly commend this book for its detailed research, for its wealth of factual information and for its fine illustrations. It is a worthy tribute to the design, development, production and operating teams which brought more than 15,000 Douglas piston-engined aircraft into airline service and to military transport operations, throughout the world.

In the way that things evolve in human affairs, the genesis of the Douglas Commercial line of transport aircraft can be traced back, on the West Coast of the United States, to the first of the classic formula of American twin-engined, low-wing, all-metal monoplanes, with retractable landing gear – to the one and only Boeing Model 215/246 (B-9 bomber), built and paid for by its originators, and first flown, in civil colours, on 13 April 1931.

From the B-9 came the twin-engined, ten-passenger, low-wing Boeing 247D, built specifically for United Air Lines and first flown on 8 February 1933, six months after Jack Frye, Vice-President (Operations) of TWA alerted to its impending arrival, had written round to five United States aircraft manufacturers – including Douglas – with an invitation, a challenge and a commercial opportunity to match – or to beat – this prospective leap forwards in civil aircraft technology.

That challenge and that opportunity were eagerly accepted by Donald Douglas and his team. It led, step by step, not only to the 'Magnificent Seven', but, onwards, in due course, to their successors of the jet age, from the DC-8 to the MD-12 – with more to come.

Look here at these aircraft – in brief summary – whose story Arthur Pearcy has recorded in detail in this fine book:

The first – the twelve-passenger DC-1 prototype of 1933. It brought forward in one classic aircraft all the most advanced features of the day: aerodynamics, structures, cabin layout and power plant – features which still can be seen in their developed forms in the latest transport aircraft of sixty years later.

The fourteen-passenger DC-2 of 1934, of which almost 200 were built. It brought the concept of the smaller DC-1 to production reality, although lacking refinement in its economic and flying characteristics, but putting into practice 'the new idea'. It won for Douglas an unchallenged place among the world's major aircraft constructors.

The twenty-one-passenger DC-3 of 1935, of which more than 13,000 were built. It remains one of the great aircraft of all time. In the words of Bill Littlewood of American Airlines, one of its instigators, 'The DC-3 was the first airplane to show clearly a potential profit – enough payload and speed at reasonable ranges, and established rates (and low enough operating costs) to give an assured margin.' Thus it made possible, for the first time, the earning of profits by the world's airlines, and – in military form – it helped to win the Second World War.

The forty-four-passenger DC-4/C-54 of 1942 – after a false start with a larger DC-4E in 1938 – launched wartime, long-range, military air services and – with the Lockheed C-69 Constellation, as four-motor transports, opened up the oceans to universal, reliable and safe international air transport.

The sixteen-passenger DC-5 of 1939 (twelve built), an early move towards regional air transport – ahead of its day, its development restricted by the outbreak of war.

The fifty-two-passenger DC-6 of 1946 (706 built). It became, in successive developments, the most economic, long-range transport aircraft of its day.

The sixty-two-passenger DC-7 of 1953 (338 built), the ultimate, fast, long-range, piston-engined transport aircraft capable of flying non-stop between London and New York, cruising at around 340 mph.

The fact is that, together, this outstanding group of seven aircraft marked a leap forwards in performance and economy, the likes of which had not been seen before. They marked both the start of a new era in air transport and, twenty-four years later, the end of the piston-engine phase which had brought the business of aviation steadily forward from the Wright brothers to the wholly new horizons opened up by the concept of the jet engines brought about by Frank Whittle and Hans von O'Hain.

Aircraft are, of course, only as good as the competence and inspiration of the people who make and operate them. Those pioneering Douglas aircraft owe their origins, and their success, to a remarkable group of design, development and production engineers and administrators. Their names deserve to be remembered in aviation history.

Foremost among them was, of course, Donald Douglas himself, President of the Douglas Aircraft Company Inc. There were three chief lieutenants, Harry Wetzel (Vice-President and General Manager), 'Dutch' Kindelberger (Vice-President Engineering) and Arthur Raymond (Chief Engineer).

With them must be mentioned – in alphabetical order – seven of the inspired team: Lee Atwood (chief of stress analysis), Ed Burton (design layout), Fred Herman (project engineer), Arthur Klein (aerodynamics), Clark Millikan (aerodynamics), Jack Northrop (structures), Bailey Oswald (aerodynamics), and Ivar Shogran (power plant).

From the airlines there were: from TWA, Howard Hughes and Jack Frye; from American Airlines, C.R. Smith, Bill Littlewood, Dan Beard and Frank Kolk.

I had the pleasure of knowing them all.

The great thing about this book is that it gathers together – in an accurate, readable and comprehensive form – the story of the conversion of air transport from an unreliable, short-haul, loss-making business into one of the world's great industries, – an industry which, more than any other, has had a profound influence upon human progress.

Douglas Aircraft did not, of course, do it alone. But they were one of the prime instigators of this transport revolution.

Arthur Pearcy has splendidly encapsulated the unique Douglas contribution.

Reigate
Surrey

Acknowledgements

The great fame generated by the ubiquitous Douglas DC-3 over the years since 1935, has tended for the many accomplishments of the remainder of the Douglas Commercial series, before and after, to be forgotten. This is despite the fact that all but the DC-1 and DC-5 survive today, if only in reduced numbers, many still revenue-earning in remote corners of the globe as cargo transports or fire bombers. This is the story of the early Douglas Commercials built prior to the introduction of jet airliners, built by the company founded by Donald Wills Douglas Sr, who served as its guiding force up until the merger with Jim McDonnell. Donald Douglas and his California-based company were responsible for resurrecting commercial aviation out of the fabric-covered wood and wire aircraft, into an era of modern, safe, and reliable air transports. That era commenced with the unique DC-1, and continues today with the MD-80 and MD-11.

My first and most sincere thanks must go to the Douglas Aircraft Company and the many personnel who, over the past thirty-five years, have made Audrey and me so welcome at the Long Beach facility. Also for their continued encouragement and guidance with the books and other publications produced over the years on their products. Our very good friend Harry Gann allows me into the Douglas archives on each visit in my continued search for those interesting unknown photos, often finding them.

Sir Peter G. Masefield, a good friend of many years standing, kindly agreed to contribute the Foreword. He was a personal friend of the late Bill Littlewood of American Airlines, and Sir Peter kindly allowed me to use extracts from his mammoth paper *The First William Littlewood Memorial Lecture* which he delivered to the National Aviation Club in Washington, DC, on Friday 19 November 1971. For this concession I am more than grateful.

In addition to Harry Gann, Don Hanson, Director External Relations at Long Beach, and Andrew B. Wilson, Director International Public Relations at St Louis, have assisted in many ways.

Fortunately many of the world's airlines who operated the early Douglas Commercials still survive, despite the many problems facing commercial air transport operators. Many have assisted with rare photos etc and include: Denis Couture (Air Canada); R. S. Iyer (Air India); Tone G. Johannesen (Braathens); Dennis Fernandes (British Airways); Thomas R. Weight (Basler Turbo Conversions Inc.); Paulette D. O'Donnell (Delta Air Lines); Coert Munk, Maarten Brouwer (Dutch Dakota Association); M. Kroon and George Evelein (KLM); Liwa Chiu (Pan American Airways); J. Deschutter (Sabena); Gunnel Thorne-Nystrom (SAS); Marlyse Bartis and Barbara Burnstiel (Swissair); Bob Takis (American Airlines); Steven Le Beau and Mary Sue Hartmann (United Air Lines).

The private photograph collections of many friends who are aviation buffs, were placed at my disposal. These include, Peter M. Bowers, Edward J. Davies, Henry M. Holden, Frank A. Hudson, William T. Larkins, Robert C. Mikesh, Boardman C. Reed, Hans-Heiri Stapfer, Michael A. Prophet, Brian Pickering of Military Aircraft Photographs, Brian Stainer of Aviation Photo News, Charles A. Cooke in New Zealand and Bruce Potts in Australia.

Lastly to the Airlife Publishing Limited company team headed by Alastair Simpson, and John Beaton (Book Editor) who have guided and encouraged with the subject. My wife, partner and mentor, Audrey, the other member of the 'A' team, who accompanies me far and wide in search of material, and is a fully-fledged member. Even so, my grateful thanks for her inspiration, patience and vigilance.

My sincere apologies if I have omitted anyone – I assure you it was not intentional.

Introduction

In the history of the Douglas Aircraft Company, there is evidence of an impressive relationship between character and integrity on one hand, and accomplishment on the other. During the Second World War, the Douglas company produced 432 million pounds of airframes – almost 30,000 aircraft. It built 10,629 versions of the ubiquitous DC-3, designated the C-47/C-53 in the US Army Air Force, the R4D- in the US Navy and Marines, and Dakota in the RAF and Commonwealth Air Forces; and known affectionately as the 'Gooney Bird' by millions of GIs. At one point the Douglas Aircraft Company was turning out a C-47 transport every sixty-five minutes on a two-shift basis.

The year 1932 was a pivotal one for Douglas. In August, along with other companies including Boeing and Lockheed, it received a two-paragraph letter from Transcontinental & Western Air – TWA – asking for bids on an order of at least ten tri-motor transports. The historic letter specified an all-metal monoplane that could carry at least twelve passengers, cruise at 145 mph, have a landing speed not to exceed 65 mph and have a service ceiling of 21,000 feet.

Donald Douglas and his team decided to bid with a design that called for just two engines, but with a retractable landing gear, advanced engine cowling design and capable of carrying fourteen passengers. TWA liked the Douglas design and the result was the DC-1, the 'DC' standing for 'Douglas Commercial'. The DC-1 first flew on 1 July 1933.

The specification laid down by TWA was exceeded by large margins. The DC-1 had 20 per cent payload, a top speed of nearly 180 mph and a remarkable one-engine performance. TWA ordered twenty of an improved model called the DC-2. The long line of Douglas airliners or propliners, had begun. A total of 198 DC-2s were subsequently built; they served around the globe and became involved in both the Spanish Civil War, along with the one and only DC-1, and the Second World War.

Probably the best known of the Douglas Propliners is the DC-3. First flown on 17 December 1935, just thirty-two years after the Wright brothers made aviation history, it was a brilliant extrapolation of the DC-2. Initially with two 1,000 hp engines, it could carry twenty-one passengers and cruise at 195 miles per hour. It removed what was then one of the great obstacles to commercial flying – the danger that the airline would go broke. The late C.R. Smith, President of American Airlines, said it was the first airplane that could make money just by carrying passengers.

The Douglas DC-4 Skymaster was an outstanding success. It was the first Douglas four-engined transport, and was taken over by the US Army Air Force and the US Navy and Marines for service in the Second World War prior to seeing stalwart service with the postwar airlines of the world. It flew over the 'Hump' from India to China and was the workhorse of the Berlin Airlift. It operated in the first United Nations conflict in Korea and the first transport for the President of the United States, the *Sacred Cow*, was a Douglas DC-4. A total of 1,241 were built.

It was a Douglas DC-4 military transport which was converted for use by Winston Churchill when he became Prime Minister. Over seventy were built as the DC-4M in Canada by Canadair and powered by Rolls-Royce Merlin engines; in addition to operation by many airlines this model was used by the Royal Canadian Air Force. In the United Kingdom over twenty DC-4 transports were converted by Aviation Traders to ATL-98 Carvair standard, and served throughout the world.

Rarely remembered is the Douglas DC-5 – just as well, according to a Douglas Aircraft Company official who will remain nameless. A high-wing version of the DC-3, it was not successful and only twelve were built. It was ordered by both British Imperial Airways Ltd and KLM but the Second World War intervened; it was however operated by KNILM in the Far East, one DC-5 being captured by the Japanese and flight tested. The US Marine Corps operated the DC-5, and a possible claim to fame may be that one was sold to William E. Boeing.

Following a policy of conservative, evolutionary development, Douglas and his team now chalked up another success with the DC-6, the company's first transport with a pressurised cabin. It was also built in all-cargo and stretched versions, and like the DC-4 was chosen for the personal transport of the President of the United States, this time named *Independence*. It entered military service initially with the US armed forces, subsequently going to many foreign military air arms. Of the 704 built quite a number are still flying, some being used as fire bombers by the US Forest Service. In the United Kingdom two are used for charter work by Air Atlantique at Coventry, who also operate a fleet of venerable Dakota transports which will shortly number ten.

The DC-7 was the last of the Douglas piston-powered propliner transports. With turbo-compound engines, it achieved a maximum speed of 406 miles an hour, and its final production version, the DC-7C, was used successfully by BOAC and many other major world airlines. It proved a winner on long international routes. The DC-7, of which 338 were built, with its turbo-compound engines, clearly marked the furthest and final advance of piston-powered propeller airliners.

A span of twenty-five years covers the period from the first flight of the DC-1 to the delivery of the last DC-7 on 10 December 1958. Like the DC-6, many DC-7 are still in operation around the globe, and a number are in use by the US Forest Service as borate bombers.

Mention must be made of the Super DC-3, the DC-3S, which was an unsuccessful attempt to market a DC-3 replacement with a stretched version. However, the US Navy came to the rescue and in addition to the three civilian DC-3S transports operated by Capital Airlines, one hundred plus two privately-operated airliners were converted from R4D- airframes and operated successfully by the US Navy and Marines in both the Korean and Vietnam conflicts.

Today there appears to be a revival of the veteran DC-3 with models being reworked, refurbished and rebuilt, fitted with new avionics etc, and powered by the PT-6 turboprop engines. Six are currently either flying or being converted with the aid of kits in South Africa, while the El Salvadorian Air Force has taken delivery of two C-47 turbo-transports fitted out as gunships. Basler Turbo Conversions Inc. in the United States are involved in the turbo DC-3 conversion and at least one cargo operator flies cargo nightly between two cities in Texas. The DC-3 has also seen service in the sub-zero temperatures of Alaska. It is estimated that many DC-3s are still flying in all corners of the world with both military and civilian operators, a great tribute to men and machine alike. The Grand Ole Lady will celebrate her sixtieth birthday on 17 December 1995. There is a well-known adage repeated extensively by a respected DC-3 historian: 'The only replacement for a DC-3 is another DC-3.'

Douglas Commercials
First flights and numbers built

DC-1	1 July 1933	1
DC-2	11 May 1934	156
DC-3	17 December 1935	10,629
DC-4	14 February 1942	1,241
DC-5	20 February 1939	12
DC-6	29 June 1946	704
DC-7	18 May 1953	338

Grand total 13,081

One or two of the Douglas team are still alive, including my very good friend, Arthur E. Raymond, who today lives in the foothills north of Los Angeles. Dr Bailey Oswald also survives, whilst Donald W. Douglas Jr and his brothers retain the family name, but are no longer active in the business founded by their father. I myself was most fortunate in corresponding with Mr Donald W. Douglas Sr, though unfortunately we never met. Ed Heinemann, who supervised the engineering for the Douglas DC-5 died in December 1991.

This is the first ever exhaustive attempt to catalogue or compile a fully comprehensive volume covering the early Douglas Commercial series of aircraft. The series did of course continue into the jet age with the DC-8, DC-9 and DC-10. After that the original identity was lost with the introduction of the MD-80, MD-90 series and a new airliner, the MD-11. Surely the very fact that only the Douglas DC-1 and DC-5 do not survive speaks volumes for the impact on air transportation made by the Magnificent Seven.

Sharnbrook,
Bedfordshire

The Curtiss JN-4H Jenny of the US Army Air Service was used under contract to the US Post Office, making first flights on 15 May 1918 from New York to Washington DC. Power was a Wright Hispano 150hp engine; all-up-weight was 2,150lb, with a cruise speed of 75mph, range 250 statute miles. Wing span 44ft and length 27ft. Depicted is a Curtiss JN-4C. (AP Photo Library)

Chapter One

Air Transport – the Beginning

The world's first fare-paying passengers were carried over the 120 miles between Frankfurt and Düsseldorf, Germany, on 22 June 1910, in the trimotor Zeppelin airship LZ-7 **Deutschland** operated by Deutsche Luftschiffahrt Aktien Gesellschaft – DELAG, the first commercial air transport company. Twenty passengers paid 200 marks each for the flight. Prior to the outbreak of the First World War in 1914, a total of 35,000 people were carried.

There has been much controversy as to whether these pre-World War I services by DELAG can be claimed to be the world's first scheduled passenger air services. The suggestion is that they consisted of a series of unconnected joy-rides and pleasure flights, but this is difficult to support in the light of reliable statistics of the service. Between March 1912 and November 1913, 881 flights were completed, covering 65,000 miles, and with 19,100 passengers carried. This is an average of more than one flight per day and whilst many must have been excursion flights, undoubtedly many others formed a regular schedule over defined routes with the important feature that they made connections with the busy port of Hamburg.

In the wake of the Zeppelins and in the tenth year after the first tentative flight by the Wright brothers, the aeroplane began to develop substantially in size and in its ability to carry loads. A leap forwards came, not from the early pioneers in the United States, nor in France, Germany or the United Kingdom – but from Czarist Russia.

Igor Sikorsky, inspired by accounts of Wilbur Wright in France during 1908, was by 1912 employed in the aircraft subsidiary of the Society of Russian Baltic Railroad Car Factories at St Petersburg – later Leningrad, now St Petersburg once more. There, on 13 May 1913, he flew for the first time a new aeroplane of lasting significance – the huge four-engined, enclosed cabin, 92-foot span biplane S-7 Grand, or Bolshoi. This successful aeroplane, named '**Rosskii Knyaz**' or 'Russian Knight', was the ancestor of all multi-engined aircraft, and was a remarkable step forwards. Its direct development, the Ilia Mouroumetz of 1914, was put into production. More than seventy-five were built. But for the Russian Revolution, the Sikorsky might have inaugurated air transport services with enclosed cabin aircraft some years ahead of their actual time.

The first all-metal cabin airliner in Europe was the German-built Junkers F-13, designed specifically as a commercial airliner. Its body was of light, strong, corrugated steel, its wings were cantilevered to eliminate external bracing. Introduced in 1919, the F-13 ferried mining and oil-drilling equipment over South American jungles, and for nearly ten years formed the backbone of European airlines.

In the United States the most extraordinary feature of the early years of air transport was the hesitancy in recognising the aeroplane as a potential passenger vehicle. Geographical conditions were considered unfavourable, there being few over-water routes, and the large cities between which most traffic flowed were already served by luxurious Pullman trains. There was little reason for the US government to take a prominent part in promoting and pioneering a new form of transport for which there was apparently no great need.

Often forgotten is the comparatively slow speed of those aircraft in the early 1920s. Average speeds, including stops, were of the order of about 80 mph. This was not a spectacular improvement over the express trains. When interest in the United States finally crystallised, it was into exploring ways of using aeroplanes to improve US mail services, so the first six years of air transport history were taken up almost entirely with concentrated devotion to that cause, although there were also some passenger services.

During 1917 the United States Post Office received an appropriation of $100,000 for starting an experimental airmail service. The tenders were opened on 21 February 1918, and it was suggested that the US Army might supply aircraft to speed up the inauguration of the Air Mail. First flights took place on 15 May 1918, the first route being from New York to Washington DC via Philadelphia; it was considered a moderate success. Curtiss JN-4H 'Jennies' training aircraft discarded from military service were used, the normal letter rate being 24 cents, which included 10 cents special delivery. The average speed over the 218-mile route was 50-60 mph.

On 12 August 1918, the US Post Office took over the air mail service, using biplanes especially built by the Standard Aircraft Corporation. On 15 December postal rates were set at 6 cents per ounce. Early in 1919, the US Post Office took over one hundred war-surplus de Havilland DH-4Ms with metal fuselage framework and powered by Liberty engines, twelve Handley Page aircraft, also powered by Liberty engines, and twelve Glenn Martin aircraft. Plans were formulated for operating an efficient transcontinental airmail service with this substantial fleet.

Excellent close-up photograph showing the front of the Imperial Airways Handley Page HP.42E G-AAXE Hengist c/n 7 and parked at Croydon Airport, Surrey. It was destroyed by fire on 31 May 1937. (AP Photo Library)

The 2,600-mile transcontinental route schedule was maintained by a combination of day and night flying. On 22 February 1921, two aircraft left San Francisco and two left New York; one of those starting from San Francisco, flown by a relay team of pilots, reached New York after 33 hours 20 minutes flying time. This proved that the transcontinental air service was practicable, so work commenced on installing a system of lighting for night operations along the routes. A regular night mail service was inaugurated on the 1 July 1924. By 1926, the lighting system was extended to cover the whole route. A regular schedule of 34 hours 20 minutes westbound, and 29 hours 15 minutes eastbound was maintained. Pilots and aircraft were changed six times en route, at Cleveland, Chicago, Omaha, Cheyenne, Salt Lake City and Reno.

However by 1926 the end of the US Post Office Air Mail was in sight. A year before, on 2 February 1925, the Air Mail Act known familiarly as the 'Kelly' Act had been passed by Congress, to provide for the transfer of airmail service to private operators, under a scheme of competitive bidding, for a period of four years. The bids were advertised on 15 November 1926 and on 15 January 1927, and the contract for the section Chicago to Cheyenne was granted jointly to the Boeing Airplane Company and Edward Hubbard. On 8 March 1927, the Chicago to New York section was awarded to National Air Transport, followed on 28 March by the joint contract west of Chicago being turned over to Boeing Air Transport.

By the time the last Post Office mail flight took place on 1 September 1927, more than ten million miles had been flown, and seven million pounds of mail carried, reaching a maximum of 67,875,000 letters in 1923. The total cost over nine years of operation was some fifteen million dollars. Standard aircraft equipment had been the de Havilland DH-4 built in the USA and fitted with Liberty engines. Each pilot was assigned a DH-4 for his exclusive use. Complete overhauls were carried out every 750 flying hours, with engine overhaul every hundred hours.

Airmail contracts started air transport in the US on its way to becoming a major industry and a massive part of national and international economic progress. However, the transfer of the airmail routes to private contractors did not produce an immediate airline industry. The contracts were for airmail only, the US government having no concern for passengers. In addition the aircraft had no room for passengers, although some operators allowed a fare-paying passenger to ride on top of the mail sacks in mid-1926 and early 1927.

Seen parked at Spokane Airport, Washington State on 15 August 1935 is an 18-passenger Boeing 80A-1 three-engined airliner which was able to operate safely over the two high and rugged mountain ranges on the route between Chicago and San Francisco. It was powered by three Pratt & Whitney Hornet engines, had an all-up weight of 16,500lb, carried 12 passengers and flew at 120mph. It had a span of 80ft and length was 55ft. (C. K. McHarg)

The first true mail and passenger transport was the Boeing 40A, a redesign of Boeing's 1925 Post Office contest entry, updated with modern construction and powered by a more efficient 420 hp Pratt & Whitney Wasp air-cooled engine. The company had developed this model early in 1927 when they decided to bid on the Chicago to San Francisco mail route. So much weight was saved by the installation of an air-cooled engine that Boeing were able to include a two-passenger cabin in the design and still carry the required mail. Boeing won the route by submitting what seemed an impossibly low bid.

The Boeing 95 was powered by a Pratt & Whitney 575hp Hornet engine and operated on the New York to Chicago route. Depicted is NC185F which carries the dual title of National Air Transport and United Air Lines. All-up weight was 5,840lb, cruise speed 120mph, range 520 statute miles. Its wing span was 44ft and length 32ft. Twenty-four were built, it going into service in April 1929. (AP Photo Library)

Pitcairn Mailwing of Eastern Airlines powered by a Wright Whirlwind engine, with an all-up weight of 3,050lb carrying two passengers. It flew at 120mph, had a wing span of 33ft and was 23ft long. Original route was flown on 1 May 1928 between Brunswick, New Jersey and Atlanta, Georgia. This was extended later that year to include Jacksonville and Miami. (AP Photo Library)

By late 1923 many of the cheap war-surplus aircraft used for instruction and charter work by unregulated US civil operators were beginning to wear out. This opened up a limited market for replacements, resulting in the formation of new small but venturesome aircraft companies and the revival of some older ones. By mid-1926 business was fairly brisk.

Since the industry had no airliners on the stocks or even under development in 1926, it became necessary to import established

European designs for passenger work. The foundation of airlines in Europe was going ahead at a rapid rate. Imperial Airways Ltd was incorporated on 31 March 1924 in the United Kingdom, whilst on the continent KLM was founded on 7 October 1919, and Sabena in Belgium on 23 May 1923. In Sweden, ABA, the forerunner of the Scandinavian Airlines System (SAS) was formed in June 1924, and in neighbouring Norway DNL was organised by Captain Hjalmar Ruser-Larsen. However, this latter company was liquidated in 1920 after operating a mail service between Bergen and Stavanger.

By 1924 there were airlines operating in seventeen European countries. The Junkers F-13 and the Fokker F.VII became the outstanding civil aeroplanes, being rugged, reliable and adaptable enough for the primitive airfields of the day. Customer requirements were combined with early success and profits, resulting in the Junkers and Fokker dominating the market for many years to come.

Back in the United States, Henry Ford, the automobile tycoon, was persuaded by business associates and his son Edsel, that there was a need for a healthy US aircraft industry, providing there was sufficient public demand. The first step was to overcome the public's inherent fear of flying. Using a Dutch-built Fokker F.VIIIA/3M tri-motor, Henry Ford set up the first of an annual series of 'Ford Reliability Tours' in which a tight schedule over a long course covering several major US cities was flown. The 1925 tour commenced on 28 September and finished 1,775 miles later on 4 October.

The Curtiss J-2 Kingbird was powered by two Wright 440hp Whirlwind engines. Gross weight was 5,870lb, carried six passengers and cruised at 115mph with a range of 450 statute miles. Its wing span was 55ft and it was 35ft long. Fifteen were built and it first entered service with Eastern Air Transport on 10 December 1930. Depicted is NC620V Fleet No.209.
(AP Photo Library)

The Fokker tri-motor was a conversion of the eight-passenger, single-engined Fokker F.VIIA airliner. With great foresight, Anthony Fokker realised that the least reliable part of any contemporary single-engine aeroplane was the engine. So he replaced the single 450-hp engine in the nose of his F.VIIA with a 200 hp American Wright Whirlwind air-cooled radial engine and added two more Whirlwinds between the wheels and the high wing. This adaption was to standardise the airlines of the world for the following eight years.

Contract mail carriers quickly saw the potential of the new tri-motors. Principal models were improved, US-built Fokker F.10s and the new Ford 4-AT and 5-AT models. Like the original Fokker tri-motor, the Fords had been adapted from a single-engine design of William B. Stout, evolved from the German

Lockheed Orion 9D NC13749 of Northwest Airlines. It had a Pratt & Whitney 500hp Wasp engine, all-up weight was 5,400lb and it carried six passengers. Speed was 191mph with a range of 750 statute miles. It entered service in May 1931. (AP Photo Library)

Junkers all-metal construction, to the Fokker F.VII outline. Henry Ford bought the Stout Metal Airplane Company and used a number of its single-engined products to set up his own company airline between Detroit and Chicago in April 1925. With the spectacular debut of the Fokker tri-motor, the single-engined Ford-Stout 'Air Pullman' model evolved into the famous 'Tin Goose' tri-motor.

To supplement the Fokkers and Fords, other new multi-engined airliners soon appeared, but they were not true competitors in either quantity or quality. The Curtiss Condor was a twin-engined eighteen-passenger design adapted from the contemporary B-2 US Army bomber. It met such limited response that only half a dozen were built. Its claim to fame is that it was the only US airliner certificated with liquid-cooled engines. The new twelve-to-eighteen passenger Boeing 80 and 80A were tri-motors that appeared to be a step backwards in that they were biplanes in the virgin years of the monoplane age, but there was method in Boeing's apparent madness. The Boeing route from San Francisco to Chicago crossed two high and rugged mountain ranges. Airports were small and at a high elevation. The current Fords and Fokkers were designed primarily for operation from large airports at sea level, so could not operate from such high fields. With this in mind Boeing deliberately used the inherent characteristic of the biplane's slower landing speed and greater payload for its power to obtain better high-altitude and short-field capability for the mountains. Added to this was an increased fuel capacity and range for the greater distance on the east-west journey. The Boeing 80s were designed for that single route operation, in a prime example of design 'trade off' to obtain certain desired characteristics at the sacrifice of others – namely range and altitude capability at the expense of speed.

Private Enterprise

As early as 1924, Colonel Paul Henderson, Assistant Postmaster General, had tried to interest the Pennsylvania Railroad in air transport for the carriage of airmail. This was not successful, but the Kelly Act of 1925 set the seal on a government decision in this direction. At first the emphasis was on setting up feeder routes to the main trunk transcontinental route, and the first five contracts were awarded on 7 October 1925. The Air Commerce Act was passed on 20 May 1926, charging the US Department of Commerce with full responsibility for maintaining airways and air navigation facilities.

Other companies obtained contracts for carriage of mail, so that during 1926 ten feeder routes were put into operation. In addition a tentative start was made to a route from Atlanta to Miami. One more was added in April 1927, so that by the time the trunk route was started by Boeing and National later in the year, every major city in the United States, except New Orleans, was connected on the airmail system.

In general only mail and express packages were carried, but two companies in the west, Western Air Express and Pacific Air Transport, the latter bought by Boeing on 1 January 1928, also carried passengers. Western's mail operation was so successful that within a month, on 23 May 1926, it began the first scheduled and sustained passenger service in the United States. The early mail contracts stimulated manufacturing interest in other civil aeroplane types. Western put the Douglas M-2 mailplane into service on 17 April 1926, and Florida Airways the first Stinson Detroiter in September 1926; Colonial had put the first Fokker Universal into service on 18 June.

By 1930 the US airline industry had developed into a healthy network, with tri-motors operating on the main trunk routes that fed the trunks. In spite of better and more powerful power-plants and more professional aerodynamics, the aircraft industry both in the United States and abroad was very conservative and some of its designs reflected features that dated back to the First World War. There were still large quantities of biplanes available, and the new monoplanes that served the shorter routes were mostly high-wing strut-braced designs such as the Ryans, Stinsons and Travel Air. Innovative designers such as John K. Northrop at Lockheed did introduce greatly improved performance for a given power and weight through close attention to streamlining. The Lockheed Vega of 1927 eliminated the struts by the introduction of a Fokker-like cantilever wing and used a sleek oval cross-section for its laminated wood veneer fuselage.

During 1932, Curtiss-Wright reopened their subsidiary plant in St Louis, Missouri, which had been closed early in the depression, to build a new twin-engined Condor transport. This was a unique combination of the old and the new, a biplane that incorporated a retractable undercarriage and cowled engines. The main feature of this new Condor II was its wide fuselage, which could accommodate fifteen day passengers plus a cabin attendant, or twelve sleeper berths. It was the first designed-for-the-purpose sleeper airliner, drawing its inspiration and detail from the railroad industry. For night routes with sleeping passengers, high speed did not offer a competitive advantage. With two 720-hp Wright Cyclone engines, the Condor II cruised at 167 mph, but due to progress in other areas its career was limited to a mere three years. This last biplane and first sleeper transport in US airline service was not an unqualified success. It was liable to engine fires and it picked up ice. However, it paved the way for airliners of the future, such as the Douglas DST.

Star Airlines Inc. of Alaska operated the Lockheed 9D2 Orion airliner. A total of 36 were built, it had a wing span of 43ft and was 28ft long. Depicted is N230Y of Star Airlines. The Orion was operated in Europe by Swissair. (Museum of Flight)

The Curtiss Condor was powered by two 1,400hp Wright R.1820 Cyclone engines, had an all-up weight of 17,500lb, carried 15 passengers and flew at 145mph with a range of 650 miles. Wing span was 82ft and it was 49ft long. Total of 45 were built and it entered service in May 1934 with American Airlines. (AP Photo Library)

Walter Folger Brown

The former US Secretary of Commerce under the Coolidge administration, Herbert Hoover, became President of the United States on 4 March 1929. He appointed as his Postmaster-General Walter Folger Brown, a Toledo attorney, who was to become one of the most controversial figures in the entire history of air transport. Under his influence, five of the largest airlines in the world consolidated their route patterns and became so powerful that a wholesale cancellation of mail contracts, upon which they depended for their livelihood, could not have an effect on them, when these became the subject of a national inquiry four years later.

Brown immediately set about the task of examining the whole structure of air transport in the USA as a prerequisite to streamlining the airmail service. Methodical, thorough and very patient, he took many months digesting the facts. During his first year of office, he took no decisive step. On 7 November 1929 he chose not to renew the first five mail contracts, electing instead to extend them for a period of six months. It was obvious that Brown was not satisfied with the state of airmail contracts under the Kelly Act.

He had due cause for dissatisfaction. Of all the thirty-two mail contracts issued up to that date, only one combination offered a mail service over the transcontinental route, where the benefits of the faster service which the aeroplane offered could be most effective. There were others which covered distances of approximately 1,000 miles. In short, the airmail map was not unlike a patchwork quilt, looking decidely threadbare in places.

Brown was undoubtedly a dedicated character. He visualised an efficient airline industry within the United States, organised to give maximum service to its customers, whether they were Post Office officials or passengers. He was prepared to subsidise the airlines in order to build up the foundations of a new industry which was not yet equipped for its major role. If the airmail network had its shortcomings, at least it was better than the passenger airline system, which was a disjointed collection of sporadic services. Commercial aircraft of the day were not fast enough to offer substantial time savings over the railroad, nor did they provide much comfort. Passengers could be forgiven for not boarding aeroplanes in large numbers. But there was no passenger services south of Washington DC. North American Aviation, later Eastern Air Transport, did not introduce such a facility until 18 August 1930.

One problem was a certain apprehension about flying at night. In the summer of 1929, a few airlines overcame the dangers of night flying by organising some ingenious schemes by which a route was divided into sections, with aircraft flying the journey by day and the railways providing service at night. The most famous of these was the 'Lindbergh Line', operated by Transcontinental Air Transport. This was a 48-hour service from New York to Los Angeles, using Ford 5-AT Tri-motors in conjunction with trains of the Pennsylvania and Santa Fe railroads. Whilst this was the most ambitious of the transcontinental air/rail services, commencing on 7 July 1929, and quoted as the fastest and most luxurious, it was not the first.

On 14 June 1929, Universal Aviation Corporation opened up a 67-hour service from New York to Los Angeles. The first portion of the journey was conducted by the '*Southwestern Limited*' of the New York Central Railroad as far as Cleveland, Ohio. Then the Fokker FXs of Universal took over as far as Garden City, Kansas, with stops at Chicago, St Louis and finally Kansas City. The rest of the journey was by the Atchison,

Topeka and Santa Fe Railroad, which was quite happy to serve more than one airline.

A third transcontinental air/rail system began on 4 August 1929, involving the New York Central Railroad to St Louis, where passengers were transferred to the Ford 5-ATs of Southwest Air Fast Express (SAFE) for the flight to Sweetwater, Texas. The Texas & Pacific Railway provided overnight travel as far as El Paso, where Jack Frye's Standard Airlines took over the rest of the journey. It was often described as a coast-to-coast adventure.

To Walter F. Brown, with an eye mainly on the goal of creating a co-ordinated and comprehensive airmail route system, the whole industry appeared chaotic. After many months his plans finally took shape. He conceived a method of airmail payment which would achieve the dual purpose of improving airmail service and encouraging passenger travel. The first requirement was a change in the law regarding airmail payments.

The Ford Trimotor was adapted from a single-engine design evolved from the German Junkers all-metal airliner, and in the United States became the famous Tin Goose *trimotor. Power was from three Pratt & Whitney 1,350hp Wasp engines; all-up weight was 12,250lb. It carried 13 passengers and flew at 110mph. Wing span was 78ft and it was 50ft long.* (AP Photo Library)

The Third Amendment to the Air Mail Act of 1925 (the Kelly Act) was approved by Congress on 29 April 1930 and became known as the Watres Act. Armed with this latest legislation the Postmaster set about the task of redrawing the United States airline map. No time was wasted; within two weeks of the passing of the Act, Brown took the first fateful steps in a crusade which was to make airline history. Between 15 May and 9 June 1930, he held a series of meetings in his Washington DC office. They were not secret, but the intention to hold them received the minimum of publicity, and actual invitations were extended to a chosen few, representing United Aircraft, the Aviation Corporation, Western Air Express, TAT, Eastern Air Transport and the Stout Line, which by this time was part of United. These companies obtained all but two of the twenty-two airmail contracts awarded under the provisions of the Watres Act. On the credit side this 'Spoils Conference', as it was called, set up a network of airmail services extending over more than 27,000 route miles. On the debit side, there was accusations of malpractice, which were eventually disproved.

Franklin Roosevelt and the Democrats swept into office in the election of November 1932, and this brought the end of the Walter Folger Brown regime. The new Postmaster-General, James A. Farley, listed nine major charges of maladministration, favouritism, collusion and illegal practices. The result of these charges was a 'Special Committee of Investigation of Air Mail and Ocean Mail Contracts' under Senator H.L. Black, which began hearings on 28 September 1933. All airmail contracts were cancelled on 9 February 1934, while the committee was in session, and the US Army Air Corps were obliged to fly the mail with a motley collection of 160 miscellaneous aircraft during a spell of bad wintry weather. The result was disaster. In the first week five Army pilots were killed and six badly injured. By 10 March all airmail flights had been abandoned.

Brown had left office in disgrace, although he was exonerated from charges made by the US Court of Claims on 14 July 1941. He left behind him thirty-four airmail routes operating an airway network of 27,000 miles. Despite economic depression, passenger traffic had increased steadily. Most important of all, the security of tenure and new opportunities offered by the Watres Act made it possible for the airline industry to set new and higher standards for its flying equipment.

The introduction of the all-metal retractable-gear Boeing 247 marked the birth of the modern airliner. It entered service with United Air Lines in March 1933, reducing coast-to-coast travel time to 19½-hours. It was powered by two Pratt & Whitney R.1340 engines, had an all-up weight of 13,650lb, carried ten passengers and flew at 160mph. Its wing span was 74ft and length 54ft. The Boeing 247 NC13336 depicted now hangs on display in the National Air & Space Museum in Washington DC. (Nut Tree Associates)

On 20 April 1934, forty-five operators attended a meeting called by Postmaster-General Farley to bid afresh for mail contracts. All those who had taken part in Brown's Spoils Conference were specifically barred. The result was a new deal on domestic air transport. Walter Farley granted fifteen temporary airmail contracts on 3 May 1934, to cover 78,000 aircraft miles a day, which compared with the 97,000 aircraft miles a day summarily cancelled by President Roosevelt on 9 February. The list of contracts was headed by the 'Big Four' – American Airlines, United Air Lines, Transcontinental & Western Air and Eastern Air Lines. There were also a substantial number of smaller companies involved. Only multi-engine equipment was eligible.

This was the basis for the great leap forwards in the United States with modern aircraft and modern operating techniques. It was also a time for re-organisation as the older airlines were restructured to undertake the new contracts. A condition of these was that, for the first time, the air transport operating industry must be separate from aircraft or aero-engine manufacturing interests.

Boeing's Airliner

One of the most far-reaching effects of the consolidation of a small number of large companies was the opportunity, through greater capital resources and long-term traffic potentials, for sponsoring the development of better flying equipment. The first example came from the Boeing Airplane Company which produced for Boeing Air Transport the first all-metal, stressed-skin monoplane designed expressly for transport work. This aircraft the Boeing Type 200, known as the Monomail, first flew during 1930. With its speed of 135 mph, achieved partly by the use of a retractable undercarriage, it was a marked improvement

on the existing Fords and Fokkers, and its tail-wheel and wheel-brakes ended the use of tail skids once and for all. However, because of its various shortcomings, it never went into production; only two Boeing Monomails were built.

Undaunted, Boeing applied the new design concept to a twin-engined ten-passenger transport. It was known as the Model 247. It made its first flight on 8 February 1933, and such was the pace in the early 1930s that it entered service on 30 March with the United Air Lines group just before the signing of the Watres Act. By the end of June, United had thirty 247s in service and had established a coast-to-coast schedule of just under twenty hours. United had made financial history as an airline by ordering an unprecedented sixty Boeing 247s off the drawing board. Altogether seventy-five were built, of which seventy were for United and three for DLH, the German airline.

The Boeing 247 was built to higher engineering standards than the Monomail and was improved by the installation of Hamilton variable-pitch propellers to the 550-hp Pratt & Whitney Wasp engine. It carried ten passengers – four fewer than the Ford – but at 160 mph it was 70 mph faster. TWA had approached Boeing for a number of 247 aircraft but had been rebuffed, as Boeing was still essentially part of the same group of companies as United. The Lindbergh Line therefore went to the Douglas Aircraft Company in Los Angeles in August 1932, with a design specification aimed at bettering the Boeing 247 which was on the drawing board.

Fate is the Hunter

Transcontinental Air Transport (TAT) had commenced operations on 8 July 1929, with a fleet of new Ford Tri-motors on the air-rail 48-hour schedule between Los Angeles and New York. A second airline, Maddux Airlines, flew smaller and older Ford Tri-motors out of Los Angeles as from 2 November 1927. Western Air Express started up on 17 April 1926, with Liberty-powered Douglas open biplanes (M-2) flying mail between Los Angeles and Salt Lake City. Within twenty-one months Western Air Express was operating luxurious Fokker Tri-motors, first from Los Angeles to San Francisco, and soon east to Kansas City. The Fokker F.10s had a fabric-covered, welded steel-tube fuselage, plywood-covered wings with spruce spars and ribs, and a tail skid. The Fokker F.10A had a tail wheel. The Ford Tri-motor was an obvious copy of the Fokker, except for its all-metal construction.

Then, as now, there were airline mergers. Transcontinental Air Transport (TAT) completed a merger with Maddux and Western Air Express and on the first day of October 1930, Transcontinental & Western Air (TWA) had come into existence. Western Air Express, however, retained one short route under their own name. Eight of their Fokker F.10A Super Tri-motors were soon transferred to the new TWA, with 'Transcontinental & Western Air Inc.' replacing the old Western Air Express name, but retaining the colours, Indian-head insignia and other markings of WAE. One of these was the very last Fokker F.10A Tri-motor built, NC999E.

It was overcast and humid in Kansas City on 31 March 1931 when TWA Flight 5 to Los Angeles was ready to depart. Captain Bob Fry and co-pilot H. Jesse Mathias were in the cockpit of Fokker F.10 NC999E ready to start the three Wasp engines. Six passengers were on the manifest, only half filling the twelve-place cabin. The Fokker took off on schedule at 9.15 a.m. The co-pilot doubled as the steward, serving box lunches, coffee

Fairchild 71 NC9726 seen in Pan American Airways Inc. markings during the 1930s. It was powered with a Pratt & Whitney Wasp engine, could carry six passengers, and had an all-up-weight of 5,500lb. It flew at 110mph and had a wing span of 50ft and was 33ft long. (AP Photo Library)

from a thermos and chewing gum to help pop the passenger's ears. The airliner maintained CFR (Contact Flight Rules) through a fast-moving weather front east of Wichita, their first stop. It was evidently a rough ride. At approximately 10.35 a.m. the airliner radioed to Wichita to check on the weather. It was satisfactory, and at 10.45 Wichita called the Fokker to enquire their intentions. Possibly due to static, from which the old low-frequency radio sets suffered, transmissions may have been inaudible.

It is estimated that between 10.45 and 10.50 a.m. Fokker F.10A NC999E crashed in a field near Bazaar, Kansas, killing all eight occupants. The cause of the crash was a wing rupture resulting from pieces of ice collected round the propeller hub breaking loose, snapping a blade with a shock sufficient to fracture a section of the wing from the outboard engine, which was missing. It was found approximately a quarter of a mile away from the site of the crash.

The crash caused not one, but three very large, separate and distinct shock waves in American life. The first was in the sports world. One of the six passengers on board had been Knute K. Rockne, one of the most famous and greatest football coaches of all time, and a highly respected household name in America in the 1920s. Rarely, if ever, has the death of a sports celebrity caused such universal grief among American athletes. Even teams regularly beaten by the 'Fighting Irish of Notre Dame' held memorial services. Some newspapers ran the story bordered in black.

A second shock wave was in the larger world of American society. Knute Rockne was amazingly well known by reputation in all walks of life, far beyond the normal reaches of football coaches. Two years later newspapers still speculated about the causes of the accident, and mourned Knute Rockne. A movie was made of his life. There was a Rockne automobile, and there is still a Rockne Memorial on the exact spot of the crash.

The third shock wave was not as predictable, perhaps, but was infinitely longer-lasting in its effect. It was in the field of commercial aviation. Aeroplanes had always been crashing, and as they grew larger, there was naturally greater loss of life.

Never before the Rockne crash, however, nor again until half a century later, had an airliner disaster caused such a public outcry, or had such an impact on commercial aviation. The US Department of Commerce temporarily grounded all Fokker Tri-motors, and new safety rules and regulations were soon established for all civil aircraft.

Business problems, exacerbated by the economic depression and the Rockne crash, caused the Fokker Aircraft Corporation of America, by then controlled by General Motors, to disappear. The major airlines feared public resistance to flying in that type of aircraft. Even the term 'tri-motor' made the old Ford airliner suspect. The major airlines all wanted new equipment, but United Air Lines had the monopoly of the new Boeing 247 production line. There was nothing else available.

TWA, badly stung by the Rockne publicity, asked several aircraft companies for an entirely new design. The rest is now well-known history. A little company making military fabric-covered biplanes in southern California received the order for an improvement on the Boeing 247. It was simply called the DC-1, and it even had flaps. And so the Douglas Aircraft Company, with its massive production of a piston-engine range, from DC-2s through to the DC-7, owes its impetus in a very real way to Knute Rockne's death in a forgotten fabric-covered airliner on a rain-soaked Kansas hillside so many years ago.

The Fairchild Pilgrim Model 100-A was the first aircraft in the USA to be built directly to an airline specification. It was powered by a nine-cylinder 575hp Pratt & Whitney Hornet, and twenty-one were put into service by American Airways in 1931. Depicted is Pilgrim 100-A NC9976V of American Airways. (AP Photo Library)

Carl A. Cover, Vice-President, Sales and test pilot with the Douglas Aircraft Company, who first flew the Douglas DC-1, DC-2 and the world-winner, the ubiquitous DC-3. Date of the first flight of the famous Douglas Commercial One was 1 July 1933, from Clover Field, Santa Monica, and was planned during the lunch hour for the company employees. It is reported that Carl Cover was wearing a tweed suit and a bright green hat for this test flight. (Douglas)

Chapter Two
Donald Wills Douglas and the Douglas Commercial

Donald Wills Douglas was a design genius. His talent flowered with the Douglas DC-1, one of the most famous single aircraft of all times; the forerunner of the lesser-known but equally successful Douglas DC-2 and the most famous transport of them all, the immortal Douglas DC-3. This chapter is written as a personal tribute to Mr Donald Wills Douglas, and reveals the man and the circumstances that led to remarkable milestones in aviation.

The eminence of Donald Douglas as a creative engineer and head of a major industrial establishment was more than once recognised by the US government and members of his own industry. Despite the many honours accorded him as a member of the top echelon of American business, he did not take on the airs of industrial royalty. One incident is illustrative of his unassuming ways. On the day the board of directors of the Douglas Aircraft Company were to meet for the last time prior to the merger in 1967 with McDonnell, the huge headquarters building located just off Lakewood Boulevard, Long Beach, California, was bustling with limousines, helicopters and busy senior executives and their aides. After the meeting, when all the VIPs had departed, an elderly gentleman stepped alone out of the elevator, chatted with the security guard in the lobby and walked to his faded Mercury sedan. Donald Wills Douglas drove himself home.

Donald Douglas earned an impressive list of awards and honours, including the Robert J. Collier Trophy in 1936, the Guggenheim Medal in 1939, an LL.D.(Doctor of Laws) degree from the University of California at Los Angeles in 1947, the US Certificate of Merit in 1948, the Commander's Cross of the Order of Orange-Nassau in 1950, the Légion de' Honneur in 1951, the USAF Exceptional Service Award in 1953, the Royal Order of Dannebrog in 1955 and the Elmer A. Sperry Award in 1956.

Friend of the author and ex-President of the Douglas Aircraft Company, John C. Brizendine, describes DWD as 'a great human being as well as a giant of aviation, and if I have any hero in the world, he was it.' Donald Wills Douglas passed away on 1 February 1981, in Palm Springs, California, at the age of 88. Through the remarkable Douglas Commercial series, he had done more than any other to make commercial aviation possible.

Born on 6 April 1892, in Brooklyn, New York, the second son of an assistant bank cashier, young Donald Douglas was fascinated by ships. He studied hard at the Trinity Chapel School in New York City and passed the necessary examination to enter the US Naval Academy at Annapolis in the autumn of 1909, at the age of seventeen. Before entering the academy, he took a trip to Fort Myer, Virginia, where the US Signal Corps was conducting acceptance trials on the Wright brothers' flying machine, the first ever military aeroplane. He saw Orville Wright put his box-kite biplane through its paces, and apparently never forgot the experience.

After his resignation from Annapolis in 1912, and prior to his enrolment at the Massachusetts Institute of Technology (MIT), Donald Douglas had attempted to join both Grover Loening and Glenn Curtiss, early pioneers in the growing aircraft industry, but was turned down by both. He graduated in the spring of 1914, obtaining his Bachelor of Science diploma after serving just two of the four years normally required, and was requested to stay on as Assistant Aeronautical Engineer. He occupied this post for only a year, but it gave him the opportunity to work with wind tunnels, the first of their kind and size in the country. One of his MIT professors was one Jerome C. Hunsaker, who later became Chief of the Bureau of Construction and Repairs, Aircraft Division, US Navy. Donald Douglas became Hunsaker's assistant, a role which played an important part in shaping his future career in aviation.

Young Douglas had applied to join both Grover Loening and Glenn Curtiss, but was turned down. He finally joined the re-organised Glenn Martin Company in Cleveland, Ohio, as chief engineer. This early photograph shows Donald Douglas working at his desk in the drawing office where he designed the MB-1 or GMB bomber for the US Army Air Service. (Douglas)

Design and construction, rather than teaching, attracted the energy of the young engineer and in 1915 he left to join the Connecticut Aircraft Company as a consultant. His association with the company was very brief, but he participated in the design of the DN-1, the first dirigible for the US Navy. In August 1915, he joined the Glenn Martin Company in Los Angeles as chief engineer and worked on a number of early Martin designs until November 1916 when, following the consolidation in August 1916 of the Wright Company and the Glenn Martin Company, with operations on the east coast of the United States, he resigned to accept a position with the US Army. Douglas was ambitious and at times restless, as he wanted to establish his own aircraft company.

Despite an attempt by Glenn Martin to dissuade him, Douglas was convinced that the 'Golden State' of California was where he wanted his children to live. His marriage to Miss Charlotte Marguerite Ogg in Riverside, California in 1916 helped him make his mind up. He also realised that the salubrious climate was particularly favourable for aircraft construction and testing. But, for the time being, his stay in southern California was to be brief. He had agreed, when terminating with the Wright-Martin Aircraft Corporation, to become chief civilian aeronautical engineer for the Aviation Section of the US Army Signal Corps. Again his employment was of short duration as Glenn Martin, following the organisation of a new Glenn Martin Company in Cleveland, Ohio, asked Douglas to resume his function as chief engineer.

With Glenn Martin, Donald Douglas was responsible for the design of the large twin-engined MB-1 or GMB bomber for the US Army; its transport derivative, the T-1 or GMP, and also its naval version, the TM-1 or MTB. Of these, the T-1 transport, with accommodation for a crew of two in a glassed-in enclosure and ten passengers, was the one which was of greatest interest to Douglas who already had great faith in the future of commercial air transport. However he was still restless and anxious to become his own master. In March 1920, on completion of the design of the Martin MTB, he resigned his $10,000-a-year position with the Glenn Martin Company and again headed west to California where, soon after, he was able to form the first of four aircraft companies which have borne his name.

The Douglas M-3 mailplane was adopted by the US Post Office in March 1926, proving faster, having a longer range, and being capable of lifting two-and-a-half times as much mail as the Post Office DH-4s. Of the 59 Douglas Mailplanes built, ten were M-3s c/n 285/264. Power was from a 400hp Liberty engine. Span was 39ft 8in and length 28ft 11in. (Douglas)

Whilst living in Ohio, Douglas and his wife often missed the mild winter climate of southern California, and so in January 1920, Mrs Douglas and their two sons left for Los Angeles. Two months later, Douglas joined them. It turned out to be a permanent move, even though the warmth of Los Angeles held an uncertain future. That his total assets were in the order of $600 proved no deterrent, but he urgently needed to find a financial sponsor. He invested some of his savings in desk space at the rear of a downtown barber's shop on Pico Boulevard and began to search for additional capital.

The Davis-Douglas Company

Keeping in close touch with his old mentor Commander Jerome Hunsaker, Donald Douglas was given every encouragement and it was suggested he join William Boeing in Seattle. The US Navy were expecting to employ contractors and Hunsaker felt that Douglas's services could be beneficial. He was not prepared to take permanent employment with another company, but within a year he would be involved in some of the US Navy contract business mentioned.

A friendly young man called Bill Henry, once public relations officer with Glenn Martin and now a sports writer on the staff of the *Los Angeles Times*, introduced Douglas to David R. Davis, a millionaire sportsman and flying enthusiast who was interested in financing an aeroplane which would fly the 2,500 miles coast-to-coast non-stop. Davis was willing to provide a capital of $40,000 to form a company with Douglas if the latter was prepared to design and built a single aircraft for an attempt on the first non-stop flight across the United States. This was not the big start Douglas had hoped for, but it was a beginning, and on 22 July 1920 David R. Davis and Donald W. Douglas formed the Davis-Douglas Company.

Douglas immediately summoned five of his former colleagues from the Glenn Martin to join him in his new venture. These were Ross Elkins, James Goodyear, George Borst, Henry Guerin and George Strompl. From then on the life of Donald Wills Douglas was closely associated with the history of the Davis-Douglas Company, the Douglas Company, the Douglas Aircraft Company and the McDonnell Douglas Corporation, and with the wide variety of aircraft they designed and built from 1920. This was the beginning of the Donald Douglas aircraft saga, including the Douglas Commercials.

The back room of the barber shop, inadequate as it was as a drawing office, was retained and a suitable place to build the new aircraft was sought. Eventually, in late July, the new company rented the loft of an old factory, the Koll Planing Mill, in Los Angeles. Before the completion of the as yet unnamed aircraft, Eric Springer, chief test pilot with Glenn Martin, who had test-flown the Douglas-designed Martin MB-1 twin-engined bomber on its maiden flight on 17 August 1918, joined the Davis-Douglas Company as test pilot. It is rumoured that when Springer saw the almost completed aircraft, he exclaimed, 'You've got a real cloud buster there, Doug.' The phrase caught on and the aircraft, the first produced in the Douglas family, was named the 'Cloudster'.

It was a single-bay tractor biplane powered by a 400 hp Liberty water-cooled engine and had a large-diameter fuselage. Two fuel tanks capable of holding a total of 660 US gallons and a 50 US gallon oil tank were housed behind the engine compartment. Behind these tanks and aft of the 55 ft 11 in span wings, there was an open cockpit with side-by-side seating for a crew of two. The rear fuselage section, tail unit and wings were of wood with fabric covering. The aircraft had a design range of 2,800 miles.

February 1921 saw completion of the 'Cloudster' components and, after being lowered in sections down a lift at the Koll Planing Mill, the aircraft was transported to the Goodyear Blimp hangar at South Park and Florence Boulevards in Los Angeles, where the company had rented space in which to assemble the new aircraft. On 24 February, the aircraft made its first 30-minute flight with Eric Springer at the controls.

The Davis-Douglas 'Cloudster' was the first aeroplane in history capable of lifting a useful load exceeding its own weight.

Donald Douglas had accomplished his part in the agreement between Davis and himself. David Davis was pleased with the 'Cloudster' and was naturally anxious to attempt, with Eric Springer, the non-stop link between the Pacific and Atlantic coasts. On 19 March, during a series of test flights made to determine the optimum cruise performance, the 'Cloudster' broke the Pacific Coast altitude record by climbing to 19,160 ft. However, on 27 June 1921, after being postponed several days due to the prevailing seasonal early morning fog at March Field, Riverside, the transcontinental flight was cut short over Texas when a timing-gear problem caused engine failure.

The 'Cloudster' was recovered from its emergency landing at Fort Bliss, Texas, and returned to March Field with the intention of fitting a slightly modified Liberty engine for a new transcontinental attempt, but David Davis had lost his enthusiasm for the project. By this time the small Douglas team was engaged on their first military aircraft, the DT- series of torpedo bombers for the US Navy, so no serious effort was made with the 'Cloudster'. On 2-3 May 1923, an Army Air Service Fokker T-2 completed the first non-stop flight across the United States. Donald Douglas was therefore very pleased to find a buyer for the 'Cloudster' later that month.

It was acquired by two businessmen, T. Kinney and B. Brodsky, who intended to use it for flying passengers over Venice, California, a popular beach resort which they were actively promoting. The aircraft was modified and accommodation for five passengers and a pilot was provided in three rows of open cockpits, with the first two cockpits replacing one of the fuselage fuel tanks. Using the first two cockpits to carry four passengers gave the 'Cloudster' a capacity of ten people.

In 1925 the 'Cloudster' was sold again, this time to T. Claude Ryan in San Diego for use with Ryan's Los Angeles to San Diego Air Line. It was used to carry passengers on that route and to fly prospective real estate buyers to San Clemente island off the coast of southern California. During a landing mishap the upper wings and propeller were damaged. Douglas repaired them, and Ryan modernised the passenger accommodation. The two-seat open cockpit was moved forward to just beneath the leading edge of the upper wings, and an enclosed cabin accommodating ten passengers, five on each side of a central aisle, was fitted behind the pilot's cockpit. The Liberty engine was fitted with a large exhaust pipe which carried the exhaust fumes over the wings and away from the cockpit. A circular radiator was fitted around the propeller shaft, eliminating the original large propeller spinner and the radiator installation beneath the engine. So modified, the 'Cloudster' was used to fly passengers between Los Angeles and San Diego on a regular schedule. Later, following the demise of Ryan's airline, the aircraft was used on charter flights.

Prohibition – the ban on the manufacture, sale or transport of intoxicating liquor – had come into force in the United States on 16 January 1919. Towns just across the US borders made a profitable business of providing an outlet for American citizens to quench their thirst. Noteworthy in this enterprise was the town of Tijuana, in Mexico's Baja California, which depended heavily on a mountain road linking it to Mexicali for its supply of beer. Shortly before Christmas 1926 this road was washed out and so the bars in Tijuana were in danger of losing substantial Christmas sales. Several aircraft, including the 'Cloudster', were chartered in this unusual airlift.

A very wealthy Chinese businessman chartered the 'Cloudster' for a flight from Tijuana to Enseñada, further down the coast of Baja California. Arriving over Enseñada after dusk, the pilot, J.J. Harrigan, had to attempt a landing on the beach. Unfortunately he miscalculated his approach and hit the water before the aircraft stopped. The pilot and passengers walked out unhurt but, during the night, the rising tide and high swell caught the stranded 'Cloudster' and it was totally destroyed.

The Douglas Company

In April 1921, the Davis-Douglas Company had received a contract from the US Navy for three experimental aircraft designated DT-1s under Contract No. 53305, worth $119,550. But David R. Davis had lost interest in the 'Cloudster' project, and showed little or no enthusiasm for financing the production of three torpedo bombers. DWD had no choice but to dissolve the company and once again search for financial backing for the expanded project.

Turning to his friend Bill Henry once more, and with the promise of partial payments by the US government for work in progress on the DT-1, Douglas needed only $15,000 to launch his new company and commence construction of the US Navy torpedo bombers. Bankers needed guarantees before making an advance. Bill Henry introduced DWD to his employer, Henry Chandler, the publisher of the *Los Angeles Times*. Anxious to promote new business ventures in southern California, Chandler agreed to co-guarantee the required loan if Douglas was able to obtain a guarantee from nine other Californian businessmen. He did, and in July 1921 the Douglas Company was incorporated in the State of California.

Rare photograph depicting William E. Douglas, his son Donald W. Douglas, and Carl Cover, test pilot for the company, taken with a large size cake made to celebrate the first round the world flight by the Douglas World Cruiser aircraft. (Douglas)

The sole single-seat DT-1, delivered late in 1921, was followed by two DT-2s with a crew of two and a modified radiator installation. Successful testing by the US Navy in competition with three other American designs and a British one in the spring of 1922 resulted in the company's first production contract. The initial order was for eighteen production DT-2s. Realising the limited production capacity of the company, the US Navy placed orders for the DT-2 with the Naval Aircraft

Factory in Philadelphia, and the Dayton-Wright Company in Dayton. Douglas completed forty-six aircraft. Two years later the Norwegian government ordered the modified DT-2B and acquired the manufacturing rights for the aircraft. These were spectacular achievements for a company which had less than a dozen employees, limited facilities and other problems.

Two Boeing-built Curtiss HS-2L flying-boats were overhauled for Pacific Marine Airways whilst the DTs were being evaluated by the US Navy. These were to be the last aircraft handled by Douglas in the original premises. It became imperative for the company to find more suitable facilities. Initial plans were to move to the Long Beach area, but instead in the summer of 1922, Douglas leased the abandoned buildings of the Herrman Film Corporation at 2435 Wilshire Boulevard, Santa Monica, where a vacant field was also available for flight operations. In the new premises the production of the DT-2s was followed by some of the most famous Douglas aeroplanes, the World Cruisers, derived from the DT-2.

The Douglas World Cruiser was ordered by the US War Department for the specific purpose of attempting the first around-the-world flight. Four US Army Air Service DWCs left Santa Monica on 17 March 1924, on the first leg of their epic journey. After 175 days and 28,945 miles, two of these aircraft arrived at Seattle. The Douglas Company thus earned its proud motto 'First Around the World'.

The order book was becoming interesting as more contracts, both military and commercial, were received. These included a series of military cargo and personnel transport types, DT-2B torpedo bombers for Peru and the T2D-1 for the US Navy. The archives reveal that 26 C-1s were built for the military, 59 mailplanes for the airlines and the US Post Office, a single, company-owned Douglas Commuter, 30 T2D and P2D for the US Navy, and a single DA-1 Ambassador. In 1922, after its first full year of operation, the company had delivered a total of six aircraft at a value of $130,890. Four years later the company's production had risen to 120 aircraft, for a total value of $1,662,724. With production increasing at such a pace, the facilities at the Wilshire Boulevard factory soon became overcrowded.

At this time the Douglas workforce included several designers who achieved fame either with DWD or later with other aircraft companies. Among these early employees was Arthur E. Raymond, a close friend of the author, who joined the company in 1924, becoming Vice- President (Engineering) of the Douglas Aircraft Company Inc. ten years later. James H. 'Dutch' Kindelberger was chief engineer from 1924 until 1934. John K. Northrop had joined DWD in 1923, leaving in 1927 to join Lockheed where he designed the famous Vega. He rejoined the team again in 1932 to form the Northrop Corporation, a subsidiary of the Douglas Aircraft Company Inc.

Donald Douglas and Henry H. 'Hap' Arnold, became friends from the early days of the Douglas Commercial series. Today the grandchildren of both are married. Depicted is General Arnold talking to Donald W. Douglas Sr. and Donald Douglas Jr. during World War II. (Douglas)

A devoted family man, Donald Douglas had a love of the sea, and animals. He is depicted here with one of his best friends, his labrador. (Douglas)

Success followed success and the reputation of the company grew rapidly. The next major achievement was the winning of the 1924 observation aircraft competition for the US Army Air Service held at McCook Field. The company entered its Liberty-powered XO-2. The Douglas Company, and its successor the Douglas Aircraft Company Inc., went on to build a total of 778 observation biplanes for the US armed forces, and 101 observation biplanes for the export market. From this line of military observation biplanes the first commercial Douglas transport aircraft, the M- series of mailplanes, was derived.

Initially test and production flying was halted at Wilshire Boulevard, and after the early part of 1927 aircraft had to be towed by night the two miles to Clover Field, still in Santa Monica. Production capacity was nearing its maximum, coinciding with the expiry of the lease on the property, due in July 1929. The City of Santa Monica had the foresight to be anxious to retain the expanding Douglas Company and was prepared to offer facilities and co-operation. However, with more capatal required, Donald W. Douglas had to once more revamp his company.

This unique photograph with a Douglas DC-3 as a background was taken at Santa Monica in 1959 by Stan Raymond, son of Arthur E. Raymond. It depicts the Douglas team and includes left to right: Arthur E. Raymond, J. L. Atwood, George Strompl, W. Bailey Oswald, James H. Kindelberger talking to Donald W. Douglas, Ed H. Burton, Franklin R. Collbohm and J. O. Moxness. (Douglas)

Douglas Aircraft Company Inc.

Donald Douglas, initially with his friend Bill Henry and later with his father, had controlled the capital of the Douglas Company, relying whenever necessary on loans from the Security Trust and Savings Bank. All but $40,000 of the net profit made since 1922 had been reinvested in the company, resulting in the net worth rising to $2,500,000 by the autumn of 1928. This was more than spectacular for a small company which, seven years earlier, had been looking for a $15,000 loan to commence operations. DWD was advised, despite the excellent cash position, to reorganise the capital structure of the company.

On 30 November 1928, a new company, the Douglas Aircraft Company Inc., came into being, purchasing the assets of the Douglas Company with an authorised capital stock issue of one million shares. The new company retained Santa Monica as the location of the corporate office and for aircraft production, but was incorporated in the State of Delaware to benefit from more favourable tax laws.

Shares were issued to the general public, whilst $650,000 went into the company cash account, with a balance to be spent on the acquisition of property and the construction of a new factory. Completed in 1929, this was located on the fringe of Clover Field, alongside Ocean Park Boulevard, Santa Monica,

and occupied nearly eight acres. At the same time, the City of Santa Monica expanded and improved the facilities available at Clover Field, permitting the company its use for experiment test and production flying under a ten-year renewable contract, at a nominal rent.

Production continued from the new facilities, with a series of observation biplanes and the company's first flying-boats, the PD-1 series for the US Navy. These were followed by a series of interesting twin-engined amphibians, the Dolphins, for which the 'Sinbad', completed in 1930, was to act as a prototype in anticipation of a booming market for luxury transport aircraft. The October 1929 stock market crash triggered the Great Depression and, unfortunately for Donald Douglas, the anticipated civilian market for the Dolphins all but vanished. However, a total of fifty-nine amphibians of the type were produced, and of these forty-five including the 'Sinbad', were delivered to the US Army Air Corps, the US Navy and the US Coast Guard. One Dolphin was even sold to William E. Boeing in Seattle.

The design and production of military aircraft continued at a satisfactory rate, keeping the Douglas Aircraft Company active and financially sound at a time when many other US companies in all fields were going bankrupt. A total of 127 observation monoplanes were built for the US Army Air Corps in the 0-31, 0-43 and 0-46 series, followed by fourteen 0-35 and B-7 types. Experimental torpedo bomber aircraft (the XT3D-1/2) and the XFD-1 naval fighter were produced.

Donald Douglas was by now a major and very highly respected aircraft designer and manufacturer. The stage was being set for the appearance of the famous Douglas Commercial series. These were not evolutionary developments of any of the earlier Douglas types. They drew their main structural features from the Douglas subsidiary, the Northrop Corporation.

After resigning from his company which had not only merged with others, but had moved to Wichita, Kansas, in September 1931, John K. Northrop formed a new company, the Northrop Corporation. This venture was financed by Douglas, who held 51 per cent of the stock. New types of aircraft were developed based on the Alpha, notably the Gamma mailplane and the Delta mail and passenger models. The company was based at Mines Field, Inglewood, California.

The financial soundness of the Douglas Aircraft Company was to prove more than valuable in enabling Donald Wills Douglas to launch his company into a new – and as yet untried by him – market, that of manufacturing passenger transport aircraft for the airlines. There is no doubt at all that the company having the right capital at the right time was a major factor in explaining the spectacular success of the Douglas Commercial series.

The United Air Lines order for sixty Boeing 247 airliners caused great panic in the industry. Other potential customers were told they would not be able to obtain the new plane for nearly two years, due to the monopoly on the production line held by UAL; ultimately this resulted in a major loss of revenue for Boeing.

Following the fatal crash of the TWA Fokker F-10A NC999E on 31 March 1931, the Bureau of Air Commerce instructed all operators of this and similar types of airliners with wooden spars and ribs to inspect the internal wing structure periodically. These inspections were both costly and time-consuming for the fledgling US airlines and resulted in the early phasing-out of most wooden airliners. A year later TWA found it imperative that they look for a new aircraft. Turning to Boeing, they were prepared to negotiate for the new Model 247, but the idea of a two-year delay on delivery placed them in a very precarious position. The choice was either to wait, or to initiate the design of a new compatible aircraft.

As history has revealed, the airline adopted the latter course, which resulted in Donald Douglas receiving a copy of the letter written by Jack Frye, Vice-President in charge of Operations for Transcontinental & Western Air Inc. in Kansas City, Missouri on 2 August 1932.

On Wednesday 1 July 1935, the third anniversary of the maiden flight of the Douglas DC-1, Donald Wills Douglas stood before the President of the United States, Franklin D. Roosevelt, to receive the coveted Robert J. Collier Trophy, US aviation's highest award. The President read the citation. 'This airplane, by reason of its high speed, economy and quiet passenger comfort, has been generally adapted by transport lines throughout the United States. Its merits have been further recognised by its adoption abroad, and its influence on foreign design is already apparent'. This was just one of the many honours which the development of the DC-2 brought to designer and constructor Donald W. Douglas. (Douglas)

ABOVE: *This right-hand passenger door DC-3-277B NC25664 was delivered to American as* Flagship Rochester *on 28 March 1940. Between 18 April 1942 and 23 August 1943 it was probably leased to the military. It is depicted in take-off sequence.* (American Airlines)

RIGHT: *Air New England commenced a third level service in April 1971 with six refurbished DC-3 airliners. The colourful interior is depicted in this view looking forward towards the cockpit. They were operated successfully until 1975.* (Air New England)

RIGHT: *Rare photograph taken during 1939 depicting right-hand door DC-3-208A NC21745* Flagship Phoenix *of American Airlines c/n 2103 delivered on 18 February 1939. The three-wheel vehicle plus the small items of freight being loaded are of historic interest.* (American Airlines)

ABOVE: *When Air New England of Barnstaple, Massachusetts, commenced third level air services in April 1971 they used six veteran DC-3s. Depicted is N18105 c/n 1953 ex-DST-A-207 NC18105 of United delivered on 16 July 1937. It was impressed into military service as C-48B 42-56100 in 1942. In 1979 it joined the fleet of PBA being re-registered N43PB.* (AP Photo Library)

RIGHT: *Modern day DC-3 cockpit packed with updated avionics and depicted is DC-3-208 VP-LVH c/n 1963 of Air BVI in the 1970s. Originally built as NC17338 for American Airlines as* Flagship Philadelphia *and delivered on 22 July 1937. Up to a few years ago this veteran was operating from San Juan, Puerto Rico.* (Austin Brown)

BELOW: *This Douglas C-48A ex-41-7682 c/n 4146 formerly a DC-3A-368 built on 30 June 1941 survived World War II being transferred to the Civil Aviation Administration on 1 August 1946. It is seen at National Airport, Washington DC on 31 July 1946 still in military marks with N86 inscribed. It was later transferred to the FAA being re-registered N1. On 27 March 1975 it crashed at Dubois, Jefferson, Pennsylvania.* (Peter M. Bowers)

Swissair (Schweizerische Luftverkehr) was formed from Balair and Ad Astra in 1931. Its initial resources were quite slender with only nine pilots and twelve other crew. In 1932 Swissair purchased the DC-2 and later the DC-3. By 1939 eight Douglas twin-engined types were in Swissair service. Fokker assembled the Douglas DC-3s and the first two were delivered in June 1937 – HB-IRA c/n 1945 and HB-IRI c/n 1946. These two served the airline until 1955. Depicted is a nose close-up of a Swissair DC-3. (Swissair)

This DC-3 HB-ISB c/n 4667 today operates pleasure flights for Classic Air from Zurich-Kloten. It is depicted in Swissair pre-war livery during the 60th Anniversary of the birth of the airline 26 March 1931. (Swissair)

LEFT: *Swissair added the DC-3 to its fleet in 1937 with more purchased post-war, the type remaining in service until replaced by Convair liners. The last DC-3 was sold in 1969. Depicted is DC-3 HB-IRN c/n 33393 ex-RAF KN683 delivered to Swissair on 28 March 1947. Today this transport is preserved in the Transport Museum (Verkehshaus) in Lucerne.* (AP Photo Library)

RIGHT: *Many Russian-built Li-2 transports are today preserved in Russia, China and eastern Europe countries, where the type was in service in large numbers. This Li-2 '03' is preserved at Norilsk in Northern Siberia. It was withdrawn from use late in 1989 and seen on 28 May 1991.* (Paul Duffy)

LEFT: *In 1941 the advance of German invasion forces dictated the transfer of PS-84 (Passazhirskii Samolet Plant 84) near Moscow to Tashkent Plant 18 and on 17 September 1944 the Russian DC-3 designation was changed to Lisunov Li-2. Production continued until 1945 when estimates suggested some 3,000 Li-2s had been built. Recently it was revealed that twice that number in fact had been constructed. This Li-2 is mounted outside the Tashkent factory.* (Paul Duffy)

Chapter Three
Douglas DC-1

The single most important date in the history of the Douglas Aircraft Company is 2 August 1932. It was on this date that Jack Frye, Vice-President in charge of Operations with Transcontinental & Western Air (TWA) wrote letters to several manufacturers. These included General Aviation (North American Aviation), Consolidated, Curtiss-Wright, the Douglas Aircraft Company and Glenn L. Martin.

Donald W. Douglas, thirty-eight-year-old President of his own company in Santa Monica, California, had been pondering for some time how to introduce Douglas Aircraft into a more productive and secure civil aircraft field. Most of the orders so far relied heavily on military contracts, and while the company had built fifty-seven mailplanes and a dozen civil Dolphin amphibians, civil aircraft had been sparse, and the company had never been in competition for airline transports.

Then there had been the loss of the TWA Fokker F-10A NC999E on 31 March 1931. The ensuing public furore created much distress in the air transport industry, resulting in a call for major design and construction changes for safer and better designed aircraft. Early in 1932 it became common knowledge that Boeing in Seattle were working on a design of a new and revolutionary all-metal airliner of twin-engine, low-wing construction based on the advanced Boeing YB-9 bomber. The Model 247 was expected to fly early in 1933.

Despite the Great Depression, these events were to signal the end of the slow, comfortable, uneconomical, wooden-winged Fokker, Ford and Stinson tri-motors, the Curtiss Condor biplanes and others. The days of the Ford 'Tin Goose' were numbered.

Jack Frye had held a meeting with the TWA executives to discuss the company's operating losses and their failure to place an order with Boeing for the new Model 247. At this time TWA was operating Ford and Fokker tri-motors, some Northrop Alphas and an odd assortment of other aircraft. A competitive airliner was needed, and quickly. Discussions were also held with pilots, engineers, technicians and Charles Lindbergh, TWA's technical advisor. What evolved was a collection of ideas covering four volumes of facts and figures. From these a simple specification was devised, and mailed to the aircraft manufacturers.

General Aviation immediately contracted to build an all-metal, tri-motor, low-wing monoplane as their GA-38 project. It was Harold Talbot Jr, GA Chairman and a good friend of Donald Douglas, who urged him to respond to Frye's letter. Here was a good chance for Douglas to enter the commercial aviation field and it was a challenge to tempt any aircraft designer's ego.

The two-paragraph letter solicited bids for ten or more tri-motor transports. The TWA specification called for an all-metal, tri-motored monoplane, but a combination-materials structure or even biplane would be considered. The main internal construction wings and fuselage must be of metal, however. Recommended power-plants were the 500-550 hp Wasp engines equipped with superchargers for high-altitude operation, being built by Pratt & Whitney. The transport must provide for a crew

A scale-model of the new Douglas DC-1 airliner was extensively tested in the 200 mph wind tunnel located at the California Institute of Technology, supervised by the physicist and aerodynamicist, Dr W. B. Oswald, who was hired as a consultant on the DC-1 project. (Douglas)

of two, pilot and co-pilot, with a cabin capable of carrying at least twelve passengers in comfortable seats and fully equipped with the many fixtures and conveniences generally expected. The most stringent requirement read as follows: 'This plane, fully loaded, must make satisfactory take-offs under good control at any TWA airport on any combination of two engines.' The fact that one of TWA's major airports was Albuquerque, New Mexico, located at an elevation of 4,954 ft and where summer temperatures often exceeded 90°F, made this requirement seemingly difficult to meet. There was no doubt about it, the specification was a challenge.

The letter concluded by asking Donald Douglas to advise whether his company was 'interested in this manufacturing job' and, if so, 'approximately how long would it take to turn out the first plane for service tests.' Donald Douglas called the letter from Jack Frye 'the birth certificate of the DC ships' and deservedly so. After thoroughly digesting the contents of the letter he called in his production and engineering team – J.H. 'Dutch' Kindelberger, Arthur E. Raymond, Fred Herman, Lee Atwood, Ed Burton, Fred Stineman and Harry E. Wetzel. The Douglas team decided to accept the challenge, exceed what TWA had demanded, but to use a different approach in achieving the end product. The requirement for three engines was scrapped. More powerful engines would soon be available as both Pratt & Whitney and Wright-Aeronautical had some new designs on the test blocks. Two of these were expected to be sufficient. The adoption of a fuselage sufficient to accommodate

This close-up photograph of the DC-1 shows in detail the 710hp Wright SGR-1820-F Cyclone nine-cylinder air-cooled radial engines driving three-bladed Hamilton Standard propellers. Photograph taken on 26 August 1933 with Eddie Allen in the cockpit. Eddie flew the DC-1A powered by Pratt & Whitney Hornets for the first time on 6 October 1933. (Douglas)

taller passengers and enable them to stand upright in the aisle, combined with effective cabin sound-proofing, were to offer greater passenger appeal and make the transport more competitive.

Donald Douglas replied to Jack Frye's letter indicating that the company was definitely interested. The team's proposal was already put on paper and there was even a name for the project – they called it the DC-1, Douglas Commercial Model No. 1. Only ten days after the receipt of the TWA specification, Arthur Raymond, deputy chief engineer, and Harry E. Wetzel, general manager, left for New York by railroad to present the proposal to TWA. The team had not been idle, and TWA wanted quick results. Kindelberger and Raymond had worked out the initial performance figures. Fred Herman, project engineer, had been involved with hardware design; Lee Atwood, wing design and stress analysis; Ed Burton, other flying surfaces; Harold Adams, hydraulics and the landing gear; Ivar L. Shogran, power plant and attendant designs.

The team involvement was evident from the start. Kindelberger thought the two engines sheathed in full NACA cowlings should be sufficient to power the DC-1. Arthur Raymond was for the use of the Northrop-designed, multi-cellular, stressed-skin, tapered wings, light in weight, but extremely strong. TWA already had plenty of experience with this type of wing on their mailplanes. The wing would be three-piece with the outer panels bolted outboard of the nacelles. The centre section would form an integral part of the fuselage, supporting both the engines and the landing gear. All agreed that the undercarriage would retract into the engine nacelles. This would add to the speed.

Wetzel and Raymond remained in New York for three weeks working out details with TWA. With Harry Wetzel negotiating all contractual and financial questions and Arthur Raymond discussing technical matters with the engineering staff of TWA, plus their chief technical advisor, Charles Lindbergh, the Douglas representatives were able to impress the management of TWA. On 20 September 1932, the contract was signed in the presence of Jack Frye, Richard W. Robbins, President of TWA, and Charles Lindbergh, who was also TWA's most famous stockholder. The price agreed for the aeroplane was $125,000 to be paid in gold bullion; if the cost exceeded that figure, Douglas would have to stand the difference. An option clause in the contract gave TWA the right to buy all, or part of, sixty additional transports in lots of ten, fifteen or twenty, at $58,000 each. This figure did not include the cost of the engines. That same day Donald Douglas signed the work order at Santa Monica to start the DC-1 project and sent it down to the workshops. The first transport would have to be hand-built. It was projected that production might reach fifty airliners. The first Douglas Commercial aircraft was underway.

Despite the depression and the secrecy surrounding the DC-1 project, Douglas stock suddenly rose from $7.12 a share to $16. The precarious economic conditions prevailing at this time and the problems facing the airline industry had done much to dampen the early enthusiasm of the Douglas team. It was Harold E. Talbot Jr who boosted morale. He was Chairman of North American Aviation Inc., which owned 89,000 shares of the Douglas stock, the largest stockholder apart from Donald Douglas himself; he was also a director of TWA.

The Douglas team, already experienced, benefitted from the valuable assistance of several individuals and companies. John K. Northrop, on returning to Douglas, contributed to the DC-1 design his multi-cellular wing construction which accounted to a large extent for the longevity of the DC-1 and its descendants, the DC-2 and DC-3. A team from the California Institute of Technology, led by Drs Clark B. Millikan and Arthur L, Klein, after conducting extensive wind-tunnel testing of the DC-1 with models, helped the Douglas team by pointing out the need to move the aircraft's centre of gravity forwards and to change the radius of curvature of the fillet joining the wing to the fuselage to improve lift and reduce drag. Douglas obtained from the National Advisory Committee for Aeronautics (NACA) information necessary for the design of more efficient engine nacelles and cowlings and for the use of an improved wing aerofoil. Stephen J. Zand of the Sperry Corporation volunteered new ideas and techniques to reduce noise level inside the passenger cabin. Finally, from the office of Frank W. Caldwell, chief engineer of the Hamilton Standard Propeller Company, came the design of the variable-pitch propellers without which the DC-1 would not have been able to meet the stringent single-engine requirements laid down by TWA. The combination of the talents of the Douglas engineers and their outside associates resulted in an aircraft which exceeded all the original performance specifications of Transcontinental & Western Air.

Into Production

From the inception of the DC-1 project, the Douglas team decided to depart somewhat from the TWA specification, to improve their competitive chances and achieve performance superior to that of the Boeing Model 247. At the Santa Monica factory detailed engineering work began at once and, in addition to the extensive use of wind-tunnel tests, this involved fuselage mock-up and independent test models for various systems such as fuel and hydraulics, to optimise the design. Work moved ahead of schedule. On 15 March 1933, TWA representatives approved the fuselage mock-up, which was about 60 per cent complete. However, in the process of adding all the luxuries, including sound-proofing, cabin temperature control, improved lavatory facilities and more comfortable seats, the weight had increased from 14,200 to 17,000 lb. A 1/11th scale model of the DC-1 was undergoing tests in the 200 mph wind tunnel at Cal-Tech. Dr W. Bailey Oswald, known as 'Ozzy', had joined the team.

Arthur Raymond went to Kansas City for ten days to confirm technical details with Jack Frye, Paul Richter, Walt Hamilton, Chief Pilot D.W. 'Tommy' Tomlinson and other operations personnel with TWA. On his return to Santa Monica on 16 October he flew in a vibrating Ford Tri-motor which was to effect his thoughts on passenger comfort. Cotton ear wads were handed to passengers to help quell the noise. Conversation across the aisle could only be accomplished by shouting. The lavatory was tiny and the entry narrow. The wicker seats covered with leather were very uncomfortable, and on climbing to altitude to fly over the mountains the temperature in the cabin was freezing.

Hundreds of structural tests were carried out before construction began. Three different wing designs were tried. Tests revealed instability brought about by the leading edge sweepback which allowed the landing gear to be forward of the centre of gravity, assisting in anti-nose over. The Northrop wing proved superior in a number of additional categories such as ease of construction, low unit stresses, low maintenance costs, and maximum rigidity. Extensive flutter tests were performed on control surfaces. Torsional tests were carried out on window and door frames. Great attention was paid to fillet design, another Northrop contribution. A hundred wing-rib tests were carried out with a hundred specimens of structure. Aerofoils selected were the NACA 2215 at root and NACA 2209 at the tip. The tailwheel fork design was tried out behind a truck with concrete blocks simulating aft fuselage weights.

The fuselage design had sufficient depth so that the centre section spars were below the floor level, in contrast to the Boeing 247 and the later Lockheed L-10 Electra. Control cables were routed beneath the floor panels. Cabin height would be 6 ft 3 in and the width 5 ft 6 in with 16 in allocated for the aisle. Metal for construction was the new 24S and 24SRT Alclad. With aerodynamic configurations finalised, the fabrication process began on two aeroplanes. One was a full scale mock-up made of a wooden framework and covered with heavy paper to simulate the aluminium skin of the real aircraft. The other was the DC-1 itself.

Selection of engines led to intense competition between Pratt & Whitney and Wright-Aeronautical, the latter with their SGR-1820 F-1 Cyclone rated at 710 hp, geared 16:11 at 1,950 rpm at 8,000 ft. Pratt & Whitney offered the R-1690 SD-G Hornet of 700 hp, geared at 3:2 at 2,150 rpm at 6,500 ft. There was both great rivalry and great secrecy. By April 1933, experts from the Wright team had moved into Santa Monica. They set up their office on one side of the ramp, while a team from Pratt & Whitney did the same thing across the way, their products hidden by large screens. The two teams did not speak to each other for fear of divulging company secrets. Both engines were

supercharged, geared, nine-cylinder radials of near-equal size and weight. It was felt in many circles that the engine selection was as interesting as the DC-1 itself.

Both TWA and Douglas agreed initially to install the Wright engines, but there were some problems with the Hornet which were not resolved in time for the first flight. The variable-pitch propeller units were not ready, so DC-1 made its first flight with fixed-pitch propellers. On Thursday 22 June 1933, little more than ten months after receipt of Jack Frye's letter, the first and only Douglas DC-1 was rolled out of its hangar and on to Clover Field. She looked gigantic. The fuselage was 60 ft long, half as long again as a Greyhound bus. A low-wing monoplane with a wing span of 85 ft, it rested on a conventional undercarriage, two main wheels on shock-absorbing struts plus a small tailwheel. This was the largest land-plane configuration ever built in the United States as a bi-motored monoplane design. It carried the experimental registration X223Y and had the Douglas factory serial number 1137.

The new DC-1, still with X223Y registration, seen parked at Grand Central Air Terminal, Glendale, California, when TWA gave demonstration flights to its regular passengers and guests. Prior to the DC-1 and DC-2 appearing in service the TWA ramp would be occupied with the airline's Ford Trimotors. (Douglas)

First Flight

On Saturday morning, 1 July 1933, some 332 days from the date of the TWA letter, the DC-1 was ready for its initial test flight. It was planned to fly it during the lunch hour so that all 800 Douglas factory personnel could watch. Taxi and brake tests had been completed by Chief Pilot Carl Cover. The weather was bright and clear with a light westerly wind blowing off the Pacific Ocean. Carl Cover was joined by Fred Herman, the project engineer, and the DC-1 taxied to the east end of the runway, turned into wind and, after cockpit checks, started its take-off roll. The transport was airborne at exactly 12.36 p.m. – all was well. That is, for thirty seconds, at which point the port engine spluttered and stopped. The pilot recovered a few hundred feet of altitude, then the starboard engine also stopped. To the dismay of the watching crowds, the maiden flight was almost the last flight as the engines failed each time the DC-1 reached its climbing attitude. The new Douglas DC-1 was saved only through Cover's skilful piloting.

A second flight was made with Frank Collbohm, flight test engineer. The results were the same, but there were no answers to the questions that arose. A third flight with Ivar L. Shogran on board produced the same frightening performance. The DC-1 was grounded. For a week every one of the systems on the aeroplane was checked, re-checked and tested, but nothing was found to explain the failure.

Investigation eventually revealed that the carburettor floats on the Cyclone engine were mounted in such a way that fuel flow ceased every time the nose of the aircraft was raised. Despite strong objections from the Curtiss-Wright Company the carburettor was reversed, and the fuel inlets and controls were changed. On 7 July the DC-1 made a further test flight and the engines worked as intended.

During the three months following the eventful maiden flights, the DC-1 was intensively tested by pilots from Douglas, TWA and the US Bureau of Air Commerce. The test programme was marked by a series of memorable incidents, including the almost complete jamming of the control surfaces due to the use of the wrong type of hydraulic fluid in the automatic pilot system. Test pilot Eddie Allen, with 'Tommy' Tomlinson as co-pilot and Frank Collbohm and 'Doc' Oswald on board, flew over to Mines Field, the airport serving Los Angeles, to do some landing tests. Oswald would assist with calibrations and handle the landing-gear pump. Through a misunderstanding he did not receive the instruction to pump the wheels down. The DC-1 suffered a couple of bent propellers but no structural damage and by mid-August it was flying again.

Gross load tests were completed on 24 August. Loaded with sandbags to 17,500 lb, the DC-1 lifted off the runway in 1,000 ft. Speed tests were conducted over a measured course at different altitudes, the best speed attained being 212 mph. Jack Frye brought over a TWA pilot, Captain Smith, to fly the DC-1. Eddie Rickenbacker, Vice-President of Eastern Air Transport,

Seen on 16 August 1933 the DC-1 is seen embarking passengers despite still carrying experimental X registration. It had become TWA property on 13 September 1933 and it had cost the Douglas Aircraft Company $306,778 to design, build and test. Of interest is the fairing built around the fixed tail wheel. (Douglas)

was another interested visitor. On 4 September 1933, the transport was put through its most difficult test to demonstrate its ability to meet TWA's most stringent requirement – a flight from Winslow, Arizona, to Albuquerque, New Mexico, with one engine shut down from take-off to landing. Personnel on board included Eddie Allen, pilot; 'Tommy' Tomlinson, co-pilot; Frank Collbohm, flight test engineer; 'Doc' Oswald, aerodynamicist; Bill Birren, Wright Aeronautical; Ralph Ellinger, TWA factory inspector; and Clarence Young, US Department of Commerce.

The following day, after one of its engines had been switched off during the take-off run, the DC-1 climbed slowly from 4,500 ft to its cruising altitude of 8,000 ft, and, single-engined, successfully flew the 280 miles between the two airports. Winslow had an altitude of 4,878 ft with runway 24/06, a length of 4,752 feet. Birren, Ellinger and Young took a TWA Ford Tri-motor schedule to Albuquerque, taking off before the DC-1, which arrived first.

Douglas had proved, without any doubt, the ability of the new DC-1 to meet all TWA's requirements. On 13 September 1933, the DC-1 became TWA property. The airline placed an initial order for twenty DC-2s, a derivative of the DC-1 with the fuselage length increased by two feet to accommodate an additional row of two seats.

Pratt & Whitney pressed Douglas to install the nine-cylinder air-cooled Hornet for comparative tests. There was some interest expressed in a Hornet-powered version of the DC-1, plus the promise of an improved and more powerful E-series Hornet, so Douglas was persuaded to design, construct and flight test a Model L SD-G-1690 Hornet installation. By late September 1933, the Pratt & Whitney technical team had completed the installation of two 700 hp engines. The aircraft was redesignated DC-1A and made its first flight on 6 October piloted by Eddie Allen and D.W. 'Tommy' Tomlinson. Extensive ground and flight tests were conducted and the Hornet engines were in and out of the DC-1 several times as various improvements were incorporated. However, it was the Wright Cyclone which was eventually selected.

On 15 November Donald Wills Douglas took his first flight in the DC-1 with Carl Cover and 'Tommy' Tomlinson as pilots on the aircraft's first cross-continental flight from Santa Monica to Newark, New Jersey. Douglas had business with Dick Robbins,

President of TWA, to re-negotiate the airframe contract price of $58,000 each to $65,000, due to the United States going off the gold standard. The DC-1 had cost the Douglas Aircraft Company $306,778 to design, build and test. The new airliner was introduced to both the press and the general public on a 'show-and-tell' public relations exercise. Numerous airports were visited during check flights.

Rare photograph of the DC-1 with not only the name Skyliner *inscribed on the tail, but its transcontinental record recorded on the fuselage, plus the fact that it was the holder of eight international and eleven national records for speed, weight and distance.* (Peter M. Bowers)

Airline Service

The DC-1 was officially handed over to TWA during December 1933, in a ceremony at Los Angeles Municipal Airport when the company handed Donald Douglas a cheque for $125,000. This was the beginning of a new era for the Douglas Aircraft, which was to become the largest producer of commercial airliners in the world. Now registered NC223Y with TWA, the DC-1 was used as a flying laboratory over the airline's network, and occasionally operated for scheduled passenger flights pending the delivery of the first production DC-2s.

Tomlinson continued experimental flying, working out the best operational cruise speeds, various altitudes, fuel consumption with both and single engines and comparing his figures with those of the factory for guaranteed performance; his results sometimes exceeded the guarantees. The DC-1 was quoted as one of the earliest transport aircraft operated basically on a manifold pressure favouring combustion chamber areas by which supercharging allowed cruise-control power up to around 8,000 ft. A major step forward, for more altitude power and less dynamic drag.

Paul Richter, senior pilot with TWA, worked out a schedule for mail flights at night between Grand Central Air Terminal, Glendale, and Kansas City. As well as being a means of checking out pilots for the new DC-2, it was a useful utilisation of the DC-1 and enabled the pilots to learn its idiosyncrasies. The steam-heating system was found to be very unreliable and on the nightly mail flights pilots found it necessary to wear heavy clothing and sheepskin boots. Tomlinson complained about the landing gear being spongy on taxying.

On 9 February 1934, President Roosevelt signed Executive Order No. 6591, cancelling all private airmail contracts. The US Army Air Corps was to carry the mail and the expiry date for airline contracts was 19 February. Jack Frye requested the use of a DC-2 from Donald Douglas to fly mail before the expiry day, but had to use the DC-1. With Eddie Rickenbacker, Jack Frye loaded the transport to the maximum with mail sacks and took off from Glendale hours before the deadline. It proved the point that the airlines could do the task of flying the mail better than the US Army.

Flying on oxygen, they crossed the Rockies at 14,000 ft, refuelled at Kansas City, then flew on to Columbus, Ohio, in very bad weather. Over Pennsylvania they flew into a blinding snowstorm, so climbed the DC-1 to 19,500 ft, where a tailwind gave them a speed of 230 mph. On landing in Ohio they were surprised to discover that they had crossed the continent in a record time of 13 hours 4 minutes. The two 690 hp SGR-1820-F engines had been changed for two 710 hp SGR-1820-F3s and later for two 760 hp SGR-1820-F52s.

Record Breaker

During the early part of 1935 the DC-1 was extensively modified before being loaned by TWA to the National Aeronautical Association for an attempt at various US and world speed, distance and weight-carrying records. For this the engines were changed once more for two 875 hp Wright SGR-1820-F25s and additional fuel tanks were installed in the fuselage to increase the total capacity from 510 US gallons to 2,100. This meant eliminating most of the cabin windows. Maximum take-off weight rose to 28,500 lb. Valves allowed the fuel to be dumped, if need be, in three minutes in order to make an emergency landing.

So modified, the DC-1, on its positioning flight to the east coast, broke its own transcontinental speed record on 30 April 1935: flown by D.W. Tomlinson, H.B. Snead, and F.R. Redpath, it flew non-stop from Burbank, California, to New York in 11 hours 5 minutes. Between 16 and 19 May, piloted by Tomlinson and J.S. Bartles, the DC-1 set or broke no fewer than twenty-two records, including eight world records. The most significant of these was accomplished on 16/17 May when the DC-1, carrying a 2,205 lb load, flew over a 3,107 mile course in 18 hours 22 minutes 49 seconds at an average speed of 169.03 mph.

Not too many DC-1 photographs depict it in flight. In 1934 TWA used the airliner for various flying laboratory tests, such as developing new equipment for use of passengers and crew in the sub-stratosphere regions, for increasing engine horsepower at high altitudes, being fitted with equipment applicable to the development of super-charged cabins. In the photograph the tail wheel fairing is fitted. (Douglas)

Also during early 1935 the DC-1 was loaned to the US Department of Commerce and US Army Air Corps to test a new Sperry automatic pilot linked to the Kreuse radio compass. The military were very interested in purchasing the DC-2, but there was a problem of funds. They were operating an assortment of military airliners such as the Fokker C-2, C-5, C-7, Ford C-3, C-4, C-9, Fairchild C-8 and C-24 Pilgrim, and the Bellanca C-27. None was very efficient compared with the new Douglas Commercial transports.

During the early part of 1936, TWA conducted some high-altitude research with the DC-1. The engines were changed to Wright GR-1820-F55 Cyclones fitted with two-speed blowers, turning Hamilton Standard constant-speed propellers, plus oxygen and an autopilot. The latter enabled the captain and crew to record data on both engine and aircraft performance, as well as cloud and wind data above 20,000 feet. At these extreme altitudes, the DC-1 was flown on instruments, and frost obscured all the windows.

Overseas

In January 1936, having completed and fulfilled its experimental tasks, the DC-1 was acquired by Western Aero & Radio Company of Burbank, California, for Howard Hughes, TWA's largest stockholder. It was re-engined with 875 hp Wright Cyclone F-52 engines for an attempt to break the around-the-world record set by Wiley Post. The original intention was to enter the transport in the 1936 Bendix air race, but for some reason this did not happen. Modified with long-range fuselage tanks, the range of the DC-1 was extended to 6,000 miles. In addition to the around-the-world flight, Howard Hughes had three record attempts in mind: Hollywood to New York via Nome, Alaska; Khabarovsk–Vladivostok–Shanghai–Khabarovsk, and Nome to Edmonton, Canada. He also planned a New York to Moscow flight via Paris. Authorisation for these flights was requested from the US Department of Commerce and the Department of State, but delays occurred and eventually Hughes lost interest in the DC-1 and used a more powerful Lockheed 14 for his around-the-world flight.

On 4 January 1937, the DC-1 appeared on a shipper's export declaration document submitted by the Vimalert Company Limited. Robert Cuse, an engineer born in Lithuania and President of the Vimalert Corporation of Jersey City, had exported reconditioned aircraft engines and other equipment to the USSR, through Amtorg, the Soviet trading organisation in the United States since the 1920s. It is believed Amtorg provided Cuse with several million pounds sterling during September 1936, in order to purchase aircraft and other material for Republican Spain. On 24 December 1936, Cuse had applied for a licence to export eighteen aircraft, 411 aero engines and parts with which to make a further 150 engines, direct to Bilbao. The list included the Douglas DC-1 c/n 1137 NC223Y. Although the sums paid were much higher, the valuation on the export certificates for the DC-1 was $70,000. Its real market value was in the region of $50,000.

The DC-1, along with seven Vultee V-1As, six Boeing Model 247s, two Northrop Deltas, one Lockheed Model 10 Electra and a Fairchild 91, was due to be shipped on board the SS *Mar Cantabrico* at New York with Bilbao as the destination. For some reason not known, the DC-1 was in the end not included in the shipment.

The DC-1 remained idle for two years, its history rather obscure, though it was rumoured to have been used briefly by the US Army Air Corps. On 27 May 1938, Howard Hughes sold it to Viscount Forbes, the Earl of Granard. Total air-frame hours had reached 1,370. It was originally intended to fly the DC-1 across the Atlantic and Hughes had it modified in preparation for the journey. It had had a new set of wings fitted which had been meant for DC-2 c/n 1292 for Eastern Air lines: the fins and rudder had been enlarged, and all the fuselage windows filled in. In fact, the DC-1 was shipped to London on the deck of a freighter. It was found too large to pass through the dock gates, so was transferred to a lighter and unloaded further down the River Thames at Dagenham, the home of the Ford Motor Company. After assembly by KLM engineers, who already had experience assembling Fokker contracted DC-2s, it was flown to Croydon Airport and registered G-AFIF.

During September 1938, Lord Forbes used the DC-1 to fly parties of journalists to Munich to cover the Sudetenland crisis. However, it soon became apparent that the DC-1 was far too large to retain and operate as a private aircraft, and later that year it was sold, possibly through a dealer, to La Société Française de Transports Aériens (SFTA). The company was small, but recognised by the French right-wing Press and by the Non-Intervention Committee in London as a major supplier of aircraft and arms to the Spanish republic.

Mysteriously, having failed to reach Spain early in 1937, the DC-1 did turn up there during November 1938 and was registered EC-AGN Fleet No. 39. It served with LAPE – Líneas Aéreas Postales Españolas, the airline operated for the Republicans. Its Alclad skin was camouflaged and it went into service on the routes Barcelona–Toulouse–Paris and Barcelona–Valencia–Albacete. While with Lord Forbes it had been returned to airline configuration. When Barcelona fell to General Franco's Nationalists during February-March 1939, members of the government were flown out of the country to France in the DC-1. The transport must have returned to Spain, though, for on 23 March it was the aircraft in which two Republican officers, Colonels Ortega and Garigo, flew from Madrid to Burgos in a vain attempt to negotiate peace terms more honourable than the unconditional surrender demanded by General Franco. The government capitulated in April.

During the last week of the Civil War the DC-1 flew parties of senior Republican officials to France. It was returned to Spain, along with Douglas DC-2s and other aircraft, during May 1939, and on 7 July was transferred to SATA – Sociedad Anónima de Transportes Aéreos, which later became Iberian Airlines. It was re-registered EC-AAE, and christened '**Manuel Negrón**' after Commandante Manuel Negrón de las Cuevas, the Nationalist airman killed during the Battle of Turuel. The Douglas transport was placed on the Seville–Málaga–Tetuán route.

In December 1940, the DC-1 arrived at Málaga on the regular morning scheduled service. Passengers disembarked and others embarked. The aircraft taxied out to the end of the runway, power checks on the engines indicated all was normal, and the throttles were opened for take-off. Just as the DC-1 became airborne, one of the engines failed and the pilot made a belly landing. The plane caught fire, but passengers got out quickly and there were no injuries. The DC-1 itself was wrecked beyond repair.

For many years during the Second World War, the wreck of the DC-1 lay corroding. It is recorded that during the Civil War the wooden float or *andas* on which the effigy of Nuestra Señora de la Esperanza (Our Lady of Hope) was carried through the streets of Málaga during Holy Week had been burned by Communist mobs during the Marxist occupation. Someone recalled the wrecked DC-1 at the airport. A new aluminium float for the cathedral was made from the fuselage metal of the DC-1.

It is all that remains of the progenitor of the most famous and successful line of civil aircraft ever produced – the Douglas Commercial series.

TRANSCONTINENTAL & WESTERN AIR. INC.

10 RICHARDS ROAD
MUNICIPAL AIRPORT
KANSAS CITY MISSOURI

August 2nd,
19 32

Douglas Aircraft Corporation,
Clover Field,
Santa Monica, California.

Attention: Mr. Donald Douglas

Dear Mr. Douglas:

Transcontinental & Western Air is interested in purchasing ten or more trimotored transport planes. I am attaching our general performance specifications, covering this equipment and would appreciate your advising whether your Company is interested in this manufacturing job.

If so, approximately how long would it take to turn out the first plane for service tests?

Very truly yours,

Jack Frye
Vice President
In Charge of Operations

JF/GS
Encl.

N.B. Please consider this information confidential and return specifications if you are not interested.

SAVE TIME - USE THE AIR MAIL

TRANSCONTINENTAL & WESTERN AIR, INC.

General Performance Specifications
Transport Plane

1. **Type:** All metal trimotored monoplane preferred but combination structure or biplane would be considered. Main internal structure must be metal.

2. **Power:** Three engines of 500 to 550 h.p. (Wasps with 10-1 supercharger; 6-1 compression O.K.).

3. **Weight:** Gross (maximum)   14,200 lbs.

4. **Weight** allowance for radio and wing mail bins   350 lbs.

5. **Weight** allowance must also be made for complete instruments, night flying equipment, fuel capacity for cruising range of 1080 miles at 150 m.p.h., crew of two, at least 12 passengers with comfortable seats and ample room, and the usual miscellaneous equipment carried on a passenger plane of this type. Payload should be at least 2,300 lbs. with full equipment and fuel for maximum range.

6. **Performance**

Top speed sea level (minimum)	185 m.p.h.
Cruising speed sea level - 79 % top speed	146 m.p.h. plus
Landing speed not more than	65 m.p.h.
Rate of climb sea level (minimum)	1200 ft. p.m.
Service ceiling (minimum)	21000 ft.
Service ceiling any two engines	10000 ft.

This plane, fully loaded, must make satisfactory take-offs under good control at any TWA airport on any combination of two engines.

Kansas City, Missouri.
August 2nd, 1932

Under the impetus of Jack Frye, Vice-President of TWA operations, a specification was drafted for a new three-engined aircraft, preferably of all-metal construction and monoplane configuration, to be powered by 500 to 550hp supercharged engines. A crew of two and at least twelve passengers were to be carried over a distance of 1,080 miles at a cruising speed of 150mph. On 2 August 1932 TWA sent its specification and an invitation to bid for the new transport design to Consolidated, Curtiss, General Aviation, Martin and Douglas. This is the TWA letter and specification. Within a few days the Douglas Aircraft Company expressed its intention to submit a proposal to TWA.

First Flagship service New York – Chicago

With just three Douglas DST airliners delivered, American Airlines launched its first non-stop Chicago to New York service on 25 June 1936 the first commercial operation with the aircraft which was to make history. The inaugural flight left Midway Airport, Chicago, at noon CST on that Thursday morning flown by Captain W. W. Braznell with First Officer Miller in NC16002 'Flagship Illinois'. The reciprocal service left Newark, New Jersey, at 1330 hours EST the same day, flown by Captain Melvin D. Ator with First Officer F. R. Bailey in NC16001 'Flagship New York'. The group of American Airline officials in the photograph include, left to right: M. D. Miller, J. T. Dunnion, Treasurer; Ralph Daman, Vice-President; and C. R. Smith, President, who later became Chairman. (American Airlines)

Chapter Four
Douglas DC-2

The performance achieved by the DC-1 led TWA to order twenty Douglas commercial transports on 4 September 1933. An order for a further twenty followed two months later. These aircraft, designated DC-2s, were fundamentally similar to the prototype, but incorporated enough minor refinements and significant structural changes to justify a new model number. The cabin was lengthened by two feet to accommodate two rows of seven passenger seats – the technique of stretching the fuselage of an airline transport to increase accommodation and payload, with a natural improvement in its operating economics, is a practice long favoured by the Douglas Aircraft Company. The DC-2 also sported a new rudder and wheel brakes. Take-off weight was 18,000 lb with fourteen passengers and 1,740 lb of freight, the maximum range was 1,060 miles at 196 mph and the fuel capacity was 510 US gallons. Several different engine installations were to be mated with the DC-2, including Wright Cyclones, Pratt & Whitney Hornets and even Bristol Pegasus VIs, but it went into production powered by Cyclone SGR-1820-F3 engines. Although it was initially equipped with two-position propellers, Frank Caldwell's Hamilton Standard fully-feathering units were later applied.

Except for the two-foot increase in the fuselage, it was outwardly identical to the finalised form of the DC-1, including the left-hand-side passenger door. To improve directional stability, later DC-2s incorporated an enlarged vertical fin. Gross weight of the new airliners varied from 18,200 lb to 18,560 lb, with some military cargo versions having a gross weight of 21,000 lb.

As 1933 became 1934, the Douglas factory at Santa Monica was a hive of industry, with a work force numbering 2,000 personnel. In one section of the factory a variety of observation aircraft for the US Army Air Corps were moving down the assembly line, whilst in another section the new DC-2s were taking shape. Initially there was a production problem. It was taking 58,000 man hours per DC-2, whereas the estimates showed a small margin of profit at 38,000 hours. George Strompl, shop foreman, had to explain to Donald Douglas that the first twenty transports had to be practically hand-made owing to the non-arrival of huge hydraulic presses ordered from Ohio. When these presses did eventually arrive the production time was cut down to 32,000 hours. During February 1934, production in the factory was at a peak level, the new DC-2 transport moving down the line at the rate of one every two weeks.

By 27 April 1934 the first DC-2-112 c/n 1237 for TWA with fleet No.301 was on final assembly, with many more to follow. It was registered NC13711 and delivered on 14 May. After stalwart service with TWA it went to the RAF in February 1941 as a DC-2K being struck off charge at Bangalore, Inida, on 8 November 1943. (Douglas)

This photograph dated 11 May 1934 shows the interior of a Douglas DC-2 airliner, looking forward with typical configuration of seven-rows of two-abreast seating. The new airliner had comfort, heating and ventilation, and was a winner for the airlines and the Douglas Aircraft Company. (Douglas)

Production and Export

Captain Eddie Rickenbacker and his team from Eastern Air Lines had now followed TWA in placing an order with Douglas, as had Western Air Lines, KLM (Royal Dutch Airlines) and ABA of Sweden. The first Douglas DC-2, NC13711 c/n 1237 designated model DC-2-112, for TWA was rolled out at Santa Monica at the beginning of May 1934, progressing rapidly through the usual acceptance formalities. The first flight took place on 11 May, with delivery to TWA following three days later. The initial proving flight was flown on 18 May along the Columbus–Pittsburgh–Newark route, and on 28 June the aircraft was certificated. By this time the order book for the DC-2 had reached seventy-five aircraft.

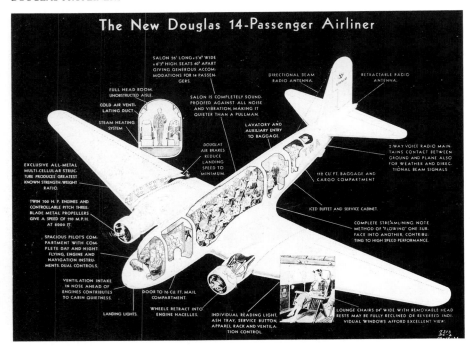

The New Douglas 14-Passenger Airliner

SALON 26' LONG x 5'6" WIDE x 6'3" HIGH: SEATS 40" APART GIVING GENEROUS ACCOMMODATIONS FOR 14 PASSENGERS.

FULL HEAD ROOM, UNOBSTRUCTED AISLE.

DIRECTIONAL BEAM RADIO ANTENNA

RETRACTABLE RADIO ANTENNA

COLD AIR VENTILATING DUCT

SALON IS COMPLETELY SOUNDPROOFED AGAINST ALL NOISE AND VIBRATION, MAKING IT QUIETER THAN A PULLMAN.

STEAM HEATING SYSTEM

LAVATORY AND AUXILIARY ENTRY TO BAGGAGE.

DOUGLAS AIR BRAKES REDUCE LANDING SPEED TO MINIMUM.

2-WAY VOICE RADIO MAINTAINS CONTACT BETWEEN GROUND AND PLANE ALSO FOR WEATHER AND DIRECTIONAL BEAM SIGNALS

EXCLUSIVE ALL-METAL MULTI-CELLULAR STRUCTURE PRODUCES GREATEST KNOWN STRENGTH-WEIGHT RATIO.

112 CU. FT. BAGGAGE AND CARGO COMPARTMENT

TWIN 700 H. P. ENGINES AND CONTROLLABLE PITCH THREE-BLADE METAL PROPELLERS GIVE A SPEED OF 210 M.P.H. AT 8000 FT.

ICED BUFFET AND SERVICE CABINET.

COMPLETE STREAMLINING. NOTE METHOD OF "FLOWING" ONE SURFACE INTO ANOTHER, CONTRIBUTING TO HIGH SPEED PERFORMANCE.

SPACIOUS PILOT'S COMPARTMENT WITH COMPLETE DAY AND NIGHT FLYING, ENGINE AND NAVIGATION INSTRUMENTS. DUAL CONTROLS.

VENTILATION INTAKE IN NOSE AHEAD OF ENGINES CONTRIBUTES TO CABIN QUIETNESS.

DOOR TO 76 CU. FT. MAIL COMPARTMENT.

LANDING LIGHTS.

WHEELS RETRACT INTO ENGINE NACELLES.

INDIVIDUAL READING LIGHT, ASH TRAY, SERVICE BUTTON, APPAREL RACK AND VENTILATION CONTROL.

LOUNGE CHAIRS 24" WIDE WITH REMOVABLE HEAD RESTS MAY BE FULLY RECLINED OR REVERSED INDIVIDUAL WINDOWS AFFORD EXCELLENT VIEW.

This publicity cutaway of the new Douglas DC-2 14-passenger airliner was released by the Douglas Aircraft Company on 10 December 1933 some months before its first flight on Monday 14 May 1934. It was a new luxury airline transport and TWA inaugurated scheduled service with the DC-2 on 18 May 1934 between Columbus, Pittsburgh and Newark, New Jersey. (Douglas)

The new Douglas transport established nineteen American and world records in the early days of its service, including a speed record – New York to Chicago – four times over a period of eight days. By March 1935, the DC-2 held the transcontinental west-east transport record at 12 hours 45 minutes and soon afterwards the east-west record at 15 hours 39 minutes.

There was nothing flying that could match the DC-2 for speed or comfort. TWA introduced the new transport on the overnight New York to Los Angeles route during August 1934, proudly advertising 'Coast-to-coast in 18 hours via 200-mile-an-hour luxury airliners'. Dubbed *'Sky Chief'*, the DC-2 left Newark, New York, at 1600 hours daily, landed at Chicago shortly after dinner time and was in the air again bound for Kansas City at 2025 hours. Departing Kansas City at 2330 hours, it made the flight to Albuquerque, New Mexico, non-stop and from there, after a brief refuelling stop, it took off once more at 0320 hours, arriving in Los Angeles at 0700 local time. This service was undoubtedly epoch-making, and acceptance of the new airliner by the public was even greater than TWA had envisaged. Passenger load factors broke all records, and it was soon evident that the TWA-Douglas team had assumed leadership in air transportation.

During September 1934, Douglas DC-2s were delivered to Pan American Airways and Panagra for services in the Caribbean and in Central and South America. The first Pan Am aircraft was a model DC-2-118A NC14268 c/n 1301, delivered on 27 August 1934, to be re-delivered to Panagra the following month, with the remaining five of the initial batch of six following at short intervals. The first Eastern Air Lines transport was a DC-2-112 NC13735 c/n 1261, delivered during October, and the first of a large fleet of Douglas transports to operate between New York and Miami. In November American Airlines took delivery of the first of ten, a model DC-2-120 NC14274 c/n 1307; they were to operate the new transports between New York and Los Angeles.

Anthony Hermann Gerhard Fokker, the internationally famous Dutch aircraft manufacturer, had met Donald Douglas during 1933, at Santa Monica, whilst looking over the Douglas DC-1. This meeting was to mark the beginning of a close relationship. On 27 October 1933, Fokker cabled Douglas to acquire the licensing and sales rights for the DC-2 in Europe, and rumour had it that $100,000 was paid immediately. A contract was signed in the USA on 15 January 1934, but no DC-2 was ever to be produced in the Netherlands under the terms of the licence; Fokker merely acted as European sales agent, an arrangement that was to be responsible for the sale of a total of thirty-nine DC-2s and a larger number of DC-3s, as a result of the efforts of

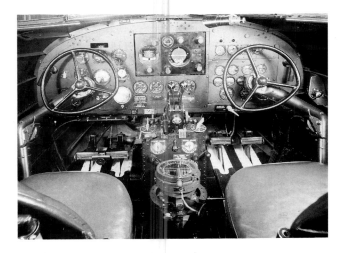

Unfortunately cockpit photographs of many early aircraft types are not always available. Depicted as an excellent view of the 'office up front' of a Douglas DC-2 airliner operated by KLM. Both Dutch and English are used on the instructions. The DC-2 had a range of 1,060 miles and carried 510 US gallons and cruised at 196mph. (KLM).

Six DC-2-112 airliners belonging to TWA lined up on the airline's ramp on 14 November 1934. The first twenty DC-2s were ordered by Trans Continental & Western Air who were the initiator of the Douglas Commercial series and the first operator of the DC-1 and DC-2. (Douglas)

Fokker's super salesman, F.W. Seekatz. Fokker, incidentally, adopted a numbering system for the DC-2s as accepted at the Douglas factory, commencing with KLM's first aircraft PH-AJU, a DC-2-115A c/n 1317, as Fokker No. 1.

On 25 January 1935, the Airspeed Company, based at a new factory in Portsmouth, Hampshire, had its capital increased by £130,000 with a new share issue for financial development following an agreement with Fokker. This included not only a licence to build Fokker-designed aircraft and to sell them throughout the British Empire, but also to build and sell in the United Kingdom the Douglas DC-2 for which Fokker held the European licence. Fokker was appointed technical advisor to Airspeed. Apart from £20,000 on the execution of the licence, a royalty of £600 was to be paid for each DC-2 manufactured up to twenty, and another £20,000 when sales reached a value of £150,000. Fokker was to receive one per cent of gross receipts, and had an option on preferred shares. The DC-2 contract even developed as far as assigning the design number AS.23 to the sub-contracted licence-built Douglas transports, and allocating the registration G-ADHO to what was presumably Airspeed's first DC-2. In the event, the agreement and any contract issued were subsequently cancelled, including the DC-2 registration from the British Civil Register.

On 11 September 1934, the Douglas representative in the Netherlands cabled the company in Santa Monica that the first DC-2s had crossed the Atlantic aboard the SS *Statendam*. These aircraft had been purchased by KLM and were, in fact, the first DC-2s to be exported. Originally allocated the registration NC14284, the first KLM aircraft became PH-AJU and was named '*Uiver*'. It had been delivered from the Santa Monica factory on 25 August 1934. Soon the new transport was in daily use on the KLM routes between Amsterdam and the principal cities of Europe and beyond, including the 9,000-mile route to Batavia, now Djakarta in Indonesia.

Less than five months after Fokker's acquisition of a licence to manufacture the DC-2, on 27 March 1934, the Japanese company Nakajima Hikoki KK also purchased a licence to build for the sum of $80,000; this was to be almost as abortive in terms of aircraft produced as the Dutch licence, and it later

became apparent that Japanese interest was primarily in the advanced technology that the Douglas DC-2 represented rather than the aircraft *per se*. In the event, only five DC-2s were to emerge from Nakajima's Koizuma facility, 45 miles north-west of Tokyo, where the programme was centred, and these were assembled from kits of major components imported from the parent Douglas company, Japanese content being limited to instrumentation and some minor items of equipment.

Both the Russians and the Japanese recognised the potential of the new Douglas Commercial series. Factory photograph of DC-2-123 NC14284 c/n 1323 seen on 16 October 1934 and registered to Douglas. On October 27 it went to Great Northern Airways in Nakajima, Japan, and was later registered J-BBOI with Dai Nippon Airlines. (Douglas)

One Douglas-built example of the transport, a DC-2-123 NC14284 c/n 1323, completed at Santa Monica on 16 October 1934, was acquired by Nihon Koku KK – Japan Air Transport Co – later to be recognised as Dai Nippon Koku KK – Greater Japan Air Transport Co – with Great Northern Airways of Canada acting as purchasing agent. This aircraft arrived in Yokohama on 22 November 1934, and by the beginning of December was on display at Haneda, where its technical features aroused immense interest. Meanwhile, the component kits for the five DC-2s mentioned earlier were ready for assembly at Koizuma. These had the Douglas c/n 1418 to 1422, and the first of them flew in February 1936, with the aircraft subsequently operating over Nippon Koku's Fukuoka to Taipei route, the airliner powered initially by Wright Cyclone SGR-1820-F2s and subsequently by SGR-1820-F52s. If the DC-2 itself was to prove of little importance to Japanese air transportation, the technology that the transport embodied was *certainly* significant, the newly-acquired Douglas techniques being applied to a series of bomber projects, while Nakajima evolved a somewhat smaller transport, the AT-2, which drew its inspiration from the DC-2.

A little known fact involved a single Douglas DC-2 acquired by the French government through Fokker. This was a DC-2-115B F-AKHD c/n 1333, delivered on 28 August 1935. Renault, the car and aero-engine manufacturers, contributed one-tenth of the purchase price for this aircraft, which was tested by the Centre d'Essais de Material Aérienne in the autumn of 1935. Renault at that time contemplated acquiring the manufacturing rights to produce a version which would have been powered by two nine-cylinder Renault engines but, even though flight trials were successful, the DC-2 was not destined to be adopted by the French. It was fitted with Bristol Pegasus engines and leased to Air France for trial flights between Paris and Algiers.

It was KLM's first DC-2 PH-AJU which was entered by the airline in the 1934 London to Melbourne Air Derby – the famed MacRobertson Trophy race. On 20 October 1934, at Mildenhall, Suffolk, twenty aircraft lined up for the start of the 11,123 mile race to Australia. The stakes were high, for, in addition to a solid gold trophy, there was a tempting $75,000 for the winner. Entries had come from France, England, the Netherlands, USA, Germany and Italy. It was announced that the Dutch DC-2 – piloted by a normal KLM flight crew, K.D. Parmentier and J.J. Moll – would fly its regular route, which was 1,000 miles longer than the prescribed course. In addition to the two pilots, '*Uiver*' was to carry a navigator and mechanic, three fare-paying passengers and 30,000 letters. Required stops included Baghdad, Allahabad, Darwin, Charlesville and finally Melbourne.

The KLM DC-2 did not win, in the event, but it did come second in both the speed and the handicap sections, and won the transport class event with an elapsed time of 90 hours 13 minutes and 36 seconds, which included a return to Allahabad in India to collect a misplaced passenger.

Back in California, Donald Douglas followed reports of the race with intense interest, particularly as the DC-2 was competing with two other US-built aircraft, both of which were in commercial service: a Boeing 247D flown by the well-known pilots Roscoe Turner and Clyde Pangborn, and a Lockheed transport.

Apparently the Douglas Company also conducted negotiations with the Soviet trading agency Amtorg, which desired to obtain manufacturing rights for the DC-2 in the USSR. These were not granted, but Amtorg purchased one DC-2-152 NC14949 c/n 1413, on 3 August 1935, for use and evaluation by Aeroflot with whom it is believed to have been registered CCP-M25.

Leading the Field

By the time the 1930s decade passed its halfway point, the DC-2 was universally recognised as the world's most advanced transport aircraft. United Air Lines faced intensive competition from the DC-2s of TWA, but had initially been able to hold its own to some extent by making modifications to its fleet of Boeing 247Ds; these improved the cruising speed by 28 mph, but increased the gross weight by 1,000 lb. This was, of course, no more than a palliative. As its DC-2s were faster – saving almost two hours on the transcontinental flight – more

comfortable and more economic than the UAL Boeings, TWA had every reason to congratulate itself on effectively initiating the development of the Douglas Commercial. But TWA was not to remain for long the sole DC-2 operator. Donald Douglas, having learned from Boeing's mistake of refusing to give prompt delivery of its Model 247s to customers other than United, had reserved the right to sell its DC-2s to customers other than TWA as long as its production capacity was sufficient to meet the contractual delivery schedule agreed with that airline. This arrangement was to prove more than beneficial to Douglas as, in spite of an agreed increase in unit price of $7,000 over the $58,000 stipulated when the original DC-1 contract was signed, the manufacturer was to show a loss on the construction of the TWA fleet of DC-2s.

Other airlines had certainly noted the remarkable performance of the DC-1 and were soon ordering substantial numbers of DC-2s. In the event, out of a total production of 193 civil and military DC-2s, seventy-five were to be ordered by and delivered to airline customers in the USA. These were to comprise thirty-one for TWA, sixteen for American Airlines, ten for Eastern, nine for Pan American, five for Panagra and four for General Air Lines. Three more were ordered by private customers. The Swiftflite Aircraft Corporation operated a Cyclone-powered DC-2-124 NC1000 c/n 1324 from October 1934 until November 1936 when it was sold to Pan American. A Hornet-powered DC-2A-127 NC14285 c/n 1328 was delivered to Standard Oil of California on 15 November 1934, but crashed on 6 October 1935 in Salt Lake City, Utah, due to fuel starvation. Finally, Captain George Whittell took delivery of a DC-2-190 NC16048 c/n 1586 on 11 August 1936. He named it the '*Thunderbird*'. The Swiftflight DC-2 was fitted out as a business executive aircraft with desk, large, comfortable chairs, filing cabinets, galley and even a telephone. The cost was upwards of a million dollars. This executive DC-2 was entered by George Pomeroy in the 1936 Bendix Air Race from New York to Los Angeles and, flown by Louis Brewer, was placed fourth.

The China National Airways Corporation (CNAC) was affiliated to Pan American Airways, who owned 45 per cent of its stock. From 1935 on the DC-2 was supplied to CNAC as depicted by this photograph taken on 8 July 1935. All CNAC DC-2s were initially registered in the USA to Pan American. (Douglas)

Typical airport ramp scene in the USA on 29 July 1935 with activity around an Eastern Air Lines DC-2, a type acquired soon after Eastern was formed as a division of North America Aviation on 17 April 1934. First DC-2 was delivered to the airline at the end of September 1934, initially in General Air Lines livery. (Douglas)

In early 1935, Captain Eddie Rickenbacker had become General Manager of Eastern Air Lines and it was he who placed an order for ten DC-2s, later to be increased to fourteen when the four originally ordered by General Air Lines were acquired. These aircraft were soon placed in service on the popular New York to Miami route. To promote the new schedule, Rickenbacker staged a one-day VIP flight in a DC-2 between the two cities, making the round trip in little more than sixteen hours. Guests took off from New York in the morning, had dinner in Miami and returned to New York the same evening. It was the beginning of the '*Great Silver Fleet*'.

Delta Air Lines took delivery of this DC-2-120 NC14275 c/n 1308 from American on 4 February 1940. A year later it was bought by the British Purchasing Commission going to the RAF as DG473 in April 1941. On 14 June 1942 it was damaged beyond repair after war service in India. (AP Photo Library)

Other domestic airlines in the USA – Western, Braniff, Northwest – converted their fleets as quickly as possible to the DC-2 transport. Pan American Airways was soon operating the DC-2 to Latin and South American destinations. Pan Am was also responsible for the fleet of four DC-2s for the China National Aviation Corporation (CNAC), the first of which arrived in Shanghai during March 1935, and the last being delivered unassembled during June 1936. CNAC was 45 per cent owned by Pan American from 1933 onwards, and both DC-2s and later DC-3s were supplied before the Second World War. The archives reveal that five DC-2s were delivered to CNAC, commencing with DC-2-118B NC14269 c/n 1302; this crashed at Nanking on 25 December 1936. A second DC-2-118B, NC14297 c/n 1369, followed and was sold in 1936. Two DC-2-221s followed – c/n 1567 delivered on 18 May 1937, and c/n 1568 on 30 May 1937. The unassembled aircraft was a DC-2-118A cn/ 1600 delivered on 26 June 1936.

A little more than a year after the first DC-2 had made its inaugural flight with TWA, the Douglas Commercial was flying under the flags of no less than twenty-one countries and had already flown twenty million miles. This was certainly an appropriate time for Douglas to survey the achievements of the DC-2, and the following are extracts from that survey:

With 108 silver-winged transports in service in the eastern and western hemispheres, flying approximately 75,000 miles every 24 hours on night and day schedules in all kinds of weather, operators claim that the Skyliners are performing work under variable operating conditions not possible heretofore. United States operators and Pan American Airways in South America report 15 million miles flown in the first eight months at an efficiency of 98.8 per cent. Douglas planes owned by foreign operators and private individuals in America and Europe made up the remaining five million miles....

TWA, American Airlines, Eastern Air Lines and Pan American Airways report their fleets of Douglas ships are negotiating 52,289 miles a day with 21,499 miles flown at night and 30,790 miles of daylight flying. Of the 26,259,665 miles flown in the US during the first six months of 1935, 7,286,437 miles were flown by Douglas planes or 27.7 per cent. However, the 42 Douglas transports available for service constituted only 7.6 per cent of the total planes in service in the US; a remarkable tribute to the Douglas operating ability....

Operating efficiency increased on the airlines using the Douglas luxury liners from the first month the planes were placed in service. Airlines report that operational efficiency – planes in the air not on the ground for mechanical delays – jumped 20 to 25 per cent. In some cases there was reported a 66 per cent gain in average 'air time' per day.

Development of the DC-2 brought many honours to Donald Wills Douglas. The new transport had been in service less than a year when he was invited to deliver the annual Wright Memorial Lecture before the Royal Aeronautical Society in London. It was with great pride that Douglas accepted the invitation. In the USA he was to receive another high honour in recognition of his work on the DC-2. On Wednesday, 1 July 1936, the third anniversary of the DC-1's maiden flight, Douglas stood before the President of the United States to receive the Robert J. Collier Trophy, US aviation's award. Franklin D. Roosevelt read the citation: 'This airplane, by reason of its high speed, economy and quiet passenger comfort, has been generally adopted by transport lines throughout the United States. Its merits have been further recognised by its adoption abroad, and its influence on foreign design is already apparent.'

Three major versions of the DC-2 were built, one powered by Wright Cyclone, one by Pratt & Whitney Hornets and one by the Bristol Pegasus. When powered by Cyclone engines – SR-1820-F2, -F2A, -F3, F3A, -F3B, -F52 or -F53 ranging from 710 hp to 875 hp for take-off, the commercial aircraft were generically known as DC-2s, with specific models being designated DC-2-112, DC-2-115, -115A, -115B, -115D, -115E, -115G and -115J to -115MO, -118A, -118B, -120, -123, -124, -152, -171, -172, -185, -190, -192, -193, -199, -200, -210, -211 and DC-2-221 depending on the engine model fitted and other special minor modifications requested by customers. With Hornet SD-G, S1E-G or S2E-G engines, the DC-2-115B, DC-2A-127, DC-2-115H and DC-2-165H were commonly

The flight crew of the KLM DC-2 PH-AJU 'Uiver' which took part in the race from Mildenhall to Melbourne, Australia, which commenced on Saturday 20 October 1934. Left to right: Bouwe Prins, Kolne Dirk Parmentier, Jan Johannes Moll and van Cor Brugge. (AP Photo Library)

known as DC-2As. Finally two DC-2-115Fs powered by Bristol Pegasus VIs were unofficially designated DC-2Bs.

Bristol Pegasus DC-2

Among other European DC-2 operators, LOT – Polskie Linie Lotnicze – must be singled out, as it was responsible for the development of the Bristol Pegasus-powered DC-2B. As Bristol engines were built under licence by the Skoda Company and were in widespread use in Poland, LOT ordered through Fokker two 750 hp Pegasus VI-powered aircraft – SP-ASK c/n 1377 and SP-ASL c/n 1378. The Pegasus VI installation was jointly developed during early 1935 by Douglas and the Bristol Company. Lufthansa, which had acquired one DC-2-115D D-ABEQ c/n 1318 from Fokker in February 1935 and named it '*Taunus*', sold it to LOT where it was registered SP-ASJ in February 1937. Lufthansa was later to operate a fleet of captured DC-2s during the Second World War. During the same period, an ex-LOT DC-2-115F SP-ASL c/n 1378 should have come to the United Kingdom as G-AGAD, but was interned by the Romanian government.

The DC-2s ordered by LOT were for use on the Warsaw to Berlin route. The Bristol Pegasus VI medium-supercharged engines, designed to run on 87 octane fuel and fitted with Hamilton controllable-pitch metal propellers, were specified for the Polish transports. The engines supplied to the Douglas Company were standard production units. They were of the moderately supercharged type and, on account of the somewhat small airscrew clearance of the fuselage, were fitted with 0.666 reduction gear ratio in order to accommodate the three-blade Hamilton controllable-pitch metal propellers of 11 ft diameter. Bristol single-outlet exhaust rings were supplied, and exhaust rings, cowlings and baffles were thoroughly tested and cleared by means of flight tests at Filton, Bristol, in a company Hawker Hart aircraft. The actual NACA – National Advisory Committee for Aeronautics – type cowlings and baffles were manufactured by Douglas from drawings supplied by Bristol, and both proved eminently satisfactory in service.

The new Douglas DC-2 airliner saw service worldwide. This DC-2-199 VH-UXJ c/n 1561 was delivered to Holymann Airlines in Australia on 10 November 1936 and was named 'Loongana'. It was withdrawn from use at Essendon, Sydney, on 15 October 1946. (AP Photo Library)

The engines left the Filton factory on 13 March 1935, being delivered to Santa Monica on 30 March. Under the supervision of a Bristol engineer and in close collaboration with Douglas engineers they were successfully installed by the beginning of July, only thirteen weeks later, an achievement which demonstrated the ease which the simple and straightforward design of the Pegasus engines lent to the process of installation. Time required for an engine change was about one hour.

With the two Pegasus VI engines, each developing a maximum output of 750 hp at 4,750 ft and a rated output at normal rpm of 655/690 hp at 3,500 ft, the DC-2 had a speed of 198 mph at 6,500 ft and 2,110 rpm and a cruise speed of 185 mph at 12,000 ft at 2,000 rpm. Take-off time with full load under normal conditions was 15 seconds. An altitude of 5,000 ft was attained in three minutes, 10,000 ft in nine minutes, and 15,000 ft in 18.8 minutes. The maximum height reached on one engine was 10,700 ft.

A fleet of five DC-2 airliners were purchased via Fokker by Ceskoslovenska Latecka Spolecnost (CLS) prior to World War II. The fleet is depicted after delivery on 29 July 1938. During the invasion of Czechoslovakia later in 1938 by the Germans they were impounded. (Douglas)

The Polish airline Polskie Linie Lotnicze – LOT – took delivery of two DC-2-115F airliners in July/August 1935 – SP-ASK and SP-ASL powered by Bristol Pegasus VI 750hp engines. Depicted is SP-ASK c/n 1377. The registration was cancelled on 5 September 1939. (AP Photo Library)

First test flights were carried out at Santa Monica on 3 July 1935, and reports transmitted by Douglas back to the Bristol Company were satisfactory. Cylinder-head temperatures in full-power climbs and at cruising nowhere exceeded stated limits. In particular, single-engine climbs with a full load of 18,200 lb were also satisfactory.

Following official type approval by the US Department of Commerce, DC-2 SP-ASK left Santa Monica on 17 July 1935, on its delivery flight to New York for shipment to Europe. The second DC-2 SP-ASL departed six days later and was flown by a Douglas test pilot, with the LOT chief pilot, and as passengers carried representatives of the Polish airline, the Bristol Company and the Sperry Gyroscope Company. At the request of the US Army Air Corps, the DC-2 visited Wright Field, Dayton, Ohio, *en route* to New York in order that the military engineering section might inspect the Pegasus engines and the installation in the DC-2.

When DC-2 SP-ASL arrived in New York the following cable was compiled: 'Second machine made perfect journey New York. No trouble of any kind. Exactly 15 hours cruising at 2,000 rpm, 22 inches. At 12,000 feet air speed 180 mph cylinder head temperatures 329°F. Fuel consumption 28.8 Imperial gallons per hour and oil consumption 5 Imperial pints per hour.' These figures, recorded on the 2,800-mile delivery flight from Santa Monica to New York, which was made at an average speed of 180 mph, mainly as 12,000 feet, demonstrate the remarkable economy of the Bristol Pegasus engine. These consumptions showed an improvement of the order of 10 per cent over other

DC-2-115E PH-AKS c/n 1365 was delivered to KLM via Fokker on 13 May 1935 and it is seen on the apron at Schiphol Airport, Amsterdam, with mail being loaded. This airliner was captured by the Germans on 15 May 1940, served with the Luftwaffe and crashed at Tempelhof Airport, Berlin, on 11 February 1944. (AP Photo Library)

engines usually fitted to the DC-2, the specification figure being 31.7 Imperial gallons per hour for the standard machine cruising at 177 mph at 8,000 feet.

In Europe the two DC-2s were re-assembled by Fokker, the European licensee for Douglas. One was used in a demonstration at Amsterdam airport and flown by several airline pilots, including a Mr Zimmerman, chief pilot of Swissair. He declared the Pegasus-powered DC-2 to be superior to any he had flown, and the take-off and smooth running of the engines to be excellent. This was an opinion also freely expressed by the Douglas test pilots at Santa Monica.

In addition, Dr S.J. Zand, an acknowledged authority on the subject of vibration and silencing, and research engineer for the Sperry Company, who were responsible for the sound-proofing of the Douglas DC-2, expressed great satisfaction with the improvement in sound conditions compared with the standard DC-2. This was attributed solely to the smoother running and absence of engine vibration. Dr Zand was a passenger in SP-ASL on the Santa Monica to Chicago stage of the delivery flight, a distance of 1,890 miles which took ten and a half hours flight time. Operating the new transport on the Warsaw–Posen–Berlin route, LOT cut the flight scheduled time from approximately three and a half hours to two hours. The DC-2s continued on schedule flights until the outbreak of the Second World War. DC-2 SP-ASK was cancelled on 5 September 1939, whilst SP-ASL was taken over by the Romanian government on 10 September.

Croydon Airport served London in the pre-war years and is depicted here with three Swissair DC-2s neatly parked. They are HB-ITO c/n 1332, HB-ITE c/n 1322, and HB-ITA c/n 1329 all delivered via Fokker. The latter DC-2 crashed at Senlis, France, on 7 January 1939. (Swissair)

Typical apron scene at Schiphol, Amsterdam, in the pre-World War II years, with two DC-2s being prepared for flight. They are PH-AKN c/n 1354 'Haan' and PH-AKR c/n 1364 'Reitvink' the latter being captured by the Germans on 15 May 1940 serving with the Luftwaffe. (AP Photo Library)

Swissair – Schweizerische Luftverkehr AG – purchased its first DC-2 via Fokker in December 1944 and continued to operate the type until 1952, becoming the longest user of the type. The fleet of six included HB-ITE c/n 1322 delivered on 17 January 1935. It crashed on 29 August 1952 at Kosti, Sudan. (Swissair)

This DC-2-115L c/n 1584 was delivered to KLM by Fokker as PH-ALE in 1936, it escaping the invasion, flying to the United Kingdom on 16 May 1940 becoming G-AGBH with KLM, returning home in December 1945. On 1 June 1946 it joined Southampton Air Services, but crashed at Malta on 3 October 1946. (MAP)

Into Uniform

As early as 1934, the US Navy purchased its first example of the DC-2. Four more followed and all carried the US Navy designation R2D-1, being assigned the Bureau of Aeronautics serial numbers 9620 to 9622 c/n 1325 to 1327, and 9993/9994 c/n 1404/5. The first three of these were DC-2-125s and the last two DC-2-142s, these latter being assigned to the US Marine Corps at Quantico, Virginia, where – subsequently and among other applications – Marines were to gain experience as paratroopers using the Douglas transports. The R2D-1s provided performance advances and advantages so far removed from the service's pair of veteran Curtiss R4C-1 Condor twin-engined biplanes and Ford Trimotor RR-4 monoplanes they replaced that the US Navy was to maintain a strong preference for military derivatives of the successive Douglas Commercials for many years to come. The first three R2D-1s served in US Navy livery at the US Naval Air Stations at Anacostia, Pensacola and San Diego, the US Marine Corps transports being assigned to Utility Squadron Six (VJ-6M), a unit to be re-designated VMJ-1 of Aircraft One, US Fleet Marine Force, with effect from July 1937. All five transports were powered by 710 hp Wright R-1820-25 Cyclone engines.

US Army Air Corps interest in the Douglas Commercial followed that of the US Navy in 1935, with the purchase at a cost of $86,788 of a single DC-2 for General Andrews. Used for evaluation from Langley, Virginia, as the XC-32, serial 36-1 c/n 1414, it was powered, like the R2D-1, by the 710 hp R-1820-25 Cyclone, and the higher echelons of the US Army were quick to appreciate the value and usefulness of such a transport. Two more DC-2s with special interiors were promptly purchased, being designated initially as YC-34s and later simply as C-34s. These were serial 36-345 c/n 1415, a DC-2-173, and 36-346 c/n 1416, a DC-2-346, delivered during April 1936. Both were assigned to the US First Staff Squadron at Bolling Field, DC, one being reserved for use by the Secretary of State for War.

Also ordered were eighteen C-33 transports at a cost of $77,929·90 cents each with serials 36-70 to 36-87 c/ns 1503 to 1520, and all were DC-2-145s. The new transports were essentially similar to the commercial DC-2, but had a cargo-loading door and the larger fin-and-rudder assembly later to appear on the DC-3. They also had a reinforced cabin floor and the normal load consisted of either 2,400 lb of cargo or twelve passengers. They were delivered between May 1936 and January 1937 and distributed between the following units: 1st Transport Squadron at Patterson Field, Ohio; 2nd Transport Squadron at Langley Field, Virginia, moving to Olmstead, Pennsylvania early in 1940; 3rd Transport Squadron at Duncan Field, Texas; 4th Transport Squadron at McClellan Field, California; 5th Transport Squadron at Olmstead, later Patterson; 6th Transport Squadron at Olmstead and the 7th at McClellan. They were absorbed into Transport Groups by 1941, and carried the brunt of domestic army transport work following the attack on Pearl Harbor.

The first Douglas C-33 36-70 was re-designated C-38 in January 1938, after improvements to the undercarriage, brakes and tailplane and the fitting of a dorsal fin. It was in fact the prototype of the series of transports sometimes referred to as DC-2½s because they combined features of both the DC-2 and DC-3. Power was provided by 975 hp R-1820-45 Cyclone engines. This one C-38 was to serve as the aerodynamic prototype for a total of thirty-five C-39s delivered between January and September 1939; these combined a C-33 fuselage

Captain E. V. 'Eddie' Rickenbacker, then Vice-President of Eastern Air Lines, was one of the first customers to buy the Douglas DC-2. Eastern pioneered the New York to Miami route with the Florida Flyer. Eastern operated all the Douglas Commercial airliner series with the exception of the DC-1 and DC-5. (Douglas)

During 1934 the US Navy Department recognised the potential of the early Douglas Commercial DC-2 transport and purchased a handful designated R2D-1. Seen at Boston, Massachusetts, during 1939 is BuNo.9621 c/n 1326 basically a DC-2-125 possibly from Utility Squadron Six of the US Marine Corps. (Wood)

and outer wing panels with a DC-3 centre section, tail unit and undercarriage, and were powered by a pair of 975 hp R-1820-55 Cyclones. The Douglas designation was DC-2-243. When delivery of the final Douglas C-39 38-535 c/n 2092 was made on 28 September 1939, it was the 139th and last of the DC-2 series to come off the Douglas assembly line at Santa Monica. It served the military until October 1944, when it was sold for commercial use. After the end of the war, the US military sold its DC-2 derivatives as surplus and also released a number of DC-2s which had been pressed into service as C-32As.

Although the Douglas Company had already built several types of commercial aircraft, it was only with the advent of the DC-2 that the company acquired its reputation in this field. Thanks to the success of the commercial and military versions of the DC-2, the company was able to recoup the loss of $266,000 incurred on the original TWA order and the programme ended with a substantial profit.

An early Douglas C-33 transport from the 63rd Transport Group seen during the 1941 War Games. Records show that this C-33 36-85 c/n 1518 had previously served with the 64th TG. It crashed at Hill Field on 8 May 1943 when the undercarriage retracted prematurely during take-off. (USAF)

The US Army Air Corps were envious of the new Douglas DC-2 transports used by the major airlines. Stress tests showed that the design could be adapted for military use. Depicted is a Douglas C-33 at the Rockwell Air Depot located at Oakland, California, during 1938. (William T. Larkins)

War Clouds

The dramatic advances in civil air transport in the USA in the early 1930s had an inevitable impact upon the US armed forces of the day, but limited budgets prevented rapid replacement of older transports. However, a number of airline DC-2s took on a military role with the designation C-32A, and it is quite astounding that of the 192 DC-2 transports eventually produced, the majority became either directly involved in conflict or donned military uniform.

Seven Douglas DC-2 transports of KLM were captured by the Germans at Schiphol Airport, Amsterdam, on 15 May 1940, and these later appeared in Luftwaffe livery. No less than three LAPE DC-2s were employed as bombers by the Spanish Republic government during the Civil War, whilst the DC-1 was allegedly utilised for reconnaissance missions as well as transport duties. Further north, in Finland, three DC-2s became involved in military activities from 1940 onwards in the battle against the USSR. A total of ten DC-2 transports, all ex-Eastern Air Lines, was acquired by the British Purchasing Commission acting on behalf of the Royal Australian Air Force, whilst the first Douglas transports to enter Royal Air Force service were undoubtedly the dozen received by No. 31 Squadron in April 1941, all being DC-2s, with more to follow.

By 1941 the US Army Air Corps C-39s had been absorbed into the mushrooming Transport Command and these were to bear the brunt of the domestic US Army transport load in the months following Pearl Harbor, being called upon to perform many rigorous transport operations. They would ferry supplies to Goose Bay, Newfoundland, and beyond, as well as fly survivors out of the Philippines to Australia in December 1941. At least two C-39s – 38-509 and 38-521 – were to serve with the US 10th Air Force in India during 1942. In that year, three others – 38-519, 38-530 and 38-532 – served with the US 5th Air Force in Australia, whilst another – 38-526 – was based at Elmendorf, Alaska, and was one of the comparatively few to survive the war.

The US 374th Troop Carrier Group, with its 6th, 21st, 22nd and 33rd Troop Carrier Squadrons, was constituted on 7 November 1942, and activated in Brisbane, Australia, five days later with the 5th Air Force. It operated with what can only be described as war-weary and worn-out transports such as the Douglas C-39, C-49, DC-3 and DC-5 plus the Lockheed C-56 and C-60 until it was re-equipped with the Douglas C-47 in

Douglas C-39 38-509 c/n 2066 seen landing at Burbank, California, during June 1941. It was based at the huge Fairfield Air Depot and later served overseas with the US 10th Air Force in India during 1942. The likeness to the DC-3 is obvious in this photo, with the centre section and tail unit of the DC-3, fuselage and outer panels of the DC-2. (Peter M. Bowers)

Rare photo depicting a C-39 38-508 c/n 2076 carrying the radio callsign 'VHCCG' and seen on the airstrip at Seven Mile Drome, Port Moresby, New Guinea, on 19 August 1942, surrounded by a mixture of war supplies. It was a DC-2-243, survived World War II, its last owners being Guinea Air Traders. It was broken up on 13 July 1950. (Australian War Memorial)

February 1943. It was engaged in supplying Allied forces in the Papua New Guinea campaign, receiving one Distinguished Unit Citation – DUC – for these missions, and being awarded a further DUC for transporting troops and equipment to Papua and evacuating casualties to the rear areas during November and December 1942. It received a third DUC for transporting men and supplies over the Owen Stanley mountain range between 30 January and 1 February 1943, to aid the small force defending the airfield at Wau, New Guinea. It also participated in the first airborne operation in the south-western Pacific on 5 September 1943, dropping paratroops at Nadzab, New Guinea, in order to seize enemy bases and cut off inland supply routes.

Two Douglas C-39 transports – 38-513 and 38-528 – were later modified up to a standard approximating to that of the Douglas C-42, which was very similar to the early military version of the DC-3. During 1942, a total of twenty-four commercial DC-2 transports was impressed for military service from the fleets of US domestic operators. Being generally similar to the sole C-32, they were logically enough designated C-32As. They were powered by the commercial 740 hp SGR-1820-F3A Cyclone, which was designated R-1820-33 by the US Army Air Force. The transport differed from the C-33 in having no special cargo door. The US Defense Supplies Corporation was responsible for taking over a large number of DC-2s and, later, even more DC-3s, from the airlines, leaving US domestic operators hard pressed for airline equipment. To enable them to carry on limited operations under military control, the corporation restored some of the impressed Douglas transports, and the airlines exchanged some aircraft internally amongst themselves in order to meet national defence needs. Several DC-2/C-32As were involved in such exchanges. On occasions, however, DC-2s changed hands for different reasons. One such transaction is reported to have taken place in 1941/42, when Northeast Airlines, owing to financial problems, exchanged three new DC-3s for five used TWA DC-2s. In service with Northeast, these DC-2s were retrofitted with DC-3 wings, becoming known unofficially in consequence as 'DC-Twees'. Later, these aircraft were taken over by the USAAF as C-32As, and sold again for civil operations after the war. The Douglas

Aircraft Company indicate that such a retrofit to the DC-2 would have required a new Type Certificate to fly.

The Spanish Civil War

Perhaps the oddest chapter in the remarkable story of the Douglas Commercial is that of the career of the DC-2 in Spain. During 1934, the Director General of Aeronautics, Ismael Warleta de la Quintana, elected to purchase the DC-2 for the state airline, Lineas Aéreas Postales Españolas – LAPE – despite considerable pressure to buy the Junkers Ju 52/3m. Five DC-2s were ordered from Fokker, of which four were destined to be delivered to Spain prior to the outbreak of Civil War on 18 July 1936.

Throughout 1934 there had been debate in Spanish aeronautical circles over whether or not to re-equip LAPE with DC-2s or the smaller Lockheed Electras. It was advocated that the DC-2 would put LAPE not only on a competitive footing with KLM and Swissair, but place LAPE in an advantageous position over both French and British airlines, countries which were without any modern airliners. A further deciding factor was the outstanding performance of the KLM DC-2 in the England-to-Australia air race in October 1934, and in fact, on the very night that news of KLM's achievement reached Europe, Ismael Warleta authorised Vicente Roa, who was in Amsterdam, to place an order with Fokker for five DC-2-115s. The order was on cigarette paper written in a cafe.

The first of LAPE's aircraft, a DC-2-115D c/n 1330, had been accepted by Fokker at the Santa Monica factory on 12 January 1935, had left the USA on 11 March for Cherbourg and had been assembled at Querqueville to where it had been transported by lighter. It arrived in Spain during April, was named '*Hercules*' and registered EC-XAX, making its inaugural flight from Madrid to Paris on 22 May 1935. It carried LAPE fleet No. 21, Douglas Export No. E-1321 and initially the temporary Dutch registration PH-AKF.

Douglas DC-2-115B c/n 1334, Douglas Export No. E-1330, was accepted by Fokker on 1 March 1935, reaching Spain on 29

May to become EC-AAY. It was christened '*Orion*' and given LAPE fleet No. 22. Confusion arose when LAPE publicity agents issued a photo purporting to show '*Orion*', with '22' on the fin. However 'AX' was visible under the port wing, and it appeared to be a retouched photo of EC-XAX '*Hercules*'. Authentic photos of EC-AAY show that, unlike '*Hercules*', it did not have a direction-finding loop behind the cabin, or a cable antenna running from a short post behind the loop to the fin. The airline title 'Líneas Aéreas Postales Españolas' appeared above the passenger windows.

It would appear that LAPE was originally to have received three of the Douglas DC-2 transports during 1935, Douglas engineering records list Spain as c/n 1331's destination. However, Fokker retained this last aircraft in the Netherlands as a demonstrator before selling it on 22 July 1935 to Swissair, with whom it was registered HB-ISI.

A further two aircraft were to reach LAPE during 1936, and both of these were DC-2-115Js with revised vertical tail surfaces. The first was c/n 1417 Douglas Export No. E-1762, leaving Santa Monica on 26 November 1935 and receiving its Spanish certificate of navigability on 31 March 1936, although it is known to have been operated by LAPE by the beginning of that month. It was registered EC-EBB and named '*Sagitario*', carrying the LAPE Fleet No. 24. It was to be joined by c/n 1521, which, registered EC-BFF, was handed over to Fokker on 24 April, and arrived at Cherbourg aboard SS *Europa* on 15 May. It had Douglas Export No. E-1906. It was reassembled at Le Bourget, Paris on 16 June, and reached Barajas, Madrid, a day or two later. Although this DC-2 became LAPE Fleet No. 25, there was for many years some doubt over both its registration and its name. Until 1979, in view of the lack of official Spanish registration records for the weeks immediately preceeding the civil war, the authorities agreed that it had been registered EC-BBE and named '*Granada*'. More recent research into post-war registrations show, however, that it was registered EC-BFF. This is confirmed by Douglas records, which indicate that it was painted EC-BFF before leaving the factory at Santa Monica. A recently discovered photo shows that it was named '*Mallorca*', not '*Granada*'.

Until the outbreak of hostilities in Spain, the LAPE DC-2s served on the Madrid to Paris route, but at times they were withdrawn from regular services to fly gold for the Bank of Spain. On 12 March 1936, it was revealed that, during the previous week, three LAPE DC-2s had flown 9,810 lb of gold to Paris.

When fighting in the Civil War broke out on 18 July one DC-2, positioned at Le Bourget, Paris, was hastily summoned back to Madrid arriving early in the morning of 18 July minus passengers. At the same time two DC-2s – EC-AAY and EC-BFF – were flown to Tablada airfield, Seville, under the command of LAPE Operations Manager, Joaquín Mellado, who had received orders to refuel, load with bombs and attack Tetuán airfield, Morocco, where the uprising against the Madrid government had just been proclaimed. There was considerable tension at Tablada when the DC-2s arrived, and a pro-nationalist officer, Captain Vara de Rey, promptly immobilised EC-BFF by firing his revolver into its starboard engine. The remaining DC-2, along with a pair of Fokker F-VIIb3ms, flew on to bomb Tetuán and returned direct to Madrid. Later that same morning, another LAPE DC-2 piloted by Mellado landed at Tablada. It hurriedly loaded up with bombs and took off to attack Tetuán. That night Tablada was taken over by the rebels, resulting in EC-BFF, which was repaired by 25 July, becoming Nationalist property.

The first task for DC-2 EC-BFF was to ferry Nationalist troops from Spanish Morocco to Spain, and, at the end of July, to drop supplies to Nationalists besieged in the Santuario de la Cabeze, a monastery near Córdoba. The pilot of the DC-2 was Capitán Carlos de Haya, who was to become one of the most distinguished of Nationalist fighter pilots. On 11 August he flew General Franco from Morocco to Spain in DC-2 EC-BFF, and Franco subsequently retained the Douglas aircraft; he was to use it as his personal transport throughout the remainder of the Civil War. The DC-2 was renamed '*Vara de Rey*' in honour of the officer who had enabled it to be acquired by the Nationalists. It received the military serial 42-1. An Irishman, William Winterbottom, is reputed to have served as co-pilot for a while.

The loss of EC-BFF left the Republicans with three DC-2s to be used both as transports and bombers. Conversion for the bombing role was primitive in the extreme, but had the advantage that reconversion for transport duties could be effected within an hour or two. The passenger door was removed and a slanting wooden chute, rather like a washboard, was affixed to the floor. Between seventy and eighty 24-lb bombs were laid on the seats and passed by hand to the bombardier, who slid them down the chute at a signal from the bomb aimer, who was provided with a Warleta bomb sight on the flight deck. Heavier bombs, between 110 and 220 lb, were laid on the cabin floor and swung into position by rope and tackle equipment.

A window in each side of the DC-2 cabin was removed for the mounting of two machine-guns, and, so equipped, the Republican DC-2s carried out numerous bombing sorties in the early days of the conflict. Targets included Tablada airfield, the Campamento Barracks outside Madrid, the Loyola Barracks at Oviedo, the Pelayo Barracks at San Sebastián, Algeciras, various airfields in Morocco, and elsewhere. During an attack on Badajos on 4 August 1936, the DC-2 EC-EBB '*Sagitario*' encountered the Nationalist-flown EC-BFF '*Granada*', the two converted airliners flying around each other while their respective gunners fired through the cabin windows. On another occasion, the gunner of one of the Republican DC-2s was credited with the destruction of a Nationalist Hispano-Nieuport 52 fighter, although this report may be considered apocryphal. It has been said that one of the DC-2s had a hole cut in the roof behind the pilot's cabin for a dorsal gunner equipped with a Lewis gun on a Scarff ring.

Between bombing sorties, the DC-2s were used to transport diplomats and other officials to and from Paris, and particularly for the transportation to the French capital of gold with which to purchase arms. Between 30 July and 12 August 1936, DC-2 EC-AAY *'Orion'* alone was to make seven gold flights to Paris, carrying about one metric ton of the metal on each flight. These gold transportation flights were to continue at a rate of several per week until the end of September, when the bulk of the remaining Spanish gold was secretly sent to the Soviet Union. The DC-2s continued to fly to Paris with silver, jewellery and other valuables until all available sources of these were exhausted by mid-1938.

Rare photograph depicting a DC-2-115H of KLM PH-AKT c/n 1366 which was captured by the Luftwaffe at Schiphol on 15 May 1940. It is depicted in June 1940 in Luftwaffe camouflage and became the personal transport of General Christiansen who was based in the Netherlands. It carried the code NA+LA and crashed on 9 August 1940 at Lammershagen. (AP Photo Library)

After the Civil War, officers of both sides were fulsome in their praise of the extraordinary qualities of the Douglas DC-2. Until the debut in Spanish skies of Bf 109s and I-16s, the Douglas transports had been able to outrun any fighter opposition; their range enabled them to reach any point on the peninsula, and their ruggedness was astonishing. The Republican DC-2s were never kept in hangars and were operated for most of the time from primitive fields, often by the seashore or in the mountains, under conditions ranging from intense heat and dust to extreme cold. Yet not once during the entire conflict did the engines of the DC-2 call for major repair, and the airframes withstood degrees of damage that Douglas engineers were later to find scarcely credible.

During May 1937, a DC-2 landed at Tarragona with no fewer than thirty-five troops and their weapons aboard. During the landing, the aircraft struck a bomb crater and the wing was bent seventeen degrees out of true on the port side. Nevertheless, the aircraft was able to take off and return safely to its base at Valencia. On another occasion, a case containing ammunition exploded beside a DC-2, tearing a large hole in the fuselage.

Rudimentary repairs were undertaken, after which the aircraft, according to the pilot, 'flew as well as she ever had'. Indeed, it was the prestige attached in Spain to the DC-2 that inspired application of the cover name 'General Douglas' to the most famous of the Soviet commanders of VVS units in Spain, Colonel Jacob Smushkievich.

Some mystery surrounds the next DC-2 to be acquired by the Spanish Republican government. This, a DC-2-115M c/n 1527, had Douglas Export No. E-1910 and was handed over to Fokker at Santa Monica on 17 August 1936, there being no indication in the Douglas records as to its intended ultimate destination. However, on 9 September, French newspapers reported that a DC-2 had been flown from Cherbourg to Paris by Lionel de Marmier, an Air France pilot deeply involved in procuring aircraft for Republican Spain and ferrying them to Madrid or Barcelona. Douglas DC-2-115M c/n 1527 was the only DC-2 shipped to Europe between April and November 1936, and all other DC-2s in Europe at that time can be accounted for. Thus, the new DC-2 recalled by LAPE pilots as having arrived in Spain some weeks after hostilities began, was most certainly c/n 1527, which reached its destination on 10/11 September and made its first gold run to Paris on the 17th. Further mystery was to be added by the apparent decision of the Republicans to register this aircraft EC-BFF and christen it *'Granada'*, repeating the registration and name of the DC-2 captured by the Nationalists on 18 July. This was presumably an attempt by the Republicans to demonstrate that the original aircraft, being in rebel hands, no longer possessed the legal right to this registration.

Yet another DC-2 was added to the Republican fleet with the acquisition of DC-2-115D c/n 1320, ex-Swissair HB-ISA. This, the second DC-2 imported into Europe, had been ordered as the personal aircraft of President Dollfuss of Austria. By the time Fokker had accepted it on 22 September 1934, Dollfuss had been murdered by the Nazis and when the DC-2 arrived in Holland, Fokker retained it as an unregistered demonstrator. In 1935 the Austrian government bought it after all as a ministerial transport, with the registration A-500 applied. On 5 April 1936, it was bought by Swissair and registered HB-ISA, though it is not certain if this registration was applied. The transport was then purchased again on 26 October 1936, through Macklerfirma, ostensibly for Air France, but was in fact part of an illicit deal involving several aircraft intended for Republican Spain. Another source indicates the DC-2 was sold to the Republicans as part of a complicated deal organised by the celebrated Swiss-Lithuanian barrister Vladimir Rosenbaum. When Rosenbaum was brought to trial and gaoled for this transaction in 1937, Swissair denied all knowledge of a 'Spanish connection' to the deal. LAPE pilot José-Maria Carreras, who ferried the DC-2 from Le Bourget to Barcelona on 26 October 1936, has indicated that Swissair had agreed to sell the DC-2, which the Spaniards wanted, on condition that they also bought three other aircraft – two Swissair Lockheed Orions and a General Aviation Clark GA 43A – which they did not want.

In Spain, A-500 was used for a time as a flying headquarters by the Commander-in-Chief of the Russian units in Spain, Major-General Jacob Smushkievich. In the summer of 1937 the DC-2 was transferred to LAPE, being registered EC-AGA, and it made three gold runs to Paris in September and October 1937. In 1938, after suffering serious damage in an accident, it was rebuilt, and on 20 November was seen at Malta, where it had taken Republican officials to Ankara for the funeral of Kemal

Ataturk, the founder of modern Turkey. A refuelling stop was made at Malta.

Somewhat surprisingly, in view of the intensity of their operations and the conditions under which they were operated, most of the DC-2s survived the Civil War. The DC-2 EC-AAY *'Orion'* c/n 1334 was one of only two that failed to see the end of hostilities – no record of this transport existing after August 1936. According to some sources, it crashed and was destroyed in France during the autumn of 1936, but this would seem very unlikely as such an incident would have had prominent coverage in the French press. The other casualty was EC-BFF *'Granada'* c/n 1527, the second DC-2 to carry this name and registration. This aircraft was destroyed on the ground at La Albericia airfield, Santander, on 6 April 1937.

After employment in evacuating personnel to France, the three remaining Republican DC-2s were returned to Spain where they were reunited with *'Vara de Rey'*, the original EC-BFF, and in 1940, a new official register of civil aircraft was created, commencing, appropriately enough, with the DC-2s. The DC-2 EC-AGN c/n 1320 became EC-AAA and was named *'Garcia Morato'* after the fighter ace; EC-EBB *'Sagitario'* c/n 1417 became EC-AAG *'Ramón Franco'*; EC-BFF *'Granada'* c/n 1521 became EC-AAC and retained the name *'Vara de Rey'*, and EC-XAX *'Hercules'* c/n 1330 became EC-AAD *'Carlos Haya'*. This latter DC-2 had been renamed *'Toledo'* in September 1936, but the name was discarded after the fall of that city on 29 September 1936.

Late in 1939, the Compania Anonima Española de Transporte Aéreo – SAETA – had been established, and the quartet of DC-2s was duly absorbed by this organisation. During early 1940 this company gave place to Tráfico Aéreo Español: but on 7 June TAE, in turn, was absorbed by Iberia, to whose fleet the DC-2s were now added. EC-AAA flew its last service on 11 April 1946, EC-AAB on 19 October 1945, and AAD on 8 September 1945. EC-AAC was destroyed in a crash at Barcelona on 3 February 1944 in which two crew and six passengers were killed and one crew and two passengers injured. All were finally struck off the Spanish civil register on 25 September 1947.

Finally, reports that the French Air Ministry Douglas DC-2 c/n 1333 F-AKHD, was sold to the Spanish Republicans can be discounted. Although it may have flown to Spain at some time, it was still in France in 1939. One publication suggests it went to Spain as EC-AGN in 1938. The official Spanish registration listing of 1940, containing four DC-2s and one DC-1, quotes the construction number 'A-540'; this has obviously been confused with 'A-500' c/n 1320, the original Austrian government registration. It is now known that this DC-2 became registered '42-5' after the Civil War.

Finnish – Russian Conflict

The Douglas DC-2s delivered to LAPE were not the only examples of their gender to undertake a more militant role than intended. An example purchased by KLM on 2 April 1935, registered PH-AKH *Haan* c/n 1354, was transferred to the Swedish AB Aerotransport on 13 January 1940, becoming SE-AKE. The invasion of Finland by Russia on 30 November 1939 served to expose Russia's weakness. Expecting a walkover, the Russians used only second-line troops, supported by some 900 mainly obsolete aircraft.

Douglas DC-2-115E, a Fokker delivered transport, originally PH-AKH c/n 1354 'Haan' later SE-AKE with ABA in Sweden before going to the Finnish Air Force during 1940. It was named 'Hanssin Jukka' and modified to carry a bomb-rack and a mid-upper gun turret. Soviet built M-62 engines were fitted, whilst the spinners and propellers came from P-36 Hawk fighters.

Count Carl-Gustav von Rosen subsequently bought SE-AKE from ABA and presented it as a gift to the Finnish Red Cross in January 1940. The DC-2 went to the Finnish Air Force, was named *'Hanssin Jukka'* and registered 'DC-1'. It was promptly converted as a bomber, which entailed enlarging the toilet compartment, removing the contents and fitting two bomb containers for twenty to twenty-four bombs, each weighing 27.5 lb. External racks were also fitted, together with a machine-gun in the mid-upper position on the fuselage. Only one sortie was, in fact, flown in this configuration during the 'Winter War' with Count von Rosen as pilot, a Finn named Winqvist as observer and a Dane named Rasmussen as gunner. On the return flight from this bombing mission, one of the two Cyclone SGR-1820-F3 engines cut and the aircraft made a forced landing.

This DC-2 was to continue in Finnish service as a VIP transport, flying Marshal Mannerheim to Luonetjarvi air base on 18 August 1940, and Foreign Minister Witting to Stockholm in March 1941. During the 'Continuation War', the DC-2 made numerous supply flights in support of advancing troops and various mapping flights in the proximity of the Soviet border. Transport of vital materiel and wounded soldiers was carried out in Eastern Karelia and on the northern front during 1941/42, as well as photographic missions. Several VIP flights overseas were made in 1942/43, whilst, during 1944, *'Hanssin Jukka'* was engaged in parachuting provisions and depositing patrols immediately behind the frontline. On flights abroad 625 personnel and 55,115 lb of freight were carried. The *'Hanssin Jukka'* encountered anti-aircraft fire on numerous occasions, and survived many air raids. During the latter part of 1942, its Cyclone engines were replaced by captured Soviet-built M-62 radial engines driving three-bladed propellers taken from Curtiss P-36 Hawk fighters. After twenty years of faithful service, *'Hanssin Jukka'*, having amassed a total of 7,500 flying hours, was finally retired on 1 June 1955, and from August 1959 was used as a cafe at Hameenlinna. Happily, this aircraft was moved in November 1981 to the Central Finland Aviation Museum at Luonetjarvi airfield, Tikkakoski, for full restoration.

Two other DC-2s were used by the Finnish Air Force during the Second World War and these had differing backgrounds. A DC-2-115K c/n 1582, assembled by Fokker during March 1936, was sold to CLS in Czechoslovakia as OK-AIB and, after capture during the German occupation of 1938, was re-registered to Lufthansa as D-AAIB. During March 1941, it went to Aero O/Y in Finland as OH-LDA 'Voima'. A similar fate befell another Fokker-assembled DC-2 sold to CLS as OK-AIC; this, a DC-2-200 c/n 1562, becoming D-AAIC with Lufthansa. It then went to Aero O/Y as OH-DLB 'Sisu' – later OH-LDB – during March 1941. The Finnish Air Force converted both DC-2s for mapping and photography, their engines being 920 hp Bristol Mercury XVs. With these engines the DC-2s were underpowered, presenting overheating problems during climb and requiring overhaul after only 320 hours of flying. The two aircraft were designated 'DO-2' c/n 1582 and 'DO-3' c/n 1562, and named 'Iso-Antti' and 'Pikku-Lasse' respectively. Based at Luonetjarvi air base, DO-3 was eventually to be written off when it ran into a snow drift on 7 February 1951, during a take-off run from Malmi air base. It was eventually sold as a summer dwelling to Mr Kuusakoski on Loparo island on the archipelago near Helsinki. The last flight of DO-2 took place on 14 March 1956, and it was later reduced to scrap. One of the Finnish Air Force DC-2 pilots, H. Kokkonen, accumulated over 1,200 flying hours in all three DC-2 military transports.

Lufthansa

Germany's first Douglas twin was DC-2-115D D-ABEQ c/n 1318 'Taunus' bought by Deutsche Lufthansa AG from Fokker in 1935. It was used on flight trials for a year before being sold to LOT in Poland as SP-ASJ. It crashed on 25 November 1937, in the Rhodope mountains, Bulgaria. Three more DC-2s were taken from CLS in 1938 and used until 1941, when the surviving pair went to Finland. These were DC-2-200 OK-AIC c/n 1562 which became D-AAIC; DC-2-211 OK-AID c/n 1565 D-AAID; and DC-2-115K OK-AIB c/n 1582 D-AAIB. The DC-2 D-AAID returned briefly to CLS in November 1939, then went back to DLH on 24 July 1940, being impressed into service with the Luftwaffe as 'VG+FJ'. It crashed in January 1944, near Plotzig, West Prussia.

During a bombing raid on Schiphol Airport, Amsterdam, on 10 May 1940, the Luftwaffe destroyed five KLM DC-2 airliners – PH-AKK c/n 1357, PH-AKN c/n 1360, PH-AKO c/n 1361, PH-AKP c/n 1362 and PH-ALD c/n 1583. Five days later, on 15 May, when the Wehrmacht occupied the Netherlands, six KLM DC-2-115E transports, all Fokker assembled, were captured.

These were: PH-AKI c/n 1355, which became D-ADBK with Lufthansa on 25 July 1940, later going to the Luftwaffe as 'NA+LD'; PH-AKJ c/n 1356 to D-AJAW with Lufthansa in July 1940, and to the Luftwaffe as 'PC+EC'; PH-AKQ c/n 1363 D-AEAN to Lufthansa in July 1940, then Luftwaffe as 'SG+KV' (this DC-2 was seized by the RAF on 6 May 1945 from the Luftwaffe air base at Flensburg); PH-AKR c/n 1364 D-AIAS with Lufthansa in July 1940, then to the Luftwaffe as 'PC+EB'; PH-AKS c/n 1365 D-ABOW with Lufthansa on 1 August 1940, and to the Luftwaffe as 'NA+LF' (it crashed on 11 February 1944, at Tempelhof, Berlin's airport); and PH-AKT c/n 1366 D-AIAV with Lufthansa on 23 July 1940, to the Luftwaffe as 'NA+LA' and reported as crashing on 9 August 1940, near Lammershagen.

One of the KLM DC-2s c/n 1366 captured was later to be used by General der Flieger Christiansen, Commander of the Wehrmacht in the Netherlands, as his personal transport with his name and title painted on the starboard side of the nose beneath the cockpit, and registered 'NA+LA' with the Luftwaffe. Incidentally, a Swissair DC-2-115D HB-ISI c/n 1331 was to be destroyed on Stuttgart Airport on 9 August 1944, during a raid by United States Army Air Force bombers.

The Royal Australian Air Force

At the outbreak of war in 1939 the RAAF was in the process of re-equipping with operational types, resulting in transports having a very low priority. Four airline Douglas DC-3s were chartered during September 1939. A total of ten Douglas DC-2s all ex-Eastern Air Lines, was acquired by the British Purchasing Commission acting on behalf of the RAAF. These were initially intended for No. 8 Squadron and assigned the RAAF serials A30-5 to A30-14. They were delivered between November 1940 and May 1941 and operated in the south-west Pacific theatre of operations by units of the RAAF, including Wireless/Air Gunner Schools, a flying training school, a paratroop training unit, communications flights and with No.s 34, 36 and 37 squadrons. Seven more Douglas DC-2s, including three ex-KNILM aircraft and four acquired pre-war by Holymann's Airways and

Rare photograph of two RAAF DC-2s A30-7 c/n 1290 and A30-8 c/n 1291 seen at the training station at Parkes, New South Wales, during World War II, home of No.2 Wireless/Air Gunner School. DC-2 A30-8 was shot down by the Japanese on 26 June 1942 whilst on a flight from Surabaya to Kupang via Waingapu. DC-2 A30-7 crashed on 15 June 1942. (D. G. Newell)

Australian National Airways – ANA – as well as three ex-USAAF C-39s were operated in the Pacific by ANA on behalf of the Allied Directorate of Air Transport – DAT – a unique transport organisation.

The Allied Directorate of Air Transport was activated on 28 January 1942, at Amberley Field, near Brisbane, equipped with two aged Douglas B-18 bombers, one Douglas C-39 flown out of the Philippines and five Douglas C-53 Skytrooper transports 'liberated' from a convoy bound for the Philippines and subsequently officially diverted to Brisbane. All US transport aircraft in Australia and all flyable combat aircraft no longer considered fit for operational use came under the aegis of the DAT. During the early months of the organisation, aircraft belonging to Koninklyke Nederlandse-Indische Luchtvaart Maatschappy – KNILM – were chartered to the Directorate on a contract basis, until negotiations for their purchase had been concluded. The aircraft included three DC-2-115G transports. Of these PK-AFJ c/n 1374 crashed during December 1941 at Darmo and was destroyed by the Australian Army. On 15 May 1942 PK-AFK c/n 1375 was allocated the USAAF serial '41-1375', the radio call-sign 'VHCXG' and 44-83226. One report indicates that 'VHCXG' may have been lost in an accident at Chartes Towers on 23 June 1942, while serving with the 21st Troop Carrier Squadron USAAF. PH-AFL c/n 1376 was allocated the radio call-sign 'VHCXH' and USAAF serial 41-1376 on 19 March 1942. It is also quoted as a C-32A 44-83227 on 17 March 1945. This latter DC-2 survived the Second World War; in February 1983 it was purchased by the US Confederate Air Force, but export restrictions kept it in Australia registered VH-CDZ. The contract for the wartime charter of these transports was finalised on 28 March 1942, and negotiations for purchase were concluded on 18 May, the purchaser being the US Armed Forces in Australia – USAFIA.

Shortages of suitable aircraft had prevented any rapid expansion of air transport in the RAAF, but during February and March 1942 four transport squadrons were formed, including No.36 Squadron raised at Laverton on 11 March. Eleven days later, the unit began to function with a personnel strength of two officers, twenty-four other ranks and a single DC-2 – A30-14 c/n 1288, originally delivered to Eastern Air Lines in October 1934 as a DC-2-112 NC13738 and imported into Australia on 1 May 1941, with the military radio call-sign 'VHCRH' and squadron code 'RE-H'. During the following month aircraft strength was increased to three by the addition of DC-2-112 A30-11 c/n 1286 ex-NC13736 radio call-sign 'VHCRE' coded 'RE-B' and DC-2-171 A30-13 ex-NC14970 radio call-sign 'VHCRG'. Douglas DC-2-112 A30-12 c/n 1257 ex NC133731 radio call-sign 'VHCRF' arrived with the squadron from Parkes, New South Wales, on 28 April and was found to be incompletely modified for use as an emergency air ambulance, modifications having to be completed by the unit's riggers. Yet another DC-2-171 A30-10 c/n 1372 ex NC14969 with radio call-sign 'VHCRD' was delivered on 26 May, giving No. 36 Squadron the distinction of being the first RAAF transport squadron to be fully equipped with five aircraft. During this early period, the air-crews were kept busy flying any serviceable transport, while ground-crews maintained the Douglas transports under the most difficult conditions, with the added burden of lack of equipment and spares.

Parkes was the home of No.2 Wireless/Air Gunner School – WAGS – which was equipped with ten Tiger Moths and the DC-2s A30-7 c/n 1290, DC-2-112 ex-Eastern NC13740, and A30-8 c/n 1291 DC-2-112 ex-Eastern NC13781. Both transport were fitted with radio transmitters and receivers to enable students to be flown on a fixed course whilst sending and receiving signals from the radio beacon on the airfield. In the DC-2s, the passenger cabin was fitted out on the starboard side with three sets of equipment equally spaced along the fuselage, the left-hand seats being left intact for off-the-air students and their respective instructors. Nine students and three instructors were taken aloft for three hours so that by rotation each student could spend an hour operating the radio set and get his required period of training in the air.

One of the No.2 WAGS DC-2 transports, A30-8, was seconded to pick up a number of US military specialists from Amberley at the end of 1942 and deliver them to an island north of Australia on a highly classified military mission. Flying Officer Webster was in command of the DC-2 with airman-pilot Sergeant Lionel van Praag as co-pilot. On its way back home on 26 January, it was jumped by a Japanese Zero fighter and shot down between Surabaya and Kupang via Waingapu. Webster, van Praag, the wireless operator and an engine fitter managed to get out before the DC-2 sank. The four crew spent thirty-six hours in the water in their Mae Wests before being washed ashore on an island from which they were subsequently rescued. Webster and van Praag took it in turns to support the wireless operator, whose Mae West had been punctured by a shot from Webster's revolver whilst he was fighting off sharks. Both pilots were subsequently decorated for bravery, van Praag being awarded the George Cross in lieu of a military decoration as he was not in the regular RAAF, but one of a special category of airman pilots taken straight into RAAF service on the basis of having a pilot's licence. These special duty pilots did no formal training and were given the rank of sergeant on appointment.

On 14 July 1942, No. 36 Squadron came under the operational control of the Allied Directorate of Air Transport – DAT. Because the unit's aircraft had to fly to Essendon to pick up freight and Australian ANA did all the 240-hour and complete overhauls on the DC-2s, a decision was made to move the squadron to Essendon for convenience. The move commenced on 16 July and was completed the following day, and during August the squadron was assigned the status of master depot for Douglas transport spares. A sixth DC-2 was allocated to the squadron on 11 August, this being A30-9 c/n 1292 ex-Eastern NC13782 with radio call-sign 'VHCRK', and a seventh, A30-5 c/n 1287 ex-Eastern NC13737, was issued on 14 September. In the event, this last aircraft was lost on its first mission with the squadron when it crashed and was burnt out whilst landing at Seven Mile Strip, Port Moresby, New Guinea.

Redeployed to a new operational base at Stock Route Strip, Townsville, Queensland, during January 1943, the unit's transport strength was greatly enhanced by the arrival of five Douglas C-53 Skytroopers on loan from the USAAF, the DC-2s being re-allocated to a parachute training unit located at Richmond, New South Wales. Only a handful of DC-2 transports survived the Second World War, one being A30-12 c/n 1257, which was struck off charge by the RAAF on 4 October 1946 and sold to a scrap dealer called S.D. Marshall at Bankstown for just £225. The previous day, Mr Marshall had also bought the airframe of A30-11 c/n 1286 for £52. On the last day of August 1979, the DC-2 was moved for preservation to Albury, New South Wales, where the work was completed on 28 January 1980. It represents the KLM DC-2 PH-AJU and is mounted on three concrete poles with the undercarriage in the down position. Douglas DC-2 A30-14 c/n 1288 is now at Schiphol Airport, Amsterdam, with the Dutch Dakota

Association – DDA – after being shipped from Australia. It will also be preserved as the KLM PH-AJU '*Uiver*', the DC-2 which came second in the 1934 England-to-Australia air race.

The Royal Air Force

The first Douglas transports to enter Royal Air Force service were the twelve received by No. 31 Squadron during April 1941 – all DC-2s. The British Purchasing Commission acquired from US airlines a total of twenty-five DC-2 transports, which were assigned to the RAF with serial numbers AX755, AX767 to 769, DG468 to 482, HK821, HK837, HK847, HK867 and HK983. Three of these aircraft, DG480/481/482, were not actually taken over by the RAF, and HK867 c/n 1311 ex DC-2-120 NC14278 of American Airlines crashed on delivery whilst landing at Hastings Site, Freetown, Sierra Leone, on 7 September 1941, when it collided with a Hurricane. This DC-2 was also allocated a USAAF C-32A designation with USAAF serial 42-53530. These DC-2K transports, as they were known in the RAF inventory, were operated by 31 Squadron in India, and by 117 and 267 Squadrons in the Middle East.

Some of these DC-2s were originally intended for use in India by Tata Airlines and Indian National Airways, and, in fact, registrations were not only allocated, but, in some cases, painted on aircraft along with the RAF serial. The DC-2s DG480/481/482 were allocated the registrations VT-APC, APD, APE. Trans World Airlines archives reveal that they were ex-NC13720 c/n 1246, NC13726 c/n 1252 and NC13784 c/n 1294 respectively, all DC-2-112s; they were destined for Tata, but a change in US policy resulted in their retention by TWA until 1942, when they were sold to Northeast Airlines and the Defense Supply Corporation, finally going to the USAAF as C-32As 42-68858, 42-57154 and 42-65579.

Operated by the RAF with 31 Squadron, this DC-2-120 c/n 1403 was intended for civil use in India as VT-APA but went to the RAF as DG478. It is seen in Egypt during 1941 with both civil and military registrations. The DC-2K was damaged at Chittagong, India, and was struck off charge on 30 June 1944. (AP Photo Library)

No. 31 Squadron spent the period commencing 12 April 1941 in converting 'B' Flight crews to the first six Douglas DC-2Ks, which became operational on 16 April. Rashid Ali had started his rebellion in Iraq at this time, and 'A' Flight with seven Vickers Valentias and 'B' Flight with four of its DC-2Ks DG468/469/470/471, were detached to fly some extra reinforcements to Shaibah on 17 April, remaining there as a detachment. During the next three days, four more civil DC-2s

were taken over by the RAF at Shaibah from their American ferry crews. The detachment moved to Basra on 19 April and continued flying men, stores and equipment to Habbaniya daily with the loss of DC-2K NC14290 c/n 1350, a DC-2-118B ex-Pan American. It was later repaired and allocated to No.117 Squadron as HK820 in July 1942, and its destruction at Habbaniya was claimed by German Bf.110s. May 1941 saw the detachment return to Karachi and in September the squadron moved to Lahore, but in late October another detachment of seven DC-2Ks flew to the Canal Zone, being based at Bilbeis, where they joined DC-2Ks from No. 117 Squadron. Here they were used for re-supply and casualty evacuation missions. Douglas DC-2K AX755 c/n 1301, ex-DC-2-118A NC14268, was to fly General Sikorski, the Polish Premier, to see Josef Stalin at Kuybyshev, the temporary capital of the Soviet Union, whilst another flight was made to Stalingrad.

When Japan entered the war in December 1941, only two of the DC-2Ks of No.31 Squadron had been serviceable at Lahore, but these transports kept open a service between Rangoon and Calcutta until one DC-2K DG474 c/n 1401, ex-DC-2-120 NC14921 American Airlines, was destroyed in an air raid at Mingaladon airfield in Burma during January 1942. In the following month, the squadron transferred to Akyab, on the Burmese coast, where, during February and March, its task was primarily the evacuation of personnel from Burma. When Akyab became untenable through Japanese air raids, the squadron moved back to Dum Dum, Calcutta. Its principal task was now the transportation of reinforcements and supplies to Shwebo and Mandalay, with casualty evacuation on the return flight. A Douglas DC-2K flew each evening to Akyab until the port finally fell to the Japanese, and a veteran DC-2K AX755 was lost on one of the sorties on 13 April 1942. Another DC-2K was badly damaged at Chittagong, but was patched up and eventually flown out.

The first three Douglas DC-2Ks received by No. 117 Squadron were AX767/768/769 on 14 October 1941, delivered at Khartoum. AX767 was c/n 1238, ex-DC-2-112 NC13712 TWA; AX768 c/n 1406, ex DC-2-120 NC14966 American Airlines: and AX769 c/n 1310, ex DC-2-120 NC14277 also of American. In November DC-2K HK821 c/n 1304, ex-DC-2-118B NC14271 of Pan American, joined the squadron, followed by HK837 and HK847 in December. The latter was c/n 1313, ex-DC-2-120 NC14280 of American. In April 1942, all the DC-2Ks, with the exception of HK837, were transferred to No.31 Squadron. In July 1942, HK820 joined No. 117 Squadron.

It must be remembered that these early Douglas transports issued to the Royal Air Force were already veterans. Some of the engines, a mixture of Wright Cyclones and Pratt & Whitney, had already accumulated 10,000 or more flying hours when the RAF took them over. They arrived in the theatre of operations at a time when they were most needed, so inspections that were routine elsewhere had to be overlooked. Yet RAF pilots had great faith in and affection for their 'new' transports and many were the tales of their survival against all odds. For example, on 14 March 1942, DC-2K AX755 was being flown to Akyab from Dum Dum, Calcutta when, midway across the Bay of Bengal, an oil pipe to the starboard engine burst. The DC-2 propellers had only fine and coarse pitch, with no feathering facility, and the aircraft lost height rapidly. The co-pilot was ordered to throw all the freight out of the rear door while the pilot jettisoned fuel, and AX755 somehow managed to limp into Akyab at about 100 ft altitude. The starboard engine had been windmilling without

Originally delivered to TWA in 1934, this DC-2-112, the second built, became AX767 at Khartoum with the RAF on 14 October 1941. It served with both 117 and 31 Squadrons. On 25 September 1942 it was registered VT-ARA with Indian National Airways and is seen parked at Willingdon, New Delhi on 31 July 1945 still with AX767 visible. (Peter M. Bowers)

oil for nearly an hour, and the pilot fully expected it to be a write-off, yet, after the damaged engine pipe had been repaired and the engine refilled with oil, it ran perfectly and AX755 continued flying. However, on 13 April 1942, again at Akyab, this DC-2 came to a sticky end when it ran into a bomb crater and was damaged beyond repair. It was felt, however, that the Douglas DC-2K was underpowered for the tasks presented to it in time of war. It also displayed a very pronounced penchant for swinging or ground looping.

The status report for the DC-2K presented by No. 31 Squadron on the first day of August 1942 indicated that all these stalwart transports were by now in a very poor state. Any aircraft that were serviceable were flying between six and ten hours each day. As mentioned earlier, many of the engines installed in the DC-2K had logged up to 10,000 hours of flying when received, with the airframes accumulating close to 17,000 hours since manufacture, many of these flown under the most arduous conditions with only elementary maintenance available. It was truly remarkable that so many of these early transports had remained operational for so long. All credit should go to the RAF ground personnel, many of whom doubled up as aircrew. By April 1942, the first Douglas DC-3 had arrived, able to carry twice the payload of the earlier DC-2K and rather easier to fly. However, the DC-2K continued to serve alongside the DC-3 in diminishing numbers until the last was finally struck off Royal Air Force charge during 1944.

Of the twenty-five Douglas DC-2Ks allocated to the RAF and procured by the British Purchasing Commission, five never saw RAF service. These included three never delivered – DG480 c/n 1246, ex-DC-2-112 NC13720 of TWA; becoming C-32A 42-68858: DG481 c/n 1252 ex-DC-2-112 NC13726 of TWA to C-32A 42-57154, and DG482 c/n 1294, ex DC-2-112 NC13784 of TWA to C-32A 42-65579. Mention has already been made of HK867 c/n 1311, destroyed on its delivery flight, whilst HK983 c/n 1312, ex DC-2-120 NC14279 American Airlines, suffered a similar fate when it crashed at Bathurst, West Africa, on 2 August 1941, also on its delivery flight. Three of the RAF DC-2Ks were leased to Tata Airlines, later to become Air India. These were DG468 c/n 1314 to VT-AOU in July 1942, cancelled on 6 July 1944; DG469 c/n 1315 as VT-AOQ on 22 August 1942, struck off charge as DG469 on 2 June 1943; and DG472 c/n 1402, leased to the airline for the month of October 1942, and struck off charge at Lahore on 8 November 1943. The DC-2K DG475 c/n 1410 was shot down by three Luftwaffe

Bf.110s some ten miles east of LG138 in Iraq on 8 December 1941, whilst DG 473 c/n 1308 was damaged beyond repair in flight on 14 June 1942, 60 miles east of Bangalore, possibly due to a bird strike. Likewise DG478 c/n 1403 was damaged beyond repair, and later struck off charge at Lahore on 30 June 1944.

Survivors

Today the US Civil Register reveals that there are two flyable DC-2s. The first is c/n 1404 DC-2-142, an ex-US Navy R2D-1 Bu No. 9993 which was delivered to NAS Anacostia, Maryland, on 7 September 1935. It went to NAS Pensacola, Florida, on 28 August 1940, back to Anacostia on 4 January 1941, and south again to Pensacola on 28 August 1941, before being struck off charge on 28 August 1944. During 1960 it appeared in General Air Lines livery. In November 1983, it re-appeared in KLM colours as PH-AJU for a special fiftieth anniversary commemorative flight to Australia of the famed London-to-Australia air race of 1934. It was shipped to the Netherlands and completed the return flight, despite an engine change.

After US Navy service this DC-2 went to the Hollingstead Corporation as NC39615 on 11 January 1946, and to North American Aviation during 1953. On 28 August 1954, it was registered to D.W. Mercer and a year later to Mercer Enterprises of Van Nuys, California. Finally, on 2 September 1968, it went to its current owner, Colgate W. Darden III of West Columbia, South Carolina.

The other DC-2 in the US is c/n 1368, a DC-2-118B NC1934D which I have had the great privilege to fly in. It is currently on lease to the Douglas Historical Foundation and based at Long Beach, California, where it is flown at least once every month, and also appears at various local air shows. It was the seventy-seventh DC-2 built, and was delivered to Pan American Airways on 16 March 1935 as NC14296. After a couple of years it was transferred to the PAA Mexican affiliate, Mexicana, during October 1937 as XA-BJL. This rugged transport was particularly valuable in Third World countries where up-to-date maintenance and repair facilities were not always readily available. On 28 November 1940 the DC-2 was sold to A/v de Guatemala SA as LG-ACA, going to Aviateca during March 1945, where it led a long and hard life as a jack-of-all-trades workhorse. On 29 October 1952, it returned to Guatemala as TG-ACA, and on 9 June 1952 it was flown back to the USA to be registered N4867V with A.J. Levin of Burbank, California. By March 1953, it was owned by Hasmer Independent of North Hollywood. Johnson Flying Service of Missoula, Montana, were the next owners and its engines were changed to R-1820-52Bs. The transport was modified for aerial spraying and for carrying smoke jumpers, flying a hazardous new role as the aircraft fought in currents of super-heated firestorm air while dropping the daring smoke jumpers near the perimeters of huge forest fires.

Amazingly, DC-2 N4867V survived the harsh battles with nature until 1973, when it was traded to Stan Burnstein in Tulsa, Oklahoma, as partial payment for a used Douglas DC-8 with which Johnson Flying Services started a disastrous airline venture. Burnstein, in turn, decided to donate the veteran to the Donald Douglas Museum & Library located at Santa Monica, the DC-2s birthplace. It was delivered on 27 January 1975. In May 1984, it was re-registered N1934D, was repainted in TWA colours to become NC13717 and named *City of Santa Monica*.

The museum was unfortunately underfunded and the bare metal of the DC-2 soon began to look more than shabby in Clover Field's salt-laden environment. In July 1982 the Douglas Historical Foundation was created by the Douglas Aircraft Company Management Club to take over the DC-2 and restore it to its former glory. Volunteers set to work at Long Beach, with thousands of man hours being expended on recreating an exact replica. The airframe was thoroughly overhauled, fresh engines fitted and all wiring restored. It was a task aided by many of the subcontractors who have supplied Douglas for many years.

On 25 April 1987, fourteen years after it had last flown, the DC-2 once again took to the air from Long Beach Airport. Currently the DC-2 is on a ten-year lease, with a few years to run, at which time it will possibly be returned to Santa Monica and the fairly new Museum of Flying under David Price.

Also in the USA, at the large USAF Museum located at Wright Patterson AFB, there is an immaculate Douglas C-39 c/n 2072. As we have seen on display at Albury, New South Wales, Australia, is mounted a DC-2 representing the KLM PH-AJU, its origin being c/n 1286 ex-RAAF A30-11, and in the Netherlands the Dutch Dakota Association at Schiphol has c/n 1288 DC-2-112 ex-RAAF A30-14.

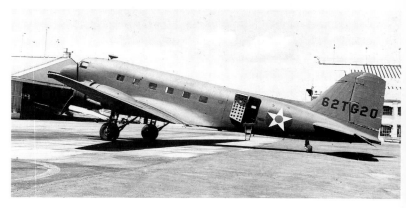

Seen parked at Oakland, California during September 1941 is a C-39 military transport, one of thirty-seven ordered on contract. They were called DC-2½s since a DC-3 centre section was added to the narrow DC-2 fuselage and short outer wing panels. Engines were the more powerful R-1820-55s rated at 975hp at 2200rpm. The C-39s were the first US Army transports to be involved in World War II. The one illustrated carries the markings of the 62nd Transport Group. (William T. Larkins)

Very rare photograph taken in Australia during World War II depicting DC-2-112 ex-NC13738 of Eastern Air Lines in RAAF markings as A30-14 with radio callsign 'VHCRH' on the fuselage. This was effective 1 May 1941. The transport survived the war and the fuselage was intact in a scrapyard as late as April 1971. (via Dutch Dakota Association)

Crashes

The Douglas DC-2 was a revolutionary aircraft, but it did have some undesirable characteristics. Landing-gear malfunctions made some landings unpredictable, with a tendency to collapse. The US Army Air Corps had four transports which were damaged during landing or taxying. A hand pump raised or lowered the undercarriage, and it took all of sixty seconds of vigorous pumping to raise the wheels in moderate temperatures. Sometimes, in cold weather, the gear was almost inoperable. Some pilots even instructed their co-pilots to commence pumping before the wheels left the runway. The DC-2 had the landing lights in the nose. In bad weather this created the same problem of reflected glare in the cockpit that had plagued the earlier Condors, Fords and the DC-1.

Author and ex-DC-2 pilot Ernest K. Gann vividly recalls the distress of the passenger in the Douglas airliner of the 1930s:

The air is annoyingly potted with a multitude of minor vertical disturbances which sicken the passengers, and keep us captives of our seat belts. We sweated in the cockpit, although much of the time we flew with the side windows open. The airplane smells of hot oil and simmering aluminium, disinfectant, faeces, leather and puke. The stewardesses, short-tempered and reeking of vomit, come forward as often as they can for what is a breath of comparatively fresh air.

On 20 December 1934 tragedy struck the DC-2, involving the first Fokker aircraft, PH-AJU c/n 1317 '*Uiver*' on its flight from Amsterdam to Java. Twenty-four hours after take-off from the Netherlands it was a charred, twisted hunk of metal, after crashing at Rutbah Wells in the Iraqi desert. There were no survivors from the crew of three and four passengers. The official KLM report on the accident revealed that the DC-2 had been struck by a bolt of lightning which killed all on board immediately. The aircraft continued to fly until it flew itself into the ground, somersaulting and bursting into flames.

In the USA TWA Flight 323 was eastbound from Los Angeles to Kansas City on 3 August 1935. The Kansas City control tower notified the captain that the field was closed due to bad weather, and advised him to proceed to an emergency field some 130 miles away. When the DC-2 arrived over the field, the captain found the area covered in clouds. He waited until the last possible moment, with his fuel nearly exhausted, before commencing his descent. Flying blind, he was looking for a break in the overcast. The airliner's angle of descent was too steep, and by the time the pilot broke cloud and saw the ground, all he could do was attempt to level off. The DC-2 narrowly missed a farmhouse, crashed through a fence and came to rest on a roadway.

Eleven people survived the crash of DC-2-112 c/n 1248 NC13722 Fleet No. 312, but the pilot, co-pilot, flight attendant and one passenger died. The passenger was senior US Senator Bronson Cutting. It was TWA's first fatality since the Rockne crash, and unfortunately also involved the death of a nationally known person. Cutting's colleagues launched an investigation. There were public hearings, charges and countercharges. The senator's death had come a year after the US Army Air Corps' tragic attempt to fly the mail. The bad taste of publicity resulting from the airmail débâcle was still fresh in the mouths of fellow senators. The hearings took on the form of a witch-hunt against the airlines in general, and TWA in particular. The US press gave even more publicity to this crash than they had to the Rockne disaster. It became evident that the reputation of the DC-2 and the Douglas Company could be at stake.

When the US Department of Commerce issued its official report, it revealed that the crash was the result of bad weather and inadequate weather reporting. The investigation cleared the DC-2 pilots, the aircraft and its designers of any wrong-doing or poor design. There was no evidence of either mechanical or structural failure. Douglas had built a rugged and reliable airliner.

Looking back, it is easy to appreciate that as a result of the Brown-Farley airmail imbroglio of 1933/34, a wholly new deal in airmail contracts and route awards came about on 20 April 1934. With it came the restructuring of air carriers from which emerged the great airlines. One of these was American Airlines Inc., with the great genius Cyrus R. Smith in command and its president from October 1934.

The newly-structured and newly-led American Airlines had inherited an order for fifteen Douglas DC-2s from American Airways to replace its existing Ford Tri-motors and single-engine Vultee V-1As and to supplement the Curtiss Condor biplane sleepers. During the latter part of 1934, the airline went bust getting its DC-2s into service. Its first DC-2 NC14274 c/n 1307 was accepted on 4 November 1934, and the tenth NC14283 c/n 1316 on 12 January 1935. By the end of 1934, with the DC-2 commencing airline service, some seventy-five aircraft had been sold – fifteen of these to American Airlines and there were hopes of more. These hopes were realised with a total of 130 DC-2s being sold to commercial airlines by Douglas. A further sixty-two were produced in military configuration and eight in parts – some 200 in all.

It is very interesting historically to recall that, in all, first twenty-five and then twelve different pioneering airlines went into the formation of American Airways in 1930, although the twelve had already been grouped into just five: Universal, Colonial, Southern, Interstate and Embry-Riddle. Up until 1932, when a single operations department was formed under C.R. Smith, American Airways flew its services under four separate divisions – Colonial, Embry-Riddle, Southern and Universal. On 13 May 1934, American Airlines Inc. as we know it today came into being.

It was accepted that although the DC-2 was clearly a marked improvement on the Boeing B.247D, which put the Ford Tri-motor out of business, it was still not wholly satisfactory. The payload of the DC-2, which carried fourteen passengers, was inadequate. It had propeller and fin-icing problems; it was nose heavy, difficult to land and directionally unstable due to insufficient vertical fin area. On handling characteristics it was, even then, said to be a 'good example of a flying barn door', with especially heavy ailerons and rudders.

Ernest K. Gann, the well-known pilot and aviation author describes the DC-2 in one of his many volumes.

Pilots assigned to fly the DC-2 were advised to take a Charles Atlas course in muscle-building. This was felt unnecessary as it was the co-pilot who provided the beef by hand-pumping the flaps up and down and sometimes the landing gear. In summertime the more fastidious co-pilots carried a small towel to wipe the sweat from their brows, thus hoping they would offend neither their captains nor the single stewardess.

The skipper of a DC-2 also developed a mighty left arm, although his exertions were of relatively short duration. When taxiing, the braking system in a DC-2 was activated by heaving on a horn-shaped handle protruding from the left side of the instrument panel. By simultaneous use of rudder and handle the desired left or right brake could be applied. Inevitably there was a time lag between motion and effect, so the DC-2 was stubbornly determined to chase its own tail on the ground and in cross winds, sometimes switching ends to the embarrassment of all on board. Taxying a DC-2 was something of an art rather than a skill, and even the best, chaste-mouthed pilots were occasionally given to blasphemy.

For reasons which are still obscure, consistent good landings with a DC-2 were impossible. A pilot might make ten perfect landings and the eleventh, regardless of related factors, would cut him back to size. Most pilots made wheels landings followed by an immediate and very firm forward shove on the control yoke to make sure the DC-2 stayed put, for once a DC-2 started bouncing the performance became so spectacular that only Herculean efforts plus grim determination could tame the beast. After a series of such humiliations even veteran pilots were known to stand glaring at their DC-2s while morosely considering another line of work.

Two other idiosyncrasies contributed to the bone-and-gristle life of DC-2 pilots. When flying in rain the windshields leaked so badly that the effect in the cockpit was that of a seriously depth-bombed submarine. Caulking did not seem to improve the fault. The steam heating system, originating from a boiler in the forward baggage compartment, was alleged to have been designed by Machiavelli. Much of the time the contraption gagged, gurgled and regurgitated ominously, and to the dismay of passengers occasionally filled the entire interior of the aircraft with vapours. A co-pilot charged with adjusting the several valves intended to control the system could make or break his esteem with both crew and passengers according to his success in keeping temperatures somewhere between intolerably hot and intolerably cold.

A further reminder that the DC-2 was not exactly a gentleman's aeroplane came when the flight had arrived at its destination and the engines were shut down. The co-pilot was obliged to crawl back into the rear baggage compartment, a very small cubicle located just forward of the tail. There, while maintaining a praying position, he passed out passenger baggage, mail and cargo to the ground crewman. If he appeared to be thoughtful in the process it was not because he knew he was erasing the creases in his uniform pants. He was kneeling on 1,000 lb of sandbags, a permanent adjustment to the weight and balance problem in a DC-2.

However, the DC-2 had a couple of endearing qualities which easily balanced their sins. They were strongly built and pilots caught while trying to sneak through thunderstorms were profoundly grateful for that strength. Pilots beset with ice during the winter months knew that if any aircraft could survive the trouble they were in, the Douglas DC-2 was unquestionably the mount of their choice.

Cyrus R. Smith and Bill Littlewood, who joined American Airlines in June 1930 as Safety Officer, experienced a flight in a DC-2 between Buffalo, New York and Chicago when the airliner yawed badly in turbulence and icing. Both were acutely conscious of the deficiencies in the DC-2 and were later to seek better things from the Donald Douglas stable.

Although Donald Douglas and his team had already built several types of commercial aircraft, it was only with the DC-2 that the company acquired its reputation as a world leader in commercial transport design. The DC-2 was fitted with some sophisticated instruments including the auto pilot and the coast-to-coast night-time navigation system, making long-distance flying much easier. Furthermore, thanks to the success enjoyed by the DC-2, the Douglas Aircraft Company was able to recoup the loss of $266,000 on the original TWA order and so turn a high-risk venture into a substantial profit. And the Douglas DC-2 was just the beginning.

Douglas C-32A

Twenty-four commercial Douglas DC-2 airliners impressed during 1942. Powered by two 740 hp SGR-1820-F3A engines – military version R-1820-33.

c/n	Model	Reg.	Airline(s)	USAAF Serial
1238	DC-2-112	NC13712	TWA/RAF	42-58071
1239	DC-2-112	NC13713	TWA/Braniff	42-53527
1241	DC-2-112	NC13715	TWA/RAF	42-70863
1242	DC-2-112	NC13716	TWA/Braniff	42-61095
1243	DC-2-112	NC13717	TWA/Braniff	42-65577
1245	DC-2-112	NC12719	TWA/Braniff	42-61096
1246	DC-2-112	NC13720	TWA/Braniff	42-68858
1249	DC-2-112	NC13723	TWA/PAA/PAA Africa	42-53528
1250	DC-2-112	NC13724	TWA/Braniff	42-57227
1252	DC-2-112	NC12726	TWA	42-57154
1254	DC-2-112	NC13728	TWA/Braniff	42-57228
1293	DC-2-112	NC13783	TWA/Northeast	42-65578
1294	DC-2-112	NC13784	TWA/Northeast	42-65579
1297	DC-2-112	NC13787	TWA/Northeast	42-68857
298	DC-2-112	NC13788	TWA	42-57155
300	DC-2-112	NC13790	TWA	42-57156
1310	DC-2-120	NC14277	American/RAF	42-53529
311	DC-2-120	NC14278	American/RAF	42-53530
312	DC-2-120	NC14279	American	42-53531
1313	DC-2-120	NC14280	American/RAF	42-58072
1367	DC-2-118B	NC14295	PAA/PAA Africa	42-53532
1372	DC-2-171	NC14969	Eastern/RAAF	44-83226
1376	DC-2-115G	PK-AFL	KNILM/ADAT VHCXH *	44-83227
1406	DC-2-120	NC14966	American/RAF	42-58073

* Previously operated as 41-1376.

Fokker Assembled Douglas DC-2 Transports

No.	c/n	Model	Date	Reg.	Del. Date	Notes
1.	1317	115A	25 Aug 34	PH-AJU		KLM 'Uiver' '44' MacRobertson Air Race
2.	1320	115D	26 Sep 34	A-500		Austrian Government
3.	1318	115D	26 Oct 34	D-ABEQ	Feb 35	Lufthansa 'Taunus' 4.
4.	1321	115B	14 Nov 34	HB-ITI	4 Dec 34	Swissair
5.	1319	115B	26 Dec 34	PH-FOK	35	I-EROS ALI 25 Apr 35
6.	1322	115B	1 Jan 35	HB-ITE	17 Jan 35	Swissair
7.	1329	115B	7 Jan 35	HB-ITA	Jan 35	Swissair
8.	1330	115D	6 Jan 35	EC-XAX	May 35	LAPE 'Hercules'
9.	1331	115D	13 Jan 35	HB-ISI	22 Jul 35	Swissair X-331 1935 Croydon
10.	1332	115B	18 Jan 35	HB-ITO	15 Feb 35	Swissair
11.	1333	115B	25 Jan 35	F-AKHD	28 Aug 35	French Government
12.	1334	115B	11 Mar 35	EC-AAY	May 35	LAPE 'Orion'
13.	1335	115E	22 Mar 35	PH-AKG	22 Mar 35	KLM 'Gaai' '13'
14.	1354	115E	3 Apr 35	PH-AKH	3 Apr 35	KLM 'Haan' '2'
15.	1355	115E	15 Apr 35	PH-AKI	15 Apr 35	KLM 'Kievit' '3' D-ADBK NA+LD
16.	1356	115E	15 Apr 35	PH-AKJ	15 Apr 35	KLM 'Jan Van Gent' '44' D-AJAW PC+EC
17.	1357	115E	17 Apr 35	PH-AKK	17 Apr 35	KLM 'Koetilang' '5'
18.	1358	115E	20 Apr 35	PH-AKL	20 Apr 35	KLM 'Lijster' '6'
19.	1359	115E	24 Apr 35	PH-AKM	24 Apr 35	KLM 'Maraboe' '7'
20.	1360	115E	26 Apr 35	PH-AKN	26 Apr 35	KLM 'Nachtegaal' '8'
21.	1361	115E	29 Apr 35	PH-AKO	29 Apr 35	KLM 'Oeverzwaluw' '9'
22.	1362	115E	6 May 35	PH-AKP	6 May 35	KLM 'Perkoetoet' '10'
23.	1363	115E	25 May 35	PH-AKQ	25 May 35	KLM 'Kwak' '11' D-AEAN SG+KV
24.	1364	115E	9 May 35	PH-AKR	9 May 35	KLM 'Rietvink' '12' D-AIAS PC+EB
25.	1365	115E	13 May 35	PH-AKS	13 May 35	KLM 'Sperwer' '13' D-ABOW
26.	1366	115H	27 May 35	PH-AKT	27 May 35	KLM 'Toekan' '14'
27.	1377	115F	Jul 35	SP-ASK	Jul 35	LOT Bristol Pegasus engines
28.	1378	115F	3 Aug 35	SP-ASL	3 Aug 35	LOT Bristol Pegasus engines
29.	1417	115J	26 Nov 35	EC-EBB	Mar 36	LAPE 'Sagitario'
30.	1581	115K	24 Feb 36	OK-AIA	24 Feb 36	CLS
31.	1582	115K	4 Mar 36	OK-AIB	4 Mar 36	CLS D-AAIB
32.	1583	115L	12 Apr 36	PH-ALD	12 Apr 36	KLM 'Djalak'
33.	1584	115L	16 Apr 36	PH-ALE	16 Apr 36	KLM 'Edelvalk' G-AGBH
34.	1585	115L	16 Apr 36	PH-ALF	16 Apr 36	KLM 'Flamingo'
35.	1521	115J	24 Apr 36	EC-BBE	24 Apr 36	LAPE 'Granada' '25'
36.	1527	115M	17 Aug 36	EC-BFF	17 Aug 36	LAPE 'Toledo' '26'
37.	1562	200	5 Nov 36	OK-AIC	5 Nov 36	CLS D-AAIC
38.	1564	211	24 Jun 37	OK-AIA	29 Nov 37	CLS
39.	1565	211	12 Jul 37	OK-AID	12 Jul 37	CLS D-AAID

Notes: (1) was originally registered NC14284; (2) (3) (5) (8) (9) (10) test-flown as PH-AKF by Fokker; (17) (20) (21) (22) bombed by Luftwaffe at Schiphol, 10 May 40; (15) (16) (23) (24) (25) (26) captured by Luftwaffe at Schiphol, 15 May 40.

William Littlewood, Vice-President, Engineering, of American Airlines, put forward ideas for a stretched wide-
bodied version of the Douglas DC-2, which eventually became a completely new design, the ubiquitous DC-3.
The first version was the Douglas Sleeper Transport – DST – which was followed by the daytime version.
Costs per seat mile were about a third less than the DC-2. It was 64½-foot long and had a wing span of 95 feet.
(Douglas)

Chapter Five
Douglas DC-3

The period 1932 to 1935, during which the Douglas DC-3 evolved from the DC-1 and DC-2, marked the transformation of the Douglas Aircraft Company from fledgling status to maturity. This was a team effort, but its success stemmed from the nature of Donald Douglas himself, whom we knew as 'Doug'. He set the tone, he established the rules, our decisions patterned his. The reputation of the company grew in harmony with his. He knew the operation had to be profitable to stay alive, but he also knew that its products had to put technical excellence first. As the company grew he had to withdraw from detail, but he always kept in touch. His other love was yachtsmanship and sailing and he always put his hand on the tiller if we deviated from course. Basically he was a superb engineer and designer and talked our language. He also learned to talk the language of lawyers, of businessmen, of financiers, and of the marketplace. The result was that by 1936 our customers had such faith in our dependability and integrity that sometimes the order came first and the contract later, even in one case after delivery. It was a lot of fun to work for Douglas in those days. The DC-3 was virtually unchallenged, for we had such a headstart that nobody could catch up. We knew each other and our customers intimately. We were not overburdened by organisation. But best of all, we were proud of our boss and felt that he was proud of us.

Line-up of at least ten DC-3s and DST airliners from the huge American fleet including DC-3-178 NC16013 c/n 1551 Virginia NC16015 c/n 1553 Kentucky and DC-3-208A NC21747 c/n 2105 Fort Worth. American was the original customer for the DST-DC-3 configuration receiving the first aircraft in 1936. (American)

So wrote Arthur E. Raymond, Vice-President, Engineering, Douglas Aircraft Company: he retired in 1985, the fiftieth anniversary year of the birth of the Douglas DC-3. Donald Wills Douglas, founder of the company bearing his name, headed a small team of engineers, which included James H. 'Dutch' Kindelberger and Arthur E. Raymond, in developing the DC-3. The new airliner was larger, faster and more luxurious than her predecessors and the airlines found her more economical to operate and safer. She was the first passenger airliner to be equipped with an automatic pilot, heated cabin and sound-proofing. Customer and passenger popularity for the DC-3 was based on these factors. Standardisation reduced maintenance and broke safety records.

Originally the DC-3 was conceived as a luxury sleeper airliner for American Airlines, when it was found that the earlier DC-2 was not wide enough to accommodate a comfortable berth. Initial design was for seven upper and seven lower berths, with a private cabin in front. The engineers soon found that by removing the berths they could fit three rows of seven seats into the fuselage. Thus the Douglas Sleeper Transport – DST – evolved into the DC-3.

It was an immediate success when American Airlines introduced it into service in June 1936 on the non-stop New York to Chicago route. Orders from other airlines in the USA and overseas for more and more DC-3s came almost immediately. The airline industry converted to the new DC-3 as fast as the Douglas factory at Santa Monica could produce them. By 1938 the transport was not only the standard equipment of the US major airlines, but it was also operating in dozens of foreign countries. Air travel coast-to-coast in the United States was reduced to fifteen hours. The President of American Airlines, Cyrus R. Smith, stated: 'The DC-3 freed the airlines from complete dependence upon government mail pay. It was the first aeroplane that could make money by just hauling passengers.'

For all its unprecedented performance, the $110,000 transport was not radically new technology, but rather a logical extension of the fourteen-passenger DC-2. The real breakthrough was economy. Because of this, the DC-3 soon became the standard airliner throughout the air transport world, confirming US manufacturing leadership and lifting American Airlines to a position amongst the leaders in the airline industry. There is always a turning point in the affairs of a company. That point for American Airlines, dramatically and decisively was the introduction of the DC-3.

Any worries that the Douglas Aircraft Company may have had were over as the order book for the DC-3 filled up. In December 1937, just two years after the first DC-3 made its maiden flight, it was announced that the company had reached an all-time high in production. That month, alone, they had produced thirty-six aircraft and parts totalling $2,700,000, with the new DC-3 airliner making up the bulk of the orders. There was a backlog of $5,250,000 in foreign orders for the DC-3 alone, and another $2 million more on the order books from the US domestic airlines. By 1939, with the DC-3 in service all over the globe, the company employed 9,000 personnel and the yearly payroll was $12 million.

Factory scene at Santa Monica on 29 November 1940 with a hive of activity centred around a Delta Air Lines DC-3 being completed, while in the background is parked a DC-3A Mainliner for United, and a Douglas Boston for the Royal Air Force. (Douglas)

Seen at Oakland, California, in January 1971 is DC-3-208A c/n 2103 N51AD from the Flying Sportsmen's Club, National Stockyards, Illinois. It was originally NC21745 Flagship Phoenix of American delivered 18 February 1939. After many ownerships it was cancelled during 1975.
(William T. Larkins)

Early Developments

Credit for the first ideas, and later more positive thinking, on the potential development of the early DC-3 must surely go to American Airlines and its Vice-President, Engineering, William Littlewood. Seen now with the benefit of hindsight, there stand out two historic dates and events, both associated with American Airlines and William Littlewood. They marked the start of air transport as we know it today in terms of equipment standards and economic performance. At the time they caused very little comment. Today, in retrospect, we can see their true significance.

They occurred as a direct result of the uncomfortable flight Bill Littlewood and his boss Cyrus Smith had in a DC-2 in the autumn of 1934, described in the last chapter. The two men had one of those discussions from which so much can emerge. What emerged in this case were two milestones in air transport history:

1. 8 July 1935. Smith sent a telegram to Donald Douglas ordering ten DSTs as a stretched, 'wide-body' development of the DC-2.
2. 25 June 1936. The first commercial service of the DC-3 was flown by American Airlines between Midway, Chicago and Newark, New Jersey.

Four people – C.R. Smith, Bill Littlewood, Donald Wills Douglas Sr and Arthur E. Raymond – were closely involved in both.

The Birth of the DC-3

The fantastic story of how the DC-3 came to be developed has often been told from many angles. The hard facts of this historic tale have not hitherto been set on record with the precision so essential to achieve historic accuracy.

The early discussions of 1934 included a longer-range, stretched DC-2 powered by the new 'G' series of Wright Cyclone engines. As these discussions developed there were three obvious requirements: a greater payload than the DC-2; a body wide enough to accommodate berths on either side of the aisle so that the new transport could be used for transcontinental sleeper services, in succession to the Curtiss Condor; and increased range to cut out stops between New York and Chicago and so achieve transcontinental services in four hops.

But for the persistence of Cyrus R. Smith there would have been no DC-3. Matters were brought to a head one evening in the autumn of 1934 when Smith telephoned Donald Douglas from the head office of American Airlines in Chicago to the company office at Santa Monica. In the course of a two-hour call Smith asked Douglas to expand the DC-2 so that it could not only carry fourteen passengers, but enable them to sleep as well, and in its day configuration, carry even more passengers. Naturally Douglas was reluctant to embark upon a new project at a time when he had a full order book for the DC-2. By the end

Six Douglas DC-3 airliners seen on 26 June 1938 minus wings and tailplane spars, at Santa Monica. In June 1937 production of the DC-2 was completed, and that year 63 DC-3s were delivered to customers in the USA, and 31 were exported. Fokker, who held construction rights in Europe, had accepted a total of 63 DC-3 and DC-3A airliners. (Douglas)

of the telephone call, Smith had made it clear that American Airlines could contemplate an order for up to twenty wide-body developments of the DC-2 if Douglas would build them; half the order could be for sleeper transports, and the remaining ten could be dayplanes with 50 per cent more payload and a longer range than the DC-2. Somewhat grudgingly, Douglas agreed to go ahead with a design study, and Smith promised to send Bill Littlewood to Santa Monica to help.

Design work started immediately under Arthur Raymond, with basic layout under Ed Burton and aerodynamics headed by Dr Bailey Oswald. They worked in close consultation with the National Advisory Committee for Aeronautics – NACA, now NASA – and the Guggenheim tunnel under Clark B. Millikan and A.L. 'Maje' Klein at the Californian Tech. Lee Atwood headed the stress department.

A great deal of knowledge stemmed from the original work on the DC-1 and DC-2 headed in 1932 by J.H. 'Dutch' Kindelberger, then Vice-President of engineering with Douglas before he moved on, in 1934, to become President of the General Aviation Corporation, which was shortly after renamed North American Aviation Inc. of Inglewood, California.

On 10 May 1935, Arthur Raymond produced 'Douglas Aircraft Report No. 1004', which outlined performance and weights of a DST – Douglas Sleeper Transport – development from the DC-2 to American Airlines' requirements. The Douglas company built a mock-up, expending some 15,000 man-hours on it.

Early in 1935 Bill Littlewood and his assistant, Kirchner, made a detailed examination of the possibilities of splitting the DC-2 fuselage longitudinally through the middle, widening it by a 26-in wide insert to make possible two seats on one side of the aisle and one on the other; and lengthening the fuselage to gain eight rows of seats of three abreast for a twenty-four-seat day plane or three double rows of berths on each side of the aisle for a twelve-berth sleeper plus two extra berths in a private 'honeymoon' sky room on the right of the front fuselage.

As it transpired, one row of seats was sacrificed to give more baggage space forward, thus reducing the day seats to twenty-one. The DC-3 was finalised with a fuselage 92 in wide inside and 78 in high from the floor, compared with the 66 in width and 75 in cabin height of the DC-2.

The busy production line at Santa Monica on 26 October 1939 with 'Ship 227' 'Factory 2169' making its way towards completion to become NC21780 c/n 2169 for Penn Central Airlines. It was delivered on 29 November. By May 1959, it had flown a total of 53,338 hours and had served with both Capital and United Air Lines. In 1980 it was based in California. (Douglas)

Cockpit photograph of Douglas Sleeper Transport (DST) the second built as DST-144 NC16001 c/n 1495 which went to American Airlines as 'New York' on 7 June 1936. The plate on the right upper gives the radio callsign of 'KHALB' along with fleet No.116 and registration. In June 1942 it was impressed as a C-49E 42-56097 and crashed on 18 December 1943 at Biggs Field, Fort Bliss in Texas. (Douglas)

Curtiss Wright had informed American Airlines of the possibility that the 750-hp R-1820-F engines fitted to the DC-2 could, hopefully, develop into 1,000-hp R-1820-G engines by the end of 1935. Bill Littlewood recalled that work started on the design of the DC-3 some eighteen months before engines were available to power it. Initial ideas were that the new airliner would be about 85 per cent DC-2 and 15 per cent new with a 50 per cent increase in payload. The original discussions were, clearly, wholly within American Airlines, between Littlewood, Smith and Kirchner. If the aircraft-mile costs could be maintained, the new aircraft would be able to make money, and it ought to be ready for service by the middle of 1935.

In the end the DC-3 turned out to be almost wholly new, with a wider and longer fuselage, larger wingspan, more tail volume with a dorsal fin to stop the 'fish-tailing' of the DC-2, a much stronger undercarriage and more power. It took two years to bring into service, rather than the one year envisaged.

There were many long telephone calls between American Airlines in Chicago and the Douglas company at Santa Monica, and on 17 June 1935, Harry Wetzel wrote to Bill Littlewood to quote prices for five, six, or ten DSTs at, respectively $82,000, $81,000 and $79,500 each for delivery at one a week from 15 February 1936, subject to the airline's acceptance within ten days. On 8 July 1935, Cyrus R. Smith telegraphed Donald Douglas: 'Enter our order 10 model DST airplanes delivery according to letter from Wetzel 27 June.' The order was confirmed by Douglas on 9 July, and on 17 July Bill Littlewood arrived in Santa Monica to work over details, flanked by a lawyer on one side and a purchasing agent on the other.

Frank Kolk, American Airlines Vice-President of development engineering, recorded: 'The Littlewood and

Douglas technical team headed by Raymond worked closely and informally together, had complete confidence in one another and tried to accommodate each other as closely as possible. This relationship was probably closer than in any other major commercial project.'

At that time there was a good deal of scepticism within American Airlines about the advisability of buying the DC-3. But both Smith and Littlewood believed that the trend must be towards more power and more aeroplane, and that it was worth the gamble that Curtiss Wright would come up with their new 1,000 hp engines in time. There was no certainty, but it happened. American Airlines flew a Curtiss Condor to Santa Monica so that the sleeping berths could be studied, and both Littlewood and Wetzel spent time lying down on the berths to prove precisely the best places for fitting the lights. However it was 8 April 1936 before any contract between the Douglas Aircraft Company and American Airlines was signed for the new DC-3.

The first DC-3 to be fitted with Pratt & Whitney engines was this DST-A-144 X-16002 c/n 1496 later NC16002. It became Flagship Illinois *with American, and is depicted devoid of airline livery, but has a A-117 on the fin.* (United Aircraft Corporation)

Depicted on 18 December 1935 the day after its maiden flight is the first DC-3, a DST-114 c/n 1494 registered X14988 and carrying only the minimum of American markings. It carries A-115 on the fin and is seen parked at Clover Field, Santa Monica. (Douglas)

Manufacture of the first DST began towards the end of 1934, with first engine ground runs taking place less than a year later on 14 December 1935. Registered X14988 and carrying the Douglas constructor's number 1494, the first DST did not have the dorsal fin, later a characteristic of all DC-3s. This was added in March 1936 to improve stability on the approach. The new airliner was fitted with the passenger door on the right-hand side. It was listed as a DST-114.

The DC-3 Power-plant

The engine is the heart of an aeroplane, and no reference to the DC-3 should omit an obeisance to the two powerplants that made it possible: first, the Wright Cyclone R-1820 G-series 9-cylinder radials and, second, the Pratt & Whitney Twin Wasp R-1830 series of 14-cylinder radials. They ranged in power from 1,000 bhp in 1936 to 1,250 hp by 1939.

The Wright Aeronautical Corporation of Paterson, New Jersey, was the engine-manufacturing division of the Curtiss

Wright Corporation, which had evolved as the result of a merger in 1931. The Cyclone engine was already in service, chiefly with the US Navy. The Wright Cyclone engine and name in fact started in 1924 as the Wright R.1656.P.1 9-cylinder radial, rated at 400 bhp at 1,650 rpm with a weight of 840 lb. The first user was the US Navy. By 1926 the Cyclone had developed into the 525 bhp R.1750 engine with a longer stroke and weight reduced to 760 lb. A total of 254 engines were supplied to the US Navy and 141 to the US Army at $14,188 each.

The Cyclone R-1750 received its civil certificate (ATC 17) on 26 January 1929, and in 1930 it was again developed to the R-1820 variant with an increase in bore. The engine was certificated on 8 September 1930 (ATC 61) at 575 bhp at 1,900 rpm. In that year 345 R-1820-E engines were delivered to the US Navy. The 525 bhp R-1820 commenced its commercial life with American Airlines in the Curtiss Condor in 1933, and then went on to power the DC-1, DC-2 and DC-3. The Cyclones in pre-Second World War commercial use were: R-1820-E 108

The Santa Monica DC-3 production line seen on 10 November 1937, with airliners reaching final assembly having had their Wright Cyclone or Pratt & Whitney Twin Wasp engines added, but still minus the outer wing panels. (Douglas)

made from July 1930; R-1820-F 2,589 made from June 1932; R-1820-G 1,547 made from April 1935; and R-1820-G100 2,258 made from July 1937. The last Cyclone was finally shipped during April 1967 to complete a total of more than 125,000 engine units.

Cyclone R-1820-F.2 engines of 725 hp were installed in the DC-2s that American Airlines introduced into service in December 1934. The prospective development of those 725 hp F.2 engines into the Cyclone G-5 of 1,000 hp for take-off at 2,200 rpm with a weight of 1,163 lb made the DC-3 possible.

Chief architect for the Cyclone's success was Phil Taylor under Arthur Nutt. Bob Johnson was the designated Wright aeronautical installation engineer at the Douglas plant from the time of the installation of the Cyclone in the DC-2s, DSTs and the DC-3. He undoubtedly deserves much credit, among all the members of the Wright team, for the commercial success of the engine in service. Bob Johnson worked with Bill Littlewood through all the saga and on into the joint activity with the unique Wright turbo-compound engines in the Douglas DC-7 series.

First Flight

Records show that the first ground run of the Cyclone engines fitted to X14988 took place on 14 December 1935, when the first DST was wheeled out of the hangar for a ninety minute engine run at noon.

The first flight of the DC-3 – the Douglas Sleeper Transport variant – took place at 3 pm on 17 December 1935, with Carl Cover, Douglas test pilot and Vice-President of sales, at the controls, accompanied by two flight engineers, Ed Stineman and Frank Collbohm, plus Jack Grant, a mechanic. The initial flight lasted thirty minutes and was followed by two more, to bring the total time that historic day to 1 hour 40 minutes.

Rare factory photograph taken at Santa Monica on 25 November 1936 depicting a DC-3-196 NC14995 c/n 1589 with right hand door destined for export to the USSR for Excello via Amtorg the importer. After flight test it was dismantled and delivered by sea to Europe to Cherbourg, France. It was delivered to Russia from the factory on 30 November. Later the DC-3 type was built under licence in the USSR as the PS-84 and the Lisunov Li-2.
(Douglas)

Few, if any, of the many onlookers at Clover Field that day could have perceived the great significance of the first flight of the Douglas DC-3. It was also the thirty-second anniversary of the first flight by the Wright brothers. The DC-3 revolutionised transportation and eventually touched the lives of people throughout the world. This new transport was twin-engined, had a gross weight of 24,000 lb and could carry twenty-one passengers. With the advent of war the Douglas Aircraft Company constructed it in large quantities at factories located at Santa Monica, Long Beach and Oklahoma City. By the time production finally ceased in 1946, some 455 had been built as commercial models, and over 10,000 as military derivatives.

After its first flight, the transport was then flown daily from Clover Field, except for 21 December, Christmas Day, and 27 and 30 December, right up to the end of the year. By 2.30 p.m. on the last day of December 1935 a total of 25 hours 45 minutes had been accumulated, most by Elling H. Veblen, Douglas test pilot, and M. Gould 'Dan' Beard, the American Airlines engineering test pilot. For the first few days of January 1936 the new airliner was exhibited at the National Pacific Aircraft and Boat Show organised by Harry Wetzel in the Los Angeles Auditorium. Test flying was resumed on 6 January, chiefly by Dan Beard, with Tommy Tomlinson from TWA getting his first flight on that day. Between 11 January and the end of the month, the plane was grounded for modification to the propeller controls and exhausts. In spite of such interruptions, including a double engine change between 18 and 26 February, test flying of the DST went on more or less continuously throughout the first four months of 1936.

Factory scene at Santa Monica on 9 December 1939 as the port wing is fitted to the first of Braniff Airways DC-3-314 NC21773 c/n 2179 named Super B-Liners. It was delivered on 15 December entering service two days later. On 17 September 1942 the DC-3 was impressed as a C-49H 42-68687.
(Douglas)

There was no prototype. Most of the engineering test flying continued to be done by Dan Beard of American Airlines – an example of the unusually close manufacturer and customer relationship, which certainly helped to get the desired results. On 29 April 1936, the first Douglas DST X14988 received its Certificate of Airworthiness – ATC 607. The second DST NC16001, a model DST-144 c/n 1495, also with a right-hand passenger door, made its first flight on 4 June 1936, a five-month interval since the maiden flight of the first DST, after which the new airliner was produced at an accelerating rate – thirty in the last six months of 1936.

During the intensive test flying there were two episodes, either of which might have brought the project to an early end. Between 6 and 10 January, a serious problem revealed itself in that X14988 was incapable of meeting the stipulated take-off unstick distance of 1,000 ft at the gross weight of 24,000 lb. So convinced was Tommy Tomlinson that the aircraft would not be able to operate from most of the small airport runways of the day that he reported adversely on the transport and departed back to his headquarters at Kansas City in mid-January with the firm belief that American Airlines had bought a 'clunk' and TWA should look seriously for more DC-2s rather than the DC-3. The result was that by the time TWA caught up with progress, it had lost valuable places on the production line in favour of both American and United Air Lines.

However, the take-off problems were genuine, and Dan Beard himself was very worried. There seemed no doubt that the two Wright G-5 engines were not giving the power required of them. In mid-February, Bob Johnson and Bill Birren of Wright, who shared Beard's concern about the take-off performance, asked for X14988 for a week, during which both engines were changed and modifications were incorporated in the replacement Cyclone G-5 engines in an effort to restore the power.

Unique photograph taken at Santa Monica on 9 September 1940 depicting a galaxy of Douglas products including three DC-3-201Ds of the Great Silver Fleet of Eastern, one DC-3 of Northwest, one military B-18 37-528 and three B-23 aircraft, the latter type using DC-3 components. Of the Eastern DC-3s NC15596 c/n 2247 and NC15597 c/n 2257 survived well into the 1980s while NC19963 c/n 2260 crashed at Chesterfield, New Jersey, after mid-air collision with a Grumman F6F- BuNo.72887 on 30 July 1949. (Douglas)

According to Johnson and Birren, both old friends of Bill Littlewood and members of the Wright aeronautical team, the crankcases of the original engines to Spec.286G were holding churned up, pressurised oil at high take-off rpm. The effort expended by the crankshaft in stirring up the oil was costing about 75 bhp per engine. The replacement engines to Spec.286H had fore and aft holes through the lower crankcase walls and a pick-up close to the rotating parts which forced out the oil. The power was thus restored. Take-off tests carried out by Veblen and Beard for the Department of Commerce on 28 February showed an unstick distance of 970 ft. All was well.

The second problem occurred on 5 March 1936, near the end of the planned test-flying period, after DST X14988 had completed a total of sixty-six flying hours. The aircraft was

ferried from Clover Field to Mines Field, Inglewood, now the site of Los Angeles International Airport, for landing and brake tests. Beard recounts that he was taking movie pictures of the runway marks out of the right cockpit window while Veblen made the landing. Suddenly he was thrown against the window as the airliner swung violently: it was later discovered that it had touched with one wheel almost locked and the other wholly free as a result of a burst actuating cylinder.

Dan Beard sensed what had happened as the aeroplane swung off the runway and headed in a skid towards one of the hangars. There was no time to correct the swerve, so he added power to the right engine in the direction of the ground loop. The plane skidded sideways through a four-foot cyclone fence and finished up with the tail within two feet of the hangar. Fortunately, the damage was small and the DST was flown back to Clover Field for repair. But had Dan Beard not reacted instinctively and had the ground loop not been successful, there seems no doubt that the cockpit would have gone through the concrete wall of the hangar and neither pilot would have survived the impact – nor might the DC-3 project have survived.

Between 6 and 22 March 1936, a fourteen-passenger day and night interior was installed in X14988 while the airliner was under repair. The fourteen day-seats were in facing pairs, the upper and lower berths were added to make up at night. The dorsal fin was also added at this time to improve control on the approach to land. The first batch of aircraft was certificated at a gross weight of 24,000 lb, this being later raised to 25,000 lb and then to 25,200 lb as more engine power became available.

On the day on which it received its certification, and now registered NC14988 – 29 April 1936 – the DST was delivered to Phoenix, Arizona, by Jake Moxness of the Douglas Aircraft Company and formally accepted there by American Airlines. The airline had initiated acceptance in Phoenix in order to avoid paying the California sales tax on its DC-2s. This was continued for the acceptance of all its DC-3s, DC-6s and DC-7s. As soon as the handover documentation had been completed, NC14988 was flown back to Santa Monica by American Airline pilots and between 2 and 7 May completed the required Department of Commerce fifty-hour proving flights between Glendale, California; Fort Worth and El Paso, Texas; Phoenix, Arizona; and Santa Monica.

United Air Lines, whose success with the new Boeing 247D airliner had been short-lived, purchased the Douglas DST and the DC-3A which commenced service on the Los Angeles to San Francisco route on the first day of 1937. This rare photograph, taken at Seattle, depicts a Boeing 247D NC13326 alongside a DC-3A-197 NC16070 c/n 1910, the latter surviving today. (Gordon S. Williams)

A period of ground work followed whilst some sixty outstanding items were sorted out between American Airlines and the Douglas company. Notable among these were unsatisfactory engine mounts, inadequate oil-cooler capacity and brake problems. They were finally resolved at a high level after Arthur Raymond moved some drawing boards into the flight hangar adjacent to the DST. The modifications were completed on the spot.

In the meantime, the second DST NC16001 had been flown for the first time on 4 June by Dan Beard and went through its flight tests so quickly that it was delivered to Phoenix on 7 June. It then completed a non-stop flight to Fort Worth and went on to Dallas, Texas. On 8 June Dan Beard landed it triumphantly in Chicago after a non-stop flight from Dallas, so making the first delivery of a DST into airline hands. Flight training with American Airlines personnel began at once.

The third DST NC16002 DST-144 c/n 1496, initially registered X16002 and fitted with a right-hand passenger door, was delivered on 17 June after its first flight only three days earlier. By this time American Airlines had allocated names and fleet numbers to its new airliners: NC14988 '*Texas*' 'A115'; NC16001 '*New York*' 'A116'; NC16002 '*Illinois*' 'A117'. The eighth airliner in the American Airlines order, and the first twenty-one-seat DC-3 dayplane NC16009 DC-3-178 c/n 1545, named '*District of Columbia*' 'A-123', was delivered on 18 August after making its maiden flight two days earlier. The Douglas production line had never seen so much activity, producing both the DC-2, the DST and the DC-3.

American Airlines DC-3-178 Flagship District of Columbia *NC16009 c/n 1545 delivered on 18 August 1936 seen parked awaiting boarding of passengers. The airline operated a large fleet of no less than ninety DSTs and DC-3s.* (American)

With two Douglas DSTs delivered to American Airlines at Chicago, the airline intensified its training programme and introduced some publicity and propaganda flying in preparation for the first commercial services involving the new plane. One of the most remarkable of these propaganda demonstrations was held on 21 June, when NC16001 was filled up to its full load of 822 US gallons of fuel and made a non-stop round trip from Midway, Chicago, to Newark, New Jersey, and back to Midway

in 8 hours 7 minutes carrying a standard American Airlines crew plus Cyrus R. Smith, Bill Littlewood, Bob Johnson and a few others. The DST landed with some fifty US gallons of fuel remaining.

First Airline Service

Before taking delivery of the Douglas DSTs, American Airlines had been busy flying the very important New York to Chicago flight sector, by way of Buffalo and Detroit; these 250-mile hops were matched to the performance of American's fleet of Curtiss-Wright Condor airliners. Apart from this airline service with its two refuelling stops, the only alternative for passengers wishing to go from New York to Chicago was eighteen hours in a train.

Prior to World War II the luxury liners of Europe and the USA ruled the Atlantic routes. The French Normandie *was one of these liners and is seen at New York with a TWA DC-3-209A NC18951 c/n 2015 'Sky Club 377' making a flypast. This airliner collided with a USAAF C-53 41-20116 in November 1942 near Kansas City, Missouri.* (Douglas)

Now, on 25 June 1936, American Airlines launched its 'American Eagle', non-stop Chicago to New York service, the very first commercial operation with the aeroplane that was to make history. The inaugural flight left Midway at noon Central Standard Time on that Thursday morning. The plane chosen was NC16002 '*Flagship Illinois*', flown by Captain W.W. Braznell with First Office W.A. Miller. The reciprocal service NC16001 '*Flagship New York*', departed Newark at 1330 hours Eastern Standard Time the same day, flown by Captain Melvin D. Ator with First Officer F.R. Bailey. In the westbound direction, against prevailing headwinds of almost 20 mph, the Douglas airliner was scheduled at 4 hours 45 minutes, which compared with 3 hours 55 minutes eastbound. On the inaugural day, both DSTs – the second and third off the Santa Monica production line – were equipped with fourteen passenger seats, each no less than 24 in wide, which, today, would be judged as 'luxury first class'.

The seating arrangements were, in fact, well suited to the circumstances of the time because, with fourteen occupied seats and associated baggage, the payload was brought up to just

Pan American Grace Airways Inc., New York, NY used a large number of both DC-2s and DC-3s on its routes in South America. The DC-3s were introduced during 1937 and some remained in service until 1960 when they were sold in Peru. Photograph depicts a typical apron scene in the USA prior to World War II with DC-3-229 NC18119 c/n 1995 delivered on 19 October 1937. (Douglas)

about the capacity available for the westbound non-stop flight against headwinds, with the standard fuel reserves of the period and a certified gross weight of 24,000 lb. Until the gross weight was increased to 25,000 lb when all the DST seats were filled westbound, there was normally no weight available for either mail or cargo against the prevailing wind, whereas eastbound with full seats and associated baggage the plane could carry 480 lb of mail and cargo.

In 1936, the one-way fare between Chicago and New York was $47.95. Once the DST was in scheduled airline service, other routes of American Airlines were added as aircraft became available. On 18 September 1936, DSTs took over the transcontinental coast-to-coast service between Newark and the Grand Central Terminal, Glendale, Los Angeles, by way of Memphis, Tennessee, Dallas, Texas, and Tucson, Arizona. The scheduled time was 15 hours 50 minutes eastbound and 17 hours 41 minutes westbound. Services were inaugurated with twenty-one-passenger DC-3s between Newark and Logan Airport, Boston, Massachusetts. On 1 October, a second transcontinental

Early World War II scene at Santa Monica with the first Douglas C-54 Skymaster 41-20137 parked outside the hangar with a Pan American DC-3A-414, minus wings, NC30002 c/n 4171 awaiting attention. Douglas DB-7s for the Army Air Corps are parked in the background. The DC-3A became a C-48C on 18 December 1941, with the US Defense Supply Corporation. (Douglas via Peter M. Bowers)

route was opened, with DSTs 'The Southerner' operating in both directions with four stops.

To launch this new era of air transport, American Airlines had exhausted its capital and its credit. Cyrus R. Smith had obtained the first loan made by the Reconstruction Finance Corporation to an airline. On 23 June 1936, American borrowed $1,235,000 to assist in the purchase of the twenty DST/DC-3 aircraft which were costing them a total of $2,060,000. For all these fundamental problems of finance and capital, the new airliner helped with the economic health of the airline. In 1934 American Airlines Inc. lost $2,313 million, in 1935 $748,000. In 1936, the first year of operating the DST/DC-3, American Airlines made its first profit – $4,590.

By the time that the United States came involved in the Second World War in December 1941, a total of 507 DST/DC-3s had been built, of which 434 had been delivered to commercial airlines. When, late in 1941, 10 per cent of the transport aircraft in service with airlines in the United States were impressed into the US Army Air Transport Service, American Airlines, United Airlines, TWA and Western volunteered to give up their DSTs because of the smaller disposable loads compared with the DC-3s – the figures quoted were 8,250 lb as against 9,155 lb. There were in fact a total of fifty DSTs built. These included fifteen for American Airlines; six for Eastern; seventeen for United Air Lines; ten for TWA and two for Western Air Express. All of them were integrated into military service.

Worthy of record is the fate of the 'Grandpappy' of them all, NC14988. On 14 March 1942 it was taxied over from the American Airlines hangar on the west side of La Guardia, New York, to the TWA hangars on the east side, destined for wartime service. It had 17,166 hours 15 minutes in its logbooks and records show it was numbered '361' with TWA. For sixty days TWA flew the DST in a stripped-down condition on cargo contracts for the military. On 15 October 1942, it departed Knobnoster air base, Missouri, to fly to Chicago. Two miles from its destination an engine failed. The aircraft crashed and burned, killing the nine men on board, all US Army personnel. Later, on the last day of March 1943, the DST was officially allocated the military serial 42-43619 and designated a Douglas C-49E. It is suspected it had carried these much earlier. So ended, some six and a quarter years after the first flight, the career of 'the First of the Many'.

DC-3 Economics

In its heyday the total operating costs of the DC-3 were down to around 3 cents a seat-mile or 22 cents a capacity-ton-mile, figures on which genuine profits could be earned. Cyrus R. Smith said: 'The DC-3 freed the airlines from complete dependency upon US government mail pay. It was the first airplane which could make money by just handling passengers. With previous aircraft, if you multiplied the number of seats by the fares being charged, you couldn't break even – not even with a 100 per cent load. Economically, the DC-3 let us expand and develop new routes where there was no mail pay.' During its first year, the DC-3 turned in a total operating cost per aircraft mile of 71.6 cents.

According to Edward P. Warner, in his Wilbur Wright Memorial Lecture before the Royal Aeronautical Society in May 1943: 'The median total cost for three of the leading airlines using DC-3s was reasonably stabilised at about 68 cents per

Air mail packages are loaded aboard an American Airlines DC-3 on 7 July 1936 some addressed to destinations in New Orleans, Louisiana. Mail was also included and was as vital as passengers in those early pioneering days. (Douglas)

revenue-mile flown throughout the period 1939-1941. The total cost of operating the DC-3 on major airlines within the United States during the spring of 1942 was 68.7 cents at a maximum take-off load of 25,200 lb.'

On a seat-mile basis, the most economic range for the DC-3 was about 800 statute miles – the maximum still-air range with twenty-one passengers and baggage and full reserves and allowances. On a ton-mile basis, where the capacity payload of 5,770 lb can be carried for up to 260 miles, the most economic sector distance worked out at 500 miles, where the optimum combination of block speed, payload, and range came together.

American Airlines eventually operated no fewer than ninety-four DC-3s and retired the last of them in March 1949 after they had carried 10.5 million passengers for the airline. Bill

Mohawk used 'Steamboat Gothic' typeface on their DC-3s to make them eye-catching. Depicted is DC-3-357 N409D c/n 3277 Mohican ex-Delta NC28340 delivered in November 1940. This unique Mohawk service was introduced on 10 October 1960 with the interior resembling a Victorian setting with red velvet curtains, Currier & Ives prints and carriage lamps. Stewardesses wore Gay Nineties costumes. (Henry M. Holden)

Littlewood wrote in 1961: 'The DC-3 was big for its time. Now it is small. It speed was good then. Now, with rising costs, it cannot make money at normal rates, even with a 100 per cent load factor, and is assigned to local subsidised services or general aviation uses.'

In the year 1936 United States airlines as a whole carried 1.02 million passengers in 272 aircraft, more than double the number of passengers carried in 1934 (462,000). At the end of the year American Airlines had in service twenty DC-3 aircraft of which twelve were twenty-one- passenger day-planes and eight fourteen-passenger DSTs, the former on New York to Boston and New York to Chicago services, the latter on transcontinental services. By the end of 1936, the Douglas order books indicated that sixty-three DC-3s had been sold: twenty-five to American, including eight DSTs; twenty to United; eight to KLM in the Netherlands; eight to TWA; and two to Eastern. Of these a total of thirty-one had actually been delivered: twenty to American, one to KLM and ten to United.

W. A. 'Pat' Patterson, United Air Line's fiery and dynamic President who wanted a Douglas DC-3 that was different. He ordered the DC-3A powered by the 14-cylinder Pratt & Whitney Twin Wasp engine. The first DC-3A entered United Air Line service on 30 June 1937 and made a profit for the airline. The company would never cease buying Douglas Commercial airliners. (United Air Lines)

United Air Lines

William A. 'Pat' Patterson, United Air Lines' fiery and dynamic President, wanted a Douglas DC-3 that was different. He ordered the DC-3A, powered by the 14-cylinder Pratt & Whitney Twin Wasp engines. The first DC-3A went into United Air Lines service on 30 June 1937, and made a profit for the airline.

During 1934 a test engineer with United, Raymond D. Kelly, stationed at Cheyenne, South Dakota, noticed that some of the early Douglas DC-2s showed less than sparkling take-off performance from Cheyenne airport with its elevation of 6,200 ft. At this time United Air Lines had close ties with Pratt & Whitney through the airline's use of engines supplied exclusively for their Boeing Model 80 Tri-motor, the Boeing Monorails and B.247s. Because of this, Wright Parkins of P & W made frequent trips to Cheyenne between 1934 and 1936 and Ray Peck was based in Cheyenne as the P & W field service representative.

At one stage Piedmont operated twenty-one DC-3 airliners. It was on 20 February 1948 that the airline commenced local services with the DC-3 it being retained in service until 20 February 1963 when replaced by more modern types. Depicted is N25621 c/n 2227 originally a DC-3A-269B delivered to Northwest on 14 May 1940. Piedmont purchased the DC-3, after lease on 21 March 1949 it later being re-registered N41V. (Piedmont)

When United commenced negotiations with the Douglas Aircraft Company for the purchase of their first batch of DC-3 airliners, Pratt & Whitney were the logical choice for powerplants. Those primarily involved were W.A. Patterson, who had just taken over as President of United from P.G. Johnson; D.B. Colyer, Vice-President in charge of the Cheyenne operations; Frank Caldwell, his deputy; and William Mentzer, who had recently joined United Air Lines from the Boeing Airplane Company. Bill Mentzer was, shortly afterwards, assigned to the Douglas Aircraft Company as the United engineer, where he handled first the new DC-3A and later the Douglas DC-4 'Skymaster', undertaking all the engineering responsibilities for the airline. Also closely involved were T.E. Tillinghast, the sales engineer for United, and Luke Hobbs and Jack Bunce, both based in Hartford, Connecticut.

So, to United Air Lines and Pratt & Whitney in collaboration as well as to the Douglas Aircraft Company, goes the credit for the developed version of the DC-3 powered with R-1830 engines which became, in due course, the definitive military and civil version. Indeed, without the Pratt & Whitney Twin Wasp-powered DC-3 there would have been an enormous gap in the United States' war effort. This is, of course, no reflection on the original Wright Cyclone-powered variant.

Ray Kelly recalls what happened:

My first association with the testing of the DC-3 occurred in December 1936, with Captain Walter Addems and Captain

Bill Williams as pilots. I was instructed to take our first aircraft – DC-3A NC16060, a DC-3A-191 c/n 1900, delivered 23 December 1936 – to Hartford, Connecticut, and run some performance tests. Even with the Pratt & Whitney 1830-B engine and the Hamilton Standard constant-speed hydraulic propeller, we were not getting as good take-off performance at Cheyenne as was desired. We ran a good many tests in Hartford, endeavouring to get the best possible match between propeller diameter, propeller pitch settings, and rpms to improve this condition.

In August of 1937, United Air Lines placed an order with Pratt & Whitney for twenty-eight each R-1830 and SICG engines to be delivered to the Douglas Aircraft Company in Santa Monica. In the meantime United had begun the conversion of DC-3 airplane No.16087 – DC-3A NC16087 DC-3A-197 c/n 1926 '*Massachusetts*', delivered 8 February 1937 – to the 1830-C engine installation with Stromberg downdraft carburettors and Hamilton Standard Hydomatic propellers. The project engineer was R.L. Heinrich. After the conversion and stress analysis approved by the Department of Commerce (with assistance and blessing from Douglas, for they would use this United installation for production drawings), and tests at Cheyenne, South Dakota, and Chicago, Illinois, we flew the aircraft to Mines Field, Los Angeles, for inspection and performance testing for the Department of Commerce.

On 18 January 1938, I sent additional data to Mr L.J. Holoubek, Department of Commerce at Mines Field, requesting certification. The ATC approval was granted 26 March 1936, for Douglas production aircraft with a gross take-off weight of 25,200 lb.

The longevity of the DC-3 is a phenomenon that today, nearly 60 years after its first flight, astounds many including the historians. There is no doubt that the robust structure allowed it to survive so long, plus the availability of spare parts etc. Long after production ceased in 1946 the type was much sought after and flown by operators large and small. Depicted is a pre-war DC-3 N21768 c/n 2167 of Florida Airlines based at Sarasota. It is ex-DC-3-277A NC21768 of American impressed during 1942 as C-49H 42-65580. (AP Photo Library)

In the fall of 1937, United furnished an airplane to the NACA – National Advisory Committee for Aeronautics – to investigate fully the stall characteristics of the DC-3 airplane. Captain Charles Thompson was the pilot, and I was the engineer, and one of our top mechanics, Earl Garber, accompanied us. The airplane – DC-3A-197 NC16070 c/n 1910 '**Reno**', delivered 25 November 1936 – was flown to Langley Field, Hampton, Virginia. The NACA applied tufts of yarn at many points on the top surfaces of the wings and installed special instrument equipment, along with movie cameras, in the cabin. Melvin Gough was the NACA test pilot who flew with us, and Floyd Thompson was in charge of the test programme. We stalled the airplane under all conceivable conditions of power, various flap positions, and in turns as well as straight flight.

The results were very enlightening. They demonstrated that while the airplane would roll abruptly in a full stall, when flown properly the DC-3 was not as critical as we had been led to believe from various pilot comments. We learned that the DC-3 airplane should not make the so-called 'three-point landing', but rather should be flown on to the runway at speeds somewhat above the stalling speed.

At that time, both the NACA and my test group developed stall-warning devices, but by the time production instrumentation was available, our flight crews had been sufficiently educated about the characteristics of the DC-3 so that United's Flight Operation Department vetoed the purchase of our stall warning unit.

One of the benefits of the NACA stall tests was to point out the increased criticalness of the DC-3 airplane under icing conditions. At Langley and again later in Chicago, United carried out further stall tests with simulated icing deposits (sawdust with a glue binder) on the leading edges of the wings. United was particularly interested in the icing problem because we had lost an airplane on its approach to Midway Airport in Chicago when it stalled out in an approach effort, presumably having been in icing conditions.

These tests demonstrated the changes in flight characteristics which must be anticipated by the flight crews during icing conditions. Further, they stimulated additional testing of de-icer boots manufactured by the Goodrich Company. Also, it emphasised the importance of maintaining a clear vision through the windshield, and United developed the first successfully heated aircraft windshield pane.

Another element of the icing problem related directly to the powerplant. I refer to carburettor ice. This problem was present with both the Wright Cyclone 1820 engine and in the Pratt & Whitney R-1830 installations. It was so serious that the Bureau of Standards in Washington DC co-operated in the running of tests, and I recall that Dan Beard of American Airlines, R.L. McBrien of my group, and I were actively involved. For the Cyclone engine there seemed to be more general reliance upon the injection of alcohol into the carburettor induction system, whereas United and Pratt & Whitney favoured the use of hot air to melt out ice accumulations around the throttles and the venturis.

We had a great many other problems related to cold weather operations with the DC-3, which required many tests in order to achieve satisfactory service. The cabin steam heating system caused no end of difficulties. In reviewing a list of United's engineering tests dating from 1937 to 1943, I noted that a large number of them related to cabin heating system modifications. Eventually in 1943 we developed a 'United Air Lines Hot Air – Type 3 for DC-3 Airplanes' heating system which proved much more reliable.

Another icing problem related to the pitot tubes and the support mast for same. We tested electrically heated pitot

tubes of various configurations, and it was found essential to put a de-icer boot on the mast in order to eliminate vibration of same.

Another item which is frequently repeated in our engineering test list relates to various types of spark plugs which were tried out in order to increase their service life and/or reduce the possibility of pre-ignition under high temperature and/or high power conditions. In addition to the spark plugs, there were numerous other ignition system problems.

I note that there was one general test that was set up in January 1939 which is captioned 'Engines – To Determine Cause of Excessive Cylinder Head Temperatures with P & W 1830C S1C3-G Engines'. The problem was associated with engine roughness and occasional detonation, when DC-3s powered with 1830C engines equipped with Bendix Stromberg 'injection' carburettors were flown at full throttle at the higher altitudes, particularly during warm weather.

This required a major and concerted investigation. Charles Manhardt of the Bendix Company, Phil Doran of Pratt & Whitney, and I spent some two months in an intensive test programme in the spring of 1939, trying to find the cause and its correction. We installed thermocouples on all the cylinders of both engines of the aircraft assigned to us. By the use of a hand-operated potentiometer we were able to judge the deviations in the fuel-air ratio of the mixture going to the individual cylinders, under all different throttle positions, with varying altitude, power output and outside air temperature situations.

We were amazed to find that in flight the position of the throttle had a very great effect upon the mixture distribution. This changed with altitude, power and rpm, and explained why it had not been reasonably anticipated by tests run on the test stand by P & W and Bendix. We then engaged in an elaborate 'cut and try' test programme whereby we modified the carburettor injection and induction flow patterns.

This was a slow and costly experience, finally ending up in a series of flight tests out over the Salton Sea (eighty miles inland from the coast of southern California – north-west of Yuma, Arizona). There, we were able to start at below sea level with reasonably warm temperatures and then climb to high altitudes, testing different power and throttle conditions as we climbed. We were able to achieve a modification of the carburettor which gave uniform mixture distribution patterns for the 1830C engine for all flight and power situations. I do not know that any better fuel-air mixture distribution pattern has ever been achieved for any other similar type powerplant. Although it was a long and costly test programme for United, Pratt & Whitney and Bendix, the eventual outcome was of considerable significance in the outstanding performance given by the subsequent P & W engine installations in the DC-3 airplane, in both civil and in military use.

I feel that the 'evolution' of the DC-2 and DC-3 aircraft, from the initial designs of Douglas, based on TWA and American Airlines specifications, to its eventual refinements in performance, reliability and safety, is a classic demonstration of the benefits of continued engineering collaboration and co-operation between the manufacturers and the airlines. 'Manufacturers' includes all of those companies producing all components and systems, as well as Douglas and Pratt & Whitney, that is, landing gear, instruments, communications equipment, cabin equipment, *ad infinitum*.

Bill Littlewood was the outstanding spokesman for airline engineering requirements as the DC-3 airplane came into being.

So from United's requirement for better performance from its airports at Cheyenne, South Dakota, Wyoming, in the state of the same name, Salt Lake City, Utah, and Reno, Nevada, came the higher power Pratt & Whitney R-1830 version, which led directly to the C-47 for the US Army Air Forces, and the R4D-for the US Navy. And from the airline's collaboration with Douglas came those significant developments in performance and reliability which made the DC-3 the tried and proved aircraft for military applications and for its later return to civil use.

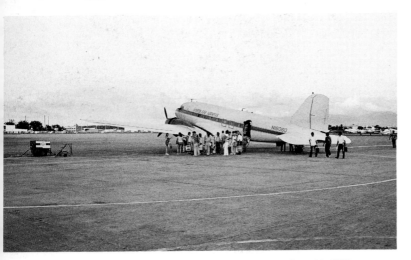

North Cay Airways of San Juan, Puerto Rico, was formed in 1970 to operate third level services with DC-3 airliners. Depicted is N16060 c/n 1902 ex-DC-3A-191 delivered to United on 3 January 1937. This DC-3 was withdrawn from use during 1980. (Lee C. Bright)

The Order Book

During 1936 orders for the new DC-3 transport began to pour into Santa Monica. Cyrus R. Smith wanted some of the twenty-one-passenger DC-3s to augment American Airlines' successful fleet of DSTs. Jack Frye and officials from Trans Continental & Western Air started negotiations for a $2 million order for a twenty-three-passenger version. Captain Eddie Rickenbacker followed suit to bolster the growing numbers of Eastern's 'Great Silver Fleet'. The Boeing B.247 airliner was the backbone of United Air Lines, and there is no question that the low-wing high-speed Boeing ten-passenger airliners were revolutionary. But the new Douglas Commercials out-performed them in every respect. As a result, in the spring of 1936, William A. Patterson, President of United Air Lines, visited the Douglas factory with a blank cheque in his pocket to buy some DC-3s. United intended disposing of its Boeings in order to meet heavy competition, and placed an order for twenty DC-3s. But the United aircraft would be powered by the 14-cylinder Pratt & Whitney R-1830 Twin Wasp engines instead of Wright Cyclones. Because of this change the DC-3As, as they were designated, cost more.

However, the DC-3A was approximately 14 mph faster, and the maximum altitude of 24,300 feet was ideal for United's routes over the highest peaks of the Rockies. Simultaneously

with the news that they were buying DC-3s, Patterson announced plans for 'Skylounge' flights, an extra fare introduced in a bid for the 'Blue Ribbon' New York to Chicago business. For an extra two dollars a ticket, passengers could have ample leg room and Club Car comfort. It was William Patterson's answer to Cyrus R. Smith's de luxe sleeper service.

Patterson had realised that his 'Mainliner Airway' with its Boeings faced an equipment and economic strangulation. During a meeting with Donald Douglas at Santa Monica, Patterson asked Harry Wetzel if he could take a flight in a DC-3 to get an idea of the aircraft first-hand. Wetzel's reply was unique: 'I'm sorry, but we don't have one of the ships here at the plant for demonstration purposes; it costs too damn much to operate them.' Later, however, Douglas borrowed a DC-3 from one of the airlines and gave 'Pat' his flight. Soon the race was on for the transcontinental airline business.

Donald Douglas, making his annual report to the Board of Directors, told them:

The DST's payload is one third more than that of any other previous airliner. Its gross weight of about 25,000 lb is half again as great as any airliner now in service. More important, our estimates show that it costs about 69 cents per mile to operate the plane, which is just about on par with the cost of operating the Ford Tri-motors. On a ton-mile basis – the capability of lifting one ton of payload and carrying it one mile – it can carry 6,000 lb in passengers, mail and freight – more than double the capacity of the Ford Tri-motors. On a typical flight, non-stop, New York to Chicago, for example, the cost of operating a DST is roughly $800. It costs about the same to operate the Ford Tri-motors between these cities with stopovers at Pittsburgh, Pennsylvania, and Cleveland, Ohio, because of limited range. The difference is the DST can carry almost three times as much in payload.

Ozark Air Lines Inc. of St Louis, Missouri, inaugurated DC-3 service on 26 September 1950 the type remaining in service until 1968. The DC-3 proved a useful freighter and nearly thirty of the Ozark fleet were converted. The photograph depicts a typical freighter carrying US mail and small items. (Ozark)

Douglas informed the board members that they had a modified version of the DST – the DC-3 – already moving down the production line – a twenty-one-seat luxury transport. Just about all the DC-2 customers were already signing up to buy the newer and larger transport.

In December 1937, only two years after the first DST made its maiden flight, Harry Wetzel informed Donald Douglas that the company had set an all-time high in production. That month, alone, they had produced thirty-six aircraft and parts totalling $2,700,000 worth of business. The new Douglas airliners made up the bulk of the orders. There was a backlog of $5,250,000 in foreign orders for the DC-3 and $2,000,000 more on the books for domestic airlines. The military business was booming and the overall picture was very bright. In 1932, at the time Donald Douglas and Jack Frye of TWA got together over the DC-1 design, the Douglas Aircraft Company employed a total of 902 personnel, with a payroll of $1,514,785 per annum. Seven years later, in 1939, with the Douglas Commercial transport in service all over the world, the personnel numbered 9,000 and the annual payroll was in the region of $12,000,000.

Braniff International Airways of Dallas, Texas, operated both the DC-2 and DC-3, the latter from 1939 until the last was sold in 1961. Depicted is DC-3A-197E N333327 c/n 4128 originally laid down as NC33649 for United but never delivered going to the military as C-52B 41-7707 in 1941. It went to Braniff on 15 August 1952 serving the airline until 5 October 1969. (Braniff)

The first DC-3A for United Air Lines went into service on 30 June 1937, and it was not long before the airline again had figures on the profit side of its ledger. The public liked the luxury of the DC-3 and her club-lounge atmosphere, including such innovations as electric razors, meals served on tables with silverware, real china and linen. There was air conditioning at terminals and aloft in the airliners. Air traffic figures more than doubled in the two years after the DC-3 was introduced into service, taking the airlines a great step forward on the road to solvency.

United Air Lines ordered more of the DC-3A powered by Pratt & Whitney engines and by December 1941 had a fleet of thirty-nine DC-3As and fifteen DSTs. Eastern Air Lines had acquired its first DC-3s in 1936. The following year it retired five of its Lockheed Electras and purchased eight new DC-3s. Air traffic on the New York to Miami route was so great during 1938 that Eastern had to lease four DC-3s from United Air Lines for use during the peak winter season. By 1941 a fleet of thirty-five aircraft, all Douglas transports, was in regular use with this airline. In August 1939 Braniff announced the purchase of four new twenty-one-passenger DC-3 airliners at a cost of approximately $100,000 each. The first DC-3 'Super-B-line', as they were called, was received in Oklahoma City, and put into regular scheduled service between Dallas and Amarillo, Texas,

on 3 February 1940. By July Braniff too had retired its Lockheed Electras and was operating thirty daily flights with DC-3 aircraft.

Milestones for the Douglas Aircraft Company production of new airliners were rapidly being reached. The hundredth DST/DC-3, a DST-A-207A NC18145 '*Mainliner Nebraska*', was delivered to United Air Lines on 25 March 1938, and on 23 May 1939, ceremonies were held to celebrate the delivery of the 350th Douglas Commercial transport. This was a DC-3-277 NC17340 c/n 2140 for American Airlines; it was named '*Oklahoma City*' and delivered to the airline on 4 June.

Pacific Northern Airlines were based at Seattle and between 1946 and 1967, when Western took over, used a handful of DC-3s on scheduled services and charter work to Alaska. Depicted is a post-war built DC-3D NC37465 c/n 42955 initially registered to Douglas and delivered on 25 January 1946. In 1964 it was TU-TIA with Air Ivoire and withdrawn from service in 1977.
(Douglas)

Exports

Progress with air transport, influenced by the introduction of the Douglas Commercial airliner, was being felt elsewhere. In South America, Panagra – Pan American Grace Airways – replaced its slow and noisy Ford Tri-motors. Panair Brasil with its large Sikorsky S.42 flying-boats reverted to land planes, whilst the Lockheed Electras and Lodestars of Línea Aeropostal Venezolana – LAV – disappeared in a huge modernisation programme. All chose the now familiar DC-3. Even the Boeing 247Ds of Compañía Mexicana de Aviación – CMA – were gradually replaced by the DC-3. The year 1936 was an important one for Australian National Airways, for in June they had introduced the first Douglas Commercial aircraft, a DC-2, into the country after exerting considerable pressure on the government to remove the ban on American aircraft imports. The single DC-2 in 1936 was followed by four DC-3s in December 1937.

By 1938 the DC-3 was carrying 95 per cent of all commercial air lines' traffic in the United States alone, and was in service with thirty foreign air lines throughout the world. By 1939, 90 per cent of the world's airline business was being flown in Douglas Commercials, mainly the DC-3.

Under the leadership of its first managing director, Dr Albert Plesman, Holland's Koninklijke Luchtvaart Maatschappij voor Nederland an Kilonien – KLM – began to consider the impressive developments being made in air transport by the US west coast manufacturer Donald Douglas. This resulted in their combined entry with Douglas for the England-to-Australia air race and, as a direct sequel, their order for DC-2 and later DC-3 aircraft. This opened the way for a major invasion of Europe by the Douglas Aircraft Company. It was KLM that set the pace in Europe, and in 1936 they placed an initial order for eleven DC-3s, with thirteen more to follow. By June 1937 Dr Plesman had put the DC-3 into operation along his routes to the Far East, in place of DC-2s.

Only a short period of operation was required to demonstrate the great carrying power of the new transport, and soon KLM was handling so much airmail that the Netherlands government abolished the airmail surcharge. In addition to mail, Plesman's aircraft now carried full capacity loads of passengers, and there was a steward to look after them during the flight. By October 1937 traffic had grown to such an extent that KLM were able to run a service to Indonesia three times weekly. By 1939 KLM were flight-planning their DC-3s as far as Sydney, Australia, and talking about a daily service, but these plans were delayed by the outbreak of war. From 1939 to 1945, virtually all services were suspended. Although Dr Albert Plesman died on 31 December 1953, the link between KLM and the Douglas Aircraft Company remained unbroken, and remains unbroken today. The airline is unique in that of all the Magnificent Seven Douglas Commercial types, the DC-1 was the only one not operated by KLM.

The vital link between Douglas and KLM remained of immense importance to both companies in terms of both prestige and business turnover. It was also crucial to world aviation in general. It was undoubtedly forged in the DC-2's race to Melbourne in 1934. Swissair and Air France were early operators of both the DC-2 and the DC-3, as were ABA – Aktiebolaget Aerotransport – of Sweden, CLS – Ceskoslovenska Letecka Spolecnost – of Czechoslovakia, Sabena – Société Anonyme Belge d'Exploitation de la Navigation Aérienne – of Belgium, LOT – Polskie Linie Lotnicze – of Poland, and others. As mentioned earlier with reference to the DC-2, Douglas built the DC-3s for Europe and shipped them across the Atlantic with Fokker in the Netherlands assembling them and making delivery under contract.

Incidents and Accidents

The Douglas DC-3 soon established a standard against which other airlines were measured. Its strength and resilience made it seem all but indestructible, and shortly after it arrived on the airways system in the United States amazing stories, many of them absolutely true, began to accumulate about it. A Capital Airlines DC-3 involved in a mid-air collision with another aircraft, lost four feet from the end of one wing, including part of an aileron. Its pilot landed the plane safely in a nearby field with no trouble, and no harm to its full complement of passengers. One DC-3 flying from Chicago to Detroit hit a downdraught so severe that several seats were ripped from the floor, a number of seat belts snapped and passengers were tossed around in the cabin. After the pilot regained control of the aeroplane and landed, it was thoroughly inspected and found to have not one loose rivet or any other sign of damage. Another DC-3, on a flight from Atlanta, Georgia, to Chicago, flew into a cold front and rapidly began accumulating ice on its wings, and carburettor ice as well. The pilot cleared the carburettor ice by causing the engines to backfire repeatedly and endured updraughts and downdraughts which flung the airliner from 5,000 feet to 13,000 feet and back down again. Eventually the pilot gained full control of the aircraft and made an emergency

landing at Indianapolis, Indiana, after breaking the ice-caked windshield with a fire extinguisher so that he could have forward vision. Looking over the DC-3 on the ground, the crew found a two-inch layer of solid ice on the wings and tail that must have weighed over a ton.

The first fatal accident to a Douglas DC-3 occurred on 9 February 1937, when a newly delivered United Air Lines DC-3A NC16073, a DC-3A-197 c/n 1913 delivered 11 December 1936, coming in for a landing at Oakland Airport, San Francisco, plunged into the bay and all on board were drowned. The weather was clear at the time, the aircraft was on its correct approach path, and was commanded by Captain A.R. Thompson, one of United's best pilots. Joe Decesaro was the co-pilot, Ruth Kimmel the hostess and there were eight passengers who had boarded at Los Angeles. The aircraft was salvaged from the sea-bed and it was found that the co-pilot's microphone had dropped to the floor and jammed the controls, so they had been unable to pull out of their glide approach. United Air Lines lost a second DC-3 on 17 October 1937, when NC16074 c/n 1914 a DC-3A-197 delivered 18 December 1936, flew into a mountain south of Knight, Wyoming.

It was natural, after a series of incidents and crashes involving the Douglas Commercial transport, that rumours that the DC-3 had bad stalling characteristics should start. In all the accidents involving Douglas airliners, the aircraft were exonerated in the investigations, and there were no indications of structural failures. The safety record which the DC-3s established even converted insurance companies to selling policies to air travellers, whilst pilots for the first time could get insurance, without paying added risk premiums. In 1939, the scheduled airlines of the United States received the Collier Trophy for flying seventeen months without a single fatality.

There were other hazards to contend with, such as bird strikes. On 30 October 1941, American Airlines DC-3-277B NC25663 c/n 2207 '*Flagship Erie*', delivered on 21 March 1940, hit a flock of wild geese and crashed near St Thomas, Ontario, killing all seventeen passengers and the crew of three. The DC-3 had accumulated 3,868 flying hours.

As a direct result of the crashes the US government took steps to increase safety in the air. There were stringent federal

Seen landing at Santa Monica is C-48C 42-38327 which in reality is a right-hand door DC-3-194H ordered by KLM Havik registered on 17 December 1939 but not delivered. It became DC-3A NC25675 with United powered by Pratt & Whitney Twin Wasp engines on 2 April 1940. On 15 March 1942 it was impressed into the military serving in North Africa with Air Transport Command. It returned to the USA and United on 5 December 1943 but crashed near Mt Elko, Wyoming, on 31 January 1946. (Douglas)

regulations for pilots and aircraft. The airlines themselves formed the Air Transport Association of America to produce better operational techniques and develop new safety devices. The pilots formed the Airline Pilots Association. There is no doubt at all that the new Douglas Commercial transports were influential in setting the pattern.

Despite the crashes, air transport in the United States was growing steadily. Each year from 1935 to 1939 air traffic figures rose about 19 per cent over the previous year. In 1939, when the majority of carriers were using Douglas Commercial equipment, the traffic increase was 42.2 per cent. The safety factor was also increasing because the larger transports were flying passengers more miles. The National Safety Council, which used passenger miles as a yardstick to measure the safety statistics, put air travel on a par with road traffic. Actual figures showed that during 1938-40 the average death rate per 100,000,000 passenger miles flown or carried was 2.8 for scheduled air transport. It was 3.7 for road transport.

Donald Douglas himself was delighted that a published survey of the airline accidents during January 1939 stated that in no incident involving a DC-2 or a DC-3 did investigations reveal any evidence of structural failure in the aircraft itself. The Air Safety Board put the blame on bad weather reporting, lack of adequate airways facilities which the new Civil Aeronautics Authority – CAA – had to remedy. Congress appropriated more money than ever before for modernising the federal airways, increasing radio facilities and improving airports. It was not long before the changes began to bear fruit.

On 26 March 1939, a Braniff DC-3 crashed near Oklahoma City killing eight passengers. From then until 31 August 1940, when a Pennsylvania Central DC-3-313 NC21789 c/n 2188, delivered on 22 May 1940, crashed near Lovettsville, Virginia, during an electric storm, the airlines enjoyed a period of peace and quiet seldom equalled by any form of transport. Apparently there was not even a minor accident.

Co-operation

The complete dominance of the DC-3 in the United States before the Second World War has probably never been fully appreciated. The fleet position just after Pearl Harbor shows that 80 per cent of the scheduled airliners in the country were DC-3s. During the period of the 100 per cent safety record mentioned earlier, for the first time the US airlines showed definite signs and intent of pulling together in an effort to further the new dimension in air transportation. A good example of this co-operation occurred during the week of 20 September 1938. Approaching from the Caribbean was one of the worst hurricanes in history. It hit the New England coastline. The whole eastern seaboard was an isolated, devastated area, completely cut off from the outside world. Pestilence threatened, thousands were left homeless and damage was extensive. The hurricane had grounded the airlines, but the following day they were airborne again, and were the only line of communication.

The nearest airline route – New York–Boston–Hartford–Maine – belonged exclusively to American Airlines. Under normal conditions the Flagships carried about 200 passengers a day. The morning after the hurricane, however, more than 1,000 passengers wanted seats. There was a desperate need for nurses, doctors and medical supplies; for rescuers, technicians and workers to help dig through the debris. American Airlines just could not cope with the task alone. It was

Edgar S. Gorrell, head of the new Air Transport Association, who answered the call from American Airlines for help. He immediately contacted the presidents of TWA, United and Eastern, all members of the ATA, pressing them to divert transports to help during the emergency. He then contacted Clinton M. Hester at the CAA and obtained permission for the other carriers to use American Airline's franchise route. For a solid week the airlines, working together, ferried in more than 1,000 rescue and reconstruction workers and flew out more than 1,500 stranded people. In addition, they carried 60,000 lb of badly needed supplies and 57,000 lb of mail. It was the busiest week in the history of air transport. The US airlines with their Douglas DC-2s and DC-3s were credited with a major role in helping to minimise a national disaster.

Hawaiian Airlines purchased its first DC-3 from the factory during August 1941, later adding more airliners from surplus post-war stocks. They remained in service until November 1968, and a dozen of the type were operated. Depicted is N33608 DC-3A-375 c/n 4808 delivered on 23 August 1941 seen modified with panoramic windows. (Hawaiian)

For the first time the Douglas Commercial transports proved the true value of an airlift in times of emergency. Little did the airlines and the Douglas Aircraft Company realise that in the not-too-far-distant future, air transport would have to put it into practice on a far larger scale. It was to be a very decisive factor in turning the tide of the Second World War.

War Clouds in Europe

Meanwhile, in Europe during September 1939, just when the whole world was about to become an inter-connecting air transport system, the nations were dividing themselves again in hostilities. By 1941 every great trading and commercial country was involved in active military operations, or was under the complete domination of the Axis Powers.

All the European services of KLM were stopped on 23 August 1939, except those to Scandinavia, Belgium and London. On 16 October the daily London service, which normally flew into Croydon airport, was transferred to Shoreham, Sussex. On 9 November it was increased to twice daily and four days later DDL – Det Danske Luftfartselskab, the Danish airline – started operating joint services on the route. After an experimental flight with a Douglas DC-2 from Amsterdam to Lisbon via Shoreham and Madrid, on 27 December, a service was opened on 20 April 1940, via Oporto to the Portuguese capital, which had become an important connecting post for the Atlantic service of Pan American Airways. Passengers were carried on the Lisbon service, which from 23 April was operated twice weekly. Meanwhile, with the co-operation of DDL, the Shoreham service from Amsterdam had been increased to four flights a day from the first day of March; but this was the end of KLM's defiant attempt to carry on as usual. Their Scandinavian service closed down on 9 April, the Belgian one on 18 April, and finally on 10 May 1940, all European services were terminated as the Nazis occupied the Netherlands.

On 26 September 1939 a KLM DC-3 PH-ASM c/n 2142 Mees *flying from Malmo, Sweden, to Amsterdam, was attacked in error by a German seaplane. One of the passengers, Gustave Lamm, a Swedish engineer was killed by machine-gun fire. The pilot was Captain J. J. Moll famous for his part in the 1934 air race to Australia in a DC-2. On 16 May 1940 this DC-3 was captured by the Luftwaffe at Schiphol Airport.* (KLM – Coert Munk)

On that fatal day four KLM DC-3s were destroyed by the Luftwaffe involved in the heavy bombing of Schiphol Airport at Amsterdam – PH-ALU *'Uil'*, PH-ARX *'Xema'*, PH-ASP *'Patrijs'* and PH-AST *'Tapuit'*. A further four DC-3s were captured intact by the Luftwaffe when they invaded both Schiphol Airport and Amsterdam on 16 May; these were flown back to Germany and impressed into military service. They included PH-ALH *'Hop'*, PH-ALV *'Valk'*, PH-ASM *'Mees'* and PH-ASR *'Roek'*. The opening of a KLM service to South Africa, proving flights for which had already been completed, had to be postponed until after the war.

Nothing daunted, KLM joined the Allied cause and with the four remaining DC-3s fled their stricken country to set up a base at Whitchurch Airport, Bristol. Here the DC-3s were allocated British registrations and during August 1940 a service was opened between Bristol and Lisbon. But the KLM fleet was reduced by half when one DC-3 had to be withdrawn on 21 September after an accident at Heston Airport, Middlesex, and a second was destroyed during an air attack at Whitchurch on 24 November 1940. During 1942, KLM extended the Bristol to Lisbon service to include Gibraltar, a valuable contribution to

the wartime communications system which continued until 1945.

The Dutch airlines' long-haul route to the East Indies soon came under fire at both ends. On 16 September 1939, the European terminus was transferred to Naples, the twice-weekly service from Amsterdam to Batavia, including the long train journey over the Alps, taking nine days. The threat from the Axis Powers increased and the route was again curtailed on 26 July 1940, when Tel Aviv became the terminus. On 15 February 1942, the Tel Aviv to Batavia service ended when the Japanese invaded Java. The KLM management, which had been transferred to Batavia in 1940, was then moved, together with its KNILM – Koninklijke Nederlandsch-Indische Luchtvaart Maatschappi – associates to New York. Seven KLM aircraft, including Douglas DC-3s escaped from Java to Australia, where they were pooled under the United States arrangements for wartime transport fleets. This unique fleet, incidentally, contained a number of Douglas DC-5 transports which had been transferred to KNILM from the West Indies fleet.

Because of the war Sabena was never able to exploit to the full the speed advantage of its Savoia-Marchetti SM.83 airliners. These were about 100 mph faster than the Douglas DC-3, components of their first Douglas transports having arrived by sea in packing cases, and been assembled in Belgium by Fokker during the early part of 1939. The first was OO-AUH, a DC-3-227B c/n 2093, delivered to Fokker on 9 December 1938, and the second OO-AUI, a DC-3-227B c/n 2094, delivered to Fokker on 27 December 1938 and registered to Sabena on 4 April 1939. The arrival of the two Douglas transports opened a new chapter in the history of Belgian aviation. Unfortunately, however, the chapter was interrupted by the outbreak of hostilities in the Low Countries on 10 May 1940, and the company's European services were then paralysed. The Sabena fleet left Belgium for the United Kingdom, where it was immediately put under requisition and used for military missions in France. On 11 May 1940, both DC-3s were attached to 'E' Flight No. 24 Squadron RAF. On 23 May, Sabena's seventeenth birthday, the company suffered a grievous war loss, when two Savoia Marchettis and DC-3 OO-AUI were shot down at Merville, France. Later the remaining Sabena aircraft were authorised to proceed to Belgian Africa, and they left the United Kingdom in June with an intermediate stop in Algeria. On 27 August 1940, four Savoia Marchetti aircraft were seized by the French Vichy government at Oran and handed over to the Italians; at Algiers two more Savoia Marchetti transports and the remaining DC-3 OO-AUH suffered the same fate and were interned. The DC-3 later went to the Italian Air Force.

In Sweden, in July 1937, ABA had taken delivery of its first Douglas DC-3 SE-BAA, a DC-3-214 c/n 1947, delivered to Fokker on 10 June 1937, and by May 1940 operated five of the type. Sweden remained neutral during the war, and its airline tried to maintain its pre-war services with its Douglas transports; the routes to Moscow, Berlin and London were all kept going under considerable difficulties. For these flights the aircraft were clearly marked with 'SWEDEN' in large letters on both sides and under the fuselage. The Russian service was suspended in June 1941, and the Berlin service withdrawn shortly before the German capitulation in 1945. In 1942 a courier service to London was started with DC-3s, two of which, including SE-BAF a DC-3-268 *Gladen*, delivered to Fokker on 20 July 1939 and to ABA in November, plus SE-BAG *Gripen* ex-Swissair HB-IRU, delivered to ABA on 16 May 1940, were shot down: SE-BAF on 28 August 1943, whilst on a flight from

Rare photograph of Douglas C-52B 41-7706 c/n 4127 the first of two right-hand door DC-3A-197E transports ordered by United as NC33648 but never delivered. On 14 July 1941 it was impressed as a military transport designated DC-3-395. On 8 July 1944 it was civilianised to Northwest as NC33326 and survived several subsequent owners until June 1980.
(Peter M. Bowers*)*

Scotland to Sweden, and SE-BAG over Hallo, Sweden on 22 October 1943.

It is believed that when the Germans overran Czechoslovakia in 1938 the complete DC-3 fleet of CLS was taken over by Tschechische Luftverkehr Gesellschaft, the German research and development organisation, as three DC-3s were later registered with Deutsche Luft Hansa – DLH. By as early as July 1940 it is reported that DLH had added at least two ex-KLM DC-3s to its fleet – the Luftwaffe had captured these during the invasion of the Netherlands. They had also included six KLM DC-2s in their haul from Schiphol, which after a period of service with the Luftwaffe found their way into the DLH fleet. It is rumoured that the Luftwaffe experienced servicing difficulties with the Douglas Commercial transports. Lack of spare parts led them to provide for interchangeability of certain critical items – for example landing-gear tyres and wheels were made interchangeable between the Douglas DC-2 and DC-3 models and the Heinkel He.111 bomber. DLH kept their Douglas transports modified with all changes which were recommended by Douglas and the Civil Aeronautics Board – CAB – during the Second World War.

This was accomplished by contracting for overhaul and other repair work with agencies operating from a neutral country such as Switzerland. Through this source, replacement parts and other information pertaining to the design were made available. DLH were not lacking in experience of the Douglas types, as during March 1936 they had obtained a DC-2 D-ABEQ 'Taunus' from Fokker for use in various tests at their air base at Staaken near Berlin.

On 26 March 1931, two Swiss companies – Balair and Ad Astra – had combined to form Schweizerische Luftverkehr – Swissair. The following year Swissair followed KLM with the purchase of the DC-2 and later the DC-3. With the advent of the Second World War, Swissair was closed down altogether after operating a skeleton network, including a number of flights between Locarno and Barcelona on behalf of US-bound passengers who continued their journeys in Spanish or Italian aircraft. The Rome and Barcelona routes were abandoned when Italy entered the war and the Berlin route was closed in 1943.

During 1935 Air France purchased a DC-2 from Douglas via Fokker, and their one and only pre-war DC-3 was registered F-ARQJ on 2 April 1939; it was a Fokker DC-3-294 c/n 2122,

delivered 26 May 1939, but it never reached Europe. Instead it was flown from Santa Monica on 23 May, arriving in Buenos Aires, Argentina on 7 June. It was used on the Buenos Aires–Mendoza–Santiago service before going to the Argentina Aviation Command in 1941 where it ended its days.

On 1 September 1939, Adolf Hitler's invasion of Poland brutally brought an end to the dynamic progress of Polish airlines – LOT. During August 1935 two DC-2s had been purchased, via the Fokker agency, to help modernise a fleet of outdated transports. A third DC-2 was purchased in 1937. Of the twenty-six aircraft in service at the outbreak of the Second World War, twenty-one managed to escape to other countries – Romania, Latvia, Estonia and the United Kingdom. One DC-2, SP-ASK, escaped to Latvia and other, SP-ASL, to Bucharest. The third, SP-ASJ, had been written off in Bulgaria on 25 November 1937, when it crashed in the Rhodope mountains. As mentioned earlier, the first two of these LOT DC-2s were powered with Bristol Pegasus VI engines.

Royal Air Force DC-3s

With the fall of France in 1940 and the almost desperate situation of the United Kingdom, the British Purchasing Commission based in the United States took immediate steps to place large orders and to take over aircraft contracts placed with the French and Belgian governments. On 11 March 1941, the Lend-Lease Act was passed in the US Congress, which increased the flow of many aircraft types for the Royal Air Force.

The Royal Air Force operated a handful of DC-3 airliners including MA925 depicted c/n 4116 a right-hand door DC-3-277D NC33653 of American bought by the US Government on 9 July 1941. It went to Pan American in Africa in October 1941 and to the RAF on 1 May 1942. After serving with squadrons and a comm flight it went to Indian National Airlines as VT-ATB.
(R. J. S. Dudman via J. D. R. Rawlings)

During 1941 the British Purchasing Commission bought a number of Douglas DC-3s from American Airlines and TWA for use by the RAF in India and the Middle East. They were dismantled in the United States and shipped as deck cargo to maintenance units in the Middle East before being allocated to RAF transport squadrons. Other DC-3s were taken over from Pan American (Africa), which had been formed by the US government and which operated the type in Africa at that time. These DC-3s supplemented the DC-2s already in service with the RAF.

In May 1941 Pan American Airways was contracted to deliver twenty Lockheed Lodestar airliners, bought by the British Purchasing Commission, and ferry them to Africa. The aircraft were delivered in the autumn of 1941, and it was this operation which started the US government in Washington DC thinking about setting up a regular service to and across Africa, in case the United States should become involved in the war. Pan American Air Ferries was organised for ferrying aircraft across the South Atlantic and Africa, and Pan American Airways (Africa) was similarly created to shuttle the spares and return the ferry flight crews. PAA-Africa actually started operations from Takoradi, on the Gold Coast, to Khartoum in Sudan on 21 October 1941, with seven DC-3s, also running a flight to Fishermen's Lake in Liberia to connect with Pan American's Boeing 314 flying-boats on the South Atlantic route. Royal Air Force ferry crews often used the PAA (Africa) DC-3s and on 29 October 1941, a flight from Takoradi to Cairo involved a DC-3 which had been delivered to TWA as a DC-3 on 17 January 1938. It was designated C-49F. A visitor to No. 2 Aircraft Delivery Unit at Cairo on 26 May 1942 was a DC-3A supplied to the US Defense Supply Corporation, impressed as a military transport on 18 December 1941 and designated C-48C. A quantity of these hybrid Douglas Commercial transports were later to join the Royal Air Force, for it was to be another year before the first Douglas C-47 Dakota would be available.

Isle, Maine, to Gander, Newfoundland, to determine the feasibility of a scheduled ferry route to Labrador and Newfoundland on what was to be the first leg of a North Atlantic ferry route to the United Kingdom. By the middle of February Douglas transports were operating over the route on a regular scheduled basis. Flying in sub-zero temperatures, often in snow storms, over uncharted wilderness, the transports carried equipment and supplies to newly established bases in the north. Unfamiliar names such as Moncton, New Brunswick, Stephenville, Goose Bay and Gander began to appear on the wartime airline map. The latter two bases were to become two of the largest and busiest gateways in the Second World War. There was a great need to extend the route north and eastwards. A military Douglas C-53 Skytrooper, operated by a Northeast Airlines crew made the first flight to Narssassuak or Bluie West One on the east coast of Greenland in April 1942. The flight, made with the transport overloaded 4,000 lb beyond its original design specification, proved the DC-3 type was capable of long over-water flights. The following month Northeast pilots and crews extended the route to Iceland, landing at Reykjavik and so adding a further 750-mile segment to the North Atlantic crossing.

This two-star general VIP Douglas transport is a right-hand passenger door DC-3A-197D NC25612 c/n 3256 destined for United in November 1940, but impressed as a C-48 41-7681 on 27 December 1940. After military service it returned to Northeast on 12 April 1945 as NC25612. (Peter M. Bowers)

This is a Douglas C-49H ex-DC-3-277D built as NC33653 c/n 4116 for American but not delivered being bought by the US Government on 9 July 1941. On 14 March 1942 the serial 42-38250 was allocated but not used and in October 1941 it had appeared in Africa with Pan American and going to the RAF on 1 May 1942 as MA925 serving with both 117 and 31 Squadrons plus the Air HQ India Comm Flight in New Delhi. It was leased to Indian National Airways as VT-ATB being bought during 1943 but not registered until 11 April 1945. (Peter M. Bowers)

US Airlines into Battle

The first major action with the DC-3 occurred on Sunday 14 December 1941, one week after Pearl Harbor, when the US War Department called the Air Transport Association for assistance in the air movement of troops. This massive operation involved some twenty DC-3s, most of them from Cyrus R. Smith's large fleet of American Airlines Flagships. They were ordered to a secret rendezvous. Aircraft already in flight were ordered to land at the nearest airport and disembark their passengers. Others took off and flew to various US Army bases. Next day, the transports were airborne, heading across the Caribbean to hot spots in Brazil. There had been a threat that Axis powers were moving to take over radio stations and other communications systems in South America. The force was small, but effective.

On 11 January 1942, a Douglas C-39 military transport, operated and flown by Northeast Airlines flew from Presque

A date of great significance was 4 July 1942, when a Douglas transport flew to Stornoway on the Isle of Lewis and to Prestwick, Scotland, which was soon to become a large transport terminal for the North Atlantic traffic. In the fuselage was a complete radio range station which was to make Stornoway a vital air link and aid the transatlantic chain. The operation was the beginning of Air Transport Command's North Atlantic Division, whose aircraft, at the peak of the war, were crossing the Atlantic ferry route one every four minutes.

Licence to Build

In Europe, Anthony H.G. Fokker's agency and construction rights for the Douglas DC-2 were extended to include the new Douglas design and eventually a total of sixty-three DC-3 airliners were sold and assembled by Fokker for the European market. The first was for KLM PH-ALI, a DC-3-194 c/n 1590 named '**Ibis**' and delivered on 21 September 1936. Fokker never put the DC-2 or DC-3 into production in Europe; instead he remained as the Douglas agent and so handled all the transports which were shipped over from the United States to the ports of Rotterdam and Cherbourg. After final assembly the new transports were delivered to the airlines. Sales were so good that at one time Fokker held a pool of DC-3s, the purchase price then being approximately £30,000 or $115,000.

The merits of the Douglas DC-3 were soon recognised by other foreign countries who were granted a licence to build the transport by the Douglas Aircraft Company. These companies in Japan, later to become an enemy, and in Russia, later to become an ally, were granted the manufacturing and patent rights.

On 27 March 1934, the Japanese aircraft constructor Nakajima Hikoki KK acquired, for the sum of $80,000, the licence rights to build the Douglas DC-2 transport and to sell such aircraft in the Japanese Empire and Manchuria. Interest in the DC-3 transport in Japan materialised as early as 1937, when two trading companies, Mitsui Bussan Kaisha KK (Mitsui Trading Company Ltd) and the Far Eastern Trading Company Ltd, began placing orders for the Douglas transport. Consequently, thirteen Wright Cyclone-powered DC-3s were delivered, the first originally intended for KLM as PH-ARA, a DC-3-237A c/n 1979, but flown to Japan on 6 December 1937 and delivered to Great Northern Airways. Seven DC-3s powered by Pratt & Whitney Twin Wasps were delivered between the end of 1937 and February 1939. Operated by Dai Nippon Koku KK (Great Northern Airways), these aircraft minus attritions through operational and combat losses, remained in service until the end of the war in the Pacific, when surviving aircraft were scrapped.

On 24 February 1938, Mitsui & Company Ltd, the US-based subsidiary of Mitsui Bussan Kaisha KK, acquired for $90,000 the licence rights to build and sell the Douglas DC-3. For this sum Mitsui obtained all necessary technical data and later purchased separately the parts for two unassembled DC-3s. Unknown to the Douglas Aircraft Company, the licence and pattern aircraft had been acquired by Mitsui on instruction of the Japanese Navy. After arrival in Japan the parts of the two DC-3s were delivered to Showa Hikoki Kogyo KK, who were instructed to assemble the two aircraft and prepare for further production. It is rumoured that Showa personnel had been trained in the United States, as the Showa factory was patterned after the Douglas factory in California. Major tools and presses were imported from the USA. At the same time Nakajima Hikoki KK were asked to participate in production.

Two prototypes, designated Douglas L2D1, or Navy Type D Transport, were delivered by Showa in October 1939 and April 1940. The delay resulted from the late completion of Showa's facilities. Meanwhile, the engineering staff of Nakajima and Showa co-operated in modifying the type for Japanese production techniques and for adoption of the 1,000 hp Pratt & Whitney SB3G engines as fitted in the L2D1s. In this form a total of 71 L2D2s – Navy Type O Transport Model 11 – were delivered by Nakajima between 1940 and 1942, and the first Showa-built L2D2 was delivered in March 1941. After November 1942, when the last Nakajima-built transport was delivered, the production of the Navy Type O Transport, which had been selected by the Japanese Navy as their standard transport aircraft, was the sole responsibility of Showa.

As production by Showa was gaining momentum, a cargo transport version, the L2D2-1 fitted with a reinforced cargo floor and large cargo-loading doors on the port side of the rear fuselage, was produced. Still later, the Navy Type O Transport

Model 22, characterised externally by the installation of an additional glazed window area behind the flight deck, became the main production version and appeared in four variants. The L2D3 was a personnel transport, powered by 1,300 hp Kinsei 51 radial engines; the L2D3G, also a personnel transport, was powered by 1,300 hp Kinsei 53 radial engines, whilst the L2D3-1 and L2D3-1a were cargo transports powered by Kinsei 51s and 53s respectively.

The L2D4 personnel and L2D4-1 cargo transports were fitted with a dorsal turret housing a flexible 13 mm Type 2 machine-gun. Two hand-held 7.7 mm Type 92 machine guns could be fired from the fuselage hatches. Designated Navy Type O Transport Model 32, this version was experimental.

Finally, the L2D5 or Navy Type O Transport Model 33 was a version of the L2D4 which was under construction when the Second World War ended. Wherever possible, light alloys were to be replaced by wood or steel and the L2D5 was to have been powered by 1,560 hp Kinsei 62 radial engines. Named 'Tabby' by the Allies, the Japanese-built DC-3s were met throughout the Pacific theatre of operations and often led to tragic recognition errors.

Production, including the two L2D1s assembled from Douglas-built parts, totalled 487. L2Ds were built by Showa Hikoki Koygo KK and Nakajima KK. The type operated with Southern Philippines Kokutai squadrons (Butais) attached to various Air Fleets (Rengo Kantai) and to the China Area and Southeast Area Fleets. Crews varied from three to five, and either twenty-one passengers or 9,920 lb of freight could be carried.

In the USSR, Dobroflot, the state airline established under the 1928 Five-Year Plan, was reorganised in 1932 as the Civil Air Line Administration – Grazdansij Wozdusnyj Flot, or Aeroflot as it was popularly called. In addition to normal scheduled transport, Aeroflot was also made responsible for non-transport activities, such as survey work, crop dusting and fire patrol. Progress from then onwards was rapid. By 1939 the USSR had almost caught up with Germany as the leading air transport nation outside the United States. By 1935 Aeroflot encompassed the whole length of the Soviet Union from Leningrad and Odessa to Alexandrovsk, on the eastern island of Sakhalin, and Yakutsk, in the depths of Eastern Siberia. There were eleven regional managements.

As the nationwide network continued to grow, more aircraft were needed and Russia looked to the aircraft manufacturers located on the American west coast. On 3 August 1935, a DC-2 NC14949 c/n 1413 a DC-2-152 was delivered to Amtorg, the pre-war purchasing agency, on behalf of Aeroflot. This machine crashed in Romania on 6 August 1937. The State Aircraft Plant's leading aviation expert, Boris Lisunov, was sent to work with the Douglas Aircraft Company at Santa Monica for two years to study the famous Douglas Commercial twin-engined airliner. The State Aircraft Plant not only bought large quantities of jigs and tools from the Douglas company, but purchased a total of eighteen DC-3s from Santa Monica between November 1936 and March 1939.

These were delivered by the Douglas Aircraft Company in the name North Eastern and Excello, both of which were represented by Amtorg. There is considerable reason to believe that these two 'airlines' were paper organisations of the Russian government. The first aircraft, a DC-3-196 NC14995 c/n 1589, was registered with Excello on 30 November 1936 and shipped to Cherbourg the following day. This transport was followed by a block of eleven delivered between May and August 1938 and

Aeroflot – (Grazdansky Wozdusnyj Flot) purchased a number of DC-3s from the Douglas factory prior to World War II. After the war Aeroflot operated the Soviet-built Li-2 transport in quite large numbers. They also operated a number of Lend-Lease C-47 Skytrains. Depicted is a Li-2 of Aeroflot CCCP-54909. (MAP)

concluded with a block of six, the last of which was delivered in March 1939. Of the eighteen DC-3s, two were delivered disassembled, ostensibly for use as spare parts.

The presence of Boris Lisunov in California with the Douglas company led to a licensed production of DC-3s in the USSR bearing the designation Li-2, of which it was originally estimated that some 2,800 were built. However, later thinking by aviation experts and historians in the United Kingdom and the United States believed the figure could be much more, with a figure of 7,000 or more being mooted. Small-scale production did not commence until 1940, but it is believed that by the summer of 1941 about thirty to forty aircraft per month were being produced by the State Aircraft Plant known as the Aircraft Production Company. Aeroflot must have been in full stride, with the new Li-2 supplementing the standard ANT-9, Tupolev's successful early design, when Germany invaded the USSR in June 1941. Immediately all air routes west of Moscow were suspended and by the following year only the trunk route across Siberia and certain indispensable Arctic services were still in regular operation.

Interpretation of the serial numbers of Russian-built Li-2s reveals a great deal of information. This Malev Li-2 HA-LIQ has c/n 23441206 which indicates it was the sixth aircraft in a batch of twelve, built in 1944 at Plant 23. Magyar Legikozlekedesi Vallalat of Budapest was formed on 25 November 1954 commencing services with nine Li-2 airliners which served the United Kingdom. (MAP)

Initially the Lisunov transport was designated PS-84, but on 17 September 1942 it was changed to Li-2. This designation applied in the USSR to DC-3 transports, plus the C-47 transports supplied under Lend-Lease during the Second World War.

During 1941, due to the German invasion of the USSR, production of the Lisunov Li-2 transport was moved from the State Aircraft Plant near Moscow to Tashkent in the republic of Uzbekskaya, north of the Afghanistan border. It is not known just how many plants were engaged in building the Li-2 and its many variants, but it is confirmed that the final assembly was at the Aviation Production Company at Tashkent, named after Mr V.P. Ckalov. It has been revealed that no less than 6,157 Li-2 transports were produced at this factory. For many years the transport was used by the USSR and its Communist satellite forces, and the type carried the code name 'Cab' in NATO aircraft vocabulary.

Aeroflot (Grazdansky Wozdusnyj Flot) purchased a number of DC-3s from Douglas before World War II. Produced as the Lisunov Li-2 the type was used by Aeroflot and post-war a number visited the United Kingdom. Depicted is CCCP-n1783 which visited London Heathrow airport during 1956. (A. T. Jones)

DC-3 Airliners into Khaki

During the early war years of 1941/42 the vital need for transport aircraft for the war effort increased beyond the ability of the Douglas Aircraft Company to supply them, despite large orders for the C-47 Skytrain and C-53 Skytrooper military transport versions of the DC-3 being placed. The US Army Air Corps acquired Douglas Commercial transports in a unique way – by drafting no less than 225 existing airliners, using two sources: airlines already in service with the US airlines, and those on order by the airlines but still on the factory production line at Santa Monica. The word draft is something of a misnomer, as the airlines were paid for the transports at the established market price on negotiated contracts. Later the airlines had the option of buying the aircraft back, though many did not do so until later in the war, or even soon after.

Many of these impressed airliners retained their passenger seats and interior fittings when used by the military; others had their interiors stripped for hauling troops and cargo into non-combat areas. They were often flown by the airline crews in military uniform and contracted to Air Transport Command – ATC – to operate and fly military transport routes. A few of the civil DC-3s taken into the Air Corps inventory and allocated military designation were never actually used by the military, but retained by the airlines and continued to fly as domestic transports, still in airline markings and with civil or military registrations.

Some of the DC-3s were in various stages of finish on the Santa Monica production line, not having received their full airline furnishings, so these were easily modified to military requirements, mainly by the installation of the C-47/C-53 type troop 'bucket' seats and military radio equipment. All retained the wooden floor of the DC-3. The transports drafted were a mixture of Wright Cyclone and Pratt & Whitney Twin Wasp-powered DC-3s, with the preference appearing to be for the Cyclone: some 152 Cyclone-powered DC-3s were acquired, compared to seventy-three Twin Wasp DC-3s.

As established and already licensed civil models, the airliners entered military service immediately, there being no need even to send an example to Wright Field, Dayton, Ohio, for routine type testing. They were very difficult to identify and after Pearl Harbor security restrictions were imposed on photographs of all US military aircraft, regardless of age, non-combat status or previous civilian service.

It must be mentioned that the DC-2 was also involved in this unique drafting exercise, the military designation C-32A covering twenty-two DC-2s, mostly series -112 and -120, but all powered with the 740 hp R-1820-F3 Wright Cyclone engines and drafted from a wide variety of scattered sources during 1941/42. In military service the Wright Cyclone engine became designated R-1820-33. During 1944, two other DC-2s were acquired in Australia, one a transfer from the Royal Australian Air Force, A30-10 c/n 1372, formerly Eastern Air Lines NC14969, and the other, a civil acquisition that was registered VH-CDZ.

Constructed as DC-3-201F NC28387 c/n 4095 for Eastern it was never delivered but impressed by the military as a DC-3-387 C-49B 41-7692 on 22 February 1941. It served in Panama with the US 6th Air Force going to the Reconstruction Finance Company on 20 January 1946. It had been used as the personal aircraft of Lt Gen Krueger who used it to fly from San Antonio, Texas, to Lake Charles, Louisiana. Photograph taken at Oakland during August 1941. (William T. Larkins)

These DC-2s were all allocated the C-32A designation, whereas all the drafted DC-3s received designations ranging from C-48 on. This has led some historians to assume that the drafted DC-2s were all production follow-ons of the XC-32 transport serial 36-1 c/n 1414.

A total of thirty-six civil DC-3As were drafted by the Air Corps as the C-48, the common denominator being the DC-3A/DST-A model powered by the 1,200 hp Pratt & Whitney Twin Wasp R-1830-SIC3G engine. These were either taken off the airline routes or drafted while still on the Santa Monica production line. It is interesting to note that these were similar in airframe and powerplant detail to the existing Air Corps C-41 and C-41A, so could easily have been designated the C-41B, C-41C etc, instead of the C-48, a completely new model

designation. The right-hand passenger door may have been an influence. However, all the C-48s were acquired under the same US Army Air Corps contract – AC-19694 – covering the lone C-48, the C-48As, C-48Bs and C-48C aircraft.

The single C-48, Army Air Corps serial 41-2681, was a twenty-one-seat, right-hand passenger door DC-3A-197S (ATC-669) intended for United Air Lines as NC25612 c/n 3256 during November 1940. On 27 December this transport had the distinction of becoming the very first drafted DC-3. No comparable military designation was allocated to the R-1830-CIC3G engines, although they were equivalent to the military R-1830-92. The principal difference from the standard airline configuration was the type and quality of the military radio installation.

In 1943, the C-48 was listed in the US Army Air Corps books at $159,884. By a year later the documental inventory system had changed to write more of the General Furnished Equipment – GFE – such as engines, propellers, and electronics included with the transport, instead of being separate items, so it was then valued at $168,384.

Three C-48A transports were left-hand-side passenger door DC-3A-368s (ATC-669) taken as a unit from the production line with c/n 4146 becoming 41-7682 on 30 June 1941; c/n 4147 41-7683 on 14 July and c/n 4148 41-7684 on 23 August. The engines were 1,200 hp military R-1830-92s. A major difference was in the cabin arrangement – as they were used by the Air Corps General Staff, they had ten swivel chairs, a typewriter desk, clothes closet and a separate cabinet for parachute storage. Military radio equipment was fitted. These three were by far the lowest-priced of the drafted military DC-3s being listed in 1943 at only $91,000, rising in 1944 to $134,487.

Quantity procurement followed of a single DC-3 variant amounting to sixteen C-48Bs, which were mostly fourteen-berth DST-A-277Bs, DST-A-277Cs and DST-A-277Cs (ATC-671) fitted with right-hand-side passenger doors and taken from orders placed by United Air Lines. One was a DC-3A-269B taken from Northwest Airlines. Records reveal that the engines were listed as R-1830-SIC3G and elsewhere as R-1830-51, the military equivalent, the latter being used in all C-48 models. The berthing feature of the ex-United Air Lines DSTs suited them for use as air ambulances, as well as VIP staff transports. Two of the airliners came from Western Air Express, later named Western Air Lines.

c/n	Model	Reg.	Del.	Serial.	Del.
2223	DST-A-207B	NC25683	29 Apr 40	42-38324	26 Mar 42
3263	DST-A-207C	NC25619	5 Nov 40	42-38325	26 Jul 42
3264	DST-A-207C	NC25620	14 Nov 40	42-38326	17 Mar 42
4113	DST-A-207D	NC33641	25 Apr 41	42-56089	8 Jun 42
1957	DST-A-207	NC18109	3 Aug 37	42-56090	8 Jun 42
1955	DST-A-207	NC18107	27 Jul 37	42-56091	8 Jun 42
1960	DST-A-207	NC18102	2 Jul 37	42-56098	8 Jun 42 Western
1958	DST-A-207	NC18110	6 Aug 37	42-56099	8 Jun 42
1953	DST-A-207	NC18105	16 Jul 37	42-56100	8 Jun 42
1977	DST-A-207A	NC18145	25 Mar 38	42-56101	8 Jun 42
2222	DST-A-207B	NC25682	20 Apr 40	42-56102	8 Jun 42
1959	DST-A-207	NC18101	25 Jun 37	42-56609	8 Jun 42 Western
3265	DST-A-207C	NC33640	7 Apr 41	42-56610	8 Jun 42
1952	DST-A-207	NC18104	12 Jul 37	42-56611	8 Jun 42
1951	DST-A-207	NC18103	9 Jul 37	42-56612	8 Jun 42
2158	DST-A-269B	NC25610	Jan 40	42-56629	8 Jun 42 Northwest

Two very rare photographs depicting a right-hand passenger door C-48B 42-56102 impressed on 8 June 1942. It was ex-DST-A-207B NC25682 c/n 2222 of United Air Lines State of New York *to whom it was delivered on 20 April 1940. It arrived in the United Kingdom on 16 August 1943 being used as a VIP transport, and is seen during a visit to AAF Station 136 at RAF Knettishall, Suffolk, home of the 388th Bombardment Group during 1944. The C-48B returned to the USA on 14 November 1944, returning to United. Col. W. B. David, CO of the 388th B Group with back to the camera in photograph on the left, watches as Col. Curtis E. LeMay greets two unidentified two-star Generals. The transport is decorated with two-star insignia forward of the cabin door.*
(Boardman C. Reed)

The C-48C was another mass procurement of sixteen airliners representing a batch of twenty-one-passenger DC-3As and one single DST-A with a mixture of passenger door locations. One Swiftflite Inc. DC-3A-363 NC1000 c/n 3275 with a right-hand passenger door was an oddity originally taken up by the military as a C-52D 42-6505 on 24 September 1941, but later re-designated C-48C and allocated the later serial 42-38260. One historical source indicates that the latter designation and serial were never taken up. Airline details of the last five in the C-48 series are not known.

c/n	Model	Reg.	Del.	Serial.	Del.
3276	DC-3A-269C	NC25623	29 Nov 40	42-38258	12 Jul 41 Northwest
4114	DST-A-207D	NC33642	21 Jun 41	42-38259	14 Mar 42 United
3275	DC-3A-363	NC1000	3 Feb 41	42-38260	14 Mar 42 Swiftflite
2147	DC-3A	NC25675	24 Apr 40	42-38327	15 Mar 42 United
4170	DC-3A-414	NC30001		42-38332	18 Dec 41 DSC
4171	DC-3A-414	NC30002		42-38333	18 Dec 41 DSC
4172	DC-3A-414	NC30003		42-38334	18 Dec 41 DSC
4175	DC-3A-414	NC30006		42-38335	18 Dec 41 DSC
4176	DC-3A-414	NC30007		42-38336	18 Dec 41 DSC
4178	DC-3A-414	NC30010		42-38337	18 Dec 41 DSC
4182	DC-3A-414	NC30013		42-38338	18 Dec 41 DSC

Unknown are C-48C 42-78026/27/28 and 44-52990/91. C/n 4114 is also listed in one document as a C-52S 42-33642 effective 10 July 1941, later coming to the United Kingdom with 267 Squadron on 4 March 1942. C/n 2147 was originally a DC-3-194H PH-AXH '*Havik*' for KLM, registered on 17 December 1939, but never delivered. DSC stands for the Defense Supply Corporation, a US government agency.

The Douglas C-49/C-51 Series

The principal difference between the C-48 and the C-49 series of military transports impressed from civilian DC-3 models was the Wright Cyclone engine in the C-49 (ATC-618) for all the series except for a few DC-3B-202s with ATC-635. However, the C-50 and C-51 models also used the Cyclones, and most of the transports from C-49 to C-52C were procured by the Army Air Corps on the same acquisition order. With the series going as high as C-49K, the C-49 was not only the most varied single model of the wartime drafted DC-3s, it was also the most numerous, involving some 138 aircraft.

Five of the six C-49s were high-density, twenty-four-seat DC-3-384s fitted with left-hand-side passenger doors. They had been ordered by TWA, but taken directly off the Santa Monica production line. The sixth aircraft was a DC-3-362, still on a TWA order. The engines were initially R-1820-71s, producing 1,200 hp at 2,500 rpm. This engine was equivalent to the civil R-1820-G202A. One quote indicates that the six C-49s later had their engines changed to Pratt & Whitney R-1830-51s; this would then have designated them C-48s or C-52s, since it was the engines which determined the military model number. The 1943 cost for the C-49 airframe and engines was only $102,570, later listed as $135,688.

c/n	Model	Reg.	Del.	Serial	Del.
3270	DC-3-384	NC1945	not delivered	41-7685	6 Feb 41
3271	DC-3-384	NC1946		41-7686	8 Feb 41
3272	DC-3-384	NC1947		41-7687	23 Feb 41
3273	DC-3-384	NC1948		41-7688	16 Feb 41
3274	DC-3-384	NC1949		41-7689	21 Feb 41
3297	DC-3-362	NC1953		41-7694	22 Mar 41

There was a single C-49A c/n 3282, an undelivered Delta Air Lines left-hand-side passenger door DC-3-385, allocated NC28345 and acquired by the Army Air Corps on 23 February 1941, as 41-7690. The engines were listed as R-1820-71 and the price in 1943 quoted as $97,069. On 4 September 1942, it joined the US 5th Army Air Force in Australia, and on 24 June 1943, went to the Royal Australian Air Force with 36 Squadron carrying the tail code 'VHCDC' and named *Miss Carriage*. After returning to the US Army Air Forces on 24 April 1944 and being flown by Australian National Airways crews, it crashed into the sea off Tacloban, Leyte in the Philippines on 13 November 1945.

The C-49Bs were three Eastern Air Lines twenty-one-passenger DC-3-201Fs with left-side doors and powered by R-1820-71 engines; these were again impressed into military service off the production line as a unit on 22 February 1941. Details were: c/n 4094 allocated NC288386 but never applied to 41-7691; c/n 4095 NC288387 to 41-7692; and c/n 4096 NC288388 to 41-7693. On 4 September 1942, the first C-49B 41-7691 went to the 5th Air Force in Australia, becoming 'VHCDD' *Eager Elaine*, later going to the RAAF before being returned to the USAAF. 41-7693 followed suit, becoming 'VHCDE' *Airline Alsie*.

There were just two C-49Cs, which were consecutive left-hand-side passenger door DC-3-375As ordered by Delta Air Lines as NC28346 c/n 4814 and NC28347 c/n 4815. The first became 41-7715 on 6 September 1941, and the second 41-7721 on 30 September 1941. For some reason these transports received more military treatment than previous draftees, with the beautiful airline interiors being stripped out and side benches installed to seat up to twenty-eight troops. No cabin soundproofing was installed and the wooden airline floor was protected from the impact of military boots and heavy cargo by a layer of heavy-duty plywood applied over it. These C-49C transports were the first military DC-3s to have the wartime olive drab and grey warpaint applied. The engines were R-1820-71s and the 1943 price quoted went up to $100,186.

c/n	Model	Reg.	Del.	Serial.	Del.
4141	DC-3-201G	NC33635	not delivered	41-7716	3 Oct 41
4142	DC-3-201G	NC33636		41-7717	3 Oct 41
4143	DC-3-201G	NC33637		41-7718	3 Oct 41
4144	DC-3-201G	NC33638		41-7719	3 Oct 41
4145	DC-3-201G	NC33639		41-7720	3 Oct 41
1923	DC-3B-202	NC17313		42-38256	14 Mar 42
1916	DC-3-201	NC16095		42-43624	9 Apr 42
4091	DC-3-201F	NC28383		42-65583	22 Jul 42
3280	DC-3-357	NC28343		42-65584	22 Jul 42
3285	DC-3-322B	NC28378		42-68860	19 Jul 42
				44-52999	

The first four DC-3-201G airliners for Eastern were allocated the Douglas type number DC-3-389 when taken over as C-49Ds. C/n 1923 went to the Royal Air Force in the Middle East as LR233 on 1 April 1942, whilst c/n 4091 is quoted as being manufactured at Santa Monica on 6 February 1941, although it was not taken over by the Army Air Corps until July 1942.

A very mixed bag of twenty-two right-hand passenger door DSTs and DC-3s made up the C-49E series. All were apparently already in full service with several airlines before being drafted into Army Air Corps service. The engines were listed in US Army Air Corps documents as R-1820-GI02A. In spite of the mixture of both day and sleeper cabins, most of the transports were fitted out as ambulances equipped with up to fourteen stretchers.

A total of 137 transports were procured by the military shortly after Pearl Harbor by simply taking over civil DC-3s and DC-3As then on the production line at Santa Monica. They were being built to different airline specifications and were powered by a variety of engines. They were assigned twenty-two different designations, whilst twelve remained undesignated.

USAAF designation	No.of aircraft	Original customer	Douglas Spec. No.	Engines	Seats
C-48-DO	1	United	DC-3A-377	R-1830-82	21
C-48A-DO	3	-	DC-3A-368	R-1830-82	10
C-48C-DO	7	Pan Am & associates	DC-3A-414	R-1830-51	21
C-49-DO	6	TWA	DC-3-384	R-1820-71	24
C-49A-DO	1	Delta	DC-3-385	R-1820-71	21
C-49B-DO	3	Eastern	DC-3-387	R-1820-71	21
C-49C-DO	2	Delta	DC-3-386	R-1820-71	28
C-49D-DO	6	Eastern	DC-3-389	R-1820-71	28
C-49J-DO	34	sundry	DC-3-454	R-1820-71	28
C-49K-DO	23	sundry	DC-3-455	R-1820-71	28
C-50-DO	4	American	DC-3-396	R-1820-85	21
C-50A-DO	2	American	DC-3-401	R-1820-85	28
C-50B-DO	3	Braniff	DC-3-397	R-1820-81	21
C-50C-DO	1	Penn Central	DC-3-391	R-1820-79	21
C-50D-DO	4	Penn Central	DC-3-392	R-1820-79	28
C-51-DO	1	Can Coloial	DC-3-390	R-1820-83	28
C-52-DO	1	United	DC-3A-398	R-1830-51	28
C-52A-DO	1	Western	DC-3A-394	R-1830-51	28
C-52B-DO	2	United	DC-3A-395	R-1830-51	28
C-52C-DO	1	Eastern	DC-3A-402	R-1830-51	29
C-53C-DO	17	sundry	DC-3A-453	R-1830-92	28
C-68-DO	2	-	DC-3A-440	R-1830-92	21
Undesignated	12	Pan Am & associates	DC-3A-414	R-1830-92	28

The military impressed ninety-three DST/DC-3 variants directly from the airlines, this constituting a third variant of military DC-3 transports. Many were leased back to the airlines for use on government approved routes, the transport not necessarily being leased to the airline from which it had come. According to engine types and internal configurations, these aircraft were given the following designations and military serial numbers.

USAAF designation	No. of aircraft	Engines	AAF serial numbers
C-48B-DO	16	R-1830-51	42-38324/42-42-38326, 42-56089/42-56091, 42-56098/42-56102, 42-56609/42-56612, 42-56629
C-48C-DO	9	R-1830-51	42-38258/42-38260, 42-38327, 42-78026/42-78028, 44-52990/44-52991
C-49D-DO	5	R-1820-71	42-38256, 42-43624, 42-65583, 42,68860, 44-52999
C-49E-DO	22	R-1820-79	42-43619/42-43623, 42-56092/42-56097, 42-56103/42-56107, 42-56617/42-56618, 42-56625/42-56627, 42-56634
C-49F-DO	9	R-1820-71	42-56613, 42-56616, 42-56620/42-56621, 42-56623, 42-56628, 42-56633, 42-56636/42-56637
C-49G-DO	8	R-1820-97	42-38252, 42-38255, 42-56614/42-56615, 42-56630/42-56632, 42-56635
C-49H-DO	19	R-1820-97	42-38250/42-38251, 42-38253/42-38254, 42-38257, 42-38328/42-38331, 42-57506, 42-65580/42-65582, 42-68687/42-68689, 42-102422, 44-83228/44-83229
C-52D-DO	1	R-1830-51	42-6505
C-84-DO	4	R-1820-71	42-57157, 42-57511/42-57513

c/n	Model	Reg.	Airline	Del.	Serial.	Del.
1494	DST-114	NC14988	American	11 Jul 36	42-43619	31 Mar 43
2165	DST-217A	NC21752	American	30 Aug 39	42-43620	14 Mar 42
2149	DST-217A	NC21769	American	24 Oct 39	42-43621	31 Mar 42
2263	DC-3-217C	NC28325	American	9 Aug 40	42-43622	12 Mar 42
2264	DST-217C	NC28350	American	23 Aug 40	42-43623	16 Mar 42
1499	DST-144	NC16005	American	12 Jul 36	42-56092	28 May 42
1976	DST-217	NC18144	American	24 Nov 37	42-56093	8 Jun 42
1549	DST-144	NC16007	American	28 Aug 36	42-56094	28 May 42
1500	DST-144	NC16006	American	18 Jul 36	42-56095	28 May 42
1498	DST-144	NC16004	American	4 Jul 36	42-56096	28 May 42
1495	DST-144	NC16001	American	7 Jun 36	42-56097	8 Jun 42
1496	DST-144	NC16002	American	18 Jun 36	42-56104	29 May 42
2216	DST-217B	NC25685	American	26 May 40	42-56103	29 May 42
1497	DST-144	NC16003	American	23 Jun 36	42-56105	29 May 42
2217	DST-217B	NC25686	American	2 Jun 40	42-56106	8 Jun 42
2127	DC-3-270	NC21751	Colonial	3 May 39	42-56107	8 Jun 42
4081	DC-3-313B	NC25695	PenCentral	10 Mar 41	42-56617	8 Jun 42
4082	DC-3-313B	NC25696	PenCentral	12 Mar 41	42-56618	8 Jun 42
1933	DC-3B-202	NC17318	TWA	17 Jun 37	42-56625	8 Jun 42
4132	DC-3-313D	NC33677	PenCentral	17 Mar 41	42-56626	8 Jun 42
2267	DC-3-313A	NC25694	PenCentral	27 Sep 40	42-56627	8 Jun 42
2271	DC-3-270B	NC28360	Colonial	19 Nov 40	42-56634	8 Jun 42

The C-49F transports were again a mixture of DSTs and DC-3s drafted from TWA, Eastern Air Lines and Chicago & South, making up a total of nine additional litter-carrier transports for the Army Air Corps, powered by R-1820-71 engines with some transports fitted with right-hand side passenger doors. The 1943 cost was quoted as $124,261 each.

c/n	Model	Reg.	Airline	Del.	Serial	Del.
2224	DST-318	NC25649	Eastern	Feb 40	42-56613	8 Jun 42
2225	DST-318	NC25650	Eastern	Feb 40	42-56616	8 Jun 42
1931	DC-3B-202	NC17316	TWA	7 Jun 37	42-56620	8 Jun 42
1932	DC-3B-202	NC17317	TWA	11 Jun 37	42-56621	8 Jun 42
2028	DC-3B-202A	NC18954	TWA	17 Jun 38	42-56623	8 Jun 42
2255	DC-3-322A	NC19977	C & S	23 Sep 40	42-56628	8 Jun 42
2226	DST-318	NC25651	Eastern	Feb 40	42-56633	8 Jun 42
4129	DST-406	NC33643	Eastern	Jun 41	42-56636	8 Jun 42
3251	DST-318A	NC28393	Eastern	8 Oct 40	42-56637	8 Jun 42

Eight twenty-one-passenger DC-3-201s taken from Eastern Air Lines became impressed as C-49G transports. Engines were listed as R-1820-G2E, a civil engine that delivered 1,000 hp at 2,200 rpm. These appeared to differ from other C-49 versions in having the more common left-hand-side passenger door.

c/n	Model	Reg.	Airline	Del.	Serial	Del.
1915	DC-3-201	NC16094	Eastern	18 Dec 36	42-38252	13 Apr 42
1949	DC-3-201	NC16083	Eastern	12 May 37	42-38255	14 Mar 42
1948	DC-3-201	NC16082	Eastern	10 May 37	42-56614	8 Jun 42
1971	DC-3-201	NC16083	Eastern	18 Aug 37	42-56615	8 Jun 42
1997	DC-3-201	NC18121	Eastern	28 Oct 37	42-56630	8 Jun 42
1998	DC-3-201	NC18122	Eastern	5 Nov 37	42-56631	8 Jun 42
2246	DC-3-210D	NC15595	Eastern	Sep 40	42-56632	8 Jun 42
1996	DC-3-201	NC18120	Eastern	23 Oct 37	42-56635	8 Jun 42

Two aircraft went to the Royal Air Force after serving in the Middle East with Pan American Airways (Africa); these were c/n 1915 to LR231 and c/n 1949 to LR235 and the transfer date was quoted as 1 April 1942.

The C-49H aircraft were a mixture of nineteen former airline transports taken from six different operators, all twenty-one-passenger DC-3s powered by R-1820-G102A engines with a broad range of identities according to the Douglas Aircraft

Company c/ns. Both right- and left-hand passenger door aircraft were included and once more two of the transports were transferred to the Royal Air Force. Two of the C-49H transports, Fokker-assembled aircraft for KLM and KNILM, were drafted in Australia.

The rather unusual history of two of the C-49H military transports cannot be ignored. 44-83228 c/n 1941 and 44-83229 c/n 1944 were allocated very late US Army Air Force serials in far-off Australia, and although there is no doubt that both transports were heavily involved in the Second World War, the allocation of both their designations and serial numbers has been rumoured in some areas to be just a paperwork exercise.

The single C-48 41-2681 c/n 3256 was originally a 21-seat right-hand door DC-3A-197D intended for United as NC25612 but not taken up. To this transport goes the distinction of being the first of many drafted DC-3s it being acquired on 27 December 1940. Price quoted in 1943 was $159,884. It is seen at Oakland, California, in November 1941 and is the personal transport of a two-star general from US Tech Training Command.
(William T. Larkins)

Douglas DC-3-194B c/n 1941 was a Fokker-assembled airliner delivered to KLM in Amsterdam on 10 April 1937, as PH-ALT 'Torenvalk' and transferred to the Far East subsidiary, KNILM, as PK-ALT on 2 June 1940. With the Japanese invasion of the Netherland East Indies the airliner managed to escape to Australia on 4 March 1942, being taken on charge by the Australian Government on 19 March. The records indicate it was transferred to the US Army Air Force on 15 May 1942, carrying ident '11941', which ties up with the Douglas c/n. Still as a military transport it was operated by Australian National Airlines as 'VHCXD' with effect from 6 December 1942, and became designated C-49H 44-83228 on 14 June 1944. It served with 33 Squadron, Royal Australian Air Force from 17 March 1945, and crashed at Higgins Field, Queensland on 5 May 1945.

Douglas DC-3-194B c/n 1944 was also assembled by Fokker and delivered to KLM as PH-ALW 'Wielewaal' on 25 April 1937 and transferred to KNILM in the Far East as PK-ALW on 1 June 1940. On 19 March 1942, after a flight from the jaws of the Japanese, it was taken over by the Australian Government, becoming '11944' with the US Army Air Forces carrying tail ident 'VHCXE' and on the strength of 21 Squadron on 15 May 1942. It was used as a VIP staff transport by General MacArthur during 1942/43. From 1 April 1944, it was operated by Australian National Airways and it became designated C-49H 44-83229 on 17 March 1945. It continued in civilian service in Australia until November 1974.

c/n	Model	Reg.	Airline	Del.	Serial	Del.
4116	DC-3-277D	NC33653	AA	5 May 41	42-38250	14 Mar 42
4118	DC-3-277D	NC33655	AA	5 May 41	42-38251	14 Mar 42
4130	DC-3-310D	NC33675	Pen Central	41	42-38253	14 Mar 42
1993	DC-3-228	NC18117	PAA	8 Oct 37	42-38254	14 Mar 42
2126	DC-3-270	NC21750	CanColonial	1 May 39	42-38257	14 Mar 42
4133	DC-3-313D	NC33678	PenCentral	26 Jul 41	42-38328	15 Mar 42
4099	DC-3-313C	NC25689	PenCentral	11 Apr 41	42-38329	26 Mar 42
2272	DC-3-270B	NC28361	CanColonial	3 Mar 41	42-38330	17 Mar 42
4107	DC-3-314B	NC28363	Braniff	20 Jun 41	42-38331	15 Mar 42
2198	DC-3-227B	NC21793	AA	24 Feb 40	42-57506	22 May 42
2167	DC-3-277A	NC21768	AA	25 Aug 39	42-65580	22 May 42
2203	DC-3-277B	NC21799	AA	9 Mar 40	42-65581	22 May 42
2205	DC-3-277B	NC25660	AA	16 Mar 40	42-65582	22 May 42
2179	DC-3-314	NC21773	Braniff	15 Dec 39	42-68687	17 Sep 42
2180	DC-3-214	NC21774	Braniff	28 Dec 39	42-68688	17 Sep 42
2181	DC-3-314	NC21775	Braniff	30 Dec 39	42-68689	17 Sep 42
2189	DC-3-313	NC21790	Pen Central	May 40	42-107422	22 Nov 43
1941	DC-3-194B	PK-ALT	KNILM	2 Jun 40	44-83228	15 May 42
1944	DC-3-194B	PK-ALW	KNILM	1 Jun 40	44-83229	17 Mar 45

One record indicates that the first three C-49H transports never received military serials. The first two were bought by the US government on 9 July 1941, and all three were operated by Pan American Airways (Africa), c/n 4116 went to the Royal Air Force as MA925 and c/n 4118 as MA943. Both subsequently operated in India. Apparently c/n 4118 had been registered G-AGEN with British Overseas Airways Corporation in July 1942 but never taken up.

c/n	Model	Reg.	Serial	Del.
4996	DC-3-454	Netherlands East Indies AF.	43-1961	30 Oct 42
4987	DC-3-455	NC14277 AA	43-1962	25 Oct 42
4988	DC-3-454	NC14278 AA	43-1963	26 Oct 42
4989	DC-3-454	NC14279 AA	43-1964	27 Oct 42
4990	DC-3-454	NC14280 AA	43-1965	30 Oct 42
4991	DC-3-454	NC14281 AA	43-1966	30 Oct 42
4992	DC-3-454	NC14282 AA	43-1967	30 Oct 42
4997	DC-3-454	Netherlands East Indies AF.	43-1968	7 Nov 42
4993	DC-3-454	NC34970 Braniff	43-1969	13 Nov 42
4994	DC-3-454	NC34971 Braniff	43-1970	12 Nov 42
4995	DC-3-454	NC34972 Braniff	43-1971	14 Nov 42
6313	DC-3-454	NC14283 AA	43-1972	14 Nov 42
6314	DC-3-454	NC14922 AA	43-1973	14 Nov 42
4998	DC-3-454	Netherlands East Indies AF.	43-1974	16 Nov 42
6315	DC-3-454	AA	43-1975	18 Nov 42
6316	DC-3-454	NC25663 AA	43-1976	20 Nov 42
6317	DC-3-454	AA	43-1977	19 Nov 42
6318	DC-3-454	AA	43-1978	21 Nov 42
4999	DC-3-454	Netherlands East Indies AF.	43-1979	5 Nov 42
5000	DC-3-454	Netherlands East Indies AF.	43-1982	5 Dec 42
6263	DC-3-454	NC33679 Chicago & Southern	43-1980	5 Dec 42
6264	DC-3-454	NC33680 Chicago & Southern	43-1981	10 Dec 42
6259	DC-3-454	Netherlands East Indies AF.	43-1983	22 Dec 42
6260	DC-3-454	Netherlands East Indies AF.	43-1984	22 Dec 42
6261	DC-3-454	Netherlands East Indies AF.	43-1985	31 Dec 42
6342	DC-3-454	NC30045 Delta Air Lines	43-1986	31 Dec 42
6262	DC-3-454	Netherlands East Indies AF.	43-1987	31 Dec 42
6343	DC-3-454	NC30046 Delta Air Lines	43-1988	6 Jan 43
6344	DC-3-454	NC30047 Delta Air Lines	43-1989	8 Jan 43
6319	DC-3-454	NC30050 AA	43-1990	5 Jan 43
6320	DC-3-454	NC30052 AA	43-1991	8 Jan 43
6321	DC-3-454	NC28359 AA	43-1992	13 Jan 43
6322	DC-3-454	NC33662 AA	43-1993	14 Jan 43
6323	DC-3-454	NC34969 AA	43-1994	30 Jan 43

The largest single series in the Douglas C-49 variants was the C-49J, made up of thirty-four DC-3-454 and DC-3-455 airliners, all taken from the Santa Monica production line after being partially completed for the Netherlands East Indies Air Force, American Airlines, Braniff and Chicago & Southern Airlines, plus Delta. Since all were drafted at once, the US Army Air Corps serial number allocation were consecutive, 43-1961 to 43-1994, but the c/ns were widespread as will be seen from the listing. The airliners, equipped with left-hand-side passenger doors, were fitted out as twenty-eight-seat troopers powered by R-1820-G202A engines. The 1943 listed price was $137,786 and the 1944 price $148,734.

The last variant in the C-49 series was the C-49K, a total of twenty-three DC-3-455s from American Airlines, TWA and Eastern Air Lines orders. The Army Air Corps serials were consecutive 43-1995 to 43-2017, following on immediately after the earlier C-49J aircraft, but preceding some late C-49H procurements. All were left-hand-side passenger door twenty-eight-seat military troopers powered by R-1820-G202A engines and priced at $147,667.

c/n	Model	Reg.	Airline	Serial	Del.
4982	DC-3-455	NC34973	TWA	43-1995	21 Oct 42
4983	DC-3-455	NC34974	TWA	43-1996	20 Oct 42
4984	DC-3-455	NC34975	TWA	43-1997	20 Oct 42
4985	DC-3-455	NC34976	TWA	43-1998	25 Oct 42
4986	DC-3-455	NC34977	TWA	43-1999	22 Oct 42
6325	DC-3-455	NC34978	AA	43-2000	28 Nov 42
6326	DC-3-455	NC34979	TWA	43-2001	25 Nov 42
6327	DC-3-455	NC34980	TWA	43-2002	28 Nov 42
6328	DC-3-455	NC34981	TWA	43-2003	30 Nov 42
6329	DC-3-455	NC34982	TWA	43-2004	3 Dec 42
6330	DC-3-455	NC34983	TWA	43-2005	3 Dec 42
6331	DC-3-455	NC30029	Eastern	43-2006	10 Dec 42
6332	DC-3-455	NC30030	Eastern	43-2007	14 Dec 42
6333	DC-3-455	NC30031	Eastern	43-2008	14 Dec 42
6334	DC-3-455	NC30032	Eastern	43-2009	17 Dec 42
6335	DC-3-455	NC30033	Eastern	43-2010	19 Dec 42
6336	DC-3-455	NC30034	Eastern	43-2011	21 Dec 42
6324	DC-3-455	NC28388	AA	43-2012	23 Jan 43
6337	DC-3-455	NC30035	Eastern	43-2013	27 Jan 43
6338	DC-3-455	NC30036	Eastern	43-2014	11 Feb 43
6339	DC-3-455	NC30037	Eastern	43-2015	4 Feb 43
6340	DC-3-455	NC30038	Eastern	43-2016	6 Feb 43
6341	DC-3-455	NC30039	Eastern	43-2017	18 Feb 43

The Douglas C-50 series were four right-hand-side passenger door twenty-one-passenger DC-3-277Ds ordered by American Airlines and allocated the Air Corps serials 41-7697/98/99/7700. The engines were R-1820-85, equivalent to the civil R-1820-G102A, producing 1,100 hp at 2,350 rpm. Price was $138,512. Two transports, c/n 4119 and 4120, went to the 5th US Army Air Force in Australia, the first arriving on 20 October 1942; in January 1943 it carried the tail ident 'VHCDK' and was named '*Laka Nookie*', but by March this had changed to '*Kwitcha Bichin*'. Arriving in Australia on 17 September 1942, c/n 4120 went to the Royal Australian Air Force to 36 Squadron with tail indent 'VHGDJ' and named '*Waltzing Matilda*', effective 28 January 1943. The C-50 transports also carried the Douglas type DC-3-396 and c/n 4122 41-7700 was eventually acquired by the Douglas Aircraft Company and became the second Douglas Super DC-3 prototype N30000 with new c/n 43159 during 1951.

c/n Serial	Model Del.	Reg.
4119 41-7697	DC-3-277D 24 Jul 41	NC33656 AA
4120 41-7698	DC-3-277D 31 Jul 41	NC33657 AA
4121 41-7699	DC-3-277D 7 Jun 41	NC33659 AA
4122 41-7700	DC-3-277D 10 Jun 41	NC33662 AA

Two DC-3-401 airliners ordered by American Airlines became designated C-50A transports and were fitted with right-hand-side doors; they were completed as military transports with twenty-eight seats for troops and powered by R-1820-85 engines. DC-3-401 NC33627 for American Airlines was never delivered and c/n 4804 became C-50A 41-7710 on 31 July 1941. It crashed on 21 April 1942, six miles north-west of Pope Field, North Carolina. DC-3-401 NC33628 was also part of an American Airlines order, but never delivered. Instead c/n 4805 became C-50A 41-7711 on 31 July 1941, being bought by American Airlines on 24 June 1944 and registered NC15577. It crashed on 28 December 1946, at Michigan City, Indiana.

The C-50B military transports were three left-hand-side passenger door DC-3-314Bs ordered by Braniff but not delivered. Airline-type seating was utilised. They were powered by R-1820-81 engines, similar to the civil GR-1820-G102A. The first C-50B 41-7703 c/n 4109 was delivered on 26 June 1941, and between 10 August 1942 and 8 October 1942 it served with the US 5th Army Air Force in Australia. The second, 41-7704, c/n 4110, was delivered on 30 June 1941 and the second, 41,7705 c/n 4111, on 9 July; it crashed on 24 July at Patterson, Ohio. These three C-50Bs were allocated the civil registrations with Braniff NC28370, NC28371 and NC28372 respectively.

A single DC-3-313B, originally ordered by Pennsylvania Central Airlines as NC25697 but never delivered, became the sole C-50C transport 41-7695 c/n 4083. The airliner was completed by Douglas as a DC-3-391 equipped with airliner-type seats. Engines were the R-1820-79, again equivalent to the civil GR-1820-G102A. The price quoted was $126,993. The C-50C 41-7695 was delivered to the US Army Air Corps on 22 July 1941, and on 4 September went to the US 5th Army Air Force in Australia. It served with the Royal Australian Air Force with tail ident 'VHCDI' and it was involved in a crash on 12 November 1942.

Four DC-3-313B airliners from a Pennsylvania Central Airlines order were completed at Santa Monica as DC-3-392 transports and equipped internally similarly to the C-50C with airline-type seats, but designated C-50D. The first, 41-7696 c/n 4084, was delivered on 8 August 1941 and would have been NC25698 with Penn Central. 41-7709 c/n 4131 was delivered on 24 July 1941 and served in Australia with the US 5th Army Air Force between 10 June and 10 September 1942. It would have been NC33676. 41-7712 c/n 4134 was delivered on 6 August 1941, and would have been NC33679. The last C-50D 41-7713 c/n 4135 was delivered on 23 August 1941, and it too served in Australia between 10 June and 10 September 1942. It would have been NC33680 with Penn Central. All survived the war and all except c/n 4131 were converted to DC-3A standard with a change to Pratt & Whitney R-1830 Twin Wasp engines.

There was just one Douglas C-51 military transport, a DC-3-270C airliner ordered by Canadian Colonial Airline to be NC34962 c/n 3289. It was fitted with a right-hand-side passenger door. The US Army Air Corps used it as a twenty-eight-seat trooper. The engines were R-1820-83s, similar to the R-1820-79 and R-1820-85 except for different reduction gear ratios, magnetos and fuel-pump drives which the Air Corps must have thought justified the change of aeroplane designation. The price listed in the inventory was $132,181. The lone C-51 41-7702 c/n 3289 was delivered to the Air Corps on 28 June 1941, and the records indicate it ended its days at Columbia, South Carolina on 20 January 1943.

Six mixed DC-3A airliners obtained from three airlines and a private owner were drafted into military service as the C-52 in 1941. All were powered by the military R-1830-92 engine, equivalent to the civil Pratt & Whitney R-1830-SIC3G. All six were equipped as troop carrier transports with reinforced floors, some being fitted with left-hand-side passenger doors, some with a door on the right. The 1943 price for the C-52 ranged from a low of $103,518 for the single C-52A to $103,973 for the two C-52Bs and single C-52C.

The single C-52 transport was initially a DC-3-197D for United Air Lines NC34999 c/n 4112, but was never delivered. It became a DC-3-398 C-50 with Air Corps serial 41-7708, being delivered on 5 August 1941. Between 15 August and 23 September 1942 it served with the US 5th Army Air Force in Australia. On 6 June 1944 it was returned to United Air Lines, being registered NC15586 and retaining the right-hand-side passenger door. The 1943 price was quoted as $103,824.

Another single, the C-52A 41-7714 c/n 4813 was initially laid down at Santa Monica as a DC-3A-394 for Western Air Lines as NC33672 with a right-hand door, but again never delivered. On 29 August 1941 it was delivered to the US Army Air Corps, being returned to Western on 10 June 1944 and registered NC19387. It was later fitted with a left-hand passenger door.

A pair of right-hand-side door DC-3A-197E airliners ordered by United Air Lines were drafted into Air Corps service and designated C-52B, both DC-3-395 models. They became 41-7706 c/n 4127 ex-NC33648, delivered on 14 June 1941, and 41-7707 c/n 4128, ex-NC33649, delivered on 22 July 1941. The latter was returned to airline service with Northwest on 4 July 1944, as NC33327, whilst its sister C-52B c/n 4127 also went to Northwest on 8 July 1944, becoming NC33326.

The single Douglas C-52C 41-7701 c/n 4136 illustrates dramatically the problem which still exists for historians and aviation buffs in calculating accurately just how many civil DC-3 airliners were produced. This transport began its career as a DC-3-201G as part of an order for Eastern Air Lines registered NC33630; it was never delivered. Instead it was drafted as a twenty-eight-seat military trooper powered by Pratt & Whitney Twin Wasp engines, making it a DC-3A rather than just a DC-3. Several other DC-3 airliners were completed on the Santa Monica production line as DC-3As when the US Army Air Corps drafted them into military service. The C-52C 41-7701 is quoted as a DC-3-402 and was delivered on 13 September 1941. It is listed as being at Columbus, South Carolina, on 15 November 1942, and ended its career on 20 January 1943.

There was a single C-52D, briefly mentioned earlier. The US Army Air Corps records reveal that the C-52D designation was cancelled but apparently that came about after the left-hand-side passenger door DC-3A-363 c/n 3275 NC1000 delivered on 3 February 1941, being re-registered NC41831 on 6 September 1941 and delivered to the Army Air Corps with serial 42-6505 on 24 September. It was subsequently re-designated C-48C on 14 March 1942, and allocated a later military serial, 42-38260, but not taken up. It served with Pan American Airways and is quoted as serving with 267 Squadron with effect from 4 March 1942, and as '26505' at Accra, West Africa, in March 1943. It served with both the North African Wing and the European Wing of the huge Air Transport Command organisation.

Additional DC-3 Draftees

Two more small batches of drafted civil Douglas DC-3s were acquired by the US Army Air Corps and were designated C-68s and C-84s. Unfortunately, no verifiable photos of these unique transports in military livery are known to exist.

A couple of left-hand-side passenger door DC-3A-414s were allocated the Air Corps serials 42-14297 c/n 4173 and 42-14298 c/n 4174, becoming designated C-68. They were constructed for the US Defense Supply Corporation and registered NC30004 and NC30005 respectively. Both were delivered to the Air Corps on the last day of 1941 and operated by Pan American Airways in North Africa with effect from 11 January 1942. These military transports had twenty-one-passenger interiors and were powered by R-1830-92 engines; on the 1943 inventory they were listed at $139,966 each. On 1 April 1942, 42-14297 went to the Royal Air Force as LR230, being delivered to 31 Squadron in India on 19 April and listed as 'D for Dog' with this famous transport unit. On 6 May it was destroyed during a Japanese air attack at Myitykina, Burma.

Unfortunately neither of the two Douglas C-68s were photographed during World War II. Built as DC-3A-414 NC30005 c/n 4174, owner unknown, it was acquired by the military on 31 December 1941 as 41-14298. Price was quoted as $139,966 and the two C-68s were leased briefly to Pan American in January 1942, flown to Britain on 12 March 1942 going to the US 8th Air Force on 31 January 1944. After World War II c/n 4174 went to Delta Air Lines as NC20752 on 26 September 1945 being eventually withdrawn from use in April 1982. (Roger Besecker)

The second C-68 42-14298 arrived in the United Kingdom on 12 March 1942. It was assigned to the US 8th Army Air Force on the last day of January 1944, returned to the United States as surplus on 17 September 1945, and was bought by Delta Air Lines nine days later, registered NC20752.

At a first glance, it would appear logical to allocate the four Douglas C-84 military transports separate designations from other Wright Cyclone-engined DC-3s, since they consisted of the rather rare DC-3B-202s plus one DC-3B-202A, of which only ten were built under ATC-635, all originally for use by TWA. DC-3B-202 NC17312 c/n 1922 was delivered to TWA on 16 April 1937, becoming C-84 42-57157 on 9 July 1942 and being returned to TWA on 3 December 1943. DC-3B-202 NC17314 c/n 1924 was delivered to TWA on 23 May 1937,

becoming C-84 42-57511 on 14 June 1942 and being returned to TWA on 17 October 1944. DC-3B-202 NC17319 c/n 1934 was delivered to TWA on 19 June 1937, becoming C-84 42-57512 on 14 June 1942. It was assigned to the South Atlantic Wing of the Air Transport Command on 1 May 1943, returned to TWA on lease on 1 April 1945, and finally bought back on 8 June of that year. The DC-3B-202A NC18953 c/n 2027 was delivered to TWA on 12 January 1938, becoming C-84 42-57513 on 14 June 1942. It was returned to the airline on 23 October 1944.

It must be mentioned that all other DC-3 airliners built under ATC-635, except one which crashed whilst in airline service, were drafted into US Army Air Corps service. They became a batch of C-49s, one C-49D, one C-49E and three C-49F transports.

Apparently there was no corresponding separate Douglas letter designation for an equivalent Pratt & Whitney-powered semi-sleeper like the DC-3B, although there were such aeroplanes. The single Douglas C-41A 40-70 c/n 2145 was designated DC-3A-253A. US Army Air Corps seating was the high-density airline type for twenty-eight passengers and the engines were civil Wright Cyclone GR-1820-G202A. Some civil sources refer to the R-1820-71 engine, equivalent to the R-1820-G202A, as a slightly different power-plant. The Douglas C-84s do not appear on either the 1943 or 1944 unit cost lists.

As mentioned earlier, all the four C-84 military transports were returned to TWA before the end of the war, receiving their original civil registrations. However, the last airliner, NC18953 c/n 2027, is a puzzle. On 5 May 1953 it was sold by TWA to Union Steel & Wrecking Co, who sold it two weeks later to Ozark Air Lines, who re-registered it N139D during 1954. Post-war Federal Aeronautical Administration – FAA – registration records confirm the manufacturers' c/n as 2027, but photos of N139D show Pratt & Whitney Twin Wasp engines, no upper-berth windows, standard main window spacing and a right-hand-side passenger door. These differences cannot easily be reconciled by the minor DC-3B-202A designation differences, so either this particular airliner must have been entirely and extensively rebuilt at some stage, or a name plate and registration number switch with another DC-3 transport must have been made – an illegal but not unheard of trick of the trade.

The C-53 'Skytrooper' Series

The first US Army Air Corps DC-3, designated C-41, was allocated a lower model designation than the C-42, which was a converted Douglas C-39 (DC-2-243), as it was contracted for and given a new model number prior to the Air Corps decision to convert a production military DC-2, the C-39, to the C-42.

A single C-41 has often been incorrectly identified as a modified C-39 ever since it was built at Santa Monica and is still often quoted wrongly. The confusion may have arisen because this C-41 was ordered as a single article on the C-39 contract involving thirty-seven aircraft. One of the C-39s on the same contract was converted to a passenger interior and delivered to the Air Corps as the first C-42. It was fairly common practice for one or more aircraft on a contract to be held back for conversion to a different configuration and so delivered under a different military designation, which might even involve a separate model number, as happened with the Douglas C-41/DC3.

The allocation of the US Army serial 38-502 gives the impression that the C-41 was the fourth C-39, when it was actually a single off-the-shelf DC-3A c/n 2053 NC15473. In keeping with the Douglas Aircraft Company practice of using a different dash number for each DC-2 and DC-3 variant built, it was identified in the factory as a DC-3A-253. It was delivered for General 'Hap' Arnold on 22 October 1938, three months ahead of the first C-39.

This VIP transport differed from commercial configuration only in interior conversion for fourteen luxury military executive passenger use, plus installation of military radio equipment. The civil Pratt & Whitney R-1830 Twin Wasp engines, generating 1,200 hp at 2,700 rpm, were given the Army Air Corps designation R-1830-21. By April 1945, the C-41 had accumulated 2,739 flying hours and was then leased to Alaska Airlines by the US government as NC15473.

There was a single C-41A military transport, serial 40-70 c/n 2145, another stock Santa Monica-built DC-3, Douglas model DC-3A-253A. It was delivered to the Army Air Corps on a one-aircraft contract on 11 September 1939. This and the earlier mentioned C-41 were the only Air Corps transports to use the R-1830-SICIG engines – military designation R-1830-21. The C-41A also carried General 'Hap' Arnold's identity, and until serial numbers appeared on the fin and rudder in 1942, could only be identified externally by the two small upper-berth windows situated above the first and third window on each side of the forward cabin. Like the Douglas DC-3B, it was a partial sleeper transport.

The Douglas C-47 'Skytrain' military transport, the most numerous of the DC-3 series, is a subject too vast to be included in this volume.

The second major production DC-3 variant ordered by the US Army Air Corps was the Douglas C-53. It was identified in the Douglas records as DC-3A-405 and the US government named it 'Skytrooper' shortly after it appeared in October 1941. A total of 379 C-53s were built on military contracts at Santa Monica, and adopted for military use without structural change; in fact, the company c/ns initially show a mixture of C-53 and DC-3 transports: c/n 4810 41-20045; c/n 4811-12 DC-3A-343B NC33670/1 for Western Air Lines, with the next C-53 41-20046 being c/n 4816. As for the C-47, power for the C-53 was supplied by the R-1830-92 Twin Wasp. The major alteration was the fitting of troop benches in most of the transports, and later the addition of an astrodome and rifle grommets to the windows. The small baggage door on the left-hand side of the DC-3 was retained, as was the passenger door, which proved something of a handicap when hauling large items of cargo.

Cabin capacity, whether for troops or litters, was exactly the same as the C-47 'Skytrain', and the gross weight was the same. Many early C-53 transports were handed over to the airlines for contract operations in support of the US Army Air Corps, later the US Army Air Force. As the Second World War eventually involved many theatres of operations, the C-53 'Skytrooper' operated over enemy territory in use as paratroopers, etc.

There were 219 C-53 transports built, covering four contracts. To those were added three draftees, including two DC-3As from a Pan American Airways order, but never delivered. These were DC-3A-447 NC34949 c/n 4960, delivered as C-53 43-14404, later going to the US Navy as a R4D-4, then to Pan American as NC30094 in December 1942. The second was DC-3A-447 NC34950 c/n 4961, delivered as C-53 43-14405 in December 1942. It also went to the US Navy as a R4D-4 and in December 1942 to Pan American as NC30095. The third drafted civil DC-3 was c/n 4809 NC30000, a DC-3A-408 registered to the Douglas Aircraft Company; after being drafted as a C-53 43-36600 on 24

September 1943; it was retained for use by the company, having been built at Santa Monica during 1941.

All the drafted Douglas DC-3 commercial transports, and their civilian airline crews, had varied careers, appearing in many remote corners of the globe where the action was, and in the widespread corners of the United States, supporting the home front. The airline crews were now in Army Air Corps khaki uniforms and included such executives as Cyrus R. Smith of American Airlines, Northeast's Vice-President Operations, Milton H. Anderson, and Frank C. Barker, Superintendent of Communications. At the head of the Atlantic Division of Air Transport Command during those busy route-finding months early in the Second World War was Major-General Lawrence C. Fritz, one-time Operations Chief of TWA. He had been among the first airline pilots to be checked out in the one and only DC-1.

A number of C-53 'Skytrooper' transports were delivered to the Royal Air Force, including 41-20081 c/n 4851, delivered from the factory on 18 January 1942 and assigned to the US Ferry Command on 4 March. It was based at Accra on the Gold Coast of Africa from 21 December, then joined 31 Squadron RAF on 1 April 1943, with a transfer to 194 Squadron in Burma on 29 April. 'Skytrooper' 42-6478, delivered on 26 May 1942, arrived in the United Kingdom on 5 August, was assigned to the US 8th Air Force on 20 October and to Oran in North Africa on 13 November. On 23 February 1944, it went to the Royal Air Force as a Dakota Mk.II TJ167 with 24 Squadron and was used as a VIP transport, being based at both RAF Hendon and RAF Northolt; it later served with the Allied Expeditionary Force Communications Flight and the Metropolitan Command Squadron. On 25 October 1945, it went into storage with 5 Maintenance Unit at RAF Kemble, in Gloucestershire, and on 3 February 1947, it received the ground instruction airframe number 6252M. It was sold in the USA in December 1947 as NC74139. Three more C-53s – 42-6479 c/n 4931, 42-6481 c/n 4933 and 42-6502 c/n 4954 – became FJ709/710/711 with the RAF. The first two were delivered from the factory on 8 May 1942, being ferried to the United Kingdom later in the month and arriving in Egypt on 12 June. Dakota FJ710 and FJ711 served with 117 Squadron in the Middle East, whilst FJ712 served with both 216 and 267 Squadrons in North Africa.

Four C-53 transports were based in Australia, serving with 36 Squadron Royal Australian Air Force; these were 41-20053 c/n 4823 radio call-sign 'VHCCB'; 41-20054 c/n 4824 'VHCCC'; 41-20066 c/n 4836 'VHCDW'; and 41-20070 c/n 4840 'VHCWA'. They were flown from the USA to Brisbane in December 1941 and January 1942 under 'Project X', being assigned to the US 5th Army Air Force. 'VHCCB' was named *Foitle Moitle* and 'VHCCC' *Kwichy R. Richin*'; 'VHCWA' was initially with the USAAF as 'VHCDV' *Dipsy Doodle* and *Natti Nikka*', being renamed *Wonga Will* in June 1943. Douglas C-53 'VHCDW' crashed on 26 February 1942, at Vansittart Bay, 150 nautical miles north-west of Wyndham, Western Australia. A further eighteen C-53s were transferred to the US Navy as Douglas R4D-3 transports in early 1942.

One C-53, 42-6480 c/n 4932, became designated XC-53A on 27 March 1943; it was tested at Wright Field, Dayton, Ohio, with effect from 15 September 1944. It was modified with full-span wing flaps, and had heated leading-edge de-icing. Neither feature of this 'Skytrooper' was adopted for wartime production, but the heated leading-edge de-icing replaced the earlier rubber boot system for new aircraft designs which appeared after 1945. This transport was named '*Old Weary Wings*'

There was a winterised version of the 'Skytrooper', designated C-53B, of which eight were modified for Arctic operations: this meant they were fitted with extra fuselage fuel tanks, improved cabin heating and a separate C-47 type navigator's position complete with astrodome. They were allocated the military serials 41-20047-50, 41-20052 and 41-20057-59. The first five served in Alaska with effect from early in 1942, while the last three went to Pan American Airways for service with the US Air Transport Command on 5 March 1942. Ironically they served in the heat of the North African Wing until at least 1944. The C-53Bs were costed at $136,399 each.

Seventeen DC-3 airliners laid down on the Santa Monica production line as DC-3A-453s for three airlines – United, Northwest and Pan Am – and acquired at $150,470 each became designated C-53C military transports. They were a specialised troop transport and had the larger port-side cargo door.

c/n	Reg.	Airline	Serial	Del.
4964	NC33685	United	43-2018	5 Oct 42
4965	NC33686	United	43-2019	4 Oct 42
4966	NC33687	United	43-2020	6 Oct 42
4967	NC33688	United	43-2021	5 Nov 42
4978	NC30025	Northwest	43-2022	13 Oct 42
4979	NC30026	Northwest	43-2023	14 Oct 42
4980	NC30027	Northwest	43-2024	20 Oct 42
4969	NC33690	United	43-2025	15 Nov 42
4970	NC33691	United	43-2026	5 Nov 42
4971	NC33692	United	43-2027	5 Nov 42
4972	NC33693	United	43-2028	5 Nov 42
4973	NC33694	United	43-2029	7 Nov 42
4974	NC33695	United	43-2030	7 Nov 42
4975	NC33696	United	43-2031	9 Nov 42
4976	NC33697	United	43-2032	10 Nov 42
6346	NC34953	PAA	43-2033	27 Dec 42
6347	NC34954	PAA	43-2034	31 Dec 42

Two of the C-53 transports, 43-2025 c/n 4969 and 43-2026 c/n 4970, were diverted to the US Navy, being allocated BuNos. 06998 and 06999 as R4D-3 transports which served respectively with VR-3 and VR-2 Squadron of the US Naval Air Transport Service on 30 and 23 November 1942. US Navy VR-3 operated out of Kansas City and VR-2 was based at Alameda in California

The 159 Douglas C-53D transports (DC-3-457) differed from the earlier C-53 mainly in having a twenty-four-volt electrical system. Their price was listed at $140,944. They were allocated the serials 42-68693 – 68851, with the last C-53D 42-68851 c/n 11778 being the last of the Douglas Commercial Threes built at Santa Monica. It was delivered on 31 July 1943 and transferred to Oran in North Africa on 18 September, returning safely to the USA on 1 September 1945. One quote indicates that the penultimate C-53D 42-68850 c/n 11777, delivered on 30 July 1943, and going to Oran on 20 September, later serving with the India-China Wing of US Air Transport Command and arriving in the United Kingdom on 7 November 1945, saw temporary service with the Royal Air Force.

US Navy DC-3 Transports

The United States Navy was a customer for the Douglas Commercial Three before the US Army Air Corps. Navy DC-3 procurement began with duplicates of Army Air Corps transports built under Navy contracts, but most were C-47s diverted from Army contracts. There was also direct purchase of off-the-shelf civil DC-3s and the drafting of other civil DC-3s.

The aircraft designation system used by the US Navy differed

notably from that of the US Army Air Corps. The Air Corps designation also covered aircraft used by the US Marine Corps and the US Coast Guard. The designation R4D- was adopted for the DC-3 transport type, the 'R' being for Transport; the '4' being the fourth transport model from Douglas, and 'D' for Douglas. The R2D- was the Douglas DC-2 equivalent, the R3D- the Douglas DC-5, and the R4D- the DC-3.

The US Navy adopted a designation system which was undoubtedly less confusing and more justifiable. An engine type change was ignored, and it did not use block numbers and factory abbreviations as the Air Corps did. The R4D-1 with Pratt & Whitney Twin Wasp engines and cargo doors duplicated the C-47. The R4D-2, on the other hand, had Wright Cyclones and deluxe DC-3 features like the C-49. What would have justified a new model number with the Air Corps, rated only a dash number with the US Navy.

In a rare example of pre-Second World War US Army Air Corps and US Navy co-operation, the two services simultaneously ordered identical cargo versions of the well-established DC-3 to be built on the same production line. As mentioned earlier, the designation R4D- was assigned to its DC-3 transports, with the first examples ordered being duplicates of the still unbuilt C-47 'Skytrain'.

Production of US Navy R4D- transports was not in sequence – the R4D-1, R4D-5, R4D-6 and R4D-7 paralleled the US Army Air Corps C-47/C47B production from the Long Beach and Oklahoma City plants. The R4D-2s were off-the-shelf airliners and the R4D-3s were transferred Army Air Corps C-53 'Skytroopers', both from the Santa Monica production line. The R4D-4s were airliners taken over on the Douglas production line at Santa Monica.

The two R4D-2 transports were the first DC-3s to enter US Navy service. They were Model DC-3-388 with BuNos. 4707-4708, originally ordered by Eastern Air Lines as NC28389 c/n 4097 and NC28390 c/n 4098, but drafted before completion. They were modified with VIP interiors as R4D-2F, later R4D-2Z with c/n 4097 being delivered to Anacostia, Maryland, on 12 March 1941 and served faithfully until 31 May 1946. The second, c/n 4098, was delivered on 25 April 1941 and became the personal aircraft of the US Naval Air Attaché based in Cape Town. It served until the last day of 1946 and remained in South Africa.

Twenty Douglas R4D-3 transports were transfers to the US Navy from production C-53 'Skytrooper' contracts and from Army Air Corps drafts involving civil DC-3s. The transports appeared in widely scattered pairs, as will be seen by the listing. The first two R4D-3s were delivered in January 1942 in US Navy livery, including rudder stripes, and stars on both wings. The last delivery from the C-53 contract was on 22 June 1942, with the first from the C-53C contract taking place on 15 November 1942 and the last in 1943. Like the drafted DC-3s used by the Army Air Corps, the US Navy transports were operated by the airlines, such as Pan American Airways, under military contracts.

c/n	BuNo.	Serial
4863/4864	05073/05074	ex 41-20093/20094
4877/4878	05075/05076	41-20107/20108
4893/4894	05077/05078	41-20123/20124
4917/4918	05079/05080	42-6465/6466
4942/4943	05081/05082	42-6490/6491
4955/4956	05083/05084	42-6503/6504
7408/7409	06992/06993	42-15891/15892
7411/7339	06994/06995	42-15894 42-15544
7350/7351	06996/06997	42-15555/15556
4969/4970	06998/06999	43-2025/2026

The early R4D-3s carried whatever cargo could be loaded through their airliner-type passenger doors, or into the baggage compartment, but otherwise served mainly as personnel transports. They were on the strength of most of the transport squadrons which made up the huge Naval Air Transport Service – NATS – serving all theatres of operations. Formed on 12 December 1941, NATS was authorised with three wings – Pacific, West Coast and Atlantic. The first R4D- squadron was VR-1 formed at Norfolk, Virginia, followed by VR-2 at Alameda, California, and VR-3 at Kansas City, in February, April and July 1942 respectively. Squadron VR-1 operated between Boston, Massachusetts, and Corpus Christi, Texas, Argentia, Newfoundland, and Trinidad in the British West Indies and later to Iceland and Rio de Janeiro. VR-2 Squadron operated between California and Alaska and to Corpus Christi. These units made up the NATS organisation in the early months of the war. The transports were powered by the Pratt & Whitney R-1830-92 Twin Wasps as used in the C-53s, the C-47s and R4D-1 aircraft.

As footholds were gained in the Pacific islands, so the Navy transport service commenced functioning from August 1942 with the South Pacific Combat Air Transport Service, known as SCAT. This carried fuel into Guadalcanal and did stalwart ambulance work, bringing wounded out of the various combat zones. In the central Pacific, the Central Pacific Combat Transport Air Group – known as TAG, came into being and both organisations were used for jungle supply air drops and transport to and from the battle fronts.

The NATS organisation continued to grow and operate over the longer strategic supply routes, flying over the Hump into China and from Karachi, India, via Africa, the South Atlantic, South America, to the United States, transporting important raw materials such as tin, rubber, tungsten and so on. More squadrons were formed – VR-4 and VR-7 in 1943; VR-5, VR-8, VR-9, VR-10, VR-11 and VR-13 in 1944; and VR-6 in August 1945, with others to follow in the early post-war years. All initially operated the Douglas R4D- transport, followed by the Douglas R5D-Skymaster.

Yet more airliners were drafted in the form of twelve R4D-4 transports, this time acquired by the US Navy from a Pan American Airways DC-3A-447 order. Two of the Navy BuNos. are not known and the rest are from two widely separated batches. The R4D-4 transports were all delivered during January 1943. Some additional Army Air Corps C-53Cs, drafted earlier from Pan American, had been transferred to the Navy in December 1942 and appear in some records as R4D-4Rs with BuNos. 33615 to 33621. These are unfortunately not identified.

The two missing BuNos. in the R4D-4 PAA listing are possibly c/n 4960/1 both delivered as C-53 in December 1942 and going to the US Navy and to Pan American Airways in the same month, becoming registered NC30094 and NC30095. They may have been operated by the airline on military contracts.

c/n	BuNo.	ex PAA
4960		NC34949
4961		NC34950
4962	07000	NC34951
6345	07001	NC34952
6348	07002	NC34955
6349	07003	NC34956
6350	33815	NC34957
6351	33816	NC34958
6352	33817	NC34959
6353	33818	NC34960
6354	33819	NC34961
6355	33820	NC34962

The DC-3 and Airline Developments

It is not generally known that, towards the end of 1938, the Douglas Aircraft Company considered the development of a four-engined DC-3. Apparently in search of four-engine reliability, Panagra initiated interest in such an airliner for operation over their Caribbean and South American routes. On 17 January 1939, Pratt & Whitney agreed to consign to Douglas by April four nine-cylinder Wasp SIHI-G engines with a take-off rating of 650 hp – 50 hp more than the standard engine – for use in a prototype aircraft. It was intended to replace the Stromberg NAY-9 float updraught carburettors with PD9-C pressure carburettors. Ultimately, an entirely new supercharger and rear section for the new engine was designed to employ Chandler-Evans carburettors. The four-engine DC-3 project was unfortunately eventually shelved, and the Pratt & Whitney SIH6-G engine, which would have powered such aeroplanes, was not produced.

Delta Air Lines moved to update its airline fleet in 1939 in response to increased passenger demand, and it concluded that the airline needed larger aircraft. The Lockheed Electra represented great advances over previous Delta equipment, but was not fully competitive with other available models such as the Boeing 247 and the Douglas DC-2 and DC-3. Delta purchased four DC-2s from American Airlines early in 1940, placing them in service on the daytime flight sector between Atlanta, Georgia, and Fort Worth, Texas, a five-hour flight segment. However the DC-2 was already semi-obsolete when Delta acquired it, and would soon be phased out in favour of its much-improved successor.

In the summer of 1940, again responding to an increase in passenger demand, the Delta board of directors decided to purchase new airliners. Two options were available: six DC-3s from Douglas, or seven Model 18 Lodestars from Lockheed. Despite the cost of $115,000 each, the airline purchased the DC-3s, the first of which arrived in Atlanta during January 1941.

In addition to carrying out regular airline operations, which were vitally important in moving military personnel and government officials, Delta contributed greatly to winning the war by performing a number of special high-priority services for both the US Army and the US Navy. In May 1942, the company headquarters in Atlanta were designated a temporary Army Air Corps modification base, under a government contract which remained in force for two years. Cargo services began to wind down in the summer of 1944, but Delta was among the last airlines still flying for the US Air Transport Command when the military took over exclusive operation of its own routes in September 1944. By that time Delta crews had logged nearly 2.5 million miles in this branch of operations, aggregating 6,632,975 passenger miles, 4,894,816,000 lb-miles of cargo, and 9,718,000 lb of mail. Many Delta pilots answered the call to duty; and by the summer of 1942 all senior Delta pilots with military experience had been recalled to active service.

The key to survival for the airlines lay in the effective use of available aircraft, particularly after the military demanded that 221 of the approximately 434 transport planes in commercial service at the beginning of the Second World War be turned over, by sale or lease, to the armed forces. Before the US entry into the war, Delta had been operating five DC-3s and four Lockheed Electras. Six DC-3s had also been ordered to replace the Electras and to accommodate the increased business expected on the company's recently expanded route structure. Shortly after Pearl Harbor, however, the US government requisitioned one of the DC-3s for use in military cargo operations. This was c/n 3280 NC28343, which became C-49D 42-65584 on 22 July 1942 and was operated by the Delta Military Transport Division with effect from 25 July.

During the summer of 1942 the Lockheed Electras were also taken, and by that time any hope of acquiring the additional DC-3s had long since disappeared. It was August 1943 before Delta obtained a re-converted military DC-3. From that point the airline received no authorisation for more transports until July 1944, when it was permitted to add a sixth DC-3; a seventh arrived in September of the same year.

In 1941 over 79,000 persons flew Delta, the airline's highest total up until then. Passenger traffic escalated sharply under the impact of wartime conditions, and in 1944 all previous records were broken, when 164,287 travellers boarded Delta's expanding fleet of DC-3s. By August 1945 the war was over and there was a mammoth leap to 274,823 passengers in that year.

Shortly after the DC-1 made its initial flight on 1 July 1933, Henry Harley 'Hap' Arnold, then a Lieutenant-Colonel in the US Army Air Corps was standing on the flight line at Clover Field, adjacent the Douglas factory, watching with interest the DC-1 airliner and talking with his long-time friend Donald Douglas. During the bad winter of 1932/33 Arnold had been responsible for organising an air drop from his base at March Field, Riverside, California to hundred of Indians who faced starvation buried in deep snow on their reservations in Arizona.

'Doug,' he said, 'what we now need is a cargo ship along the lines of the DC-1. The day is almost upon us when the ground forces will be fully dependant upon an aerial supply line. The hell of it is, if the Air Corps were to buy some of these planes, the appropiations people would think the top brass wanted plush jobs to fly around in. It would be very hard to convince them we were buying an aerial mule. Maybe, that's what we need – an aerial mule.'

Little did Arnold realise that his aerial mule would become a reality and perform so many Herculean tasks. Donald Douglas undoubtedly already had the idea of building a cargo version of the Douglas Commercial, and he knew his sales team were working on a presentation for the Air Corps procurement personnel from the Materiel Division at Wright Field. Jack Frye of TWA had approached Douglas about converting the DC-2 into an aerial freighter. Chief of the US Army Air Corps at that time was Major-General Benjamin D. Foulais, who was initially against the Air Corps including the DC-2 in the competition for a new contract for the procurement of thirty-six cargo aircraft of the single-engine type. Douglas had submitted a formal proposal to build twenty transports – modified DC-2s – for the Air Corps at a cost of $61,775, plus $20,500 for the engines.

Competing with the Fokker and Ford Tri-motor, a Bellanca and a Fairchild entry, the Douglas DC-2 was placed first with the aggregate figures of merit of 786 points, with the Fairchild entry second. Despite General Foulais's reservations, he finally approved an order for eighteen Douglas transports, to be designated C-33. Performance-wise they could carry a useful load of more than 6,000 lb, and fly at speeds in excess of 165 mp for non-stop distances of over 900 miles. The planes were modified to meet the Army Air Corps needs for carrying bulky cargo and introduced many new innovations.

On 24 December 1935, 'Benny' Foulais was replaced as Chief of the Air Corps by Brigadier-General Oscar E. Westover, and on 27 December Donald Douglas' friend 'Hap' Arnold, promoted to Brigadier-General, became Westover's new Assistant Chief. There was nothing coincidental about Arnold making a phone call to Douglas shortly after his appointment. He had been reading reports about the new Douglas DST/DC-3 transport and wanted first-hand news on the DC-3 to back up Air Corps interest in larger, faster transport planes. Arnold urged his personnel to study the prospect of converting the DC-3 into a military cargo aircraft. Douglas accepted the challenge, and the Air Corps responded by ordering the C-39 hybrid aircraft. It had a DC-2 fuselage, a DC-3 tail unit and was powered by Wright 975 hp R-1820-55 Cyclone engines generating 2,200 rpm. At this time Santa Monica was busy with a flood of orders for DC-3s from airlines all over the world and was also snarled up by change after change in the military specification and requirements from the Air Corps. It was 16 January 1939 before the first C-39 (DC-2-243) c/n 2057 serial 38-499 was nicknamed. It became known as the 'DC-2½', but had a DC-3 centre section added to the narrow DC-2 fuselage and short outer wing panels. A total of thirty-five were ordered and delivered.

Air Transport Operations

Along with the earlier C-35s, the new C-39s became the nucleus for the US Army Air Corps' first systemised air transport operation. They equipped the 10th Air Transport Group, organised during 1939 at Patterson Field, near Dayton, Ohio. Patterson was the home of the huge Fairfield Air Depot, one of a nationwide system of supply depots, coming under the Materiel Division based at Wright Field. The group started their own military-type airline, linking Fairfield with other depots located at Middletown, Pennsylvania, Sacramento, California, and others in Oregon and Utah. The silver aerial freighters of the newly-organised seven transport squadrons flew daily schedules between the depots. The 1st Transport Squadron was located at Patterson Field; the 2nd at Langley Field, Virginia, moving to Olmstead, Pennsylvania, early in 1940; the 3rd at Duncan Field, Texas; the 4th at McClellan Field, California; the 5th at Olmstead, then moving to Patterson; the 6th at Olmstead; and the 7th at McClellan. Day and night the transports flew, carrying aircraft engines, vital spare parts and key personnel to and from the expanding Air Corps squadrons, all part of the build-up of US air power as the war clouds gathered over Europe. The need for adequate air transport was vital.

The ubiquitous Douglas Commercial Two and Three, still wearing the insignia and livery of the US airlines, went on war emergency status long before their military counterpart, the C-47 'Skytrain', was even out of the jigs in the Douglas factory. A United Air Lines converted cargo-liner made headlines early in 1941 when it carried a bulky half-ton diesel-engine crankshaft from Chicago to San Francisco. It was bound for Pearl Harbor. It was the first time such a huge piece of machinery had been moved by air. On another cargo flight, a DC-3 flew a complete telephone exchange from Chicago to a large magnesium plant near Las Vegas, Nevada. It was to be the nucleus for a vital communications centre for Los Alamos, White Sands in New Mexico, site of the 'Manhattan Project'.

At Fort St John, a vital Alaskan outpost, there was a need for a sawmill to build barracks for personnel working on the Alcan Highway, a cog in the huge wheel of defence logistic plans. A commercial cargo DC-3 flew in the complete unit. On another occasion, when fire destroyed the infirmary at Nome, Alaska, two DC-3 airliners flew a twenty-six-bed hospital complete with X-ray equipment, hypodermic needles and rubber gloves etc. The shipment arrived forty-eight hours after the teletype request was received. After hostile Japanese submarines had been sighted off the Pacific seaboard, air defences were strengthened and there was an urgent need for pursuit aircraft. Curtiss P-40s were flown over the Rockies in United Air Lines cargoliners. The tiny fighter fuselages were packed inside the DC-3s, whilst the wings were slung in special brackets underneath the fuselage.

When General Claire Chennault, head of the American Volunteer Group (AVG) – the 'Flying Tigers' – needed aircraft tyres, American Airlines DC-3s, the 'Flagships' of the fleet, flew 20,000 lb of rubber tyres from New York to Los Angeles. The shipment was then transferred to Pan Americans' Boeing Clipper flying-boats and flown across the Pacific for onward transportation to the air bases in China.

Flying the new air routes worldwide the Douglas Commercials pioneered them daily, writing a new chapter in transportation history. Anything and everything was moved by air: dynamite, eggs, gold bullion, beetles from the Fiji Islands to fight other beetles which were destroying war crops of hemp in Honduras. All went into the cargo holds of the aerial mules.

Postwar DC-3 Production

After the end of the Second World War the air transport system of the free world quickly reorganised, utilising the hundreds upon hundreds of airfields, large and small, which had been constructed during the conflict, enabling an air service to be provided in previously remote areas. To support these air services there was a generous supply of surplus military transports, among them the Douglas DC-3/C-47/C-53, easily adaptable for commercial service as fully-licensed civil aircraft at a moderate conversion cost. Both United States and foreign airlines were quick to purchase surplus DC-3s at prices quoted between $8,000 and $15,000. Many that were based overseas at the end of the war were assembled for storage at the huge maintenance units and air depots, a substantial number being sold locally without ever returning to the USA. Some of the DC-3s built pre-war and confiscated by the Germans were 'liberated', and either returned to their original owners or found new ones. It was an open market.

Surviving Douglas Commercial transports in Japan both US- and Japanese-made versions, were scrapped rather than declared surplus to requirements. A few 'Tabby' transports based in China at the time of the surrender were transferred to – or rather confiscated by – the Chinese Air Force. Russian-built Lisunov Li-2s plus Lend-Lease C-47s were used by the Russian state airline, Aeroflot and supplied to both military air arms and civil airlines of countries under Russian influence, including Poland and Hungary – certainly none of the C-47s were returned to the US government which had supplied them.

In the United States, the Douglas Aircraft Company felt there was still a demand for the DC-3 equipped to full post-war civil standards and so put on the market converted surplus military C-47s, plus some completely newly-built airliners.

The initial post-war DC-3 transports were twenty-one former military C-47s modified by Douglas at Santa Monica to pre-war airline standards, fitted out with twenty-one-passenger seating. The large cargo door was replaced by a hinge-down air stair, and

a DC-3 left-hand-side baggage door installed. New c/ns were allocated to these rebuilds – 43073/43092 and 43154, all licensed under the pre-war DC-3A Type Certificate A-669. The first, formerly a Long Beach-built C-47A-DL 43-30674 c/n 13825, was used briefly as a company demonstration aircraft before being sold. Whilst with the Douglas Aircraft Company it made the second use of the NC30000 registration, initially used on the DC-3A demonstrator c/n 4122 which the US Army had taken over as a C-53 'Skytrooper' in 1942.

Thousands of surplus C-47 military transports were converted worldwide, mostly by small independent companies pleased to do the work assisted by Douglas-approved drawings. This cost much less than having the transport converted at the Douglas factory. Some airlines did their own conversions at a cost of approximately $10,000. Following conversion, the DC-3Cs received supplementary nameplates issued by the converting agency, giving the new designation, date, agency title, etc. The original Douglas factory nameplate carrying the c/n, the contract number and engine model, etc, was also retained. The plates were to be found on the right-hand bulkhead immediately behind the co-pilot's seat. Unfortunately, on odd occasions, the DC-3 buff would find these vital plates missing. The author is the proud owner of at least two nameplates from disposed Douglas Commercial transports. However, there are two inspection panels located in the main wing centre section which, when opened, will reveal the factory c/n.

It was discovered that surplus C-53 'Skytrooper' transports required less modification; they became licensed as DC-3As under ATC A-669.

There was no standardisation of doors, seating or even windows among the non-Douglas post-war DC-3C conversions. Many retained their large double cargo doors even though they were used for passenger-carrying. Others used smaller DC-3-type doors modified to hinge downwards and serve as an air stair for simplified passenger use. Some transports modified for high-density passenger work were fitted with eight cabin windows on either side. Many former military C-47s were fitted with a standard DC-3 tail cone, but others retained the cut-away used when towing gliders. Those used primarily for cargo work naturally retained the double cargo doors, tilted rear floor and the tie-down points in the metal floor, plus the six left- and seven right-hand-side windows. None of these many variations, or subsequent changes with new owners, affected approval under ATC A-669.

At the Oklahoma City factory, from which the Douglas Aircraft Company produced a total of 5,381 military DC-3 transports, twenty-eight surplus C-117A airframes were completed as civil DC-3D airliners. These differed very little from their original military configuration and were allocated c/ns 42954/42981 under ATC A-669.

The twenty-one Douglas DC-3s built post-war at Santa Monica were the last of 10,655 transports built. The last of all, c/n 43154 ex-c/n 12276, was delivered on 21 March 1947 to Sabena in Brussels as OO-AWH. Unfortunately it crashed in thick fog whilst attempting a landing at London (Heathrow) Airport on 2 March 1948. Many of the remainder were built and sold to oil companies, banks, and the last seven to Sabena. Waterman Airlines purchased three, the huge Vanderbilt empire one, the Chase National Bank of the City of New York one, the Gulf Oil Corporation one and the Creole Petroleum Corporation one. The United Aircraft Corporation of Hartford, Connecticut, which had designed and built so many power-plants for the DC-3, also bought one of the last models.

The Swan Song of the DC-3

It was evident to the Douglas Aircraft Company that due to the deluge of the secondhand market by war-surplus Douglas Commercial transports, mainly from the C-47 'Skytrain' family, there was just no need for new DC-3 transports. A substantial order book never materialised after 1945. In Europe conversions were carried out by Avio Diepen and Fokker NV in the Netherlands, and Scottish Aviation and Field Aircraft Services in the United Kingdom. In Canada ex-RCAF transports were converted to civilian use by Canadair Ltd. Some of these companies carried out simple conversions, whilst several specialist companies in the United States carried out a complete modification and refurbishing programme. These included the huge Garrett Corporation AiResearch Aviation Service, located at Los Angeles and Long Beach airports, which installed extra fuel tanks in the DC-3s outer wing panels, so increasing the range by 800 miles.

For executive DC-3s, AiResearch installed more powerful engines which boosted take-off power from 1,200 to 1,350 hp; they also substituted the Pratt & Whitney R-1830-92 Twin Wasps for R-1830-94 engines. The cruising speed was increased by 20 mph and, having a better single- engine performance, added 1,700lb to the permissible gross weight for a total of 26,900 lb. The larger engines were also 'teamed' with geared rudder and aileron trim tabs incorporating mechanical boost systems, so increasing flight safety under all conditions.

One of the greatest single advances in modernising the DC-3 was a new 'maximiser kit', designed by AiResearch. With no increase in engine horsepower, the kit provided an increase of 20mph whilst adding a measurable margin of safety, payload, economy and revenue. The maximiser kit included a completely integrated and newly-designed system of engine cowling, baffles, oil cooler ducting, wheel-well doors and exhaust system. The streamlining restricted buffeting and vibration.

To bring the modified DC-3 up-to-date and also to compete with more modern, radar-equipped aircraft, AiResearch designed a nose modification kit and radome for weather radar installation involving Radio Corporation of America (RCA), Bendix and Collins equipment without any change in air speed limitation. The company also introduced the DC-3 with the new Madsen light system, which substantially lessened the chances of a mid-air collision by indicating the aircraft's position, altitude and direction. For the plush executive airliner DC-3 they introduced four large panoramic windows replacing the conventional fourteen 12 by 16 in windows with a Viewmaster version which consisted of eight 17 by 17 in and four giant 17 by 57 in panoramic windows of extra-thick plexiglass.

Inside, the DC-3 was completely transformed with special fabrics, colours of any hue, wood panelling from any country, wing-backed, contoured, reclining chairs, luxurious divans, private sleeping quarters if requested. The whole decor and furnishings were lightweight, fireproof and blended to individual taste with infinite care and skill.

Houston Lumber had a DC-3 fitted with mink-covered door knobs. The furniture in the Alcoa DC-3 was naturally all gleaming aluminium. It was not uncommon for such executive Douglas Commercials to be fitted out with hi-fi, tape recorders and telephones, plus refreshment consoles and bar. Pillsbury Mills, the biscuit manufacturer, equipped a DC-3 as a flying laboratory to test the quick-rising properties of biscuit mix at varying altitudes, whilst a number of other firms used the DC-3 as a flying showroom and real estate agents gave prospective home buyers the chance to view property from the air. One of the plushiest of the plush DC-3 was one modified for Conrad Hilton. There was wool carpeting on the floor, a light beige ceiling of vinyl-backed fabric wall covering, lightweight walnut paneling with contrasting band of bamboo mat. Large view-master windows replaced conventional DC-3 windows, one on each side, with six other large-size windows on each side. Reclining seats and a divan were fitted in the main cabin, plus tables, lamps, TV, AM radio, stereo tape recorder etc. A large galley occupied the front of the cabin, whilst in the rear a modern lounge with modern toilet and washing facilities was installed.

Montgomery Ward employed a pair of DC-3s to fly its executives around, and Sears Roebuck had a DC-3 that flew a shuttle between its big store outlets up and down the length of California. The huge Ford Motor Car Company operated no less than three DC-3s for short-haul flights. They were fitted with dictaphone and typewriter facilities. Goodyear used a DC-3 to test a new crosswind landing gear that it had developed. As late as 1966 an executive DC-3 fitted with sixteen-place interior, latest avionics, an autopilot and radar could be purchased for $125,000 cash.

A pre-war DC-3-201A c/n 2102, built for Eastern Air Lines as NC21743 and delivered on 9 February 1939, was heavily modified during 1951 for the TV personality Arthur Godfrey and refitted with Pratt & Whitney R-2000 engines, giving it the unofficial designation DC-3A-2000. The 1,450 hp engines were used in the Douglas DC-4/C-54 'Skymaster' transport and, being slightly larger, had the propeller proud from the nacelle, a few inches further ahead of the tip of the cowling. Registered NIM, the Godfrey DC-3 also had panoramic windows fitted and later became the private executive transport of the Governor of South Carolina.

More common, and less costly, was the engine change to replace the Wright Cyclone engines of pre-war DC-3s and fit the more popular Pratt & Whitney Twin Wasps; these DC-3s were then re-designated DC-3A. Such modifications did not affect ATC A-669; they were documented as Supplement Type Certificates (STC) to A-669 and approved by the US government. Other changes were relatively minor and included the removal of the right-hand passenger door, where fitted, and installing either a single left-hand door or the large double cargo doors, enlarging cabin windows and replacing the exhaust-muff cabin heating system with separate gasoline-burning combustion heaters. These were just a few of the many modifications made.

As the many DC-3s were phased out of the trunk airline routes they became the mainstay of a new type of airline, known as the regional carrier. These served the smaller cities off the main trunk routes on a 'hub and spoke' system; low cost and fast turn-around became the hallmarks of their operation, which used small terminals with few facilities. However, the odd trunk carrier such as Mohawk Airlines still had DC-3s in its fleet in 1960. On 10 October 1960 Mohawk introduced its 'Gas Light Service' and to make the DC-3s more appealing they dressed up the interiors to resemble a Victorian setting, adding velvet curtains with gold tassles, Currier and Ive prints, and carriage lamps. Stewardesses dressed in Naughty Nineties costumes complete with sequins and ostrich feathers, served five-cent cigars, free beer and cheese and pretzels.

Initially, men only were allowed on the 'Gas Light Service' because Mohawk felt that women would find the atmosphere unpleasant. The airline stressed that women and children were, of course, most welcome aboard all of Mohawk's other flights.

Mostly businessmen filled the seats, but women charged the airline with sexual discrimination. Bowing to their objections, Mohawk boxed off a 'family parlour' in the front of the DC-3. The men retained their 'Naughty Nineties club car', where they drank the free beer and puffed on smelly cigars.

More than 23,000 passengers flew the 'Gas Light Service' DC-3s, drinking 31,700 cans of beer, smoking 17,600 five-cent cigars, and consuming a ton of pretzels and half a ton of cheese in the one year of operation.

The Douglas Aircraft Company took just twenty days to convert a military C-47 into a commercial DC-3. They modified the wings and the undercarriage, gutted the interiors and removed all the military equipment. Carpeting, air conditioning and other comforts were installed. By 1947, more than 500 conversions were flying for the US airlines, plus several hundred elsewhere in the world.

Remmert-Werner of St Louis, Missouri, was another major company which transformed the Douglas transport, converting the first in December 1946. By the early 1950s it had revitalised more than 200 Second World War 'Gooney Birds'. One all-freight and unique airline – The Winged Cargo Company – even used war surplus Waco CG-4A gliders towed by DC-3s to haul cargo. The Civil Aeronautics Board (CAB) issued a licence in May 1946, allowing the airline to use two converted C-47s and two CG-4A Hadrian gliders.

In 1949, William Littlewood, then Vice-President of American Airlines, spoke at the retirement ceremonies for '*Flagship Newark*', the last DC-3 in their fleet.

'The DC-3 is the victim of progress,' he said. 'There are so many advantages in speed, comfort and safety in the newer Douglas DC-6s and Convair Flagships that the old DC-3 is outmoded. Delivered to American Airlines on 28 August 1936, the '*Flagship Newark*' was the seventh ship built. She has spent four of her thirteen years in the air. She has been through a war, and survived with no more than a damaged wing-tip. She has been through two conversions and seven complete overhauls. Somebody will buy and fly the '*Flagship Newark*' because she will probably never wear out.'

The Douglas records show that '*Flagship Newark*' NC16007, a DST-144 c/n 1549 was the twelvth aircraft built, delivered to the airline on 28 August 1936. On 31 May 1949 it was sold to the L.B. Smith Aircraft Corporation in Miami, Florida; it later served in South America but by 1977 had been withdrawn from use.

If and when the Grand Old Lady is ever grounded completely, it will not be because it ran out of work. It will be a combination of many things, including economics, lack of spare parts, fuel costs and availability of hundred-octane fuel. Already the DC-3 has suffered separately from most of these, and still survived.

Finally, Arthur Raymond explained its longevity this way: 'It survived for more than fifty years because it was the best. It was an extremely simple structural design. There were no concentrated load points, except for the landing gear, thus making its life virtually endless. Replacement of individual parts was so easy.'

Interior modifications to the DC-3 were many as depicted here with DC-3-201B N21728 c/n 2144 of North Central Airlines. Wall-to-wall carpeting, reclining seats, couch, enlarged windows plus a TV set, stereo type tape system were just some of the many comfort features. In June 1975 this DC-3 was donated to the Henry Ford Museum at Dearborn, Michigan, after completing 84,875 flight hours. (North Central)

This Super DC-3 registered N30000 is c/n 43301 N21270. It was the first of 100 converted for the US Navy. It is registered to the Lan Dale Corporation and based at Tucson, Arizona. It was rolled out in this livery during May 1990. After US Navy use as BuNo.17175 and storage it was registered to Hawkins & Powers Aviation Inc. based at Greybull, Wyoming. (Ed Davies)

On 27 October 1982, the second commercial DC-3S was purchased by Aero Union Corporation and based at Chico in northern California as N567M. During November 1983 they sold it to an operator based in Missouri. It is seen parked at Chico on 21 June 1983. (Jay Wright)

Based at Whitman Field, Oshkosh, Wisconsin, Warren Basler founded Basler Airlines in 1957, and today is involved in converting and rebuilding DC-3s to turboprop standard. These are for the civil market and for US Government contracts for South American Air Forces. Depicted is N300BF c/n 26744 ex-N300TX in smart livery. (Jan Stroomenbergh)

Early in 1991 Basler received a contract from the US Forest Service to convert their two vintage DC-3s with turboprops at a cost of $2.7 million each. Depicted is N142Z c/n 20494 after conversion and seen parked at Bellingham Airport, Washington State, whilst in transit to Alaska. (Ralph Peterson)

Douglas DC-4 NC90423 c/n 18932 seen in American Airlines System livery as Flagship Washington. *It was delivered to the airline on 7 December 1945 and was one of 50 ex-military transports procured post-war. This one was ex-USAAF 43-17192.* (AP Photo Library)

This Douglas C-54 was unique in that it still retains its USAAF serial 42-107439 c/n 7458, yet is in American Airlines livery as Flagship America. *It was later registered as a DC-4 NC90414 and was one of 50 converted to airline standards by Republic Aviation.* (AP Photo Library)

This Braathens S.A.F.E. (South America & Far East) poster depicts one of its DC-4s LN-HAT c/n 10358 Norse Skyfarer *delivered to Oslo on 11 February 1947. Three DC-4s were purchased at the end of 1946. A group of shipowners Braathens commenced operations with the type in February 1947 operating a 'tramp' service along the main shipping routes initially.* (Braathens)

ABOVE: *This VC-54 42-107451 c/n 7470 was specially modified to serve as the personal transport for President Roosevelt and was named* Sacred Cow. *It was fitted with a state-room, three conference rooms, and was equipped with six bunks. It was delivered on 4 December 1943.* (Douglas)

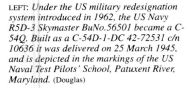

LEFT: *Under the US military redesignation system introduced in 1962, the US Navy R5D-3 Skymaster BuNo.56501 became a C-54Q. Built as a C-54D-1-DC 42-72531 c/n 10636 it was delivered on 25 March 1945, and is depicted in the markings of the US Naval Test Pilots' School, Patuxent River, Maryland.* (Douglas)

LEFT: *Delta's first DC-4, NC37472 c/n 10444 ex-C54B-1-DC 42-72339 was delivered on 12 February 1946 after conversion at Santa Monica. This was Douglas's tenth post-war conversion and it served Delta until 6 February 1953 when it was sold to Irving Herman, owner of Super Coach.* (Delta)

Chapter Six
Douglas DC-3S (Super DC-3)

After the end of the Second World War, a number of Douglas DC-3 replacement transports appeared on the market; the Martin 202/404 and the Convair 340/440 series of airliners were two examples, but these were considerably faster, had a larger passenger and cargo capacity and were naturally much more expensive designs than the Douglas DC-3. After rebuilding some war surplus C-47s and C-117s as the DC-3C and DC-3D, the Douglas Aircraft Company quickly decided to act on the old adage 'that the only replacement for a DC-3 was another DC-3'.

Production of the DC-3 had ended in 1946, and a search for a successor began. Naturally Douglas had a vital interest in finding the right replacement, and some preliminary work was carried out during 1947. Later, the threat of impending US Civil Air Regulations, too stringent to allow a renewal of airworthiness certificates for the standard DC-3 and converted wartime C-47s, lent a new urgency to the replacement project.

While it is quite true to say that the origins of the DC-3S or Super DC-3 lay in the original DC-3, the practical origin dates back to 12 July 1944. It was on this date that the US aircraft manufacturers were granted permission to construct prototype civil aircraft for the post-war airline market. Up to that time, all the effort had been devoted to military aircraft production on an enormous scale. By mid-1944, however, the supply of aircraft was more than adequate, and the course of the war suggested that the final outcome would be favourable to the Allied powers. Consequently, critical resources and raw materials could begin to be diverted to meet the requirements of the post-war period. While many US aircraft manufacturers saw their post-war sales markets as related to wartime contracts, a number of manufacturers such as Martin and Convair were quick to look at the market for short-haul aircraft for delivery in the early post-war years. Most aircraft manufacturers had groups of engineers tasked with research into products to keep the production lines intact after the cessation of hostilities – many contracts for wartime transports were cancelled as victory came into sight. Douglas was busy with the extended C-54 'Skymaster' series up to the DC-6, and Lockheed was equally busy with the C-69 'Constellation' family.

At the Douglas Aircraft Company, the post-war era appeared to be heavily involved with transport aircraft. They were the leading supplier of both short- and long-range transports for the military services in the United States and for the Allies under Lend-Lease. The Douglas products were readily adaptable to civil airline operations. The C-54 'Skymaster' in particular was being stretched, re-engined and pressurised under the guise of the military XC-112. After building almost 11,000 civil and military DC-3s in three factories, Douglas was clearly aiming at the long-haul airline market with its DC-6 and DC-7 design. As both monetary and human assets could be stretched so far, Douglas elected to forgo the short-haul airline market and concentrate on long-haul transports. It was assumed that the many surplus C-47s would provide most of the short-haul civil air transport capacity in the post-war era, and this initially proved correct as thousands of war surplus C-47s opened the world to modern air transport.

However, the US Civil Aviation Administration – CAA – was considering withdrawing the type certificate for the DC-3, as it did not satisfy the latest International Civil Aviation Organisation – ICAO – safety regulations on single-engined operation. Although this threat never did materialise, the Douglas Aircraft Company decided that there might be a market for a modernised version of the DC-3. The huge Reconstruction Finance Corporation, a United States storage body formed to dispose of government surplus materials, handled thousands of C-47s up to March 1946, when the task was taken over by the War Assets Administration; many of these transports were converted for civil use either as airliners or cargo aircraft.

In the late 1940s there was a sudden demand from the airlines for a short-haul aircraft which had many features until then associated with the larger long-haul aircraft, such as pressurisation, engine commonality, high cruising speeds and improved airfield performance to include the new landing aids then being introduced. Consequently, the airline order books began to grow for the Convair 240 and its derivatives, and the series of Martin twins. Even Curtiss-Wright received orders from Eastern Air Lines for pressurised versions of the civil CW-20 design derived from the military C-46 Commando. Market research showed that there was indeed a market for a short-haul aircraft, with better performance and amenities than the Douglas DC-3. However, since the DC-3 was still available in such large numbers at very low cost, with adequate stocks of spares, it continued to be the backbone of the US civil transport fleet providing local-service and non-scheduled carriers with the bulk of their fleet equipment.

Conversion from the DC-3

Despite the DC-3 being the most widely used transport aircraft throughout the world, there was a threat to its future. In the United States the new generation of transport aircraft were being certified to Civil Air Regulations (CAR) Part 4b, whilst the earlier generation of aircraft, which included the DC-3, were being certificated under the less stringent performance requirements of Part 7. The new Part 4b criteria, referred to as 'Transport Category', called for improved engine-out rates of climb, better fire-protection equipment and better safety margins of operating performance than had previously been required. After any accident involving a non-scheduled carrier DC-3, the clamour grew to ground the 'unsafe' DC-3. The CAA examined the situation and proposed that after a certain date, no DC-3 aircraft would be eligible for certification as a passenger aircraft. The protests of the many airline operators were heard in Washington DC, and a battle for the DC-3's survival had begun. With hundreds of DC-3s still in service with US carriers the impact of such an action would have been disastrous. The practicalities of the situation demanded that the DC-3s continue to fly, and the deadline for its non-airworthiness was put back several times until finally in 1953 the CAA admitted defeat, accepted that the DC-3 would have to continue flying and scrapped the proposed regulations.

During this period of uncertainty over the future of the DC-3, a number of options were explored to improve the transport. At this point the Douglas Aircraft Company became involved. To save engineering time and cost and to reduce the price whilst providing new life for the large number of DC-3s and derivatives which were menaced by the expiry of their airworthiness certificates in 1952, the company decided to concentrate its efforts on modernising existing aircraft rather than designing an entirely new one. After initial design work had been completed by a team comprising many of the original designers of the DC-3, the new project was transferred to a special group headed by M.K. Oleson. To meet the new civil air regulations, the aircraft's stability, single-engined performance and take-off had to be improved, and competitive pressures made it necessary to improve its speed.

Whilst it was true that some larger air carriers could afford the new Martin and Convair airliners, many operators of the DC-3 could not. Most of the major US scheduled airlines were still relying on the DC-3 with large fleets, and a potential market for the replacement or modification of this unique Douglas product still existed. Even Douglas felt that a new design would be prohibitively expensive, but that the modification of existing airframes might provide the answer with a significant improvement in performance at modest cost. Engineering design studies were carried out to meet the problems identified by the CAA. These included stability, single-engine performance, and take-off and landing distance. The company reviewed service difficulty reports for the previous ten years in order to correct operating problems which were not directly of a safety nature. Initially it was felt that modification of the DC-3 would be advantageous from a parts commonality viewpoint, as well as being able to offer the choice of Wright or Pratt & Whitney engines which had been previously available as an option to DC-3 operators.

The team, lead by M.K. Oleson as the Super DC-3 Project Engineer, was soon involved in the huge task of developing the

This model of the new DC-3S Super DC-3 is outlined with the extremities of the original DC-3 transport. There were six major areas where modification was necessary, these being so extensive that a new Type Certificate resulted. This certificate was issued on 24 July 1950. (Douglas)

solutions to the problems, as well as engineering and supervising the actual conversion of an airframe which was carried out at the Santa Monica factory. By late 1948, the decision had been taken to go ahead with the Super DC-3 project, and work commenced on detailed drawings, wind-tunnel testing, etc.

Specification

The engineering evaluation revealed six major areas in which modification work needed to be carried out in order to convert a standard DC-3 to a DC-3 fitting the Super specification. These were power-plants, drag reduction, cabin modification and expansion, the outer wing panels, the vertical and horizontal tail surfaces, and other ancillary systems and modifications. These planned modifications were so extensive that a new Approved Type Certificate – 6A2 – was issued to the Super DC-3s in addition to new Douglas factory constructors' numbers. When the Type Certificate was awarded on 24 July 1950, the new DC-3 had finally achieved Part 4b performance standards.

As with all new aircraft designs, the choice of a suitable power-plant was important. The two available were a nine-cylinder Wright R-1820-C9HE single row offering 1,475 hp, or a fourteen-cylinder, twin-row Pratt & Whitney R-2000-D5 or -D7 rated at 1,450 hp, both of which compared favourably with the standard 1,200 hp R-1820 or R-1830 engines which powered most DC-3s. Both engines were in full production at the time the Super DC-3, now designated DC-3S, was being marketed, and the choice would be made on the basis of airline fleet commonality. The 25 hp difference made for very slight variations in gross weights and performance, and there was a weight penalty of about 200 lbs per engine with the R-2000 compared to the R-1820.

Whichever engine was selected, the redesigned nacelle fully enclosed the main undercarriage and included low-drag air scoops for both the oil cooler and the carburettor. A short type exhaust stack was used, which provided a jet thrust effect when exhaust gases were discharged. The engine thrust line was tilted down by two degrees to increase nose down pitching movement caused by the enlarged horizontal tail surfaces. The use of dynafocal engine mounts reduced the transmission of engine vibration to the airframe structure.

Drag reduction was considered vital to the new DC-3S design and included a partially retractable tail wheel with a fairing, the use of flush riveting on the new outer wing panels and tail surfaces, a low-drag radio antennae, flush riveting the lower centre section tank covers, replacement of external air scoops with flush units, and flush mounting of the cockpit windshields using strengthened glass to resist bird strikes.

Donald Douglas was fortunate in being able to consult most of the team which had designed and developed the DC-1: Arthur Raymond and Fred Stineman were chief designers deeply engrossed in a design study of a DC-8 jet airliner; 'Doc' Oswald with his team of aerodynamicists was involved; and the structures branch experts sat in on the many conferences involving the new DC-3 project, with Douglas himself presiding.

The most obvious change to the fuselage was the insertion of a 39 in-long plug at about the leading edge of the wing. This, combined with the movement aft of the rear compartment bulkhead, provided an increase of 79 inches in usable cabin length. The forward cargo compartment in the standard DC-3 was eliminated and combined with a larger cargo compartment in the tail area which was easily accessible from the ground. An airstair door was incorporated to eliminate the need for ground equipment for passenger or cargo loading.

The completely redesigned outer wing panels were required to improve stability and stall characteristics, and to eliminate the tip stall characteristics of the old DC-3 wing, 3½ degrees of wash-out at the wing-tip was added and the new aerofoil section was tapered to meet the old section at the wing root. To move the centre of pressure further back to accommodate a wider range of centre of gravity travel, the sweepback of the outer wing panel leading edge was increased to 15½ degrees. The final improvement brought about by the new wing panels was an increase in strength to handle higher gross weights as well as minimising induced and parasitic drag by the use of flush skin joints and flush riveting.

Considerable work was carried out to the vertical and horizontal tail surfaces in order to accommodate the increased engine power, fuselage length and centre of gravity range. The span of the tailplane was increased by some 42 per cent, and completely new aerofoil sections used. In addition, a downspring was added to the elevator control system further to improve stability over the entire centre of gravity range. Geared trim tabs were incorporated in each elevator. Vertical stabiliser and rudder areas were increased significantly, and a geared trim tab was included on the rudder to reduce engine-out control forces. The first Super DC-3 built was flown with a triangular rudder which more closely resembled that of the original DC-3. This design proved inadequate, so additional area was added to the leading edge and this became standard. When completed, the redesigned vertical tail surfaces bore a striking resemblance to the tail design of the Douglas DC-6, which, as we shall see later in this book, was already in service.

There were other less visible changes made to improve the performance of the DC-3, particularly in respect of its take-off and single-engined performance. An autofeather system was incorporated in the engine torque nose case to speed feathering of the propeller in the event of an engine failure. This together with an improved hydraulic system – 750 psi increased to 1,100 psi – led to a much quicker landing-gear retraction time which improved take-off distance and second segment climb performance significantly. The undercarriage also received an additional compressed air extension system as well as the normal and back-up hydraulic systems. As jet exhaust pipes prevented the use of exhaust collector-ring heating for the cabin, a separate gasoline combustion heater was installed below the cabin floor.

DC-3S Prototype

According to one reliable source, the Douglas Aircraft Company paid about $8,000 each for two DC-3s purchased from airlines for use in the new Super DC-3 conversion programme. When the 'Super Three' was ready for the airline market its price tag ranged from $140,000 to $200,000, depending upon the interior configuration required by the purchaser. However, it was almost an entirely new aeroplane.

With the engineering and design well under way, the company needed a standard DC-3 to become the prototype DC-3S. There was no need to go far in the search for a suitable candidate: Western Air Lines sold DC-3 NC56592 c/n 6017 to the company for cash. The transport had been built at Long Beach as a military C-47 41-18656, delivered to the USAAF on 5

Hangar scene at Santa Monica on 4 March 1949, with the first DC-3S fuselage under conversion. The gap in the fuselage for the thirty-nine inch insertion is evident in this photograph. The aircraft had been operated by Western Air Lines as NC56592. (Douglas)

November 1942, and had served with the 5th Army Air Force in Australia during the war. After being declared surplus it had been purchased by Western on 9 October 1945.

On completion of the extensive modernisation programme, c/n 6017 emerged from the Santa Monica factory as the first DC-3S, received the new c/n 43158 and registered with the company as N30000. Powered by two Wright R-1820-C9HE engines, the aircraft made its first flight from Clover Field on 23 June 1949, with John F. Martin at the controls. Flight test results exceeded all hopes and there was little doubt that the Super DC-3 would meet all expectations and Civil Air Regulations requirements while offering increased payload and improved performance. Compared with the DC-3C, maximum speed increased from 230 mph to 270 mph, cruising speed from 207 mph to 251 mph, and initial rate of climb from 1,130 ft per minute to 1,300 ft per minute. Following completion of the flight trials programme the new aircraft was used by the Douglas Aircraft Company for a sales tour of the United States.

Just over a year elapsed before the Super DC-3 was awarded its Approved Type Certificate on 24 July 1950, and the project which had commenced as a modification of the tried and true DC-3 in reality had produced an aircraft which the chief engineer on the project declared was 60 per cent new.

The tour of the US commenced in October 1949, in California and eventually covered some 10,000 miles within the USA, Canada and Mexico. The large potential market thought to exist overseas caused Douglas to examine the possibility of licensing service centres in Europe and South America to make potential conversions. Furthermore, discussions were held with the Canadian Car & Foundry Ltd, located in Montreal, for production of DC-3S conversions in Canada. Scottish Aviation, located at Prestwick airport, south of Glasgow, would have been a likely centre for any conversions required in Europe, as they had done military C-47 overhauls for the USAAF, plus civil conversions which had sold throughout Europe and Asia. They had converted British European Airways' fleet of over fifty DC-3s to the super-luxury 'Pionair' standard, and these conversions may well have turned out very differently if the DC-3S programme had gone ahead. In fact, the only Douglas Super DC-3 conversions were those processed at Santa Monica.

The new Super DC-3S N30000 c/n 43158 made its maiden flight from Clover Field on 23 June 1949, and is depicted during October during flight tests and airline demonstrations. This was the first of five commercial models.
(AP Photo Library)

The prototype N30000 c/n 43158 had an executive interior, and both thirty-one and thirty-seven seat capacities were offered. All the major US carriers operating the DC-3, as well as many local service operators, were able to witness the new DC-3S in action and take demonstration flights. The aircraft was demonstrated at Dallas, Houston, Memphis, Atlanta, Washington, Chicago, New York and Kansas City. Many of the trunk carriers visited still had significant fleets of the standard DC-3 in service. United and TWA still operated sixty-nine each, Eastern Air Lines had fifty-one, Delta and Mid-Continent twenty each. Smaller airlines such as Capital operated twenty-four, Braniff fifteen, Colonial and Chicago & Southern thirteen each. The type still represented a very important market, and Douglas research revealed that a total of approximately 400 DC-3s were still in regular service with trunk and feeder airlines in the United States. The main exception was American Airlines, which by this time had phased out its large fleet of DC-3 airliners, and had ordered a huge fleet of Convair 240s, so was not considered in the market for the new DC-3S.

When this first prototype 'Super Three' had passed all its initial flight tests as NC30000, a registration allocated to the Douglas Aircraft Company and used successfully on at least five DC-3 variants, preparations were made to demonstrate it to the airline executives as the DC-3 replacement. It was accompanied by top men from the company, including Ed Burton, Donald Douglas Jr and for some of the demonstrations by Donald Douglas Sr himself. First airline reactions in fact did look quite favourable. Leland Hayward, a director of Southwest Airways in San Francisco, an operator of the DC-3 since 1946, took a flight. In Houston, Texas, General Bob Smith of Pioneer Air Lines made several flights, then laid out a two-and-a-half hour flight plan over Pioneer's route with the airline's own chief of flight operations at the controls, accompanied by Donald Douglas. There was a lot of talk after a successful flight but no signatures for an order.

It was only in Washington DC, with Capital Airlines, formed in April 1948 from Pennsylvania Central Airlines and operating a large DC-3 fleet, that the attitude was more confident. The President of Capital Air Lines, J.H. Carmichael, took the controls of N30000 himself for a demonstration flight from Washington National Airport; by the time he returned he was so impressed that he immediately signed up for three of the aircraft and expressed the hope that a further seventeen could be purchased at a later date. Douglas was naturally elated at this commitment, but as it transpired these three would be the only DC-3S aircraft sold to an airline.

Production

In spite of offering markedly improved performance and notwithstanding the extensive sales tour, the commercial Super DC-3 programme proved a failure. Only the interest of Capital Airlines was converted into an order for three R-1820-C9HE-powered aircraft, while the second prototype was acquired by a construction company. Major airlines preferred the more modern and faster Convair Liner series with pressurised cabins. Smaller airlines, including the many US local service airlines which had been the prime sales target, found the Super DC-3 too expensive for their tight budgets, and in any case they were finally able to obtain current airworthiness certificates on their large fleets of standard DC-3s, despite the many threats to ground them. There was at one time a suggestion that airline customers could turn in a standard DC-3 and, for a price, get a Super DC-3 in return. The airlines, however, did not bite, since the modification price was just about what a pre-war DC-3 cost new.

The second DC-3S was N15579 c/n 43159 and retained by the company for demonstration activities etc. It was re-registered N30000 in 1951 as the original N30000 c/n 43158 had gone to the USAF for flight test, and then to the US Navy. This transport had a series of owners and became registered N222HC, N223R, N6811, XB-NIW and N567M. (Douglas)

Back at Santa Monica, work had begun on the second DC-3S, which was given the c/n 43159. Years before, this aircraft had appeared on the production line as a DC-3-277D NC33662 with a right-hand passenger door and destined for American Airlines, but was never delivered. It was impressed on the production line by the USAAF to become a military DC-3-369 and delivered on 10 June 1941, as C-50 41-7700. After military service it was in fact purchased by American Airlines on 3 July 1944, becoming NC15579 *'New Jersey'*, and was one of the many DC-3s withdrawn from use in 1948 when the American fleet was replaced by Convair 240s. On 15 February 1949 it was bought by Douglas for use in the new DC-3S project. Prior to conversion the airframe hours amounted to 16,321.

This aircraft was distinguished from the first DC-3S by having a standard left-hand-side passenger door rather than the new cargo door. It also had Pratt & Whitney R-2000-D7 engines instead of the Wright R-1820s, and a thirty-one seat interior rather than an executive layout. It made its first flight during October 1949, subsequently conducted another sales tour and was registered N15579. This second DC-3S was later fitted with an executive interior and re-registered N30000 on 20 April 1951. Even later, it was converted with Wright R-1820 engines and issued an experimental Certificate of Airworthiness on 30 August 1957, for operation with two left and one right-hand overwing exits removed. The total flying time by 7 August 1957 had reached 2,687 hours.

The third commercial DC-3S N540S c/n 43191 visited Europe in 1977 and Scottish Aviation at Prestwick for modifications. Based at Frankfurt on geophysic research, it was owned by the Geodata International Corporation based at Dallas, Texas. It is depicted at Stuttgart-Echterdingen Airport in the snow on 16 January 1977. (Helmet Lorenz)

Capital Airlines purchased three newly converted DC-3S airliners during 1950, and depicted is N16012 the third transport c/n 43193 delivered on 15 September 1950. It was named Capitaliner Cotton Queen *and is seen at Pittsburgh, Pennsylvania on 12 April 1953.* (K. Sumney)

The only three Douglas DC-3S aircraft to experience airline service had c/ns 43191, 43192 and 43193 and flew with Capital Airlines for less than two years. All three aircraft had been early DC-3-178 airliners, all fitted with a right-hand-side passenger door with original c/ns 1557, 1554 and 1548 and registrations NC16019, NC16016 and NC16012, these being retained when the aircraft were converted to DC-3S standard. They had been delivered to American Airlines in September and October 1936. All three had been spared the huge impressment into military service during the war and served faithfully on American's routes until they were withdrawn at Tulsa, Oklahoma, in late 1948 and early 1949 with total airframe hours of 35,585, 34,909 and 36,087 respectively. Douglas bought them on 10 May 1949, and ferried them to Santa Monica to join the conversion programme.

The Douglas Aircraft Company signed Contract No. 49-34 with Capital Airlines, which called for the delivery of three DC-3S to the Douglas design specification TS-1189A at a price of about $275,000 each. Work commenced immediately on the three aircraft with delivery planned for spring 1950. Although this scheduled slipped, the first Capital DC-3S N16019 was delivered to the airline on 24 July 1950, and entered service four days later. The second and third aircraft were delivered on 22 August and 15 September respectively. They carried fleet numbers 540, 541 and 542.

Capital Airlines assigned the new DC-3S airliners to Air Mail Route 51 – AM-51 – a route which started the day in Washington DC at 6.30 a.m. and arrived in Memphis, Tennessee, at 1.25 p.m. (Central Time). During that 7 hours 55 minutes, Flight 201 flew twelve route segments ranging in length from 16 to 194 statute miles. It was on such routes that young pilots learned their trade, for these were the days before Very High Frequency Omni Ranges – VORs – weather radar, autopilots, etc. Consequently all the flying had to be manual and when the weather was bad over the Great Smoky Mountains and the Appalachians, the flight crew knew that it was instrument-approach flying, taking bearings from beacons and other early radio aids along the route as there was no such thing as Instrument Landing Systems – ILS. The following is a listing of the stops on AM-51 after leaving Washington DC. with sector distances in statute miles: Norfolk, Virginia (143); Elizabeth City, North Carolina (44); Rocky Mount (91); Raleigh-Durham (57); Greensboro (66); Winston-Salem (16); Charlotte (75); Ashville (89); Knoxville, Tennessee (88); Chattanooga (87); Huntsville, Alabama (83) and Memphis (194).

Into Service

The most critical airport on route AM-51 was Ashville, North Carolina, with a 2,100 ft elevation and 4,000 ft runway length. Gross weight restrictions were applied at this airport if the winds were less than a specified strength, but the penalties to the payload were significantly less with the DC-3S than with a standard DC-3. Daily operations with Capital usually involved one Super DC-3 being on maintenance at Washington National, whilst a second aircraft would fly the Washington to Memphis route, remaining overnight in Memphis. The third DC-3S would start out from Memphis in the morning on the reciprocal route to Washington. The ground operations for handling the new $300,000 airliners along the route were well planned, giving the minimum turn-round time on the ground. Between Norfolk and Memphis, six of the stops were scheduled for two minutes each, two at three minutes each and one each at eleven and sixteen minutes, the latter two being refuelling stops. Operations of a standard DC-3 on the same route produced a total ground time of over one hour, approximately seven and a half minutes per stop.

Several new features on the DC-3S helped to contribute to this reduction in ground time. All baggage and any cargo was located in the large tail compartment, so was easily accessible. The airstair door eliminated the need for any boarding stairs.

The cargo compartment was large enough for a steward who was able to sort both baggage and cargo in flight between stops, so that once the aircraft was on the ground no time was wasted in unloading from the waist-high baggage hatch. At most touchdowns, the port engine only was stopped.

On part of the AM-51 route the Capital DC-3S airliners flew in close competition with American Airline's Convair 240s. Both carriers flew between Memphis and Knoxville, with Capital making a stop at Chattanooga – 358 miles total – and American making a stop at Nashville – 352 miles. The scheduled time for the DC-3S was 1 hour 57 minutes, while the Convair's time was 2 hours 10 minutes. The Convair was faster in the air, but its stop required eighteen minutes, to the DC-3S's two.

Capital Airlines still experienced difficulties with introducing a new aircraft into the fleet, despite the fact that the DC-3S drew heavily on the original DC-3 design. Problems with the high-powered Wright engines headed the list. The autofeather system and valves and cylinders seemed to cause the most troubles. The autofeather system could be bypassed, but this resulted in a reduction in gross take-off weight of 3,000 lb. Various modifications to the valves were tried, but an engine failure rate of once every 400 hours was significantly greater than that experienced on Capital's regular R-1820s. It was on the Capital DC-3S airliners that the Wright R-1820-C9HE was first introduced to civilian flying, so it is reasonable to expect that the numerous take-offs and short flight stages would expose any design difficulties very quickly. Flying time between overhauls on the high-powered Wright averaged 900 hours, compared with 1,200 to 1,400 for the standard R-1820s. The more complicated nature of the C9HE engine also accounted for the fact that, at first, the time required to overhaul this engine was about 500 man hours compared with 250 for the normal Wright. However, experience and learning curves soon reduced this time.

Other minor introductory problems included tail-wheel centring, wing skin cracking on the outer panels, and strengthening of the horizontal stabiliser attachment fittings. The new Douglas Super DC-3S was the first transport aircraft to be fitted with Goodyear crosswind landing gear, but because of problems with the Civil Aeronautics Authority certification, Capital Airlines was never able to operate the swivelling devices, so these remained locked in their normal positions.

Despite the difficulties, Capital was pleased with the DC-3S. Pilots liked the aircraft for its improved performance, and passengers liked it for its speed and comfort, despite the fact that it had thirty-one seats as opposed to twenty-four on the standard DC-3s operated by Capital. On a direct operating cost comparison, the DC-3S cost about four cents per mile more than regular DC-3s, but the additional seating capacity enabled an extra 20 cents per mile more revenue. In other words, the DC-3S could potentially net some 16 cents per mile more than the standard DC-3, before taking into account depreciation and insurance costs. The Super DC-3S burned less fuel per aeroplane mile while at the same time flying some 35 mph faster, carrying ten more passengers and weighing 6,000 lb more.

Capital examined and evaluated the possibility of converting another nine of their existing DC-3 fleet to DC-3S standard. The estimated cost per conversion was $260,000, excluding the value of the original airframe. They also considered increasing the seating on their standard DC-3s from twenty-four to twenty-six or even twenty-eight seats as some other carriers had done, but found this was an advantage only on short routes with little or no cargo potential.

Demonstration Flights

Despite the great marketing efforts by the Douglas Aircraft Company aimed principally at the commercial airlines, the company did not neglect the possibility of selling the DC-3S to the military. Both the US Air Force and the US Navy still had sizeable fleets of C-47-type military transports which were becoming candidates for upgrading. Proposals were made, specifications developed and demonstration flights arranged. The US Air Force evaluated the prototype DC-3S, but its continued purchases of Convair C-131s for passenger and cargo operations, and Convair T-29s for navigational training, etc, precluded any development of a Super DC-3 programme at the same time. The start of the Korean war in July 1950 turned the attention of the US Air Force away from transport aircraft conversions and towards combat aircraft once more. However, during November 1950 the prototype DC-3S, now designated YC-129 with the serial 51-3817, carried out landing trials at Edwards Air Force Base in California using a 60 ft diameter Pioneer cargo parachute.

The prototype DC-3S underwent stringent trials with the US Air Force and is seen on 22 November 1950, in a spectacular take-off from Edwards AFB, California. It was sold to the USAF and was heavily modified with the addition of a twin-wheel main landing gear and could be fitted with JATO packs for added take-off thrust. (Douglas)

During the evaluation programme the US Air Force had reserved the designation C-47E to cover any reworked C-47s which may have been contracted for. It was never used. However, Douglas did sell c/n 43158 N30000 to the USAF in late 1950 as the YC-129 Escape & Evacuation Prototype Military Transport with Douglas Specification 1244. It was later re-designated YC-47F. Mention has already been made of the dual landing wheels to handle increased weights as well as rough field landing requirements. Reversible propellers were installed and fuselage fuel tanks totalling 1,600 gallons capacity supplemented the existing 800 gallon wing tanks. The 60 ft Pioneer ribbon parachute had electrical and mechanical controls in the cockpit. The autofeather system was not installed.

Flight tests including take-offs with and without jet assisted take-off (JATO) and landings with and without reverse pitch and/or drogue parachute were conducted. Take-offs were made from hard surface runways at 30,000 and 32,000 lb gross weights. Tests included take-offs with no JATO, with eight JATO bottles of 1,000 lb thrust each, and with fifteen JATO bottles. The firing times for JATO ranged from 1½ to 5½ seconds after start of take-off roll. Lift-off distance without JATO averaged 2,000 ft, but with fifteen JATO bottles fitted and a dual main wheel landing gear, distances as short as 540 ft were achieved with a 32,000 lb gross weight. The distance required to clear a 50 ft obstacle ranged from 2,700 ft with no JATO to as little as 800 ft with a maximum of fifteen JATO bottles fitted. The field performance of the YC-129 easily matched that of the best light observation aircraft of the day.

Landing tests proved almost as spectacular as the take-offs. Touchdown distances of about 2,100 ft were achieved with wheel brakes and reverse thrust at landing weights of about 30,000 lb. The addition of the huge drogue chute being opened at touchdown further reduced the distance to 1,100 ft at a weight of 29,000 lb. On touchdown, the parachute was unreefed to its full 60 ft diameter to assist in slowing the aircraft.

Unfortunately the YC-47F, née YC-129, was found no mission to perform for the US Air Force, and in the interest of inter-service fraternity the aircraft was transferred to the US Navy as the R4D-8X. It was delivered to NAS Jacksonville, Florida, on 28 July 1953, and allocated the BuNo 138659.

Seen at Los Angeles International Airport during 1971 is the second commercial DC-3S c/n 43159. On 13 August 1966, it was registered in Mexico as XA-NIW with Banco Mercantile & Supermercado SA and named Ave Fenix. (AP Photo Library)

Meanwhile the second DC-3S was still touring the United States powered by R-2000 engines and registered N15579 c/n 43159. On 20 April 1951, it was re-registered N30000 after the sale of the first N30000 to the US Air Force in November 1950. The engines were changed to Wright R-1820s. It was painted in the same stylish livery as the first prototype and its airline interior gave way to a corporate seating configuration. By the late 1950s the lower fuselage had been returned to bare metal, and for some months prior to its sale in late 1958 even the company markings had been removed. During August 1957 it was issued with a restricted Certificate of Airworthiness for flight operations with the two aft left-hand and one aft right-hand emergency exits removed for aerial photography, with or without the removal of the main cabin door. Presumably this was in connection with the Douglas DC-8 flight test programme,

which was being carried out at this time. In December 1958 the company sold the DC-3S to the Harbert Construction Company of Birmingham, Alabama, with whom it was registered N222HC. By this time it had accumulated 2,700 flying hours. After leaving the Douglas Aircraft Company it passed through the hands of a dozen owners, having half a dozen registrations including one in Mexico, before coming to rest with its current owner in South Carolina. On 22 January 1986, it was registered to the US government – General Services Administration – by Aviation Enterprises, having been donated to Beaufort County, South Carolina, on 26 November 1985 for use as a mosquito sprayer. Its market value was estimated at $95,000.

Airline Sale

Given Capital Airlines' favourable reaction to the new Douglas DC-3S, it was quite a surprise to learn that not only did they decline to have any more aircraft converted to DC-3S configuration, but that on 15 April 1952, after less than two years' service, all three Capital Super DC-3S were sold to the US Steel Company and converted to an executive configuration. The aircraft were based at US Steel's Pittsburgh headquarters, and Capital contracted to provide flight crew and maintenance. It is interesting to record that in much the same manner, in the late 1950s, Capital operated a Douglas C-54 'Skymaster' and three Vickers Viscounts for US Steel.

All three DC-3S aircraft served with the steel company until the early 1960s. One, now registered N541S c/n 43192, was damaged beyond repair when it ran off the runway at Bluefield, West Virginia, on 10 May 1962. There were no injuries to the three crew and one passenger. The plane had amassed an estimated total flying time of 7,000 hours.

Douglas DC-3S c/n 43193, registered N542S to US Steel, continued to serve as an executive aircraft and was sold to Northwestern Refining Company of Minneapolis in 1963. On 6 August of that year it was re-registered N111SA and carried on flying much as it had done with its previous owner. It was then sold to Western Company of North America at Fort Worth, Texas, on 7 May 1969, and registered N156WC. Western was an oil company run by Eddie 'I'm Mad Too' Chiles, who was far better known for his right wing political views than for his oil production. The aircraft served as a corporate transport, shuttling back and forth to Mexico. The size and speed of the DC-3S were ideal for this work, but unfortunately the engines had a high failure rate and the story goes that this made 'Mad Eddie' even madder. The solution seemed to be a conversion to turboprop engines, and the long story of turboprop DC-3s is the subject of the next chapter in this volume.

At long last the Douglas Aircraft Company did find a major customer for the Super DC-3. The US Navy awarded Douglas a contract to modify one hundred Douglas R4D-5s, R4D-6s and R4D-7s to Super DC-3 configuration, designated R4D-8. Powered by two 1,475 hp Wright R-1820-80 engines, the converted aircraft were assigned new Douglas factory c/ns – 43301 to 43400 – but retained their original BuNo identities. Some of the new transports were modified to fulfil a variety of tasks and became specially re-designated as trainers, staff transports and cold-weather operations in the Antarctic under the code-name 'Operation Deep Freeze'. A few were used by the US Marine Corps. Under a US Department of Defense Directive dated 6 July 1962, the R4D-8 designations allocated were standardised with those of the many US Air Force variants, all standard R4D-8s becoming C-117D transports.

The fact that two of the three Capital Airlines DC-3S aircraft still exist some half a century after their original delivery as standard DC-3s is almost incredible. In recent years a number of surplus R4D-8 transports have appeared on US, Canadian and South American civil registers, primarily as cargo haulers, and it is felt that this type will join the standard DC-3 in flying on well into the next century.

To summarise, it is interesting to look at the overall success of the Douglas Super DC-3S programme. The Douglas Aircraft Company certainly did not recoup their $3 million investment in the conversion of five civil aircraft produced, nor did they recoup anything on the hundred military examples similarly converted. The DC-3S was a technically good transport that just did not find a market. At a conversion price of $250,000 to $300,000, excluding the original price of the DC-3 airframe donated, it was a new airliner offering up to thirty-seven seats and cruising at 240 mph; one would have thought this was more than attractive to any potential buyer at the time. However, there were two major items of competition. One, ironically, was the original DC-3, which was still available at low cost and in large numbers, and eventually avoided the threat of grounding the Civil Aeronautics Authority had made so many times. The other competition was from the products of Martin and Convair. In 1952 United Air Lines took delivery of its initial Convair CV-340s at a price of about $570,000 each. For this price, United received a brand new, pressurised, forty-four-seat airliner which was faster over the routes, and could fly into most of the airfields used by the many DC-3s.

For many of the trunk airlines in the United States, the temptation to dispose of their DC-3s and project the same comfort offered by large airliners proved irresistible. As a result, despite their encouraging initial market research, Douglas did not receive the massive conversion orders they expected. This was not the first time a technically good aircraft had effectively failed because of market forces, and history will show that it will certainly not be the last. However it is significant that this was the first time a failure of this nature had involved a product of the Douglas Aircraft Company.

Chapter Seven
Douglas DC-3 Turbo

At the end of the Second World War, the Douglas DC-3/C-47, of which nearly 11,000 were manufactured in either civil or military form, became surplus to requirements and was in service in virtually every country around the globe. It was a workhorse which was relatively cheap to operate, and many civil airlines and military air arms had quickly taken advantage of its availability. There were plentiful stocks of the Pratt & Whitney power-plant, and other spares were also readily available.

Since 1945 there have been many unsuccessful attempts to produce a Douglas DC-3 replacement. In the immediate post-war years there were new airliners on the drawing board to be powered by the first of a series of turboprop engines developed in the United Kingdom by Armstrong-Siddeley Motors Ltd (ASM) at Parkside, Coventry, a branch of the Hawker-Siddeley Group, and by Rolls-Royce of Derby. The Douglas DC-3 airframe was recognised as the most suitable experimental test-bed for these installations, which were being developed for commercial airliner use.

First photographs of the Dakota fitted with two 1420 s.s.hp Armstrong Siddeley Mamba turboprops were released on 15 September 1949. Depicted is Dakota KJ839 the only Mamba Dakota flying test-bed based at Bitteswell, Rugby. It carried prototype markings and flight tested several versions of the Mamba engine. (AP Photo Library)

On 1 June 1949, therefore, Douglas DC-3 Dakota, designated RAF Dakota Mk.IV KJ839, which had served with both 47 Squadron and 1382 Conversion Unit, was procured by Armstrong-Siddeley Propeller Turbines. It had low airframe hours and was unfurnished. In place of the Pratt & Whitney Twin Wasps, the company installed its own Mamba turboprop engines. An advertisement which appeared in aviation journals on 7 October 1949 described the Mamba DC-3 as being a simple

conversion to enable the Dakota to meet the full future International Civil Aviation Organisation – ICAO – take-off requirements at a weight of only 1,300 lb less than the present maximum of 28,000 lb. The Mamba DC-3 Dakota offered increased speed, improved payload on short hauls and increased comfort due to the great reduction in noise and vibration, the advertisement claimed.

The Mamba ASM.3 produced 1,475 equivalent shaft horsepower, and a later engine, the ASM.6, was also flight tested in KJ839, which retained its RAF identity. Scottish Aviation at Prestwick, who were well known for their overhauling and conversion of wartime military and civil DC-3s, were involved in the modification of the airframe necessary for the installation of the new turbine engines. Its first flight took place from the company's airfield at Bitteswell, near Rugby, on 27 August 1949. The test pilot was Waldo Price-Owen, who continued to pilot KJ839 on many hours of test-bed research.

Worldwide interest was aroused by the new Mamba Dakota as a commercial proposition to extend the useful life of the now ubiquitous DC-3, although the first conversion – KJ839 – was retained as a demonstration aircraft and employed by ASM to build up experience on the 1,475 hp Mamba propeller turbine. As the advertisement had announced, the installation of the new turboprop engines was the only structural modification required to enable the Dakota to meet the full ICAO standard. Fulfilling all ICAO conditions and with full fuel allowances, at a range of 200 miles the Mamba Dakota was able to carry a 8,250 lb payload at 165 mph at 10,000 ft; the Twin Wasp version over the same range managed 4,700 lb payload at 175 mph and 8,000 ft. Corresponding payload figures for a range of 800 miles were 5,300 lb for the Mamba and 3,200 lb for the Twin Wasp version.

The aircraft which became the Mamba Dakota was built at Douglas' Oklahoma City factory as C-47B-1-DK 43-48362 and delivered on 16 August 1944, but was diverted as a Lend-Lease transport to the Royal Air Force as KJ839. After flying many hours as the Mamba engine test-bed its Pratt & Whitney Twin Wasp engines were re-installed and on 4 June 1958 it was sold to Skyways Ltd. Today, after being registered in the Bahamas, the Leeward Islands and Antigua, this test-bed is still flying and earning its keep. It currently serves in the United States, registered N4797H with Ago Airways Inc. of Miami, Florida.

Dart Dakota

It was pure coincidence that also on 1 June 1949, a Dakota Mk.IV KJ829 was transferred from the RAF to Rolls-Royce at Hucknall, Nottingham, for the installation of turboprops and for flight test trials. This was also on Oklahoma-built C-47B-1-DK 43-48352, delivered on 14 August 1944, prior to being included in a Lend-Lease order for the RAF. It appears to have had a more extensive service life, but its airframe was sound and it had a comparatively low number of flying hours. The new Rolls-Royce Dart turboprop engine was under development for

On 1 June 1949 Rolls-Royce at Hucknall, Notts., took on charge Dakota KJ829. First flight powered by Dart turboprop engines took place on 15 March 1950 and the aircraft became the flying test-bed for a variety of versions of the successful Dart engine. This photograph emphasises how further forward this engine installation was compared with the A.S. Mamba engine. (Rolls-Royce)

installation in the new Vickers Armstrong Viscount airliner, and again the Dakota was selected as a suitable flying test-bed.

The Dart engines were fitted further forward on the airframe than the Armstrong-Siddeley Mambas, putting the propellers ahead of the cockpit instead of in line as with the Mambas. With ground runs complete the first flight took place on 15 March 1950, and this airframe became the test bed for many variants of the successful Dart. The Dakota carried the Class 'B' registration G-37-1, but was registered G-AOXI when it flew to Dakar in French West Africa for tropical trials. It was fitted with a Dart 510 engine on one side and a Dart 526 on the other. The trials commenced in October 1956.

The Rolls-Royce Dart proved eminently successful as a commercial power-plant, and with the imminent delivery of the

first Vickers Viscount four-Dart-engined 40-59 passenger airliner ordered by British European Airways, the airline decided to give both its pilots and its ground maintenance personnel some experience in turboprop operations. BEA had two Dakotas converted to Dart configuration by Field Aircraft Services in 1951; this company had had great experience with both the Dakota airframe and the Pratt & Whitney Twin Wasp engines for many years at its Croydon Airport facility, later transferred to Tollerton airfield, Nottingham.

The aircraft involved were G-ALXN '*Sir Henry Royce*' and G-AMDB '*Claude Johnson*', both certificated for freight operations only. For eighteen months the two Dart Dakotas were used on cargo work and to give experience to BEA personnel. They often flew at a far higher altitude than was normal for a Dakota, much to the surprise of other aircraft crews and air traffic control, who often queried both the type and the speed. A pure night cargo service from Northolt was initiated on 15 August 1951 by G-ALXN carrying 1½ tons of freight to Hannover in Germany. Later cargo services were extended to serve Copenhagen, Paris and Milan. The result of the Dart Dakota conversion was an aircraft with a maximum gross weight of 28,000 lbs, a cruising speed of 202 miles per hour at 25,000 ft and a fuel consumption of 120 Imperial gallons of kerosene per hour.

Interesting developments were revealed as the flight tests continued, and there were certain restrictions on freight. A bottle of champagne bursting open in an unpressurised cabin at 25,000 ft could cause a literally ear-shattering explosion. So bottled goods were not carried. Nor, for health reasons, were livestock or fresh fruit. The pilots liked the freedom from engine vibration which plagued the Twin Wasp Dakota. Even the maintenance appeared to be satisfactory. However, the Dart Dakota conversions were not practical. A letter to L.S. Casey, Director of the National Air & Space Museum in Washington DC, from A.J. Hergeworth, Assistant General Manager at Rolls-Royce at Derby said, 'Due to the lack of cabin pressurisation on the Dakotas, it was not possible to fly as a passenger-carrying aircraft at altitudes where the full advantage of the Dart engine could be obtained.'

All three Dart Dakotas, G-AOXI, G-ALXN and G-AMDB, were later refitted with standard Twin Wasp engines and sold. The records show that the two British European Airways Dart Dakotas flew some 5,319 hours in airline service as freight carriers up until March 1953 when they were reconverted.

The second BEA Dart Dakota G-AMDB seen in flight. In all, the two unique DC-3 conversions flew 5,319 hours in BEA service up to March 1953, when they were converted back to standard transports as Pratt & Whitney-powered 'Pionair' class aircraft. (BEA)

The Conroy Conversion

During the late 1960s and early 1970s, Conroy Aircraft of Santa Barbara, California, proposed a number of interesting schemes involving the fitting of surplus Dart 510 and 512 turboprop engines from ex-Continental Airlines Viscount 812s to low-time Douglas DC-3 airframes. John M. (Jack) Conroy introduced a Conroy Turbo Three N4700C c/n 4903, a Second World War C-53 'Skytrooper' transport operated by TWA after the war and purchased by Conroy in January 1968. It was fitted with two Rolls-Royce Dart 7/510 engines taken from a crashed United Airlines Viscount, and made its first flight on 13 May 1969. These engines were torque limited to 1,350 hp and drove British Rotol four-bladed propellers.

Despite the aircraft appearing at the Paris Air Show in May 1969, and subsequently completing a twenty-eight nation

The Conroy Tri-Turbo Three had made its first flight on 2 November 1977 and was later registered to Santa Barbara Polair Inc. and conducted flight trials with the US Navy in the Arctic Circle and was fitted with skis. It was demonstrated in Europe and attended the Paris Air Show. It is depicted at Boeing Field, Seattle, on 17 May 1981. (Peter M. Bowers)

demonstration tour, there was a general lack of interest from the airlines. Conroy claimed that conversions would take only thirty days at the Santa Barbara facility, but kits would be made available for installation by airlines or conversion specialists overseas. It was proposed to certificate the Conroy Turbo Three at 32,000 lb maximum take-off weight and a maximum cruise of 215 mph at the maximum all-up-weight was claimed, plus a standard fuel range of 940 miles. The Rolls-Royce Darts were certificated at 1,600 shp, but could be torque limited to 1,350 shp to match DC-3 certification and performance limits.

During 1977, the Turbo Airliner Manufacturing Company – TAMCO – proposed a major modification which would entail the fitting of either 1,535 shp Rolls-Royce Dart RDa.6s or 1,835 shp Dart RDa.7s to a modified and zero-timed DC-3 airframe equipped with a tricycle undercarriage, enlarged tail surfaces and a longer, pressurised cabin accommodating thirty passengers. A prototype, named Turbo-Commuter, was certificated to FAR Part 298. However, at a price of $880,000, ten times the unit price of the first Douglas Sleeper Transports, it failed to gain acceptance.

The next Conroy turboprop Douglas DC-3 conversion was undertaken on behalf of Eddie 'I'm Mad Too' Chiles of the Western Company of North America. Somehow Eddie had got together with Jack Conroy who had founded Aero Spacelines at Santa Barbara and who was no stranger to aircraft conversions, having previously done the Dart DC-3 conversion and a Dart-powered Grumman Albatross. The engines for these conversions came from withdrawn United Airlines Viscounts which had been sold to Sam Goldman, a Maryland-based used aircraft merchant. In essence, Goldman supplied the engines, while Conroy did the engineering and marketing. With this background it is not difficult to see why the Dart re-engine package was chosen for the Western Company's Super DC-3S c/n 43193.

At this point, Jack Conroy saw the potential of the Super DC-3S airframe powered by Rolls-Royce Dart engines, and he reactivated Turbo-Three Corporation, which had initially been established to market the original package developed for N4700C c/n 4903. About this time US airline regulations were being eased to allow the operation of larger aircraft by the so-called 'commuter' airlines. Conroy saw this as an opportunity to tap this emerging market and drew up specifications for the Super Turbo Three. In addition to the commuter carriers, the

North Slope of Alaska was hot as an oil-drilling site at this time and a cargo version of the aircraft was envisaged which would have utilised numerous surplus US Navy R4D-8 airframes now being retired. Gross weight was increased to about 35,000 lbs and the cruising speed approached 250 mph. The cost of the conversion was estimated at about $475,000 for a cargo model, with slightly higher cost for one in a passenger configuration.

Unfortunately, the market for the Super Turbo Three never materialised as commuter airlines moved on to newer, larger and more sophisticated aircraft. Meanwhile the FAA certification programme was not going well. Because of the way the Dart engines were mounted and because they used the Viscount-type propellers, the props did not extend beyond the so-called 'robin's breast' area of the cowling, which included the bulging wheel-well doors and fairings which gave rise to the nickname. Due to the poor aerodynamic interaction between the engine, prop and landing-gear areas, the balanced field length – the accelerate/stop distance – was some 6,000 ft, a totally unacceptable distance given the runway lengths available at most commuter-served airfields.

The Western Company apparently lost interest in the project at this point, and the death of Jack Conroy meant the work required for FAA certification was halted. It was now that the President of Pilgrim Airlines of Groton, Connecticut, Joseph Fugere, became involved.

In addition to its short-haul routes, Pilgrim had route authority from Hartford, Connecticut, to Montreal, Canada. The 230-nautical-mile route would generate good traffic figures, but the relatively slow de Havilland Twin Otters operated by Pilgrim would take too long to make the flight, while their rather cramped cabins would certainly test passenger comfort to its limits on the two-hour sector. Fugere had heard of the Conroy Super Turbo Three conversion programme, and traded a Twin Otter to Western in exchange for their Super DC-3S, which had been flying under a Temporary Inspection Authorisation, and the engineering data.

Fugere had carefully studied the performance of the Super Turbo Three and came to the conclusion that later model Rolls-

The 'Turbo Three' DC-3 Dart conversion by Conroy Aircraft in the USA involved N4700C c/n 4903 fitted with Dart 7/510 engines. It made its first flight on 13 May 1969 and is depicted at Bakersfield, California, during January 1970. It visited South America on a demonstration tour and on 27 July 1974 was demonstrated from the high-altitude airport at La Paz, Bolivia. (Ed Davies)

Royce Dart engines and large diameter propellers would go a long way towards solving Pilgrim's problems. Several engine and propeller combinations were tried, but the one which worked most efficiently was the 532-2L Dart 7 with -212 propellers, as fitted to the Hawker-Siddeley 748 airliner. In addition the 'robin's breast' was eliminated and, despite the fact that the wheel wells were now open, there was a significant reduction in drag and a consequent improvement in performance. During dive tests, the transport was reaching a staggering Mach .68 with no problems. These later engine modifications were completed at Van Nuys, California, by Dick Slip, a former FAA pilot. 'Fish' Salmon, a former Lockheed test pilot, was also involved with Jack Conroy in the early days of the Super Turbo Three programme during 1974.

With all FAA testing completed, Fugere was awarded a Supplemental Type Certificate for the aircraft in 1978. The aircraft was allocated the registration N156PM on 27 January 1979, but this was never applied. He had no fewer than fourteen R4D-8 airframes stored in Arizona, but was unable to find a financial partner to underwrite the cost of such a massive programme.

The second Dart conversion undertaken by Conroy involved a commercial DC-3S N156WC c/n 43193 fitted with engines taken from a United Airlines Viscount airliner. There were problems in obtaining certification. It was the fourth commercial Super DC-3 built by Douglas and is depicted parked at Santa Barbara, California, after conversion. (W. T. Larkins)

By this time circumstances had changed, and Pilgrim was able to purchase the Dutch-designed and built Fokker F-27 Friendship now certified in the United States, so sadly c/n 43193 was to remain parked at Groton, Connecticut. Unfortunately the Super Turbo Three was allowed to deteriorate and was hit by the wing of a Trans American Lockheed Hercules on 24 February 1984. The cockpit of the Douglas transport was severely damaged and remained unrepaired. The DC-3S became known locally as 'Fugere's Folly', but this was unjust – the aircraft was far from being a folly.

Having remained at Groton suffering the effects of the environment, the DC-3S was sold to Erickson & Remmert, Roswell, New Mexico, during 1989. By November 1990 the last portion of the aircraft had been moved by road to Fort Sumner, New Mexico, on a specially-built trailer. Again for the record this aircraft was awarded Supplement Type Certificate SA3241WE on 18 August 1976, under Approved Type Certificate 6A2.

Tri Turbo Three

By 1976, John Conroy had established a new firm, the Specialised Aircraft Company, located at Camarillo, California. The next turbine DC-3 effort was the conversion of the original Turbo Three airframe to a tri-motor, with new 1,174 eshp Pratt & Whitney of Canada PT6A-45 turboprops, two positioned in the conventional nacelles and the third in an extended nose. The port and starboard propellers, now with five blades, were located aft of the cockpit. The registration for c/n 4903 was changed to N23SA.

Powered by the three Pratt & Whitney PT6A-45A turboprops driving Hartzell five-bladed propellers, the aircraft made its first flight on 2 November 1977. The use of three engines was not intended to be a steady-state condition; the centre engine to be used for take-off, climb and high-speed cruise, but could be shut down with the propeller feathered for extended cruise flight. The weight saved by the lighter engines allowed a payload increase to 12,000 lb. Cruising speed on three engines was 220 mph at 5,000 ft and 230 mph at 10,000 ft. On two engines the cruise was 180 mph. Range on three engines at normal cruising speed was 1,135 miles and on two 1,395 miles. Extended ranges were 2,700 miles and 3,200 miles for three and two engines respectively.

The cost of a conversion at that time was quoted at $525,000 and around 3,000 man-hours of labour would be required. Optional outboard wing tanks gave a range of more than 3,000 miles and the aircraft could climb to 10,000 ft, shut down the centre engine and fly a 3,000 mile mission with an hour's fuel reserve. The twin-engine cruising speed was 180 mph with a fuel consumption of 108 US gallons per hour. The weight reduction of 2,500 lb from the standard DC-3 was said to give STOL – short take-off and landing – characteristics with reverse-pitch propellers giving a short landing run. Maintenance costs were considerably reduced compared with the normal DC-3. John Conroy claimed that around 90 per cent of maintenance costs and man-hours on a standard DC-3 were involved in power-plant maintenance, and on the Tri-Turbo Three this would be reduced to an average of fifteen minutes per flight hour.

In September 1978 the aircraft appeared at the Farnborough Air Show – the first ever DC-3 to do so – and attracted considerable attention. It was fitted with dummy radar sited above and below the fuselage. Demonstrations were made to a number of potential customers, but failure to obtain an FAA certification restricted the conversion to the prototype only. In 1979 it appeared at the Paris Air Show equipped with skis and was still being demonstrated in the early 1980s under the title of 'Polair', in support of a programme involving the US Navy in installing automatic hydrophones and electronic devices beneath the ice to measure the movement of marine life. It was evaluated in the Arctic regions, operating from Fort Barrow, Alaska, operating from remote landing sites, and also in Antarctica, some 700 miles from the South Pole. It was named '*Spirit of Hope*'. A swing-tail version was projected for military cargo operations, but unfortunately neither civil or military sales were forthcoming.

Whilst in the United Kingdom, pilots had an opportunity to fly the Tri-Turbo Three and one Captain Kershaw, a Britannia Airways skipper, reported that the modified DC-3 was a delight to fly, but because the exhaust outlets were in line with the cockpit window when taxying for take-off, one was blinded by watering eyes and virtually asphyxiated by the exhaust fumes. Take-off brought little relief as the vibration and noise produced by the close proximity of the third engine in the nose seemed to loosen all the bones in one's body. Cold air caused innumerable problems with the PR-6A-45 engines and it was noted that half the demonstration flight to which these remarks refer had been completed with at least one failed engine.

Turbo Express DC-3

One of the most successful DC-3 turbo conversions was the Turbo Express, sometimes referred to the DC-3-TP, produced in 1982 by the United States Aircraft Corporation – USAC – initially of Burbank, California, and Van Nuys. The prototype conversion utilised an ex-Royal Canadian Air Force Dakota Mk.4 KK160 which had been delivered in November 1944 and first registered in the United States as N502PA in August 1968. After its acquisition by the USAC on 8 August 1981, it was registered N300TX on 11 July 1982. The Vice-President of USAC was none other than Robert W. Lillibridge, who had previously been Vice-President Engineering and Manufacturing with the Conroy Aircraft Corporation.

In order to maintain the correct centre of gravity with the lighter 1254-eshp Pratt & Whitney of Canada PT6A-45R turboprops, the DC-3 Turbo Express was fitted with a 40 inch plug in the forward fuselage just ahead of the wing which extended the nose. This kept the propellers well aft of the cockpit as on the Super DC-3. One source quotes the plug extension as being 3 ft 4 in. A number of other airframe modifications were incorporated, but externally the only one visible was the modified square-tipped tailplane. Extra tanks in the outer wings increased fuel capacity by 800 US gallons. Fuel consumption was an improvement on the earlier Turbo Three at 100 gallons per hour at 190 mph at 10,000 ft, with a stalling speed of 64 mph.

The first flight of the USAC Turbo Express was made on 28 July 1982, and a year later apparently the company received an order for the first production version, a mixed configuration aircraft with capacity for eighteen passengers in the front cabin and cargo in the rear. Other changes included an entirely new electrical system with 300-ampere starter-generators, modified wing leading edges, a modified hydraulic system, new solid-state electronics and improved instrumentation. With the fuselage extension, the interior length of the cabin was increased, but passenger seating was restricted to thirty. The cargo door of the Douglas C-47 was retained. On 1 December 1983, STC SA2221NM was issued as a supplement to Approved Type Certificate A-669 on a 'one-airplane-only' basis. Gross weight remained at 26,900 lb and the usable kerosene fuel at 741 gallons out of the 800 gallon total. With wing structure reinforcement, the fast-range cruising speed was quoted as 236 mph.

After conversion the Turbo Express was purchased by Harold's Air Service Inc. of Galena, Fairbanks, Alaska, on 9 November 1984, having made an appearance at the Experimental Aircraft Association convention at Oshkosh, Wisconsin, during August of that year. In March 1987, the company was renamed Friendship Air Alaska. The Turbo Express was later sold to Basler Air Lines, located at Oshkosh and registered N300BF. Price for the conversion is quoted at $2 million with $200,000 for the new avionics and instruments. In Alaska the thirty-six passenger aircraft was used to fulfil the Civil Aeronautics Board requirement that the airline provide essential air service to communities in the outback that rely on air transportation.

President of the airline Harold Esmailka and Bill Fisher, the executive Vice-President, stated that they just could not afford the hundred-passenger aircraft on the market, so felt justified in operating the Turbo Express. This was endorsed by the chief pilot Bob Mason, who claimed that the modified DC-3 flew more quietly and was more responsive, with take-off and climb vastly improved. Cruise was at 215 knots compared with the 165 knots in a standard DC-3. Climb was 1,350 ft per minute compared with 1,050 ft per minute.

In March 1984, it was announced that United States Aircraft Corporation was working on a second Turbo Express DC-3 conversion for Harold's Air Service with an option to purchase or lease. It would be equipped with more powerful PT6A-engines. The company revealed that this second conversion was to be N607W c/n 20875. It was also rumoured that USAC was holding discussions with the government of Colombia for the purchase of nine Turbo Express DC-3 conversions, an order representing some $13 million. Neither the second Turbo Express nor the foreign order appeared.

Warren Basler

Warren Basler, President of Basler Flight Services and other subsidiary companies, all associated with the DC-3, bought his first Douglas DC-3 aircraft from the Kimberley-Clark Corporation in 1960 and immediately sold it to a businessman in Green Bay, Wisconsin. Five years earlier, in 1955, Basler had bought the aviation business at Oshkosh from aviation pioneer, aircraft designer and racer Steve Wittman, after whom Oshkosh named its airport. The price was $30,000. Eventually Basler operated DC-3s for the freight charter business and at any one time would have seven aircraft in the air at once, carrying everything from football and hockey teams to packages for Federal Express and parts for General Motors. On the ground Basler was involved in DC-3 overhaul, and since 1960 has handled well over a hundred of the type.

Today the business has more to do with economics than nostalgia. The freight operator is in big business in Wisconsin, converting and fitting out Douglas DC-3s with turboprop engines. A modern small cargo jet or a commuter aircraft such as the Fokker F-27 Friendship now commands anything between $5 million and $8 million. Warren Basler can deliver his converted DC-3s for less than $3 million. A turboprop DC-3 averages eighteen minutes of maintenance for every flying hour, appreciably less than the fifty-five minutes of work needed to keep an F-27 in the air for an hour.

Initially Basler purchased surplus DC-3s from corporate fleets and airlines as they upgraded their fleets. Then the search spread worldwide. The French Air Force and the Aéronavale were disposing of their last military C-47s, two of the French Air Force being based in New Caledonia, in the Pacific; Basler negotiated for them and, after fitting extra fuel tanks, flew them back to the United States in seventeen-hour flight stages. The Aéronavale C-47s were based in southern France at Nîmes Garon, and these were immediately allocated US registrations ending in 'BF' and ferried back to Oshkosh via Prestwick, Scotland.

Basler commenced an ambitious project that has culminated today in the DC-3 Turbo 67 aircraft. Certification of the new Turbo 67 began in April 1988, with full approval of the type being issued on 11 December 1990. Meanwhile, a completely new building containing a DC-3 conversion and production line was constructed at Wittman Regional Airport, Oshkosh, which included the earlier mentioned French Aéronavale C-47s. Employing some 124 personnel, the conversion of an airframe to Turbo 67 takes approximately six months.

Under 'Operation Peace Turbo', two standard C-47 transports from the El Salvadorian Air Force were ferried to Oshkosh for conversion and rebuild with PT-6A-67A engines under a US government contract No. F41608-89-C-2493 dated 25 August 1989. The transports were in fact AC-47 gunships. The cost of the conversions was listed as $4,330,380 and involved several US government departments including Kelly AFB and the San Antonio Air Logistics Center in Texas, and the Goodner Brothers at Inter-Mountain Regional Airport, Mena, Arizona, who stripped and painted the two AC-47s. Delivery date was given as 30 June 1990.

Two DC-3 Turbo 67s ordered for Air Colombia became involved in a scandal when these aircraft plus two others in the Basler hangar at Oshkosh were seized by the US Drug Enforcement Agency on 21 September 1990; it was believed the aircraft were to be used for drug smuggling. Warren Basler knew nothing of this, and understood that Air Colombia planned to use the Turbo 67s in support of its business of flying men and equipment between Bogotá and distant oil-drilling installations. Basler had earlier demonstrated a Turbo 67 in Bogotá to Air Colombia, the Colombian government and local airworthiness officials. All seemed quite legitimate, and Basler was shown much of the operations and aircraft used by Air Colombia. In their specification for the turboprop DC-3s, Air Colombia had specified a requirement for long-range capability with the understanding that Omega navigation equipment be fitted. As the airline flew into many remote destinations in Colombia, the request did not appear unusual.

Today, a glance at the US Civil Aircraft Register reveals that no fewer than fourteen DC-3s are registered to a variety of companies associated with Basler, ranging from Basler Flight Service, Basler Airframes Inc. and Basler Turbo Conversions Inc., the latter having as its President Thomas R. Weight. A Turbo 67 DC-3 N96BF is registered to Turbo Power & Marine Systems Inc. of Farmington, Connecticut. This was conversion five, which was involved in autopilot certification testing and became the demonstrator for United Technologies who manufacture the PT-6 engines. In December 1990, the first Turbo 67 to enter service in North America was conversion six, acquired to undertake freight contracts for Federal Express.

Demonstration Tour

In May 1991 a Turbo 67 DC-3 in the camouflaged livery of the Bolivian Air Force and registered N387T c/n 20507 appeared at the McClellan AFB Open House in California. It was seen at Oshkosh, flight demonstrated at the 1991 EAA convention and destined to be delivered shortly afterwards, possibly under 'Operation Peace Turbo' although in this instance the DC-3 was supplied by Basler. Earlier in the year it had been announced that two DC-3 transports operated for many years by the US Forest Service for hauling smoke jumpers and cargo to backwood forest fires would receive a $2.7 million overhaul and conversion to Turbo 67 configuration by Basler. The two DC-3s were indeed completely overhauled and virtually rebuilt with expanded cabin space, stronger wings and room for 10,200 lb of cargo or nineteen passengers. The aircraft were originally N146Z c/n 16819 and N100Z c/n 20494, both registered to the

US Forest Service at Ogden, Utah, although one has been re-registered N142Z. The Douglas transports can airlift as many as twenty smoke jumpers to a forest fire within an hour of receiving the report. Prior to operating the Turbo 67 the USFS only allowed smoke jumpers to travel, since they at least could bale out in case of an engine failure.

Basler is hoping to receive more orders to support a production of Turbo 67s estimated at twelve aircraft annually. During March 1991, Basler pilots Bob Clark and Paul Votava, accompanied by President Tom Weight, flew N96BF across the Atlantic to demonstrate the aircraft to interested organisations in the United Kingdom, basing the Turbo 67 with Air Atlantique at Coventry airport. The DC-3 Turbo 67 was on a delivery flight to Thailand and after the UK demonstrations was flown to Sion, Switzerland. A cargo of 3,800 kg (over 8,000 lb) of mail was flown to Glasgow on a demonstration cargo flight requested by the Post Office. Captain Andrew Dixon of Air Atlantique was at the controls and was favourably impressed. N96BF's speed performance had the Air Traffic Control centres fooled for a while.

In developing the conversion, Basler had in mind the needs of military air arm operators as well as the civil market. For the benefit of the military operator, the engine exhaust is vented over the wing to reduce the infra-red signature. The payload has been increased to 13,000 lb while the 'hot and high' single-engine ceiling, range and cruise speed are enhanced. Other modifications to the airframe introduced by Basler include wing reinforcements to support the increase in payload, wing leading edge and wing-tip changes to improve flight characteristics, and a new control pedestal for the turbine power controls.

The electrical systems of the Basler Turbo 67, as the modified DC-3 is now becoming well known, have been completely renewed to conform to FAR Part 25, while the hydraulic system has been upgraded to speed up the retraction time of the undercarriage. The fuel system has been modified to accept kerosene. The proven simplicity of the DC-3 will ensure that ease of maintenance will remain a steadfast feature of the Turbo 67, but just as important to military operators as to airlines these days is the fact that the cost of the converted DC-3 is about one-third that of other aircraft with comparable performance.

Since the military air arms of many countries are evidently determined to retain their fleet of C-47 military transports as long as possible, the conversion to turboprop power may now be judged to make economic sense. It is no secret that the South African Air Force, with possibly the largest fleet of C-47 Dakotas in the world, and the Venezuelan Air Force have already indicated an option to apply Basler Turbo 67 modification to some of their fleets – in the case of Venezuela, to two transports. It is also now general knowledge that the turboprop modification is so versatile that either conversion can be carried out at Oshkosh, or kits can be made available through company distributors currently located in Taiwan and Poland.

AMI Cargomaster

During May 1987, the Federal Aviation Administration issued a multiple-use Supplemental Type Certificate No. SA3820SW for retrofit DC-3/C-47 transports powered by Pratt & Whitney PT-6A-65A turboprop engines to Aero Modifications International Inc. of Fort Worth, Texas. AMI was formed by J.B. Williams in 1985 for the express purpose of carrying out the research and flight development necessary to retrofit DC-3/C-47 aircraft with Pratt & Whitney PT-6A-65AR turboprop engines. Earlier, Williams had engaged Earl Schafer of the Schafer Aircraft Company to retrofit a Piper Chieftain with PT-6A engines, and the result was so successful that Embraer of Brazil obtained a licence from Williams to retrofit Chieftains in Brazil, where they were named Carajas.

In 1985, several companies asked Earl Schafer to retrofit their Douglas DC-3s and, following several meetings with J.B. Williams, Aero Modification International Inc. was formed, with corporate offices in Fort Worth and a DC-3 rework facility at Waco. The company envisaged that at least a hundred DC-3s would be retrofitted with the PT-6A-65AR turboprop engines within three years. AMI negotiated interest in DC-3 retrofits in Asia, South and Central America, Africa, Canada, China and the Middle East. Import licences for retrofit kits were sought in India. Interest was shown by Air Atlantique in the United Kingdom, and evaluation by the flight engineers from the CAA envisaged no problems with a UK type certification.

In 1988 AMI converted three DC-3 transports and assembled two conversions kits, the latter being exported to Wonder Air in Pretoria, South Africa, along with converted DC-3 N240GB c/n 26713, which was used as the delivery aircraft for the kits. An oil company in Venezuela called Corpoven, previously the Mobil Oil Company and today renamed yet again Maraven, had their DC-3 YV-32CP c/n 13143 converted by AMI; it is now based at Curaçao. It was observed at Waco awaiting conversion on 11 October 1987. Douglas DC-3 N70BF c/n 27085, ex-Basler, was registered to Aero Modifications Inc. in March 1986, and sold to Rhoades Aviation of Columbus, Indiana, after conversion to turboprop configuration; it was registered N887AM and is used on nightly freight contracts between Houston and Dallas.

During October 1988 an AMI turboprop DC-3 N146JR c/n 27085 ex-N70BF made a personal appearance in Bogotá, Colombia, after a request for flight demonstrations for both military and commercial operators by Aviones de Colombia. Earl Schafer as pilot in command flew twenty-five passengers on three demonstration flights. Later, the DC-3 was flown to the military air base at Aplay in the Colombian Llanos, where there are many unpaved short runways suitable only for the Douglas DC-3 and the Curtiss C-46 Commando. A static line was fitted in the AMI DC-3, and on three flights, 140 Colombian paratroops and their equipment were air dropped. Take-offs and landings were accomplished on short grass landing strips, while single-engine operations, turns and stalls repeatedly impressed all those who witnessed the demonstration.

Although the C-47 and the R4D- aircraft have long since disappeared from the inventory of the US Air Force and Navy, the USAF showed interest in the AMI DC-3 retrofit. The C-47 is still in operation with the military air arms of Colombia, El Salvador and Honduras, the US Air Force having a military aid programme with all these countries as demonstrated with 'Operation Peace Turbo'. In early 1989 the AMI DC-3-65TP, as it is normally designated, was demonstrated to representatives of the US military and after a flight in the aircraft a senior VIP gave his support for the DC-3 retrofit.

Conversion

The conversion process is straightforward. The original fuselage is cut just forward of the wing leading edge and stretched 40 inches by the insertion of a new plug structure. All control

cables are tested and lengthened, the aircraft instruments are removed and modified for turbine operations, and a new throttle quadrant is installed. A new wiring harness and dual 24-volt battery system are fitted to facilitate simultaneous engine starts. Finally, a 118-gallon AVTUR fuel tank is added to each nacelle.

Many original DC-3/C-47 aircraft are still in use in South America, Africa and other Third World countries and it is here that AMI are hoping to sell most of their DC-3 conversions. The transport is large enough to provide for flexibility of operations and the values of load, speed, range, runway length and fuel economy can be selected to obtain an infinite number of combinations to give versatility. Some alternatives quoted include 1,505 nautical miles range at normal cruise – 197 knots at 12,000 feet – or 1,000 nautical miles range at a direct operation cost of 91 US cents per nautical mile; a total operating cost of $250 US an hour; a maximum load of 11,100 lb; and a maximum rate of climb of 1,580 feet per minute.

With a current time between overhaul – TBO – of 4,500 hours on the Pratt & Whitney PT-6A-65A turboprop, maintenance costs and downtime are considerably reduced, says the company. A complete training programme for type rating on the AMI DC-3-65TP can be provided. Initial cost for the conversion performed on a customer-owned aircraft was $1.35 million, and $1.25 million for a conversion kit. Aircraft production facilities are centred in a new 35,000-square-foot hangar at Madison Cooper Airport, Waco, Texas. The first flight of the AMI DC-3-65TP took place from Waco on 1 August 1986. The conversion took nineteen months to complete. Studies conducted by the FAA and the Douglas Aircraft Company indicate that, with proper maintenance, the airframe of the DC-3/C-47 will give service for an unlimited period of time. The studies have shown that the airframe of these veterans has no life-limiting components. Only the limits of the piston engines are keeping the transport on the ground.

Update

As early as 1985 J.B. Williams of AMI was involved in discussions with French officials when they were approached by representatives from Ethiopia about retrofitting up to forty-one DC-3s, then considered vital to the Ethiopian economy. In 1988 Donald Douglas Jr visited the company to look over the new AMI DC-3-65TP aircraft. Representatives from several Latin American countries, including the Honduran, Guatemalan, Costa Rican and El Salvadoran governments, as well as representatives from Thailand, South Africa and a number of Pacific Basin countries have visited the facility. It can now be revealed that in 1988 the US Air Force was looking for one or more contractors to provide maintenance, repair and supply support services for some 385 foreign-owned C-47 transports located in a dozen different countries. This was to be negotiated through the huge Warner Robins Air Logistics Center at Robins AFB, Georgia.

Mention has already been made of the AMI DC-3-65TP demonstration in Bogotá, Colombia, commencing on 24 October 1988. The trip was not without some moments of anxiety for the AMI crew, which included the AMI Marketing Vice-President, Dan H. Williams. The aircraft, with a full fuel load, took 6,400 lb of cargo, including barrels of kerosene, from Granada to La Macarena and 8,000 lb from Granada to La Uribe, the elevation being 1,500 ft and the airstrips 2,700 and 2,900 ft respectively. Across the river from La Uribe was the stronghold of Manuel Marulanda, a Tiro Fijo – sureshot – the infamous guerrilla of

South America. When the DC-3 landed at La Uribe, small arms fire could be heard from Señor Marulanda's side of the river.

General Paz and General Ortega were among those who observed the AMI DC-3 perform. They were eager to have a complete report of the tests and demonstrations. Captain Salazar, of Fuerza Aérea Colombia, had the report ready the day after the military demonstration, and AMI flew him in the DC-3 to Bogotá to present it. Aviones de Colombia told AMI that several commercial orders and a sizeable one from the Colombian government could be imminent. On the return flight to the United States the DC-3-65TP flew non-stop from Bogotá to Miami, a flight of 1,335 miles covered in seven hours and thirty-five minutes, with one hour and forty-five minutes of fuel remaining.

A second South American demonstration was undertaken in 1990 and involved demos to high-ranking officials in Guatemala, El Salvador, Honduras and Paraguay, including the Presidents of Guatemala and Paraguay as well as the ruling General of Honduras and his cabinet. The DC-3 took off from La Paz, Bolivia weighing 25,300 lb with an elevation of 13,500 ft in 5,000 ft and 37 seconds. An order from Mexico for twelve retrofits would hopefully mean a contract worth more than $24 million to the company. By this time Dan H. Williams had taken over as President of AMI.

Since AMI commenced research and development on the Douglas DC-3TP project in 1985, their retrofits have spread far and wide. After DC-3-65TP N240GB c/n 26713 was converted for Aeronautical Enterprises, it went to South Africa carrying two conversion kits for Wonderair in Pretoria. The first South African DC-3 to be converted was ZS-DHX c/n 32656, followed by ZS-LJI c/n DBL-0047. Wonderair acquired more DC-3s and it was rumoured that these would eventually be fitted with PT-65A turboprop engines. Two were ZS-GPL c/n 9581 and ZS-PTG c/n 13331.

Currently the Wonderair aircraft are fulfilling a contract to fly mine workers between Mozambique and South Africa. The DC-3-65TP which was ferried out to South Africa, N240GB is still resident and a further kit conversion was DC-3 ZS-LYW, demonstrated at the Farnborough Airshow in 1992, by Professional Aviation. If the South African Air Force continues to retrofit some of their faithful C-47 workhorses in the future, this will ensure the type will continue to serve for many years in a country that has always been a stronghold of the Douglas DC-3/C-47.

In April 1965 Rhoades Aviation Inc., based at Columbus Municipal Airport, Indiana, was formed, and in November 1988 the President, Jack L. Rhoades, began a demonstration tour of the turboprop DC-3 at the locations occupied by the top air freight companies in the United States, prior to accepting a contract from Federal Express. When they took delivery of DC-3-65TP N146JR from Aero Modifications International in April 1989, Federal Aviation Administration approval was immediately granted.

The South African Air Force

On 26 August 1991, the first South African Air Force turbo Dakota conversion was introduced to the public at a ceremony held by 44 Squadron at the air base located at Swartkop, near Pretoria. Deputy Minister Breytenbach and the commanding officer of Swartkop, Colonel Daan Badenhorst, accepted the aircraft from Colonel Boy du Preez, the project officer. It was officially announced that the SAAF had embarked upon a programme to modify its Dakota fleet extensively. The life of these versatile medium-transport aircraft will be extended considerably, while their operational ability and performance will be dramatically enhanced.

A dedicated SAAF project team planned and implemented the upgrading of the Dakota, making maximum use of local resources. The objective was a quality product at the lowest possible price. A production line was set up with existing facilities at two SAAF bases, using logistic personnel. These are located at Ysterplaat, near Cape Town, home of 11 Air Depot, and Swartkop. Engineering and technical support depots, plus many other facilities, are involved in the project. This has resulted in a saving of some 41 million rand. The first production model Dakota was completed in less than four years.

The integrated conversion programme encompasses the following: updating the avionics with locally-developed equipment, using experience gained from other SAAF aviation projects; replacing the Pratt & Whitney R-1830-92 Twin Wasp engines with modern turboprop engines; extending the fuselage by one metre to counterbalance the engine weight loss; updating the hydraulic and electrical systems; improving control surfaces to meet the improved performance; increasing the cargo-carrying capacity by 1,000 kg (about 2,200 lb). The cruising range is increased by almost 400 km (250 miles) and the cruising speed by 80 km (50 miles) per hour.

Development of a maritime version is planned. The Dakota will be fitted with long-range fuel tanks which should improve the operational range to 4,800 km (3,000 miles) and increase the endurance to approximately 13 hours. The converted Dakotas will be deployed to various squadrons as they emerge from the production line.

Designated C-47-TP, the new Dakota was demonstrated at the Ysterplaat air show with Commandant Trevor Hill flying 6858 c/n 3333, the first Cape TP conversion off the production line. Also seen at Ysterplaat were several more turboprop conversions including 6825 c/n 12160, 6857 c/n 33375, 6864 c/n 12580, 6884 c/n 12064 and 6885 c/n 12596.

The outlook for the DC-3 is cautiously optimistic, but with some estimated 1,000 DC-3/C-47s still flying around the globe, it is at least safe to assume that the Grand Ole Lady will make her seventy-fifth birthday – be it powered by a turboprop engine combination.

Chapter Eight
Douglas DC-4

As early as the second half of 1935, initial discussions regarding the possible development of a four-engined transport aircraft with twice the capacity of the DC-3 and a range of 2,200 miles were held between the Douglas Company and United Air Lines. The DC-3 had yet to make its first flight. Naturally Donald Douglas was wary of committing himself to such a complex and expensive project. Likewise United Air Lines, who proposed the aircraft, admitted to not having the financial resources to underwrite the project and they were certainly in no position to guarantee sufficient orders for their own use.

Nevertheless, William Patterson, President of United, was convinced that such a transport was needed and he persuaded other US carriers to support the project. The result was that, by mid-March 1936, initial design studies by the Douglas team were under way, and Patterson's efforts had persuaded four other airlines to show considerable interest. A month later, American, Eastern, Pan American, TWA and United each committed $100,000 towards the design and construction of one prototype known initially as the DC-4.

This was the fourth in the Douglas Commercial series of transports, so was logically designated DC-4. However, when it was shelved in favour of a less complex type, the DC-4/C-54 series, the original DC-4 became the DC-4E – E for Experimental. The Douglas team, under chief engineer Arthur Raymond, went ahead with design studies and built a mock-up of the forward fuselage and cockpit layout. Initial engineering costs were estimated at $300,000.

Factory photograph taken on 15 March 1938 showing the huge DC-4E under assembly in the main hangar at Santa Monica. It took nearly half-a-million man hours to produce this one prototype at a cost, prior to its first flight, of some $3 million. (Douglas)

Development of the DC-4 was unique. The one and only prototype DC-4E was built to specifications laid down by United Air Lines. Bill Patterson had asked for a forty-passenger, 54,000 lb, 175 mph transport, the basic outline being drawn up by G.T. Mead, chief engineer of United's associated company, United Aircraft, in 1935, with assistance from Jerome C. Hunsaker, an aerodynamicist from the Massachusetts Institute of Technology. After trying without success to influence several other aircraft manufacturers in the United States, Patterson took his idea to Donald Douglas and even offered to pay for half the $300,000 engineering costs of the prototype.

Preliminary design conferences took nine months, and as the DC-4E began to take shape, the aircraft appeared even more revolutionary than the earlier Douglas Commercial aircraft. Despite being initially planned to accommodate forty-two passengers with a gross weight of 61,500 lb, the transport expanded to a 65,000 lb machine capable of carrying fifty-two passengers in the roomy fuselage. A production order for forty aircraft was signed between Douglas and the five participating airlines, and all six pooled design resources for the new project.

New, indeed still embryonic, Pratt & Whitney 1,450 hp R-2180-S1A1-G Twin Hornet fourteen-cylinder air-cooled radial engines were specially developed for the new transport and the nose wheel installation was the first of its type to be installed in a large aircraft. The specification called for full pressurisation and air conditioning for the production versions, and the use of a hydraulic power-boosted flight-control system. The latter was planned, though may not, in a final form, have featured in the prototype. Original ancillary features included the use of a 115-volt, 800-cycle AC electrical system in place of the more conventional 24-volt DC system. Eclipse-built auxiliary power-plants, mounted in the inner main engine nacelles and driven by 20 hp supercharged flat-four engines, provided electrical power on the ground. Initially at least, they were designed to provide all electrical and hydraulic power for the aircraft. To enable the DC-4E to fit in to existing hangars, a triple tail was incorporated with marked dihedral. It would also provide adequate control in an engine-out situation. The four engines were canted outward from the line of flight.

The wings, fitted with slotted flaps, were to some extent on the pattern of the DC-2 and DC-3 construction, with a swept leading edge and straight trailing edge. The sweep, however, extended full span and not from a square engine-carrying centre section, as in the earlier Douglas Commercials. The multi-spar centre section of the form was evolved by John K. Northrop, one of whose companies had been formed as a subsidiary of Douglas Aircraft in 1932. The wings housed the inward-retracting main undercarriage. Under-wing pressure refuelling was another advanced feature of the type. In order to cope with the heavier than usual ancillary loads, the hydraulic system operated at a high pressure of 2,000 lb/sq in.

Accommodation on the flight deck was for the two pilots plus a flight engineer, with a separate external entrance. The passenger areas were divided into seven compartments, with roomy and luxurious arrangements. These included two lounges, with washrooms, lavatory and other appropriate facilities, forward for the men and aft for the women. There was a steward's galley and an independently-equipped stateroom for two passengers, as well as the main passenger compartment, wardrobes, hand baggage area and cargo/baggage compartments with exterior doors.

Although they were initially impressed by the Douglas proposal for the DC-4E, the sponsoring airlines began to show great concern over its complexity and by mid-1936 both Pan American and TWA had decided to withdraw their support and to sponsor the smaller and somewhat less complicated Boeing 307 Stratoliner. This decision left Douglas with only $300,000 in airline funds for the development of a costly aircraft.

Over 100,000 man hours went into laboratory research, as all the jigs and systems were much longer than anything yet fabricated. Nearly half a million man hours were required to produce the one prototype at a cost before its first flight of some $3 million. After more than two years of construction, which included wind tunnel and extensive testing of structure and systems in special rigs located at Santa Monica and elsewhere, the DC-4E NX18100 c/n 1601 was completed in May 1938.

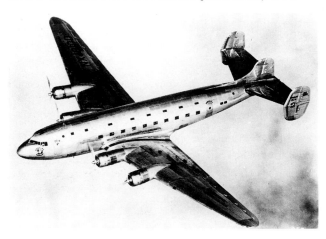

This rare photograph gives an excellent profile of the one and only DC-4E airliner NX18100 c/n 1601. Pleasant to handle with no vices, its performance was not good. However, Benny Howard a project pilot demonstrated its twin-engine take-off capability by taking off from Cheyenne Airport, Wyoming, located 6,200ft above sea level. (MAP)

First Flight

Roll-out was during the evening of 7 June 1938, at Clover Field, Santa Monica, for the initial flight by Carl Cover, test pilot and Vice-President, with co-pilot John Cable. Preliminary taxying and checks of the elevator power and braking were followed by an uneventful take-off, followed by a 90-minute test flight and a landing at Mines Field – now Los Angeles International Airport – the municipal airport, which was more suitable for preliminary test work. A further three landings were made. On the following day more flights were made from Mines Field with a larger test crew and with the chief pilot of United Air Lines as one of two observers.

Over 500 hours were flown in the next six months, during which a number of minor modifications were made before the US Department of Commerce issued an Approved Type

Certificate for the DC-4E. The ATC was finally issued on 5 May 1939, the delay being due to the numerous minor teething troubles with the aircraft's intricate systems. The DC-4E was then handed over to United Air Lines, named '**Super Mainliner**' and painted in the airline's livery; it subsequently made numerous proving flights on the United network. During this period the aircraft demonstrated its ability to take off on only two engines when Benny Howard, a project pilot with United, lifted it off from Cheyenne Airport, Wyoming, which had an elevation of 6,200 ft AMSL (above mean sea level).

Both on the ground and in the air the DC-4E was reported to be pleasant to handle and to possess no vices, but the performance did leave something to be desired. Proving flights were continued and pilots from each of the other participating airlines had the opportunity to fly the airliner. However, the complexity of the systems presented excessive maintenance problems and the operating economics were very disappointing in spite of an increase in passenger capacity from forty-two to fifty-two and an increase in the gross weight from 61,500 lb to 65,000 lb. The profit-making prospects were not very good given the expected engineering costs in initial airline service with such complexities of systems and structure.

There was no doubt that the fifty-two-seat airliner was far too ambitious, too complex and too large, as well as too costly for US domestic operation and current demand. In addition, the empty weight was above estimates and the performance was below expectation in some respects. Accordingly, the sponsoring airlines agreed with Douglas to suspend further development in favour of a new, less complex, DC-4 project, which was to lead to the military C-54 'Skymaster' and to the DC-4, which are still in service in many corners of the world.

Very few photographs exist of the DC-4E in United Air Lines livery. Seen on 20 June 1939, now registered NC18100, the transport is titled Super Mainliner. *The engines were 1,450hp Pratt & Whitney R-2180-SIAI-G Twin Hornet fourteen-cylinder air-cooled radials.* (Douglas)

Now registered NC18100, the DC-4E was returned to Douglas and during 1939 was sold, through a trading company in Japan, ostensibly for use, after tests, as a VIP transport by Japan Air Lines – Dai Nippon Koku KK. It was shipped to Japan on 29 September 1939, reassembled by Douglas technicians and registered JA6005. According to some reports, it crashed in Tokyo Bay on a test flight during 1940, whilst

The one and only DC-4E NC18100 never went into service with United Air Lines but sold by Douglas to Japan and shipped as depicted by sea on 29 September 1939. It was re-assembled by Douglas technicians on arrival and became registered JA6005. (Robert C. Mikesh)

attempting a full-flap landing with one engine out. Another report indicated that it was dismantled by Nakajima on behalf of the Japanese Navy, for which the airline had acted as cover.

Long-range Bomber

Even before the first flight of the DC-4E in June 1938, the Japanese were purchasing detailed blueprints, complete with notes, on its construction. The Japanese aircraft industry had little or no experience of such large aircraft. However, Japan had purchased the licence rights to build several US military and commercial aircraft prior to 1938, including manufacturing rights for the Douglas DC-3. Their interest in the DC-4E arose from their undertaking the construction of a large four-engined bomber for the Japanese Navy. This bomber was already well advanced in design when the DC-4E was purchased.

After dismantling the Douglas airliner during the winter of 1939/40, Japanese engineers studied its components and utilised knowledge for modifying what was to become the Nakajima G5N1 'Shinzan' bomber, known under the Allied aircraft code 'Liz'. In that project, the wing platform of the DC-4E was transposed almost exactly, although its position was moved from a low-wing to a mid-wing layout. A similar tail configuration was incorporated, but the fuselage layout was entirely Japanese.

In retrospect, both the United States and Douglas received more than the $950,000 the Japanese paid for the DC-4E. After deducting the $300,000 received from the three sponsoring airlines – American, Eastern and United – but including the unspecified price paid by Mitsui, Douglas lost a total of $1,344,600 on the DC-4E airliner project.

The Definitive DC-4

During mid-1939, American, Eastern and United shared Douglas's view that there was a need for an aircraft similar in capacity to the DC-4E. But it would have to use less complex systems, be cheaper and easier to maintain, and offer substantially improved operating economics. The Douglas engineering team, led by Arthur Raymond and Ed Burton, decided to design a completely new airliner. The new transport was to be twenty-five per cent lighter than its predecessor, smaller and simpler, its fuselage cross-section reduced by 10 in to 118 in. It had a much revised straight wing, unlike the swept-back configuration of the DC-4E. Much of the experience gained in building and testing the DC-4E was incorporated into the design.

The new DC-4 was unpressurised and built to accommodate forty-two passengers by day in ten rows, with two seats on either side of a single aisle, or twenty-eight passengers by night. It had conventional hydraulic and electrical systems and a single fin and rudder. It was powered by four well-proven 1,050 hp Pratt & Whitney SIC3-G Twin Wasp fourteen-cylinder radial engines. Apparently there was a choice of engines, which included 1,000 hp Wright SGR-1820-G205A Cyclone nine-cylinder radials. The wing span was reduced from 138 ft 3 in on the DC-4E to 117 ft 6 in, while the length was shortened by 3 ft 8 in. Power boost to the controls was deleted, as was the Auxiliary Power Unit – APU. Although the tricycle undercarriage was retained, the main wheels retracted forwards into the engine nacelles, rather than sideways into the wings. This allowed for the transfer of fuselage tanks into that area made available by the layout change. The initial proposed gross weight of the new DC-4 was 50,000 lb, compared with the eventual 65,000 lb of the DC-4E.

The new DC-4 had an entirely new wing of reduced area and high aspect-ratio with an equal taper on leading and trailing edges, a single fin and rudder and a tailplane minus dihedral. The fuselage was slightly shorter and of smaller diameter. Initial reactions from the airlines – Eastern, American and United – were very enthusiastic, and after a change in engines to four 1,450 hp Pratt & Whitney Twin Wasp R-2000 2SD1-G fourteen-cylinder radials had been agreed upon, Douglas accepted the first commercial orders. By January 1940 airline orders totalled sixty-one. Military orders from the USAAF also flowed in. These included orders for nine C-54s and sixty-two C-54As, with reinforced cabin flooring, special cargo doors and built-in loading hoists.

War Clouds

For a while it appeared that the new DC-4 was doomed before it ever flew. The conflict in Europe had resulted in an increase in military orders for the Douglas factory from both the British and French Purchasing Commissions, as well as from the US Armed Forces. The US War Department instructed Douglas to concentrate on the design and manufacture of combat aircraft and of the DC-3 and its military derivatives.

Donald Douglas, however, was intent on producing his new four-engined transport for which he had received commercial orders. He assured the War Department that the DC-4 programme would not interfere with prompt delivery of military aircraft on order. Then came the Japanese attack on Pearl Harbor. With the outbreak of war and the pre-war build-up, the Santa Monica factory was bulging with military orders – for SBD Dauntless dive bombers, A-20 Boston attack bombers, C-47 'Skytrain' transports, plus experimental work on the new B-19 heavy bomber. However, after some uncertainty regarding the disposition of the commercial DC-4s already under

The first production C-54-DO Skymaster 41-20-137 c/n 3050 first flew from Santa Monica on 26 March 1942 with Douglas test pilot John F. Martin at the controls. There was no prototype, and this transport was delivered to the US Army Air Force just four months later. (Douglas)

construction, they were taken over by the US Army Air Force and designated C-54-DOs and C-54A-DOs. These airliners were pressed into service by the War Department as a stop-gap until *bona fide* C-54As came off the production line – at the time they were the only civilian land-based transports capable of flying the Atlantic non-stop, from Newfoundland to the United Kingdom.

There was no prototype DC-4. The first production aircraft c/n 3050 had the USAAF serial 41-20137 and was completed as a C-54-DO in February 1942. It was finished in drab military markings, making its first flight from Clover Field on 14 February with John F. Martin at the controls. The first successful maiden flight and its subsequent development trials programme was trouble-free, providing the USAAF with a long-range heavy logistic transport – a type urgently needed, given the worldwide scale of operations into which the United States had been forced without proper preparation.

The first C-54 'Skymaster' for service use, c/n 3060 41-20138, was delivered on 20 March 1942, and by October the first twenty-four military personnel transports constructed from civilian DC-4s were delivered to the Atlantic Wing of the huge US Air Transport Command. These revised military transports were fitted with four long-range 464 gallon auxiliary fuel tanks in the fuselage to bring the total up to 3,700 gallons, providing a range of 2,500 miles with a 9,600 lb payload. In this configuration only twenty-six passengers were carried, but they met a need for trans-Pacific flights.

A total of ninety-seven improved C-54As, fitted with thirty-three bucket seats and slightly larger wing tanks, were built, their gross weight being increased to 68,000 lb from 65,800 lb. As production progressed the fuselage tanks were gradually eliminated, the C-54s relying increasingly on integral tanks in the outer wing panels and the fuselage tanks in the C-54B models.

Production

The first 121 of the 'A' and 'B' versions of the DC-4 were built by Douglas at Santa Monica. Early in 1942 when the factory was literally unable to keep up with new orders, which included 1,335 C-47 transports, A-20s and SBDs, a new factory was

established on the site of what is now O'Hare International Airport at Chicago. It was one of a series of factories constructed by the US Defense Plant Corporation, a subsidiary of the Reconstruction Finance Corporation, for leasing to manufacturers. The first 155 C-54A-DCs, identical to the Santa Monica transports, were completed at the Chicago plant. This facility would eventually produce nearly two-thirds of all C-54 'Skymasters'.

Santa Monica produced a hundred C-54B transports including one C-54B-1-DO 43-17126, given the RAF serial EW999, which served as the personal transport for the British Prime Minister, Winston Churchill. Chicago delivered 120 similar C-54B-DC versions. In the VIP range, one C-54A-5-DO c/n 7470 42-107451 was specially modified to serve as the presidential transport for President Roosevelt. Named '*Sacred Cow*', the aircraft was fitted with a stateroom, three conference rooms and six bunks. The normal accommodation for the President was a staff of fourteen and a crew of seven. The total fuel capacity was increased to 4,510 gallons by fitting integral tanks in the outer wing panels. An electric lift was fitted to accommodate the President's wheelchair. This was the only version of the C-54C to be delivered. In the event, President Roosevelt only used '*Sacred Cow*' twice, one of the flights being to the Yalta Conference in February 1945. Later President Harry Truman used it to fly to no fewer than fifty-five countries. After assignment to the huge Military Air Transport Service – MATS – it was transferred to the Smithsonian Museum in November 1961 and restored to its original Second World War livery.

The C-54 presented as a VIP aircraft to Winston Churchill on 3 June 1944 was delivered to the United Kingdom as an empty shell, and was refitted by Armstrong Whitworth Aircraft Ltd into a super-plus airliner with accommodation for only ten VIPs and separate compartments for a crew of six. Unique in the annals of air transportation was the installation of electrically-heated toilet seats. When the Elsan aircraft water-closet seat was lowered, the electric current switched on automatically. In November 1945, after Churchill had been voted out of office, the VIP C-54 EW999 was returned to the United States. What happened to the electrically-heated toilet seats remains a mystery.

Prime Minister Winston S. Churchill's Skymaster EW999 seen at RAF Boscombe Down, Wiltshire, during August 1944, still retaining its USAAF fin serial. It was a C-54B-1-D0 43-17126 c/n 18326 delivered to the USAAF on 3 June 1944. Captain and pilot was Wing Commander 'Bill' Fraser, RAF. (Via C. C. H. Cole)

The US Marine Corps operated the Skymaster. Depicted is R5D-3 BuNo.92003 built as a C-54D-1-DC 42-72484 c/n 10589 and delivered on 24 February 1945. It later went to the RAF as KL978 being returned to the USA in 1946, reverting to 42-72484 with the US Air Force. (Douglas)

Ten four-engined C-54 Skymasters parked on the ramp at Tempelhof, Berlin, during the Berlin Airlift. First transport in line is 42-72523 c/n 10628 from the 19th Troop Carrier Squadron, second being 42-72223 c/n 10328 from the 20th Troop Carrier Squadron. Cargoes ranged from engine crates to milk bottles. (USAF)

This excellent photograph of C-54A-DO 41-37283 c/n clearly shows the profile of the Skymaster and the wartime paint scheme. This transport was delivered on 15 April 1943, later being civilianised as NC90400 with American Airlines before sale to Air France as F-BELH. (IWM)

The C-54 and R5D- Skymasters were the life-saver of Berlin during the Russian blockade in 1948-49 some 200 Douglas four-engined transports being involved. This view shows the huge cargo door of the Skymaster. The transport is from the 20th Troop Carrier Squadron US Air Force.
(AP Photo Library)

Some two million occupants of Berlin required feeding during the Russian blockade of the city in 1948-49. This was a daily event as Berliners watch the approach of yet another load of supplies carried by a C-54 Skymaster.
(Landesbildstelle)

Seen at Nichols Field, Manila, Philippines, on 19 April 1945, is 'Bataan' the personal aircraft of General Douglas MacArthur. It is a VC-54E-1DO 44-9027 c/n 27253 delivered on 15 June 1945. Surviving World War II it became N5525V, later in 1966, OB-R-847 with Faucett Airlines.
(National Archives)

The C-54D was similar to the 'B' model but had improved R-2000-11 Pratt & Whitney engines generating 1350 hp each. It was built exclusively at the Chicago plant, and was the version delivered in largest numbers, with a total of 380 built. Later modifications led to the appearance of several specialised versions.

Differing from the C-54D mainly in having a new fuel-tank arrangement in which the two remaining cabin tanks were replaced by collapsible bag-type tanks, the 'E' model was a twenty-seat long-range version that retained the cargo door. The internal cabin configuration was modified to permit rapid conversion from 32,500 lb cargo to a troop carrier with fifty canvas bucket seats. The payload was limited and only 125 were completed at Santa Monica, though one C-54E 44-9027 was specially modified and assigned to General Douglas MacArthur in January 1945; it was named '***Bataan***'.

Next in sequence should have been the C-54F, but instead a XC-54F-DC designation was applied to a single C-54B-1-DC c/n 10426 42-72321 fitted with two paratroop jump doors for use by the US Troop Carrier Command. The planned C-54F production version was to have been based on C-54D airframes, but none was built.

Production of the C-54G model commenced during June 1945 with the more powerful R-2000-9 Pratt & Whitney radials and a troop carrier interior. Before production was terminated after VJ-Day, a total of 162 were completed at Santa Monica, with most of the 'G' models being sent to India for China–Burma–India (CBI) operations over the Hump. After VJ-Day a total of 235 C-54G-20-DO transports were cancelled and components for these were used by Douglas to produce the post-war civil DC-4-1009s.

'Skymaster' Projects

There were many projected developments for the C-54 and its US Navy R5D- series. For trans-Atlantic and trans-Pacific operations the 'Skymaster' had a limited payload-range envelope necessitating either stopovers or a sizeable reduction in payload. There was no room for additional tanks within the aircraft beyond the installation of collapsible bag-type tanks fitted to C-54Es, and the only possible method of increasing fuel load was to use external tanks. Douglas conceived a novel system of large winged tanks which were to be attached to the wing-tips by means of flexible joints linking each aircraft wing-tip to one of the wing-tips of the external tanks. Each tank was fitted with a retractable outrigger undercarriage to bear the weight of the tank whilst on the ground. With wings fitted to the tanks this reduced the total aircraft wing loading, a critical factor once the weight of the tanks and fuel was added to an already fully loaded C-54. As new transports with an increased payload range capacity became available, this unique development was suspended. This enabled the large fleet of 'Skymasters' operated by the US armed forces to be assigned to shorter routes.

One C-54E-DO was experimentally fitted with the nine-cylinder air-cooled Wright Cyclone radials, a power-plant originally offered as an option on the pre-war DC-4. The designation allocated was XC-54K-DO, but the type was not proceeded with. One C-54A-DO was modified to test a new fuel system; it was never produced, but was designated C-54L-DO. Thirty-eight C-54E-DOs were stripped to carry coal during the Berlin Airlift of 1948/49, with the payload increased by 2,500 lb to 35,000 lb. These were designated C-54M-DO. During the United Nations Korean conflict, thirty C-54E-DOs were specially modified for aeromedical evacuation for which mercy role they were fitted with thirty stretchers and accommodation for medical attendants. These were designated MC-54M-DO.

There was a projected development of the C-54 series with a pressurised cabin and four Pratt & Whitney R-2800-22W eighteen-cylinder air-cooled radials. Designated XC-112, the project was abandoned in favour of the XC-112A. One XC-114-DO prototype 45-874 c/n 36327 was built with an airframe basically similar to that of the C-54E-DO but with the fuselage

Tempelhof Airport, Berlin, during the height of the Berlin Airlift with a line of C-54s being unloaded at night. Seventeen minutes after landing, the Skymasters were airborne on the return shuttle to Frankfurt or Wiesbaden for more supplies. The first C-54 is 45-529 c/n 35982, the second being 45-610 c/n 36063. (USAF via Eldon Ferguson)

length increased from 93 ft 10 in to 100 ft 7 in; it was powered by four 1,620 hp Allison V-1710-131 twelve-cylinder vee liquid-cooled engines. Gross weight was increased to 80,500 lb. The projected XC-115-DO was a development of the XC-114 which was to have had four 1,650 hp Packard V-1650-209 twelve-cylinder vee liquid-cooled engines, but this was not built. There was also one XC-116-DO 45-875 c/n 36327, which was similar to the XC-114 but fitted with thermal de-icing equipment instead of pneumatic boots.

A large number of C-54 'Skymasters' of various models were transferred to the US Navy and US Marine Corps. Contracts for these were included in contracts from the US War Department on behalf of the USAAF. They received R5D- designations and included fifty-six R5D-1s, thirty R5D-2s, eighty-six R5D-3s, twenty R5D-4s and thirteen R5D-5s obtained by the US Navy Department mainly for use by the US Coast Guard. There was a projected R5D-6 version equivalent to the C-54J, but again none was built.

Post-war

With the end of hostilities in 1945, the airlines of the free world were keen to rebuild their operations, and the Douglas 'Skymasters' attracted the attention of many commercial customers. Already, the Douglas Aircraft Company was anticipating a strong demand for the commercial DC-4, incorporating all the improvements progressively introduced in the C-54 series. The Company now offered two new versions, the DC-4-1009 and the DC-4-1037.

The DC-4-1009 had no cargo door and was purely a passenger transport with accommodation for a crew of five and forty-four passengers, baggage and freight for day use, or twenty-two passengers, baggage and freight as a sleeper transport. The accommodation was equivalent to first class seating but later DC-4-1009s and ex-military C-54s had a capacity for eighty-six seats in a high-density configuration. The DC-4-1037 was fitted as a commercial cargo transport retaining the large cargo door of the military C-54s on the left-hand side. Both these new versions were to be powered by Pratt & Whitney Twin Wasp R-20000 radials rated at 1,450 hp for take-off. Normal fuel capacity was 2,868 US gallons, which could be increased to 3,592 gallons. Cabin pressurisation was available for the DC-4-1009.

Due to the cancellation of 235 C-54G-20-DO transports, which left a large surplus of partially built aircraft and parts, Douglas were able to offer the benefit of rapid delivery. Nevertheless they met with little success, as cheaper surplus military C-54s were available in large numbers. In the event only seventy-nine DC-4-1009s, all unpressurised, were built. The first was NC10201 c/n 42904, delivered to Western Airlines on 18 January 1946. Not a single DC-4-1037 was ordered by the world's airlines. The needs of both airlines and foreign air arms could be satisfied by modified surplus C-54s. Douglas performed a substantial number of conversions in the Santa Monica and El Segundo plants, whilst other aircraft were modified by the airlines themselves and by specialised companies. Production of the DC-4 was finally halted in 1947, following delivery of the last DC-4-1009, ZS-BMH c/n 43157, to South African Airways on 9 August of that year.

Over the North Atlantic route a converted Douglas C-54 belonging to American Overseas Airlines introduced a commercial landplane service on 23 October 1945 by flying the route between New York and Hurn, near Bournemouth, in Hampshire, in 23 hours 48 minutes, including stopovers at both Gander, Newfoundland, and Shannon, Eire. During the following years, six other airlines – Pan American, KLM, Air France, SAS, Sabena and Swissair – initiated post-war North Atlantic services with DC-4s. In addition, the DC-4 pioneered other intercontinental routes, including trans-Pacific services by both Pan American and Australian National Airways. ANA flew on behalf of British Commonwealth Pacific Airlines, making a first experimental flight on 3 May 1946, before initiating a fortnightly service from Sydney to Vancouver. On the South Atlantic route from South America to Europe, the DC-4 was first introduced by Flota Aérea Mercante Argentina – FAMA – commencing on 17 September 1946. Prior to this, following a proving flight which left Amsterdam on 10 November 1945, KLM and KNILM used DC-4s to reopen their pre-war route linking the Netherlands with the Netherlands East Indies. As more DC-4-1009s were delivered from the Douglas factory, and conversions of surplus C-54s were made at an increasing rate, Douglas DC-4s saw worldwide service with a large number of scheduled and non-scheduled carriers.

In the United States, on the domestic route system, the market for which the DC-4 had originally been designed, the airline was first operated by its three original sponsors. American Airlines commenced DC-4 service on the New York to Chicago route during February 1946, and United Air Lines and Eastern began DC-4 operations shortly after. On 7 March 1946, American started a DC-4 service between New York and Los Angeles and, by making only one stop *en route* as against three stops for the DC-3, reduced the westbound flying time from 17 hours 40 minutes to 14 hours 30 minutes and eastbound, from 16 hours to 13 hours 15 minutes. Other trunk carriers operating the DC-4 in the United States included Braniff, Capital, Colonial, Delta, National Northwest, TWA and Western. Northwest also operated Pacific routes whilst TWA operated only on cargo services and mainly on international routes.

The first DC-4 for Delta NC37472 c/n 10444 ex-C54B-1-DC 42-72339 was delivered after conversion at Santa Monica on 12 February 1946. It was the tenth post-war conversion by Douglas and served Delta until 6 February 1953 when it was sold to Irving Herman, owner of Super Coach. (Delta)

On 16 February 1946, Delta received from the USAAF the first of seven C-54B 'Skymasters', which were modified by Douglas at Santa Monica to civilian DC-4s between October 1945 and May 1946. It was NC37472 c/n 10444. The company designed new ramp equipment for the forty-four-seat airliners, whilst the chief engineer designed the galley. Reviving its old custom of naming its most important services, Delta listed the entry of the DC-4 to its route system on 6 March 1946 as 'The Rocket'. It operated between Chicago and Miami, and was joined a few weeks later, on 1 April, by the Atlanta-to-Dallas 'Comet'. In November, after receiving CAB approval, the DC-4s flew the Chicago–Miami route non-stop. There was a fatality, when on 10 March 1948, DC-4 NC 37478 c/n 18390 crashed at Chicago. The last DC-4 operated by Delta, NC37477 c/n 18333, was sold to North American Airlines on 15 June 1953.

Delta operated eight DC-4s, all ex-military, including NC37477 C-54B-5-DO 43-17133 c/n 18333 the 34th conversion by Douglas and delivered on 27 April 1946 serving Delta until 15 June 1953, when it was sold to North American Airlines. After operating in Germany and the United Kingdom it was sold to United Air Ferries in September 1964 and converted as ATL-98 Carvair No.11 G-APNH. (Delta)

Noteworthy highlights in the operational life of the DC-4 included the use of JATO by Braniff Airlines during 1949/50 to enable flights to operate out of La Paz, Bolivia, at high gross weights and still comply with regulations, in spite of the high altitude of the airport which was 11,800 ft above sea level. It is reported that some airlines, including Capital, operated DC-4s in a scheme to deceive uninitiated passengers into believing they were in fact boarding DC-6 airliners. A square of dark paint edged with a white strip was painted around the circular cabin windows. An interesting modification resulted from Sabena in Belgium fitting a swing tail to an Air Congo DC-4 to make it capable of accepting outsized cargo loads.

As larger, pressurised airliners such as the DC-6 and the Lockheed Constellation came into service, the career of the DC-4 with major world airlines on major commercial routes was comparatively short-lived. It nevertheless continued to be used on non-scheduled routes and with cargo and charter operators. Today the type is still in operation, primarily in less developed countries and with some military air arms.

The C-54 was recognised by the US Armed Forces as a very dependable transport. In a 1981 survey, it was revealed that C-54s had made some 80,000 crossings of the Atlantic and Pacific with only three ditchings, of which only one had fatalities. After the Second World War, surplus C-54s were sold by the US War Department via the Reconstruction Finance Corporation for about $90,000 each. Overhaul and conversion to

airline standards took another $200,000 and three months, which was longer than it took to build the 'Skymaster' in the first place. Although this proved a bonanza for airline and freight operators, the bargain prices seriously undercut the market for the new DC-4s with the Douglas Aircraft Company.

Some of the proposed modifications and projects involving the military C-54 have already been mentioned. During July 1941, a design study was carried out by Wright Field, Dayton, Ohio, to see if the C-54 'Skymaster' could fly with an externally mounted T9E1 tank or a 105 mm howitzer M-2. According to a non-classified USAAF document, it was observed that because of its effect on the aerodynamics and range of the transport, such material could be carried externally only as a last resort. However, it was discovered that both items of military hardware could be carried internally by widening the C-54 cargo door from 67 to 96 in.

The largest civil customer for the post-war DC-4-1009 'Skymaster' was Air France, who ordered fifteen, followed by Sabena with nine, National in the USA with seven and Australian National Airways with five.

Achievements

Pan American Airways conducted an epoch-making survey flight with a DC-4 to establish land-based routes to the Far East. This began on 21 October 1945 and covered 25,000 miles in order to set up routes in the Pacific area, draw up approach and departure procedures, and establish FAA and diplomatic formalities. The twenty-six-day flight took over 140 hours of flying. Stops were made in Honolulu, Midway, Wake, Guam, Tinian, Saipan, Manila, Iwo Jima and Tokyo. Then on to Nanking, Tsingtao, Shanghai, Hong Kong, Hainan, Saigon, Batavia (later Djakarta), Bangkok, Singapore, Calcutta and Rangoon.

At the conclusion of the mammoth 'Skymaster' survey flights, Pan Am replaced its Boeing 314 four-engined flying-boats, which cruised at 183 mph and carried a crew of ten and forty to seventy passengers, with the DC-4. The Boeing flight from San Francisco to Honolulu took twenty hours, the DC-4

This Sabena DC-4 00-CBI c/n 43096/72 was a post-war built airliner delivered on 23 April 1947. It was used by the United Nations organisation in the Congo conflict during 1961 and then went to Air Congo registered 90-CBI, later 9Q-CBI. Sabena commenced a Brussels to New York service via Shannon and Gander with the DC-4 on 4 June 1947. (Sabena)

took ten, and with the inauguration of the 'Skymaster', the fare was reduced from $278 one way to $195. Pan American had taken delivery of ten DC-4s by the end of 1945, followed by twenty more in 1946, and prior to their replacement with the pressurised DC-6 and DC-7, operated a total of ninety-two 'Skymasters'.

A subsidiary of Pan Am, the China National Airways Corporation – CNAC – based in Shanghai, also used the DC-4 for their international routes. During the Korean conflict, PAA and other civil operators were pressed into service using their DC-4s for the massive airlift to supply forces with men, materiel and armaments and providing aeromedical evacuation services. Civil airlines carried 67 per cent of the passengers, 56 per cent of the cargo and 70 per cent of the mail into Japan during what was known as the Tokyo Airlift, an uninspiring operation. It was not dramatic, but an airlift made for the civilian carriers. They operated three crews per 'Skymaster' available and could respond immediately. Since the airlift was into Japan, not Korea – the combat zone – the civil airlines had all the advantages. Over sixty DC-4 four-engined commercial transports were chartered to fly into Japan. Earlier, during the Berlin Airlift, Pan American was the airline operator at the time the Russians closed the ground transportation routes used for food, fuel and all other supplies. The Douglas C-54 became the saviour of Berlin.

All pilots familiar with the DC-4 were astounded and often grateful for its structural integrity in the severe turbulence for which the Pacific is famous. In those days, meteorological data was scarce and came only from a few ground stations and ships. Lightning strikes were common, with radio masts being severed in some instances. St Elmo's Fire would usually envelop the aircraft, rolling down the fuselage or waving like a snake in front of the cockpit.

On the Atlantic routes, notably the North Atlantic, the DC-4 proved its worth just as it had in the Pacific and Alaska until it was gradually replaced by the 'double-bubble' Boeing 377

Seen on final approach to land at Oakland, California, is DC-4 NC30040 of UAL Mainliner Yosemite c/n 18379 ex-C-54B-15-DO 43-17179 on 1 April 1946. On 10 March 1964 whilst owned by Slick it crashed into Boston Harbour whilst on final approach to Logan Airport. The accident was due to tail icing. (William T. Larkins)

'Stratocruiser'. The DC-4 again proved its structural integrity in a bizarre and extremely stupid incident that could easily have killed the crew of five plus fifty-four cabin passengers. The date was 10 August 1947; the flight, American Airlines AA331 from Dallas to Phoenix. There were three pilots on the flight deck, one a veteran of eight years flying and the company check pilot, who was in the jump seat. The two normal pilots were in the left- and right-hand seats, only one having his seat belt fastened.

The official FAA accident-incident report read:

While in flight, the Captain, who was sitting in the jump seat in order to allow another Captain on board to acquire type experience, moved the gust lock into the locked position, unbeknown to the pilot at the controls. The nose started to rise and the pilot in the left seat moved the flattener control, or trim tab, to nose-down position to correct this. Having no effect, he continued to move it to correct tail heaviness. At this time, the Captain in the jump seat released the gust lock, and the DC-4 entered a violent manoeuvre, actually becoming inverted. The co-pilot was able to roll it out to the left after which the flight returned to El Paso where the co-pilot made the landing.

During the confusion, when the two unstrapped pilots were thrown to the top of the cockpit, feathering buttons on No. 1 and No. 2 and No. 4 engine were hit and the propellers feathered. The airliner did a half outside loop and was rolled to the left by the co-pilot between 200-400 feet above the ground. The aircraft had minor damage to the de-icer boots and damage to the cabin lining by passengers hitting the roof.

The check pilot resigned after the accident and the DC-4 was returned to service five days later.

Another documentation of the ruggedness of the DC-4 design occurred when, on a night flight between Newfoundland and the Azores, one flew into a waterspout. The Captain was quoted as saying, 'While I was struggling to get up to my seat, I distinctly saw the airspeed needle pegged at 300, and after a lot of wild confusion, gravity returned.' Following the safe landing at the Azores, an inspection disclosed that the entire fuselage had been twisted out of line with the wings and the DC-4 had to be scrapped.

Domestic Boom

After the Second World War, the US airlines were in no hurry to lower fares, finding themselves with a good sellers' market. It was pressure from the many enterprising non-scheduled operators which brought about a change of heart.

The New York to Chicago route had always been the vital high-density air route of the United States, ever since operations with the DC-3 showed that profits were possible over the 740-mile stage distance, without a mail subsidy. In the post-war period, American started the first DC-4 four-engined service on the route in February 1946 and United followed with DC-4s in March. Another competitor had earlier been added to the New York to Chicago route when, on 16 December 1944, the CAB authorised Pennsylvania Central Airlines to operate via Pittsburgh and Detroit. Service was started in July 1945 and was allowed to omit the Detroit stop in February 1948. On 21 April 1948, the company was renamed Capital Airlines and on 4 November made airline history by starting the first sustained low-fare coach-class service in the United States. Called the

This C-54G-5-DO 45-571 c/n 36024 registered NC88943 was leased from the USAAF in order to train Pan American Airline pilots. It is seen on a very low approach to San Francisco Airport on 26 March 1947. It later went back to the USAAF. The author's good friend, Bill Larkins, took this photograph stood on the roof of his Model B Ford using his 3¼ x 4¼ Graflex camera – 1/1000th @ f8. (William T. Larkins)

'Nighthawk', it used DC-4s during the off-peak hours. Capital charged 4 cents per mile instead of the standard 6 cents, which brought the fare down to $33.30 one way, or about two-thirds of the first-class fare. It justified its case before the Civil Aeronautics Board by using high-density seating arrangements – sixty in a DC-4 – with a minimum of amenities in the way of cabin service. The fare remained in force until competition from the large airlines brought a further reduction, to $30,80, on 1 April 1952.

Capital's action was soon copied by other scheduled airlines and by the end of 1949, coach-class travel had reached major proportions on scheduled networks. On 27 December both American and TWA began coast-to-coast services using sixty-seat DC-4s, at a single fare of $110. United started its first post-war coach service on 14 May 1950, with a DC-4 service from Los Angeles to San Francisco. The fare was $9.95 one way, or about 3 cents per mile. Western Airlines added daylight services at the same fare on 1 June 1950, and the two airlines engaged in a minor rate war down the Pacific coast during the next few months.

Chicago and Southern Airlines held the north-to-south Mississippi River Valley route. Just before the war the CAB had given the airline a route to Houston and immediately after the war added a north-eastward extension to Detroit, which the airline opened on 1 June 1945. It then covered a broad stretch of territory from the Great Lakes to the Gulf of Mexico. In June 1946, DC-4s were put into service and, on 1 November of that year, Chicago and Southern became the first airline to put into effect a route awarded by President Truman in the momentous Latin American Case of 1946; not solved until 1957. This was from New Orleans to Havana, Cuba, and in August 1948 a further penetration across the Caribbean saw the airline serving Caracas, Venezuela. Unfortunately the airline was unable to

survive independently, and negotiated a merger with Delta Air Lines on 1 May 1953.

Eastern Air Lines held a comfortable monopoly on the New York to Miami route which was broken on 19 February 1944, when National Airlines was awarded the Jacksonville to New York segment. Encouraged by non-stop authorisation, National then began to set the pace by introducing the DC-4 on a direct over-water route from Miami to New York on 14 February 1946. Eastern followed shortly afterwards in competition which intensified over the years.

During the early post-war years the DC-4 'Skymaster' became heavily involved in both domestic and international air-cargo work. By the end of 1947 the Flying Tiger Line had acquired the DC-4 which were later used in the airlift to Korea and Japan. Riddle Airlines with its headquarters in Miami inaugurated scheduled freighter services from New York to Atlanta on 15 November 1956, and included two DC-4s in the fleet by 1958. On 16 September 1946, Seaboard & Western Airlines became established as a North Atlantic all-cargo airline. The first flight to Europe was made on 10 May 1947, with a DC-4 to Luxembourg which was developing as a trading and communications centre through its leniency in bi-lateral agreements and foreign operating rights.

In December 1951, following sustained growth of business partly through contracts with the International Relief Organisation – IRO – Seaboard & Western's fleet of five DC-4s was increased to twelve. A $3 million six-month military contract awarded in September 1954, and subsequently renewed, gave the airline sufficient corporate strength and stature to apply for permanent schedule certification. This was recommended by the CAB, and President Eisenhower gave his approval for a route from major north-eastern cities in the United States to Europe, effective from 16 August 1955. Seaboard's scheduled

Depicted at Oakland, California, on 22 February 1953 is DC-4 YV-C-EVB c/n 10408 ex-C-54A-15-DC 42-72303 which went to Avensa (Aerovias Venezolanas) in Venezuela in 1952 on a lease from Californian Eastern. It was delivered to Bournemouth (Hurn) in the United Kingdom as G-APID in November 1957 and served with several UK operators. (William T. Larkins)

Almost every major airline, including Chicago and Southern, began four-engined airliner service with the Douglas DC-4. Depicted is N53102 c/n 7467 City of New Orleans, ex-C-54A-5-DO 42-107448, the fifth of the airlines and converted at Baltimore, Maryland, by the Glenn L. Martin company. It served the airline until 15 December 1950 when sold to Brown & Brown. It crashed whilst operated by REAL in Brazil on 2 November 1957. (Delta)

Seen at London Airport (Heathrow) in 1948 is DC-4 G-AJPM Sky Freedom of Skyways under charter to BOAC. It is ex-C-54A-15-DC 42-72271 c/n 10376, ex-KLM. It went to Air France in 1950, to Air Viet Name in 1955, and to India the same year, being destroyed on 7 May 1962. (AP Photo Library)

Swissair commenced their Zurich to New York, via Geneva, Shannon and Gander service with the DC-4 on April 29, 1949. Depicted over New York is DC-4 HB-ILA Geneva c/n 43072/66 delivered on 26 November 1946. It was later renamed Uri and transferred to Balair in 1959. It crashed at Toli, Jebel Marra, Sudan, on 16 May 1960. (Swissair)

This DC-4 of Pan American, NC88928 c/n 10384 ex-42-72279 C-54A-15-DC was converted as a sleeper at El Segundo in 1946 and delivered as Clipper Union on 24 May, 1947. It later went to Iranair and on 4 August 1961 had to force land on a beach beside the Caspian Sea due to fuel starvation. (AP Photo Library)

Rare photo of UAL DC-4 with experimental NX30052 registration. It is c/n 10497 ex-C54B-1-DC 42-72392 named Mainliner Chicago delivered from Santa Monica after conversion. It was later re-registered NC30052 and became Cargoliner Lake Erie. Many other cargo operators used this DC-4 including Slick, Zantop, etc. (United Air Lines)

As early as 1943 SILA, the privately-owned Swedish airline, had ordered seven, later increased to ten, DC-4s from Douglas. They were delivered in 1946 just as SAS was being finalised. Depicted is SE-BBA Nordan c/n 42905 delivered on 1 May 1946 in Swedish Air Lines colours. On 16 September 1946 a DC-4 service from Stockholm/Copenhagen to New York via Prestwick and Gander commenced. (SAS)

freight services to Europe were inaugurated on 10 April 1956, using a DC-4 'Skymaster'.

The 'Skymaster' was involved in the inclusive tour charter business, one of the pioneers being Resort Airlines of Southern Pines, North Carolina. The tours combined a round-trip flight, connecting ground transportation and hotel accommodation. In October 1953, the airline augmented its fleet of Curtiss C-46s by purchasing three DC-4s from National Airlines. Typical of the operation was the programme of 'Caribbean Flying Houseparties' between 19 December 1953 and 15 April 1954, a series of DC-4 'cruises' lasting either two or four weeks. One itinerary involved departing from New York, calling at Washington or Philadelphia, and visiting Nassau, the Virgin Islands, Puerto Rico, Haiti and Miami, at an inclusive fare of $575. An extension period at Haiti would cost a further $105 and could be fitted in by dropping off the passenger and picking up again on the next DC-4 round trip. Trans-Caribbean Airways' goal was also the Caribbean, running a parallel course with Resort. It was organised as a non-scheduled airline on 18 May 1945, and its first DC-4 went into service to Puerto Rico during August 1946.

On 7 March 1946, British Overseas Airways Corporation withdrew its Boeing 314 flying boats from trans-Atlantic services, and for a short period US airlines operating DC-4s were free from European competition. This monopoly was short-lived, for very soon afterwards the well-established airlines of Europe, plus the odd newcomer, began services to New York, also utilising the popular DC-4 'Skymaster'.

One newcomer was the Swedish airline Svensk Interkontinental Luftrafik – SILA – who were granted permission to operate across the Atlantic on 23 March 1945. Other flights were made. On 27 November 1943, Per Norlin, representing Scandinavian Airlines System – SAS – had ordered DC-4s for use by the huge combined international airline, jointly owned by Sweden, Denmark and Norway. KLM operated a DC-4 which departed from Amsterdam on 21 May 1946, reaching New York via Glasgow and Gander in twenty-five hours of flying time. The Dutch airline was quickly followed by Air France and SAS with DC-4s in 1946; Canada and Sabena from Belgium in 1947; Iceland in 1948; and Swissair in 1949.

The North Atlantic route had grown from being the preserve of a single operator, Pan American, to become the world's number one air route, producing ever-increasing traffic, at high revenue rates, and stimulating fierce competition between major international airlines. The Atlantic had ceased to be a barrier dividing two world airline systems, and had become a bridge linking the old world with the new in a day's flying time. The Douglas DC-4 'Skymaster' was heavily involved, and was followed in due course by the pressurised DC-6 and DC-7 series of airliners, all popular products of the Douglas Aircraft Company stable.

Chapter Nine
Canadair DC-4M

During 1944 Canadair Ltd was formed to take over the management of the Crown plant located at Cartierville, Montreal. Its first goal was the development and production of a Rolls-Royce Merlin-powered version of the 'Skymaster'. Conceived as early as 1943 by the engineering department of Trans-Canada Air Lines – TCA – the Merlin-powered C-54 was anticipated to meet the requirements of both the Royal Canadian Air Force and of TCA. In order to save time, the first aircraft used a Douglas-built C-54G unpressurised fuselage plus other components, while later production aircraft would be built entirely by Canadair, with a pressurised fuselage incorporating several refinements then being planned by Douglas for the new DC-6. The use of Merlin engines fitted with annular radiators was dictated by the desire to improve performance. Also, the selection of these British-built engines resulted in cost savings for, in accordance with the Commonwealth trade agreement, they were imported duty-free into Canada; the R-2000 engines produced in the USA would have been subject to customs duties.

There were three main versions of this Canadian-built transport, initial production being centred around the unpressurised C-54GM, twenty-three of which were produced for the RCAF. Actually twenty-four had been ordered, but one was destroyed while in service with TCA before it could be handed over.

The C-54GM was based on the USAAF C-54G and, apart from the Merlin engines, had only minor differences, such as the position and size of the cargo doors. It even incorporated some surplus DC-4 parts.

The second production version was the pressurised DC-4M-2, twenty of which were built for TCA. These were sub-divided into two variants – the DC-4M-2/3, which had four-bladed

propellers, and the DC-4M-2/4, which had three-bladed propellers. The last production version was the Canadair C-4 for British Overseas Airways Corporation and Canadian Pacific. This aircraft was also pressurised and incorporated several small refinements. Including the prototype, a total of seventy aircraft were produced.

The first Canadair aircraft was designated DC-4M-X as an experimental Merlin-powered DC-4, was registered CF-TEN-X and carried the Canadair c/n 101. It was powered by four 1,750 hp Merlin 620 liquid-cooled engines and made its first flight at Cartierville during July 1946, crewed by Bob Brush from Douglas and Al Lily from Canadair. Although serving as the prototype for the Merlin-powered DC-4 version, this aircraft was part of the RCAF order designated C-54GM and named 'North Star'. It was retained by the manufacturer until November 1952, then taken on inventory by the RCAF with serial 17525. In service with the RCAF it was preceded by seventeen 'North Star' Mk.1s – 17501 to 17517, c/n 108 to 124, powered by Merlin 620s and taken on RCAF strength between September 1947 and April 1948. These were followed by five 'North Star' Mk.M1s – 17518, 17520 to 17523, c/n 102, 104 to 107, powered by Merlin 622s and initially operated by TCA pending availability of the pressurised DC-4M-2s they had ordered.

Military operations with the C-54GM began officially on 1 April 1948, and between 1950 and 1954 the planes were used to airlift material to Korea. When these flights ceased in June 1954, the transports had carried 13,000 personnel and seven million pounds of freight and mail, involving some 600 round trips. Other RCAF long-distance operations were in support of Operations 'Leapfrog' and 'Jumpmoat', which involved the ferry delivery flight to Europe of both Canadair-built F-86 'Sabres' and Canadair CF-100 'Canuck' aircraft for the RCAF Air Divisions which supported NATO. At a later date, during Operation 'Starlight', the 'North Star' supported the delivery of Lockheed T-33s to Greece and Turkey. The RCAF also supported the United Nations UNEF operations in both the Belgian Congo and the Middle East.

The DC-4M-2s, with their pressurised fuselage and square windows, were intended to take full advantage of the better performance at higher altitudes obtained by the installation of supercharged Merlin engines. However, development of the DC-4M-2 was going to delay its availability, so TCA obtained the loan from the RCAF of six unpressurised 'North Stars', c/n 102 to 107. Designated DC-4M-1 while in service with TCA, these airliners, registered CF-TEK to CF-TEM and CF-TEO to CF-TEQ, were powered by Merlin 622s and later fitted with Douglas DC-6-type undercarriages to enable the certificated gross weight to be increased from 73,000 lb to 78,000 lb. On 15 April 1947, TCA introduced the DC-4M-1 on their London to Montreal route and, after delivery of their own DC-4M-2s, returned the five surviving DC-4M-1s to the RCAF between March and October 1949.

TCA services to Bermuda, from both Montreal and Toronto using their own DC-4M-2s, began on 1 May 1948, and internal

Titled as Canadair Four *is CF-CPR c/n 148 delivered to Canadian Pacific Airlines during 1949 Fleet No.402 and named* Empress of Vancouver. *The Certificate of Airworthiness was issued on 21 May 1949. It crashed at Tokyo Airport, Japan, on 9 February 1950.* (MAP)

Canadair DC-4M-2 CF-TFT c/n 144 was delivered on 4 June 1948, to Trans Canada Fleet No.220. It was purchased by Overseas Aviation being delivered to Gatwick on 6 July 1961. After the collapse of Overseas it was ferried to Baginton, Coventry and by May 1965 had been broken up. (MAP)

flights to Vancouver and Calgary during May 1948. The new pressurised aircraft were registered CF-TFA to CF-TFT, c/n 125 to 144, and delivered between October 1947 and June 1948. The Merlin-powered DC-4M-2s were substantially noisier than the Douglas DC-4 'Skymasters'. Later TCA developed the cross-over exhaust system to reduce the noise level in the cabin, but this resulted in all-up weight reductions to 79,575 lb from 79,600 lb for the -3 model and to 79,850 lb from 80,200 lb for the -4 model. Accommodation was provided for forty first-class or up to sixty-two economy-class passengers. Depending on weight and altitude, the cruising speed exceeded that of the Douglas DC-4 by 60 to 80 mph. During 1954 the aircraft were replaced on the Atlantic route by Super Constellations; the DC-4M-2s were then operated on TCA's domestic system and as freighters.

Flights were undertaken to Greece during August 1953 with 9,000 lb of Red Cross supplies, and later, during December 1958 and January 1959, some 16,460 lb of Red Cross supplies were flown to Ceylon (now Sri Lanka). Humanitarian work of this nature was repeated in March 1960, when 6,647 lb of medical supplies and personnel were flown to Agadir, Morocco after it had been completely destroyed by an earthquake. In May 1960 further medical supplies were airlifted to Chile after it, too, had been devastated by earthquakes. Finally, in June 1961, Trans-Canada Air Lines disposed of all its remaining Canadair DC-4M-2s.

Overseas Orders

TCA had operated the 'North Star' successfully as a freighter on the important Montreal–Toronto–Winnipeg–Edmonton–Calgary –Vancouver route with effect from 2 May 1955. It was 30 June 1961 when the last freight flight was undertaken from Vancouver to Montreal. During fourteen years of service, the combined TCA fleet logged a total of 193 million miles. During the operational life of the 'North Star', TCA undertook various interior modifications, including an arrangement whereby the airliner could be operated with fifty-two first-class seats, rather than the original forty.

After the unfortunate failure of the Avro 'Tudor' airliner, BOAC ordered twenty-two Canadair C-42 for the Empire routes, which, powered by four 1,760 hp Merlin 626s, differed from TCA's DC-4M-2s in making maximum use of British equipment to reduce non-sterling payments to about $200,000 per aircraft, and in having a separate crew entrance door. They were issued the registrations G-ALHC to G-ALHP and G-ALHR to G-ALHY with c/ns 145, 146 and 151 to 170. The Canadair C-4 was given the BOAC class name 'Argonaut'. The first aircraft was rolled out on 25 February 1949 and delivered on 29 March, some two months ahead of schedule. The final aircraft was delivered in November 1949, some eight months ahead of the contract date. The first BOAC 'Argonaut' service was inaugurated to Hong Kong on August 23, 1949.

Replacing Short 'Sandringhams' and Avro 'Yorks', this was BOAC's first all-landplane service to the Far East. Flights to

This RCAF C-54GM c/n 121 was delivered as '17514' being struck off charge on 27 September 1965, and sold to the National Research Corporation and in 1966 was registered CF-SVP-X and fitted with an MDAP type sting tail. (APN)

Canadair C-4 G-ALHG c/n 153 of BOAC was delivered on 5 July 1949, and named Aurora. This airliner operated BOACs last Canadair Argonaut on 8 April 1960, and was also operated in the livery of West African Airways during 1957, and Kuwait Airways in 1958. On 4 April 1967, it crashed at the junction of Upper Brook Street and Waterloo Road, Stockport, whilst with British Midland. (MAP)

Canadair C-4 G-ALHY was delivered to BOAC on 11 November 1949, and named Avion. *It was sold to Overseas Aviation in March 1960, and after repossession by Lombank Credit was sold to Derby Aviation in October 1961, transferred to British Midland with change of title on 1 October 1964.* (MAP)

Tokyo began on 26 August 1949, but trouble with cooler pumps caused the entire fleet to be withdrawn within a fortnight. However, the trouble was quickly cured, and services to the Middle East commenced in November 1949 and to South America on 16 March 1950.

BOAC 'Argonauts' were selected for various royal tours, including those to East Africa and Nigeria, between 1952 and 1956. Modifications during its service life included the TCA-developed cross-over exhausts, and in 1953 strengthening of the floor to enable the airliner to carry fifty-six tourist-class passengers. The Corporation finally withdrew its last aircraft from service on 8 April 1960.

The fourth and final original customer for the Merlin-powered Canadair transport aircraft was Canadian Pacific Air Lines who, between May and July 1949, took delivery of four C-4-1s, registered CF-CPI, CPR, CPJ and CPP with c/ns 147 to 150. On 10 July 1949, they inaugurated an overseas service from Vancouver to Sydney via San Francisco, Fiji and Auckland. A Vancouver to Hong Kong service via Anchorage, Sheyma and Tokyo followed on 19 September. In the autumn of 1951, however, the three surviving airliners were taken over by TCA.

Once BOAC found it necessary to replace their Canadairs, the aircraft were passed to BOAC's associated companies, such as East African and Aden Airways. East African Airways put the 'Argonaut' into service during 1957, firstly in April on the Nairobi to Durban route. London was served with effect from 3 September, and the following month a route to Bombay was opened. Five airliners were operated by East African, and three by Aden Airways; these were received at the beginning of 1960, first going into service on 28 February on the Aden to Bahrain

route. Later, Cairo, Nairobi and Mombasa were also served. The aircraft were eventually retired and scrapped.

Early in 1960 the Royal Rhodesian Air Force – RRAF – took delivery of four 'Argonauts'; these served until 1964, when they were sold to Air Links. This brought the company fleet of Canadair transports to seven, but they were phased out when the company changed its name to Transglobe Airways, and changed its image at the same time.

Trans-Canada Airlines 'lease-sold' most of their 'North Stars' to Overseas Aviation in the United Kingdom in a package deal in June 1961. Scarcely two months later, however, the company was forced to suspend operations and was declared bankrupt. The twelve aircraft which had been ferried across the Atlantic were left static, although three were eventually sold to LEBCA in Venezuela, and a further two reached Miami. Two more were allocated US registrations, while another crashed in Africa in distinctly illegal circumstances. Before its collapse, Overseas Aviation transferred some of its ex-BOAC 'Argonauts' to an associated company, Flying Enterprise, based in Copenhagen, These aircraft were eventually broken up.

Three 'Argonauts', G-ALHG, HS and HY, were acquired by Derby Airways during October 1961 from the liquidator of Overseas Aviation, and in May 1962, they first entered service on schedules from Cardiff and Bristol to Palma, Majorca, and on inclusive tour services from the Midlands to Austria, France, Italy and Spain. During the winter of 1962 these airliners were used on inclusive tour charters to Tenerife in the Canary Islands. On 30 July 1964, Derby Airways became British Midland and in April 1965 moved to its present operating base at East Midlands Airport. On 4 June 1967, 'Argonaut' G-ALHG crashed in Stockport on an approach to Manchester Airport, inbound from Palma with a full load of passengers. Power had been lost on two engines and the aircraft was unable to maintain height. Tragically, almost all those on board were killed. The remaining two 'Argonauts' were grounded, and one was sent to Boscombe Down for extensive tests to determine the cause of the accident.

Powered by Pratt & Whitney R-2800-CA15 engines, Canadair produced a single pressurised C-5 transport in 1950. The four 2,100 hp radials were similar to the engines fitted to the Douglas DC-6. Intended as a VIP transport and long-range crew trainer, this aircraft had c/n 171 and was operated for over eleven years with 412 Squadron RCAF; it was initially allocated the serial 17524. Taken on strength on 20 July 1950, the C-5 was numbered 10000 on 17 February 1951 and eventually struck off charge on 5 July 1967. Its radio call-sign was 'Victor Charlie 10000' and in its time it carried many dignitaries, including the Queen and the Duke of Edinburgh, Princess Margaret, the Duchess of Kent, and Queen Juliana of the Netherlands. During 1955, the future Canadian Prime Minister, Lester Pearson, then Secretary of State, made a three-continent, twelve-country tour in the Canadair C-5. Sir Winston Churchill also requested the use of the VIP airliner, to take Sir Anthony Eden to Boston, Massachusetts, for urgent surgery.

The Royal Canadian Air Force sold all its 'North Star' transports, although eight were written off whilst in RCAF service – 17501, 17503, 17505, 17518, 17519, 17520, 17522 and 17523. 17509 was burnt in a fire at Trenton, Ontario on 24 March 1960, while 17513 was also burnt, on 4 January 1951 at the Central Experimental & Proving Establishment, Uplands, Ottawa. 17515 is preserved in a museum, and most of the remainder went to the Crown Assets Disposal Corporation – CADC – prior to sale on the civil market. Three companies in southern Florida, Trans Florida Aviation, Cavalier Aircraft and the D.D. Allyn Group, took the surplus transports, with Cavalier returning to Canada to begin a freight service. In the late 1960s Keegan Aviation were reported to be negotiating with Cavalier for the sale of four 'North Stars' to Botswana.

Training for RCAF crews on the transport took place at 4 Operational Training Unit at Trenton, and two squadrons – 412 and 426 – operated the type travelling far and wide around the globe as operational and humanitarian situations demanded.

The development and production history of the Douglas DC-4/C-54 'Skymaster' and its successors provides an excellent example of the way in which competition, though sometimes wasteful and time-consuming, is generally advantageous for all concerned. Despite a long head start in terms of operational and production experience, the post-war DC-4-1009 was a year or more behind the technically superior Lockheed L-049 Constellation when the Second World War ended in August 1945. The competitive atmosphere of those immediate post-war years forced it to catch up.

Chapter Ten
ATL-98 Carvair

The Aviation Traders ATL-98 Carvair is a Douglas DC-4 'Skymaster' conversion intended primarily for use as a vehicle ferry. The conversion, developed in the 1960s, involved replacing the entire forward fuselage with a complete new nose section embodying a hydraulically operated sideways-opening nose-door and an elevated flight deck over the forward portion of the cargo hold. Douglas DC-7-type vertical tail surfaces were introduced, but the remainder of the airframe was unchanged.

A total of twenty-one Carvairs were converted at both Southend and Stansted Airports by Aviation Traders, and today two which have remained dormant in storage in New Zealand for many years, and the last two Douglas DC-4s to be converted, have been taken to Hawaii for inter-island ferry services by a new owner and operator, Hawaii Pacific Air.

Over the years, the Carvair has been chartered, leased and owned by more than twenty-five operators, including the International Red Cross organisation and the United Nations. It has operated car ferry services from the United Kingdom across the English Channel to Europe, from Naples to Palermo and from Palma, Majorca to Barcelona and Valencia in Spain.

Design and Development

The Carvair is an outstanding example of an aircraft, designed initially to the specific requirements of a particular operator, which has since found many wider applications. The specification for the Carvair was laid down for Aviation Traders (Eng.) Ltd, by their associate company, Channel Air Bridge, later British United Air Ferries, in 1959. Channel Air Bridge had built up their vehicle ferry services around the Bristol Type 170 Freighter, but were then requiring a replacement aircraft with a longer range and higher work capacity. The outline specification called for a hold length of approximately 70 ft, which would give ample space for five British cars and accommodation for twenty-five passengers. A payload of eight tons, space for a toilet and galley, higher cruise speeds and lower noise levels than the Bristol Freighter was also on the list of requirements. Most important was the price.

Examination of existing and proposed new aircraft was alarming and showed none suitable at a first cost of anything less than £500,000. On a seven-year depreciation scale this would signify an amortisation charge of about £50 per flying hour, which was considered excessive for this type of operation. It was during 1959 that Freddie Laker, Executive Director of British United Airways, conceived the idea of converting the Douglas DC-4 'Skymaster'. By raising the cockpit and extending the nose of the fuselage by 8 ft 8 in, a hold length of 80 ft 2 in was obtained, which was divided in the British United Air Ferries configuration to accommodate five cars and twenty-two passengers, with the necessary toilet and galley facilities. The maximum payload of approximately eight tons was reached.

Wind-tunnel tests were performed on a 1/24th scale model,

initially as the DC-4, then with the new modified nose added, and with various fin and dorsal shapes. The nose fuselage fairing was so designed to prevent flow separation until angles of attack considerably higher than wing stall. Appreciable body lift, associated with a nose-up pitching: moment increment, necessitated forward movement of the centre of gravity limits. This, however proved to be an operational advantage with the increased freight volume available in the nose fuselage. Detail design and construction of the ATL-98 Carvair presented a number of interesting problems.

As the aircraft was unpressurised, the structural design was fairly straightforward, and in the majority of cases it was possible to follow the design philosophy of the DC-4. In elevating the crew compartment, it was necessary to re-route all services and controls which had previously run straight aft from the cockpit. The use of some hundreds of cast brackets, and about 2,000 additional control pulleys, enabled these services to be brought down the sides of the freight hold, carried inboard again, and routed aft under the freight hold floor. The only basic DC-4 system which had to be redesigned to meet modern concepts of flight safety was the electrical distribution system. In the DC-4, a tubular light-alloy bus-bar ran the length and breadth of the transport. For the new Carvair, the basic generating system was retained, but the distribution was revised by the introduction of main and essential bus-bars, with isolating control, segregated and protected in the crew compartment junction box. All services were protected separately. In the passenger compartment, specially designed seats at 30-inch pitch gave excellent comfort. Large picture windows and low noise and vibration levels contributed to the very favourable passenger reaction.

The problem of loading freight and vehicles through the elevated nose door, with its sill height of 10 ft was solved by the design of the Hylo range of self-propelled hydraulic scissor lift. Certification flight testing occupied some 156 flight hours and necessitated only one very minor rigging change. A full British Certificate of Airworthiness was issued in January 1962, and the United States Federal Aviation Administration certificate followed soon afterwards. The maximum certificated weights for the Carvairs on the British Civil Register were 73,800 lb for take-off and 64,706 for landing. The FAA figures were 72,900 lb and 63,800 lb respectively.

Requirements and Alternatives

The Bristol Freighter was slow, noisy and generally uncomfortable even for the short flight across the English Channel. Although these were not critical factors in the short-haul cross-channel operations, they were indeed relevant in the context of the longer-haul routes into Europe and even further afield then being planned. The specification for a new car-ferry aircraft presented both a challenging and seemingly irreconcilable set of requirements for an aspiring manufacturer.

The first essential was a drive on/off capability, dictating either a nose or rear drive-in loading. On short-haul operations it had to offer good economics, and it needed to be faster and much quieter than the Bristol Type 170 for any longer-haul routes. Perhaps the greatest challenge was to maintain economics at the low inherent utilisation which symbolised short-haul, high-seasonal car-ferry business.

In Europe there were only two aircraft manufacturers who became involved in a serious attempt to produce a car-ferry design. These were Armstrong Whitworth Aircraft – AWA – and the French company Hurel-Dubois. The Baginton-based AWA produced the AW.670 derivative of the AW.650 Argosy freighter, which featured an extended upper deck area with accommodation for passengers, while the main deck could carry up to six cars. The design was later refined for the car-ferry role, the main deck being extended to cater for up to eight cars, and thirty-two passengers on the upper deck. Front and rear loading of the Argosy was retained, but the new aircraft was optimised for short-haul operations with a fixed undercarriage and other simplified systems. The major drawback of the AWA project was its high initial cost. This was quoted at around £650,000. Amortisation at typical car-ferry utilisation of approximately 1,000 hours per annum was quoted at £75 per hour, compared with a mere £15 per hour on the Bristol Superfreighter.

The Hurel-Dubois proposal included the famous very high aspect wing based on the HD.34 survey aircraft used with success by the Institut Geographique National. The design featured a completely new deep double-deck fuselage with nose loading. The lower deck had a 53 ft long hold which could accommodate three or four cars. An additional car could be carried on the forward upper deck, a section of which could be lowered on a winch to permit loading via the lower deck. The aft upper deck, separated from the forward area by the wing spar, could carry twenty-four passengers. This French design would have a fixed undercarriage and be powered by two Rolls-Royce 527 Dart engines. It was proposed in 1959 and evoked interest from Silver City Airways, who indicated a possible requirement for fifteen aircraft. Unfortunately, like the Armstrong Whitworth AW.670 design project, the Hurel-Dubois project suffered from a very high capital cost plus a limited market, so both designs faded into obscurity.

The concept of the Carvair actually dates back to January 1959, when Freddie Laker asked the chief designer of Aviation Traders, A.C. Leftley, to investigate the conversion of existing types of suitable aircraft to give a car-ferry type with a hold 65 ft long and accommodation for twenty-five passengers. He wanted a type which had a good fatigue life, was available in reasonable quantity and for which spares were readily obtainable at not too high a cost. All possible types were studied and the one eventually chosen was the Douglas DC-4 'Skymaster'.

At the time there were over 300 DC-4/C-54s still in service with an average hours flown of around 30,000; the type had an ultimate airframe life of 60,000 hours, representing many years of service. Secondhand DC-4/C-54s were available in the United States for around $110,000 and the estimated cost of a Carvair, including conversion, was quoted as under £150,000. The initial order would be for ten car-ferry conversions for Channel Air Bridge and if the Carvair proved popular, Aviation Traders envisaged there would be a demand for similar conversions involving the Douglas DC-6 and DC-7 aircraft.

The project was allocated the designation ATL-98 and the name Carvair – a deliberate contraction of the descriptive tag 'car-via-air' adopted after two local Southend businessmen suggested it in response to a special naming competition. While detailed design of the new car ferry continued, a full-scale mock-up involving a derelict KLM DC-4 PH-DBZ ex-C-54B-1-D 42-72375 c/n 10480, was built at Southend in 1960. The salient modification embodied in the new design was the replacement of the original nose section by a bulbous forward fuselage, the final configuration of which was determined after wind-tunnel tests at the Cranfield Institute of Technology in Bedfordshire.

The first ATL.98 Carvair G-ANYB Golden Gate Bridge *seen in Channel Air Bridge livery. Conversion commenced in October 1960, and flight testing occupied 155 hours. It first flew after conversion in June 1961, and made its final flight in March 1967 with British United Air Ferries.* (Aviation Traders)

Work commenced on the conversion of the first aircraft, a DC-4 G-ANYB of Air Charter which had 37,000 hours on the airframe, during October 1960. At 8.26 a.m. on 17 June 1961, the new Carvair was rolled out of the hangar at Southend to make its maiden flight later in the day. Pilot for the occasion was the senior Aviation Traders test pilot, Captain D.B. Cartlidge. The busy two-hour first flight was incident free. An extensive flight-test programme then commenced, including a series of special flight trials using the 8,038 ft long concrete runway at Filton, Bristol. Take-offs and landings were made at different weights and a large ventilating pipe was fitted under the fuselage to enable the Carvair to dump water ballast in flight.

The aircraft returned to Southend where unfortunately the flight-trials programme received a setback, due to an accident in which a fork-lift truck rammed the fuselage of G-ANYB, causing extensive damage. The aircraft was repaired and on 31 January 1962, after 156 hours of extensive test flying, the APL-98 Carvair received its Certificate of Airworthiness. The go-ahead for its production was given. The DC-4 G-ANYB was built as a C-54B-DC 42-72423 and delivered on 22 January 1945, with c/n 10528, becoming NC88723. It eventually went to Braniff as N59952, then to E.J. Daly in June 1953, and to Rich R. Riss who operated as World Airways out of Oakland Airport, San Francisco. It was sold via the Air Carrier Service Corporation to Air Charter in February 1955, when it was registered G-ANYB and named 'Atlanta'. It was sold to British United Airways on 16 June 1960.

Production

The first Carvair was officially handed over to Channel Air Bridge on 16 February 1962. The aircraft, G-ANYB, was named '**Golden Gate Bridge**' by Mrs Daeniker, wife of the Swiss ambassador in London, and it then made its first flight across the English Channel to Ostend. The inaugural revenue-earning flight was made on the following day, when the Carvair flew a cargo of new cars to a motor show at Malaga, Spain. Scheduled cross-Channel car-ferry flights got under way on 1 March with the inauguration of the Rotterdam service.

After some excellent publicity and press reports, orders and enquiries about the new Carvair flooded in from all over the world. The most unexpected were those from the Portuguese and Spanish Air Forces, both of whom operated a number of Douglas C-54 'Skymasters' on various military tasks. One newspaper in India, the New Delhi *Hindu*, showed great interest in buying a Carvair for delivery of their newspaper from the publishing house in Delhi. However, nothing materialised. The price of a Carvair was eventually fixed at £120,000 per aircraft minus the avionics. Nearly all the subsequent Carvairs were built at Stansted and then flown to Southend for painting and test flying. All the nose conversions were constructed at Southend and moved by road to Stansted on special 'Queen Mary'-type low-loaders. It was necessary for a watchful technician to be positioned up in the cockpit section of the nose to advise the low-loader driver of any obstructions such as trees or power cables.

Of the twenty-one 'Skymasters' converted to ATL-98 Carvair configuration, eighteen were manufactured at Stansted and three at Southend. The last one was for Ansett-ANA in Australia, using their own DC-4 VH-INM ex C-54E-DO 44-9088 c/n 27314, delivered 17 April 1945, going to Douglas at Santa Monica after USAAF use on 14 November 1945, to become the thirteenth conversion to civil DC-4. It was delivered to Pan American Airways on December 23 1945 as N88881 *'Clipper Kit Carson'*, later renamed *'Clipper West'* and later still *'Clipper Red Rover'*. On 15 February 1958, the DC-4 was sold to Japan Air Lines as JA-6015 *'Amagi'*. On 18 March 1965, it was sold again, this time to Ansett-ANA, and became VH-INM. It arrived at Southend for conversion on 1 March 1966, and had to be converted there as the production line at Stansted had closed down. After conversion it made its first flight on 12 July 1968, and was delivered to the airline five days later, on 17 July.

Operations

Airlines and air-freight operators from all over the world bought Carvairs, from Canada and Australia and through to the Middle East. The second Carvair G-ARSD first flew on 25 March 1962. Channel Air Bridge and its successors, British United Air Ferries, eventually purchased eleven Carvair conversions, and orders came in from Aer Lingus for two, later three, for use on vehicle ferry and cargo services. Interocean Airways of Luxembourg ordered two for contract cargo work, whilst the Iberia subsidiary Aviaco in Spain wanted two for vehicle-ferry operations. Ansett-ANA eventually had three of its DC-4s converted for scheduled cargo work in Australia. Carvairs were converted from Douglas C-54A, C-54B, C-54E and DC-4-1009 airframes, and were delivered between July 1962 and July 1968. Plans for similar conversions of the Douglas DC-6 and DC-7, some fitted with Rolls-Royce Dart turboprops, were sadly never proceeded with.

The only serious accident in an otherwise almost perfect safety record, happened at Karachi, Pakistan, on 8 March 1967, when Carvair F-BMHU ex-G-ARSH c/n 10338 of Cie Air Transport – CAT – crashed on take-off. The aircraft failed to maintain height after lift-off and subsequently ploughed into a busy road bridge near a railway line, killing the four crew members and seven unfortunate pedestrians on the highway.

Carvairs were ideally suited for long-haul work and extra large items of freight, and in this respect made one or two unusual flights. These included the transportation of a large radio mast to Zambia for the BBC in 1965 in order for broadcasts to be made to Rhodesia. Carvair G-APNH, the eleventh built, c/n 18333, was used for the flight, departing with its unusual load from RAF Lyneham, Wiltshire.

Two Carvairs – G-ASKG and G-APNH – were leased to Air Ferry for use by RAF Transport Command for six months in a support role for the civil involvement for the Zambian oil airlift. This involved flying out 45-gallon drums of fuel oil to Zambia. Other interesting cargoes have ranged from a baby killer-whale to aircraft engines and even oil-rig drilling equipment for use in the Middle East. By far the most unusual cargo carried was a 'Black Knight' rocket which was flown out to Woomera, Australia, from Southend on 11 January 1965. However, the Carvair had to turn back, as due to a failure of the air conditioning, the rocket's sensitive equipment developed a malfunction.

The Carvairs of British Air Ferries – BAF – were used for a few interesting projects whilst on the ground. One unidentified ATL-98 was used as a backdrop for a series of photographic models, specific type not revealed. Another Carvair, G-AKSD, was used for creating 'crosswind' effects for the much publicised Invacar tests for the BBC at Southend during August 1973.

Aer Lingus

One of the many worldwide cargo operators to show interest in the new Carvair was Aer Lingus who conducted a detailed study of a possible car-ferry operation on the Irish Sea routes to the United Kingdom and France during the winter of 1961/62. The Irish airline finally narrowed down the choice of car-ferry aircraft to four types – the Armstrong Whitworth AW.659 Argosy, the AW.670 project, the ATL.98 Carvair, and the Bristol 170 Mk.32 Superfreighter. The latter was eliminated because of its restricted size and uneconomical operation. Aer Lingus had considerable experience with the Rolls-Royce Dart turboprop, and so showed great interest in the AW.670 design, becoming quite involved with the manufacturer, but the idea was abandoned before studies were completed. The AW.670 Argosy had the advantage of being a firm contract, but it was not ideally suited to the car-ferry role, and cost effectiveness was also a factor.

In addition to the seasonal car-ferry operations, Aer Lingus were also interested in the Carvair for their all-cargo services. However, the airline finally decided that its fleet of Douglas DC-3s would be adequate for this role until at least 1965/66, and that if completely divorced from a car-ferry requirement, the chosen freighter replacement would be the AW.650 Argosy.

Circumstances changed when BKS Air Transport encountered financial difficulties towards the end of 1961 and dropped their car-ferry service from Liverpool to Dublin. The Southend-based Channel Airways applied to operate a replacement service, but were turned down. The Irish tourist authority, Bord Failte, naturally became concerned at the effect on tourism if there were no car-ferry services. Consequently the Irish government asked Aer Lingus to provide a service, despite the forecasted uneconomical nature of such an operation.

Carvair EI-AMP c/n 6 of Aer Lingus St Ailbhe *clearly showing the specially-built hydraulic lift for car loading. Conversion commenced in June 1962 and took six months to complete. After a crash in Labrador the remains were returned to Southend to be used as spares.* (Aviation Traders)

In August 1962, an order worth £700,000 was placed for two Carvairs including spares and ground support, delivery to be in time for car-ferry operations to begin in the summer of 1963. A minor addition was a strengthened floor with Rolamat rollers for palletised cargo operations. The first Carvair EI-AMP '*St Ailbhe*' was delivered on 14 March 1963 and was immediately involved in a crew-training programme. It had entered all-cargo services by the time the second Carvair EI-AMR '*St Jariath*' was delivered on 29 April and Irish Sea car-ferry services began from Liverpool on 8 May. The schedule of Aer Lingus routes was ambitious – thirteen flights weekly between Dublin and Liverpool, five per week Dublin to Bristol and four between Cork and Bristol. With effect from 17 June car-ferry services were introduced twice weekly between Dublin and Cherbourg, France.

The first season figures reported 4,324 cars and 12,532 passengers, exceeding the estimated 4,000 car figure. Extra passengers were carried to Cherbourg, the configuration being three cars and thirty-five passengers. There was no car-ferry service during the winter. Unfortunately the Carvair reliability was causing problems, so it was decided to order a third aircraft for the 1964 season to improve back-up. The Carvairs were able to replace the DC-3 on all-cargo services, resulting in three of these being sold. Combined passenger and freight services to Liverpool and Glasgow were introduced.

During the winter of 1963/4 both Carvairs were returned to Aviation Traders for modifications, including increasing the headroom under the flight deck to enable horse bloodstock charters to be undertaken, some 700 horses subsequently being carried. A night-mail service from Manchester to Dublin was introduced, with the Carvairs taking over from the ubiquitous DC-3s. With the delivery of the third Carvair, EI-ANJ '*St Senan*' on 23 April 1964, Aer Lingus were able to operate the type on all its cargo services and so retire their last two DC-3s.

Also the car-ferry frequency was stepped up and in 1964 a total of 5,101 cars were carried.

Meanwhile, sea ferries were being introduced into service across the Irish Sea and in 1965 the airline reduced the frequency of car ferries. On 31 October 1966, the last air cargo service Dublin–Liverpool, Manchester–Dublin was flown by EI-AMP. The three Carvairs went into storage and in September 1967 a prospective sale to an airline in Ecuador prompted EI-AMR to be brought back to flying status. That sale fell through, but on 10 January 1968, all three Carvairs were acquired for $500,000 by Gander-based Eastern Provincial Airways.

Between February and May 1968, delivery took place via Southend for modification by Aviation Traders, all three being ferried via Dublin in Eastern Provincial Airways livery to collect spares. Carvair EI-AMP became CF-EPX, EI-AMR became CF-EPV, and EI-ANJ CF-EPW. On 28 September 1968, the first Carvair was damaged beyond repair in a landing accident at Twin Falls, Labrador. The second, CF-EPV, was ferried back to Southend in 1973 to be cannibalised by British Air Ferries, while CF-EPW went to Norwegian Overseas as LN-NAA. It was subsequently ferried to Bangkok in 1975, where it remained for a long time in poor condition.

British Air Ferries

As the successor to the pioneering car-ferry airline Silver City Airways, who commenced operations in 1946 with three Avro Lancastrians and some DC-3s, British Air Ferries was formed in 1962 with the amalgamation of many independent carriers in the United Kingdom. As part of the general consolidation, Silver City was bought by the newly-formed British United Airways – BUA – of which Channel Air Bridge had already become a part.

The two vehicle-ferry operators then amalgamated as British United Air Ferries. The next year, 1963, saw the introduction of the new long-distance Carvair penetrating deep into Europe on routes to Geneva, Basle and Strasbourg, flight time on all these routes being two and a half hours. All were operated from Southend.

In 1963 British United Air Ferries operated a fleet of twenty-eight aircraft, all Bristol Freighters and ATL-98 Carvairs. Over the next few years, further distinct changes emerged in the pattern of their market and operations. The new long-haul routes, although they clearly filled a need, did not prove to be quite the money-spinners hoped for. Fare levels were kept as low as possible, but this meant that high load factors were required to achieve profitability. The longer routes were made viable in their own right, but did not offer hope of further great expansion. Carvair services to Europe were even attempted from Coventry Airport to try and capture a market in the Midlands.

Greater emphasis was, however, being given to the carriage of passengers on flights with two, one or even no cars at all. This applied in particular to Carvair operations, as the huge passenger-cum-cargo-hold ratio on these aircraft could readily be altered to accommodate up to sixty-five passengers, still leaving room for two cars or an equivalent cargo load. Increasing use was made of the Carvair's flexibility as an all-cargo aircraft, on charter work, for it had sufficient range to reach most airfields in Europe non-stop. In 1967 the airline's name was shortened to British Air Ferries – BAF – and it was decided to discontinue all 'deep-penetration' long-haul services, which for the time being at least were deemed non-viable. The Carvairs continued to operate short-haul operations from Southend only.

In October 1971, following the takeover of British United Airways by Caledonian Airways, British Air Ferries was bought by the Stansted-based all-cargo carrier Transmeridian Air Cargo. From the outset, it was intended that the two carriers should preserve their separate identities. This left the brunt of BAF's operations remaining with the seven-strong fleet of ATL-98 Carvairs at the beginning of 1973. Although these DC-4 conversions had been in vehicle-ferry service for some ten years, no replacement for them seemed likely in an era when even turboprops were unmentionables for many short-haul operations. However, car-ferry operations demanded an unorthodox aircraft, and the Carvair was accepted as such. However, by 1972 the Carvairs were beginning to look a bit run-down, so British Air Ferries set about improving their appearance and comfort in readiness for the 1973 season. An extensive face-lift programme was carried out, providing bright new colours for the passenger cabins, and the interiors were completely refurbished to give extra comfort as well as more attractive decor. Accommodation in the rear cabin was reduced from twenty-two to seventeen seats, affording more leg-room. When fewer than five cars or corresponding freight were carried, extra passenger seating was provided further forward, up to a maximum capacity of sixty-five. The forward passenger cabin was similarly improved, and save for the absence of pressurisation and higher levels of noise the comfort standards in the BAF Carvairs were now up to the level experienced on most international scheduled services. Even taped music was introduced.

Externally, the Carvair fleet was repainted in a new colour scheme featuring a mid-blue cheat line with dark blue for the wings and lower fuselage. The introduction of these smart colours proved easier to maintain, and the dark areas masked the effect of oily discharges inevitable from large piston engines. The Carvairs were also lightheartedly humanised by the use of such apt names as '*Porky Pete*' and '*Fat Albert*'. Such was the effort put in to attracting the travelling public.

However, by late 1975, with a drop in both vehicle and passenger numbers, three Carvairs were allocated to *ad hoc* charter work. Carvair G-ASDC '*Plain Jane*' was converted to an all-cargo aircraft with the payload increased to 8½-tons and it was available twenty-four hours a day. Encouraging results on the long-distance vehicle-ferry route to Basle led to BAF introducing new services from Southend to Lyons and Düsseldorf in 1974, but unfortunately these did not show signs of justifying themselves economically and were discounted after the summer season. High landing and handling charges proved an obstacle on the Dusseldorf service, created a break-even load factor as high as 70 per cent.

This was not the demise of the Carvair, however. Rather, it enabled British Air Ferries to develop its role as an all-cargo aircraft more effectively. In February 1975, Carvair G-ASDC emerged from the airline's engineering base completely stripped of internal furnishings and trim, and bereft of its external paintwork except for essential titling. The weight saved enabled the maximum payload to increase by over 2,600 lb to 18,750 lb. By the beginning of 1976 the total operational Carvair fleet was reduced from a peak of eight to four. One was retained on scheduled passenger/cargo services, while two other standard Carvairs enjoyed full employment on general charter work. Touring pop groups, for example, found the aircraft ideal, with plenty of room for their equipment, perhaps a vehicle or two, and seventeen passengers in the rear cabin. The Carvair was on regular cargo charter within the African continent. It was also well suited to carry livestock, a field which BAF were keen to develop, and prided itself on the 'instant charter' availability of its fleet.

Worldwide Operations

In its flying characteristics, the Carvair is very similar to the Douglas DC-4, while its performance is only slightly affected by the conversion in certain *en route* configurations. No separate type rating was necessary. Pilot reaction was very favourable, and crews converted from the DC-4 to the Carvair after half a dozen landings and take-offs. The ability of the Carvair to handle large and awkward loads over stage lengths of up to about 2,000 miles made it an attractive and profitable proposition for many operators. Two Carvairs saw service with the United Nations in the Belgian Congo, carrying many hundreds of tons of military equipment up to the size of three-ton trucks. Vehicle-ferry services were operated by Carvairs between Naples and Palermo in Sicily, and the Spanish operator Aviaco introduced scheduled services for passengers and vehicles between Barcelona or Valencia and Palma, Majorca.

The Italian company Alisud-Compagnia Aerea Meriodionale, leased a Carvair c/n 10 from BUAF for daily car-ferry services between Naples and Palermo. Operations commenced on 15 August 1963, and continued on a once-a-day basis until February 1964, when the service was suspended owing to traffic rights problems. At the end of 1965, two BUAF Carvairs, c/n 10 and 11, were leased for five months to Air Ferry to carry fuel

Interocean Airways Carvair LX-IOG/N9757F c/n 5 one of two operated under dual registration. They had a strengthened floor for cargo, and featured an Aviation Traders designed ramp capable of loading up to four-ton vehicles. The ramp folded and was stored in the transport. Until 1964 these Carvairs were used on a United Nations contract in the troubled Congo. (Aviation Traders)

from Dar-es-Salaam in Tanzania to Lusaka in Zambia after the surface route via Rhodesia (now Zimbabwe) was closed following the unilateral declaration of independence. British Car Ferries were unwilling to let their good name be connected with this operation, and consequently the two Carvairs were painted in Air Ferry colours, with G-ASKG leaving Southend on 28 December and G-APNH following two days later.

The French company Compagnie Air Transport operated vehicle services from Le Touquet, near Paris, to Lydd in Kent in conjunction with BUAF, and also from Nîmes to Corsica and Palma. The two Interocean Carvairs, c/n 4 and 5, were purchased in 1965, enabling the company to add Bournemouth, Nice and Perpignan to the network originally operated by Bristol Superfreighters. The Carvair lost in the take-off accident at Karachi, Pakistan, on 8 April 1967, was replaced by c/n 10, and a third – c/n 15 – was added to the fleet, by which time CAT was serving Southend and Ibiza on its vehicle-ferry services. Operations ceased in 1970 and the three Carvairs were sold to the French charter company Transports Aériens Réunis – TAR. This Nice-based company cannibalised c/n 15 for spares in November 1972. The remaining two aircraft were leased to, and eventually purchased by, BAF.

As mentioned earlier, the Gander-based regional carrier, Eastern Provincial Airways, had purchased all three Aer Lingus Carvairs in 1968. These were returned to Aviation Traders for installation of high-capacity cabin heaters. They were used to ferry personnel, supplies and materials to remote construction sites in Nova Scotia and Newfoundland. One, CF-EPX c/n 6, was written off in a landing accident at Twin Falls, Labrador, on 28 September 1968, shortly after delivery. The two remaining aircraft were returned to the United Kingdom after the EPA construction contract expired.

In 1969 the two Aviaco Carvairs, c/n 16 and 18, were purchased by Dominicana for cargo hauling. On 23 June 1969, c/n 16 crashed into a built-up area while taking off from Miami, with subsequent heavy loss of life. The remaining aircraft was withdrawn from use in the early 1970s and removed to Santa Domingo city, where today it resides alongside the Hotel Embajador, being used as a bar and cafeteria.

In late 1974, Norwegian Overseas Airlines acquired a Carvair c/n 14 from British Air Ferries. In May 1975 it was flown to the Far East on contract to the International Red Cross, but it was abandoned on arrival in Bangkok. Also in 1974, the construction company Pauley wet-leased G-AREK c/n 5 from BAF to

Titled Croix Rouge Internationale Carvair LN-NAA c/n 14 is seen appropriately marked for the International Red Cross use. In the 1970s it operated in Norway on lease, and for many years was reported in storage at Bangkok, Thailand, in poor condition. (MAP)

support remote construction works in the Arabian Gulf area; and Air Cambodge arranged for the lease of one of the three Ansett-ANA Carvairs, VH-INJ c/n 19, which was re-registered N33AC. It did not remain in service for long, and was stored at Phnom Penh, Cambodia.

In 1975, the Indonesian scheduled passenger and cargo operator, Seulawah Air Service, acquired two ex-Ansett-ANA Carvair aircraft c/n 20 and 21. These never entered service, but were placed in storage at Singapore-Seletar, returning to Australia in 1978. They carried the names '*Kasby 1*' and '*Kasby 2*'.

Based at Addison, Texas, Falcon Airways purchased two British Air Ferries Carvairs, c/n 7 and 9, early in 1979, adding a third ex-Uni-Air aircraft c/n 5 later that year. It was envisaged that the Carvair would be useful in carrying items of freight such as drilling shafts for the oil industry, and it undertook charters to Alaska, and Central and South America. When the company ceased operations in 1980, Carvair N83FA c/n 5 went to the Kodiak-based third-level operator Kodiak Western Alaska Airlines in 1981 for contract work in the area.

The two Nationwide Air Carvairs were reportedly sold to Air Cargo Panama in 1980, but it was reported that ACP was just another dubious company intending to operate the Carvairs under the convenience of the Panamanian flag. A plan to operate these same two Carvairs was put forward by Air Express in Australia, but authorisation was not forthcoming and plans were abandoned. Likewise in 1982, a Canadian operator, Calm Air, planned to purchase the two Falcon Airways Carvairs then in storage at Love Field, Dallas.

The Gabon-based construction company Société Anonyme de Construction – SOACO – acquired Carvair c/n 10 in March 1975, the second, c/n 13, followed in June 1976. Both were withdrawn from service and stored in 1979, being sold to Société Aéro Service, based at Brazzaville, in the Congo, in 1982. TN-ADX c/n 10 was noted parked at Brazzaville on 2 February 1982, fresh from overhaul and retaining the British Air Ferries name '*Big Joe*'. It is reported that TR-LWP c/n 13 was purchased for spares, and stored minus engines and control surfaces. In early 1984, Jim Blumenthal of Arizona completed the restoration of Carvair N89FA c/n 9 at Tucson. It was last heard of with Academy Airlines of Griffin, Georgia.

With two Carvairs operating today in Hawaii, it is of interest to record that in 1983 Pacific Air Express began operations out of Honolulu with Carvair N80FA c/n 7, which became registered N103, and a second aircraft, N55243 c/n 17. The company flew regular flights from Honolulu to the islands of Maui and Hilo. Outbound they carried general cargo, while inbound the cargo was usually pineapples, papayas and other exotic perishables. The two former Nationwide Air Carvairs, today with Hawaiian Pacific Air, had been stored at Nelson in New Zealand since 1979. They had initially been ferried from Brisbane to Auckland with c/n 20 N54598 on 17 September 1978, to be registered ZK-EKY, and c/n 21 N54596 on 28 November 1978, which became ZK-EKZ. They were reregistered ZK-NWA and ZK-NWB. They were ferried north to Hamilton, near Auckland, for refurbishing in March 1983. Rumours of a sale to either the USA or Panama turned out to be false, but it was confirmed that Pacific Aero Lift in Hawaii were interested. Each Carvair was valued at $600,000 and it was believed that PAL had connections with Pacific Air Express, another Hawaiian carrier. Both aircraft appeared in Pacific Aero Lift livery with ZK-NWA named '*Ruth 1*' and ZK-NWB '*Ruth 2*'. The deal fell through prior to delivery.

Epilogue

When the Carvair story began with Freddie Laker during 1959, with work commencing on the first conversion at Southend in October 1960, it was certainly not envisaged that the type, built in relatively small numbers, would perform such a multitude of tasks with so many operators worldwide.

A look back at the history of British United Air Ferries reveals many 'firsts' with the ATL-98 Carvair. On its formation the airline was involved in a thriving vehicle-ferry business, not only across the English Channel, but deeper into Europe. There was great competition from the sea ferries, and to help the increasing traffic with Bristol Freighters and Superfreighters, an airport was built on the sand flats at Lydd, Kent. On 13 December 1963, BUAF Carvair G-ASDC made the first landing at Lydd. On 31 October 1964, the same Carvair introduced the type on the Jersey to Hurn service.

On 13 January 1972, Carvair G-AOFW made a proving flight between Guernsey and Castle Donington – now East Midlands Airport – on behalf of a consortium of Guernsey businessmen who had hoped to operate a five-times-a-week service between the United Kingdom and the Channel Islands. However, the service never got off the ground, although services were started from Jersey and Guernsey, carrying both cargo and passengers. On 19 March 1972, Carvair G-ASDC inaugurated a Coventry to Jersey and Guernsey schedule for both passengers and cargo. It had been hoped to open further services from Coventry to Ostend and Le Touquet, but these routes were never started and all services from Coventry were suspended at the end of the 1973 summer season.

With more Carvairs in service by 1972, BAF introduced a three-times-weekly service from Southend to Basle, and the following year entered into an agreement with Intra Airways for the joint operation of the freight services between the Channel Islands and Bournemouth. *Ad hoc* charter work included many flights on behalf of the Ford Motor Company from West Germany to Southend and Liverpool carrying spare parts. As we have seen, the Carvairs were ideal for carrying outsize loads and in this capacity they occasionally visited Aberdeen airport in connection with the oil-rig support work being built up in the North Sea. Late in 1974 a dock strike in Northern Ireland caused BAF Carvairs to fly numerous night services between Belfast and Southend carrying cigarettes. In 1975, Carvair G-AOFW was used for transporting pop groups and their equipment on tours around Europe, the aircraft acquiring a 'Startrekking 75' emblem on the fuselage. Other *ad hoc* charters that year included an oil-rig charter flight from Norwich to Pescara, Italy on 9 September and a flight from Humberside to Groningen, Holland by Carvair G-AXAI on 23 September. This took the aircraft into the newly-opened airfield at Humberside for the first time.

For long-range work one Carvair was fitted with eight fuel tanks instead of six, giving it an advantage over other Carvairs in the BAF fleet. This aircraft, G-APNH, left RAF Lyneham on 11 January 1965, on the first British government charter flight to the Woomera Rocket Range in Australia. As mentioned earlier, the 'Black Knight' rocket on board had a malfunction and the flight only got as far as San Francisco. Further government contracts matured to the Mediterranean and the Middle East.

How long the remaining two Carvairs currently operating in Hawaii will remain in service is hard to envisage, but Douglas DC-4 spares are fortunately still plentiful. Over thirty years of service for a conversion from a Second World War-built Douglas C-54/DC-4 'Skymaster' transport is surely unique.

Aviation Traders Ltd. ATL-98 Carvair Production

c/n	Carvair	DC-4	c/n	First flew	Model	USAF serial	Operator
1	G-ANYB	G-ANYB	10528	21 Jun 61	C-54B-1-DC	42-72423	Channel Air Bridge
2	G-ARSD	G-ARSD	10311	25 Mqr 62	C-54A-10-DC	42-72206	Channel Air Bridge
3	G-ARSF	G-ARSF	18339	27 Jun 62	C-54B-5-DO	43-17139	Channel Air Bridge
4	G-ARSH	G-ARSH	10338	5 Sep 62	C-54A-10-DC	42-72233	Interocean Airways
5	N6757F	G-AREK	10365	2 Nov 62	C-54A-15-DC	42-72260	Interocean Airways
6	EI-AMP	G-ARZV	7480	21 Dec 62	C-54A-5-DO	42-107461	Aer Lingus
7	G-ASDC	LX-BNG	10273	19 Mar 63	C-54A-1-DC	42-72168	British Air Ferries
8	EI-AMR	N88819	10448	18 Apr 63	C-54B-1-DC	42-72343	Aer Lingus
9	G-ASHZ	N9326R	27249	8 Jun 63	C-54B-20-DC	44-9023	Britsh Air Ferries
10	G-ASKG	LX-BBP	10382	29 Jul 63	C-54A-15-DC	42-72277	British Air Ferries
11	G-APNH	G-APNH	18333	4 Jan 65	C-54B-5-DO	43-17133	British Air Ferries
12	EC-WVD	G-AOFW	10351	11 Feb 64	C-54B-15-DC	42-72246	Aviaco
13	G-ABKN	G-ABKN	8088	8 Dec 64	C-54A-DO	41-87676	British Air Ferries
14	EI-ANJ	G-ASKD	10458	17 Apr 64	C-54B-1-DC	42-72353	Aer Lingus
15	G-ATRV	OD-ADW	27311	24 Mar 66	C-54E-10-DO	44-9085	British Air Ferries
16	EC-WXI	EC-AEP	10485	4 Jun 64	C-54B-1-DC	42-72380	Aviaco
17	G-AXAI	LX-IOF	18342	2 Apr 69	C-54B-5-DO	43-17142	British Air Ferries
18	EC-AXY	EC-AEO	18340	12 Mar 65	C-54B-5-DO	43-17140	Aviaco
19	VH-INJ	VH-INJ	42927	14 Sep 65	DC-4-1009	SE-BBD	Ansett-ANA
20	VH-INK	VH-INK	42994	28 Oct 65	DC-4-1009	LN-IAE	Ansett-ANA
21	VH-INM	VH-INM	27314	12 Jul 68	C-54E-10-DO	44-9088	Ansett-ANA

The design of the DC-5 was entrusted to a team led by project engineer Leo Devlin and supervised by Ed Heinemann at the El Segundo factory. Depicted in front of the prototype DC-5 is Ed Heinemann on the left, and Carl Cover the Douglas test pilot for the new airliner. (AP Photo Library)

Chapter Eleven
Douglas DC-5

The Douglas DC-5 was designed and built at the El Segundo, California, factory of the Douglas Aircraft Company, and was intended to meet an airline requirement for a twin-engined, sixteen-to-twenty-two-seat transport with the ability to operate in and out of small airports and requiring very little routine maintenance. Unlike the DC-4, it was undertaken as a private venture without any airline backing. It was the only Douglas Commercial to originate from El Segundo, and the design was entrusted to a company team lead by project engineer Leo Devlin and supervised by the well-known Douglas designer, Ed Heinemann.

Drawing-board work began during the summer of 1938, in anticipation of the demand for a short-haul feeder transport with a performance similar to that of the Douglas DC-3, then employed on a wide variety of routes by the airlines of the world, especially in Europe and South America. With the benefit of experience gained with the Northrop Delta series, and from production experience on the Model 7A and 7B attack bomber in the Havoc and Boston series, the El Segundo team decided to design a twin-engined high-wing configuration and a fully retractable undercarriage with the main wheels retracting laterally into the wings outboard of the engine nacelles. The new transport bore a strong Douglas family resemblance to the Model 7B. In fact, one source reveals that the production order for the DB-7 medium bomber paid for most of the development costs of the DC-5, quoted as a commercial version.

Interesting features of the DC-5 were a high wing combined with a tricycle undercarriage. The areas forward of the firewall, collector rings, control runs, rudder pedals and pilots' seats came from the DC-3. As detailed engineering design progressed and construction of a prototype was initiated, the new transport took on a look of great elegance. Accommodation for a crew of three and sixteen passengers was planned as standard, but provision was made in the design for increasing the passenger capacity to twenty-two in high-density configuration. Customers were offered a choice between Wright Cyclone or Pratt & Whitney Hornet engines driving fully- feathering propellers. On the prototype two 900 hp Wright Cyclone GR-1820-F62 nine-cylinder air-cooled radials were selected for initial installation. The Pratt & Whitney R-1690 Hornet engines were fitted with 11 ft 6 in propellers, and 550 gallons of fuel were carried in two wing tanks. The design gross weight was quoted as 18,250 lb with a still air range of 1,600 miles at 202 mph at 10,000 ft.

The Douglas DC-5 prototype, registered NX21701 c/n 411, was completed in February 1939, and on 20 February Carl Cover flew it on its maiden flight. When the first orders were placed it appeared that the enterprise was to be fully rewarded. KLM placed an order for four aircraft, Pennsylvania-Central of Washington DC ordered six and the Colombian airline Sociedad Colombo-Alemana de Transportes Aéreos – SCADTA – ordered two. Shortly afterwards the US Navy Department approved a contract for three of a military version of the DC-5, designated R3D-1 for the US Navy, and for four for the US Marine Corps designated R3D-2.

The Douglas DC-5 prototype, NX21701 c/n 411 seen in flight on 17 April 1939, almost two months after its maiden flight on 20 February. It was initially powered by two 900hp Wright GR-1820-F62 Cyclone nine-cylinder air-cooled radial engines. (Douglas)

It is not generally known that the original pre-World War 2 British Imperial Airways Ltd, made a comparative analysis of the potential of the de Havilland Flamingo and the Douglas DC-5 on the European London-to-Berlin route that had been prepared during the spring of 1939. On 30 August 1939, the airline signed an agreement with the Douglas Aircraft Company for the purchase of nine DC-5s and made a down-payment of some 25 per cent towards the price, which included ferry flight charges to Floyd Bennett Field, New York, cost of lighters to the freighter, ocean freight charges and import duties. The aircraft unit cost was estimated at £27,912. The first British Imperial Airways DC-5 was scheduled for delivery to New York on 15 December 1939, the second on 29 December and the third on 22 January 1940, with six remaining to follow at weekly intervals. In anticipation of their delivery to the United Kingdom, the British Imperial Airways DC-5s were allocated the registrations G-AFYG to G-AFYO inclusive. However, following the outbreak of war the British Air Ministry instructed British Imperial Airways to cancel the order with Douglas and the down-payment funds were transferred towards the purchase of other Douglas wartime types for British military use.

Despite the early enthusiasm, the success of the DC-5 was short-lived, as the aircraft experienced aerodynamic difficulties during its test-flight programme because of excessive tail buffeting. The trouble was traced to interference between the drag of the high-mounted wings, the engines and the tail surfaces. This problem was corrected by modifications which smoothed out the turbulent airflow over the tail: the engine exhaust tail pipes were changed, to dampen the exhaust flow; and the tailplane was given a marked dihedral to remove it from the wake created by the wings and engines. With these modifications completed the DC-5 flew correctly and was able to take off in less than a thousand feet. It climbed at 1,500 ft per minute and cruised a little faster than the DC-3. With flight tests completed, the gross weight was increased to 21,000 lb, the aircraft certificated for more powerful engines, including the Pratt & Whitney R-1830, and was offered with a maximum passenger seating of twenty-two.

Sales Promotion

The El Segundo Division of the Douglas Aircraft Company produced a neat sales brochure on the new DC-5, from which the following is quoted:

The Douglas DC-5 is presented to fulfil the very definite need for a safe, economical, comfortable airplane primarily designed for short-range operation. It is a high wing monoplane with accommodation for sixteen passengers and a crew of three. Additional payload in the form of mail or express cargo may be carried in compartments totalling approximately 272 cubic feet.

To ensure safety, which must always be the prime requisite of any mode of transportation, the designers have combined a wing loading of only 22.1 pounds per square foot (a value almost 30% less than other recent designs), and a low power loading, to give a wide range of flying speeds with such features as improved wing and tail sections that provide exceptional stability near the stalling speed, simple type wing flaps, small center of gravity travel, a nose-wheel landing gear which prevents nosing over and ground looping, as well as offering greater passenger comfort, a substantial keel to absorb the shock of a landing made with the wheels retracted, and a cockpit which reduces pilot fatigue by the convenient location of all instruments and controls.

Economical operation has been achieved in the DC-5 by simple, rugged design, ease of maintenance, and excellent aerodynamic qualities.

To the passenger, seated in the luxurious upholstery of the scientifically-designed chairs, the DC-5 offers the unsurpassed visibility found only in high wing airplanes. At his fingertips are ash trays, cold air vents, reading lights, and curtains to be adjusted to suit the whim of the moment. His feet rest on deep carpeting which blends into the soft restful interior, his ears are unassailed by sharp noises, and his eyes need not combat sunlight reflected from large surfaces previously located below his line of vision. No stray drafts annoy him, yet the air is always fresh and at the proper temperature. He finds that he is relaxed, comfortable and secure.

Here, then, is the doorway to a new phase of aerial transportation, to profitable short-range operation. The DC-5, scion of an illustrious family, completely modern, yet not radical, following time-proven practices to new efficiency is presented to become the always ready, dependable workhorse of the industry.

Ironically, by the time any DC-5 difficulties had been overcome, the brochures printed and the Douglas sales teams made ready

Seen on 12 April 1940 this photograph depicts William E. Boeing (in hat) and his wife, plus the sales team officials of the Douglas Aircraft Company with the DC-5 NC21701 parked behind. It was delivered a week later. (Douglas)

for action, the war in Europe and the build-up of military hardware in the United States made it necessary to concentrate the effort at El Segundo on current military War Department programmes. In addition, SCADTA and Pennsylvania Central Airlines, like British Imperial Airways, had withdrawn their orders for the DC-5, leaving KLM as the only civil airline customer. This resulted in only five commercial DC-5s, including the prototype, and seven military R3D-s being built. After the completion of its flight trials programme, NX21701 was re-registered NC21701 and re-engined with 1,100 hp Wright R-1820-G102As; it was delivered on 19 April 1940 to William E. Boeing and named '**Rover**'. The DC-5 became the second Douglas aircraft to be used by the founder of the Boeing Airplane Company. The first was a Douglas Dolphin 117 NC14205 purchased in 1934.

It might seem surprising that William Boeing should choose a Douglas product for his personal use, but his own factory at Seattle was then heavily engaged in building four-engined transports and bombers. The only Boeing product that might possibly be available was a 247, an older and smaller aircraft than the DC-5. Mr Boeing took delivery of the aircraft at Las Vegas, where it had been taken the day before from El Segundo. Vegas was a favourite delivery centre for Douglas Commercials, probably because of the more lenient tax levies in the state of Nevada. The DC-5 had been converted to a plush eight-passenger executive transport and cost $87,000. As part of the down-payment, Bill Boeing traded in the Douglas Dolphin which he had purchased from the Douglas Aircraft Company in 1934. It too had been named '**Rover**'.

The DC-5 was designated in company records as DC-5-G102A. It sported full-span flaps, and the outboard wing panels were slotted, giving the transport a near STOL performance. Clayton L. Scott, who flew the Boeing executive DC-5 for nearly a year, described it as a nice aircraft to fly, about 15 mph faster than the DC-3, but without its fuel capacity; one disadvantage was that it was powered by Wright Cyclone engines, which the airlines of the day did not care for.

On 2 February 1942, NC21701 was impressed into military service with the US Navy under Contract No. C-97175, its first assignment being at the Naval Air Station at Norfolk, Virginia. It was transferred on station to the Naval Air Department as well as being used by AirLant on 29 July 1943. On 22 January 1944, it was assigned to the Banana River Naval Air Laboratory in Florida, on Project 'Baker'. In February 1945, it moved north to Whidbey Island in Washington State, not far from the Boeing factory. Another source indicates that BuNo. 08005 was used in the Aleutians in the Pacific for aerial mapping and survey tasks, after which it was stationed at NAS Alameda, California, on utility transport duties. On 30 June 1946, it was declared surplus to requirements by the US Navy and broken up.

A unique engineering feature of the DC-5 was the wing-to-fuselage structure. In shoulder-wing designs spars extending through the fuselage severely reduce headroom. In the new Douglas twin this was eliminated by two heavy fuselage frame and bridge structure units to which the wing spars were attached. These were hidden in the bulkheads forming the passenger compartments. In addition to the wing-attach frames, the fuselage had a heavy keel beam running from the nose wheel-well to aft of the passenger compartment as a safety measure in the event of a wheels-up landing. The floor was close to the ground for ease and speed of loading and unloading passengers and cargo. This was also useful for maintenance, which could be accomplished without the use of stands. Also, the floor was level at all times for passenger comfort. A lavatory, buffet and stewardess station were located in the rear. Cargo compartments totalling 272 cubic feet, forward and aft of the passenger compartment, carried luggage plus revenue-producing mail or cargo. Fuel was carried in two oval tanks in the wing. Each engine had an independent supply but could draw from either tank.

Cockpit of a Douglas DC-5, one of four ordered by KLM for its European route network. Due to World War II the fleet were diverted to Curacao and Batavia, and three of the four fled to safety in Australia being operated by the Allied Directorate of Air Transport. (Douglas)

Experience with the Douglas DB-7 bomber influenced the El Segundo design team to use a twin-engined high-wing configuration for the new DC-5. As will be seen by the photograph, the high-wing assisted with the loading of cargo and passengers. Wing span was 78ft and length 62ft 2in. Cruising speed was 202mph and range 1,600 miles. (Douglas)

Production

The first flight of the prototype DC-5 had taken place from Mines Field, now Los Angeles International Airport, and from here the first flights of all subsequent DC-5s took place. Although the aircraft for Penn Central and SCADTA were cancelled before being built, they were allocated Douglas c/ns and type numbers in the DC-5 series. DC-5-518 were Penn Central aircraft with c/ns 422, 423, 427, 429, whilst the SCADTA DC-5 was allocated DC-5-535 c/n 425, although the

The production line for the DC-5 at El Segundo showing three DC-5s in the final stages, including PH-AXE DC-5-511 c/n 430 Eend which was diverted to Batavia with KNILM as PK-ADA. It was damaged during a Japanese air raid on Kemajoran Airport on 9 February 1942 being captured and flown by the Japanese. (Douglas)

Douglas DC-5 PH-AXB was repainted at the factory as PJ-AIZ and renamed Zonvogel prior to delivery to Curacao. It is seen parked at the Douglas factory with the nose of a Douglas C-47 military transport in the foreground of the photograph. After a very chequered career this DC-5 survived World War II ending its days in Israel. (Douglas)

Very rare photograph of DC-5-511 PK-ADA c/n 430 of KNILM seen during its evaluation by the Japanese Army and the Tachikawa Aeronautical Institute (Engineering) from its base near Tokyo. The airliner was captured and after repair flown to Tachikawa in February 1942. It ended its life as an Army radio-navigation trainer with the Japanese. (Peter M. Bowers)

airline order was for two aircraft. In the factory order for building the DC-5 follows a sequence with the c/ns, then it is possible that these cancelled aircraft were partly assembled at El Segundo, as one record shows 'not completed'. KLM had ordered four DC-5s for use on its European network; these were powered by R-1820-G102A engines and tentatively allocated registrations and names as follows: DC-5-510 c/n 424 PH-AXA '*Alk*'; DC-5-535 c/n 426 PH-AXB '*Bergeend*'; DC-5-511 c/n 428 PH-AXE '*Eend*'; and DC-5-511 c/n 430 PH-AXG '*Gruto*'.

Adolf Hitler invaded Poland in 1939, starting the Second World War before KLM took delivery of their four DC-5s. The subsequent German invasion of the Netherlands forced the airline to divert these aircraft to its overseas operations, resulting in two being delivered in May 1940 to KLM West Indies Division, based in Curaçao, in the Netherlands Antilles, and registered PJ-AIZ '*Zonvogel*' c/n 426, and PJ-AIW '*Wakago*' c/n 424. For a year these operated from Curaçao Island on the Curaçao–Venezuela–Surinam route. However, the scarcity of spares made maintenance difficult. The planes were flown back to the United States for repairs and overhaul, then crated and shipped to Java, joining the DC-5s of KNILM and being re-registered PK-ADC c/n 426 and PK-ADD c/n 424.

Koninllijke Nederlandsch-Indische Luchtvaart Maatschappij – KNILM – was a subsidiary company of KLM based in the Dutch East Indies. They took the other two DC-5s intended for KLM in Europe, which were registered PK-ADA c/n 430 and PH-ADB c/n 428. These were all in service when the Japanese attacked Pearl Harbor, and they were employed in flying refugees to Australia; they continued this humanitarian task until the Dutch East Indies were overrun by the Japanese in the

autumn of 1942. The war in the Pacific, rather than ending the already chequered career of these four DC-5 aircraft, led them into a new and colourful life.

Into Battle

The two KLM DC-5s to be operated from Curaçao Island arrived there at the end of May 1940. One was fitted out to carry twenty-two passengers, while the other was supplied with a forward freight compartment and could carry eighteen passengers, the fuselage being divided into four compartments. The Douglas Aircraft Company dismantled these two DC-5s after overhaul and they were sent by ship to Java. One record shows that '*Zonvogel*' – 'Sunbird' – left for Java on 29 May 1941, followed by the '*Wakago*' on 10 June 1941.

The career of DC-5 PK-ADA was unique. During a Japanese air raid on Kemajoran Airport, Batavia (Djakarta) on 9 February 1942, when it was about to take-off, piloted by Captain Rupplin, the DC-5 was damaged and had to be abandoned. It was later captured by the Japanese, repaired and taken to Japan, where it was flown to Tachikawa for flight testing by the Japanese Air Technical Intelligence Group. It remained there until December 1943. The pilot who flew it to Japan and later conducted many of the flight tests was Captain Haruo Odagirl, who had also flight-tested the Douglas DC-4E purchased by Japan from the United States. Apparently this DC-5 ended its days as a Japanese Army radio-navigational trainer, and in 1944 was displayed in Tokyo along with other captured Allied weapons. Unfortunately, its ultimate fate is unknown.

DC-5 PK-ADB c/n 428 escaped the war zone to Australia and was impressed into service by the 21st Troop Carrier Squadron USAAC, using the radio call-sign 'VH-CXA', but during 1942 it was destroyed at Parafield near Adelaide, South Australia. Later all remaining DC-5s were 'purchased' by the USAAC, designated C-110-DE (Douglas El Segundo) and allocated the serial numbers 44-83230/31/32, despite the fact that two, including c/n 428 'VH-CXA' had been destroyed earlier.

It must be recorded that three other DC-5s managed to escape to Australia. These were PK-ADB, -ADC and -ADD, which were flown to Darwin in northern Australia in February 1942, shortly before the fall of Java. One crashed *en route* at Charleville, Queensland, and was reduced to spares. The other two were taken over by a unique organisation operated by the joint Allied forces and known as the Allied Directorate of Air Transport. ADAT had been formed by the USAAC to organise transport with the civil airlines within Australia to be used on charter work for the US Army. PK-ADD served with the 21st TCSq at Brisbane, Queensland, allocated radio call-sign 'VH-CXB'. It was delivered to the USAAC in May 1942 and in May 1944 was allocated the USAAC serial 44-83231.

The 374th Troop Carrier Group, with its four Troop Carrier Squadrons – 6th, 21st, 22nd and 33rd – was activated in Australia on 7 November 1942, as part of the huge US 5th Army Air Force, and was employed in transporting men and materiel from Australia, New Guinea, Biak and the Philippines until the end of the war. It operated a mixture of war-weary and worn-out aircraft, including Douglas B-18s, C-39s, C-49s, Lockheed C-56 Lodestars, Lockheed C-60s, DC-3s and DC-5s, the latter designated C-110. It was re-equipped with Douglas C-47s in February 1943. The group was engaged in supplying Allied forces in the Papua New Guinea campaign, and received a Distinguished Unit Citation – DUC – for transporting troops, equipment and evacuation casualties to rear areas during November/December 1942.

A further very rare photograph depicting two Douglas DC-3 military transports, and a Douglas C-110-DE ex-DC-5, in flight. The three ex-KNILM DC-5s were impressed into service by the US Army Air Force during 1944. The transports were operated by the 374th Troop Carrier Group of the US 5th Air Force in Australia. (Australian War Memorial)

Douglas DC-5 PK-ADC was to be the only one of the three Australian based DC-5s to survive the war. It carried RAAF radio call-sign 'VH-CXC', was allocated the USAAC serial 44-83232 and after arrival in Australia was assigned to Australian National Airways in late 1942 along with several Lockheed C-60 Lodestars of the Netherland East Indies Air Force – NEAIAF. ANA based the DC-5 at Archerfield, near Brisbane and it was test-flown prior to acceptance on 25 December 1942. The allocated radio call-sign 'VH-CXC' was painted on the fin and rudder, over the dark wartime camouflage, and it also carried the USAAC insignia on the fuselage and wings. During 1943 it was involved in four minor accidents at different bases in Queensland but it was kept flying. During May an attempt was made to remove the camouflage and the paint stripper caught fire in the hangar at Archerfield. It was

then flown in metallic finish, minus the US insignia but retaining 'VH-CXC' in black on the fuselage and on the fin and rudder.

During 1944 it was transferred to Melbourne and used on the ANA Melbourne to Tasmania service. Apparently it was very unpopular with passengers and ANA received a continuous stream of letters of complaint. As a result, the USAAF gave ANA permission to have the interior redesigned and more comfortable seats fitted, with the result that the payload was reduced to 3,000 lb. At the end of the Second World War, the Australian companies operating USAAF ADAT types were allowed to retain the aircraft, so ANA was left with DC-5 'VH-CXC' and two Douglas C-39s (DC-2s), 'VH-CCG' and 'VH-CCH'.

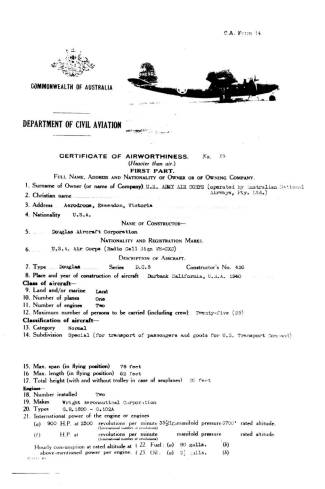

Correspondence between Australian National Airways in Melbourne and Harry Gann, historian with the Douglas Aircraft Company in Long Beach, California, have revealed more information about the career of 'VH-CXC'. On arrival with ANA it was granted the US Army Air Corps Certificate of Airworthiness No.X5 by the Australian Department of Civil Aviation, and its radio call-sign registration was allocated in Melbourne on 7 January 1943. It was then hired by the USAAC to ANA to operate a charter service on behalf of the US Air

Transport Command from Australia to various points in the south-west Pacific theatre of operations. After being taken over by ANA, it continued to be used on the courier run, carrying personnel of the various Allied Armed Services until May 1944, when the move of the war theatre north and the introduction of larger, faster aircraft such as the Douglas C-54 'Skymaster', enabled it to be released for civil use.

ANA used the aircraft on internal domestic services until May 1946, when it was finally purchased outright by ANA. A new C of A was issued, dated 24 May 1946, the DC-5 was re-registered VH-CXC on the Australian Civil Register. On 4 June it suffered an accident with the nose-wheel at Kingsford Smith airport, Sydney. It was finally withdrawn from regular ANA service on 19 July 1946 and held in reserve until November 1947.

During May 1946 ANA applied to the Australian Department of Civil Aviation to register the three Douglas transports they had acquired, prior to resale. The DC-5 became VH-ARD and the two C-39s VH-ARB and VH-ARC. For two years the DC-5 was parked in amongst other aircraft on a dump on the boundary of Essendon Airport, Melbourne awaiting a buyer. On 2 January 1948, Gregory R. Board from Sydney purchased VH-ARD from ANA and on the same day two ANA pilots were hired to fly the DC-5 to Sydney. Initially there was a dispute over the Certificate of Airworthiness as the aircraft had been dormant for so long. Trading as New Holland Airways, Gregory Board and the company stationery boasted 'Luxury Charter Flights to All Parts of the World.'

On 29 January 1948, the DC-5 VH-ARD had its undercarriage collapse whilst landing at Schoefield airport, Sydney, but the keel of the transport had been strongly built by Douglas, so very little damage was sustained. On 3 May 1948, the company was granted permission to fly to Rome with VH-ARD to bring Italian migrants to Australia. It departed from Darwin in the Northern Territories on 10 May. Nothing was heard from the company or the DC-5 until 2 July when the Department of Civil Aviation were informed by New Holland Airways that the DC-5 had gone unserviceable in Rome, and permission was requested to bring the migrants in a DC-3 the company had purchased. This was granted and a few weeks later DC-3 I-TROS arrived in Sydney, becoming VH-BNH. As no export licence had been issued for VH-ARD the DCA wrote several letters to the airline, finally receiving a reply to the effect that ownership had been transferred to an American citizen on 28 May, a Martin A. Rybakoff, whose address was Grand Hotel, Sicily.

After enquiries to the new owner by the Australian DCA, during which it was revealed that the DC-5 was being used for the personal use of Mr. Rybakoff, the matter was transferred into the hands of the Australian Customs Authority, as VH-ARD was now a very illegal export, with no permission to be sold overseas. What happened next is rather vague: apparently no proceedings were actioned immediately, but a full investigation was ordered after the Australian Consul in London wrote to the Department of Civil Aviation informing them that aircraft bearing Australian civil VH- markings had been reported in use for both bombing and transport duties by the Israeli Air Force in Palestine. One pilot who had flown six Lockheed Hudsons with Australian registrations from Sydney to Israel in 1948 was found in London, and he stated that the DC-5 VH-ARD was grounded in Palestine during 1949 due to lack of spares, and was in a depreciating state of repair.

New Holland Airways had named the DC-5 '***Bali Clipper***' and it is reported that from its new owner in Sicily it was sold to

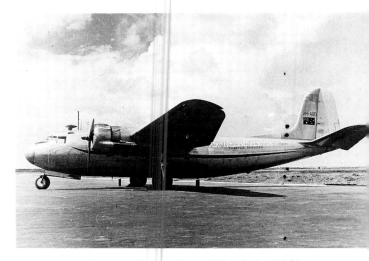

Seen parked at Lydda Airport, Israel, in March 1948, is the last DC-5 in service. It is VH-ARD of New Holland Airways charter service named Bali Clipper. *It ended its days at the Tel Aviv Aeronautical Technical School.* (H. Simon)

an agent for use by the embryonic Israeli nation. As the sale of any equipment 'constituting a potential weapon of war' to Israel was banned in Australia, so the three Hudsons used as bombers and the DC-5 became illegal exports. One can only emphasise that the Douglas DC-5 appears to have been involved in some very, very clandestine operations, was never registered in Israel, and was possibly used as a 'kick 'em out of the door' bomber in the early Jewish/Arab conflicts, with one report indicating it was named '***Bagel Lancer***'. It was last seen in Tel Aviv in 1955, stripped of its engines and being used by the Technical School as a ground training aid. Fortunately the first member of the Civil Aviation Department in the government of Palestine, Heinz H. Simon, in office for forty-two years since May 1937, was a keen aircraft photographer and captured the DC-5 VH-ARD with his camera when it passed through Lydda Airport in March 1948. This was the last survivor of the DC-5 family.

Yet another source reveals that the three Douglas C-110-DE serials 44-83230 to 44-83232 are from a batch approved on 14 June 1944, under AC 6838, Funds NPR Program UN. The other aircraft involved were two DC-2s, two DC-3s and three Lockheed 14s, the USAAF designations being C-32A, C-49H-DO and C-111-LO respectively. There is a report that the two DC-2s, two DC-3s, three DC-5s and three Lockheed 14s, formerly of KNILM, were delivered to the US Army Air Forces in Australia between 15 and 18 May 1942. Certainly, on 21 May, 21st Squadron RAAF at Brisbane included on its strength two DC-2s, two DC-3s, three DC-5s and three Lockheed 14s.

A formal contract between KNILM and Pan American Airways, acting as agents for the US War Department, was signed on about 28 March 1942, for the lease of KNILM aircraft, but to be operated under KNILM management. However, a few days later, the US Army Air Corps negotiated to purchase the transports. The USAAF records indicate the three Douglas C-110-DE aircraft with serials 44-83230/31/32 as being held on inventory from 17 March 1945 through to 31 December 1945, and being based in the Philippine Islands. It appears virtually certain that the allocation of these USAAF serials was a paper exercise, as there is proof that only two of the transports remained airworthy. There is no evidence to show that the

USAAF serials were ever carried by the C-110s (DC-5s); indeed, if they had been allocated to individual aircraft, they would possibly be allocated in sequence with the RAAF type radio call-signs – VH-CXA 44-83230, VH-CXB 44-83231 and VX-CXC 44-83232. The author has no evidence whatsoever to support this assumption.

US Navy and Marines

Production of the Douglas DC-5 was abandoned at El Segundo in October 1940. Due to the world crisis, other Douglas aircraft types were needed more, notably the military variants of the DC-3, the new C-54, the A-20 attack bomber and its export sister for France, the DB-7. The US Navy required the SBD Dauntless dive bomber, and the US Army Air Corps the B-18 and B-23. Work on the new B-19 bomber was then receiving top priority and there were other designs waiting as the United States prepared for war. So the DC-5 never really had its chance to make history, although it must be admitted that the antics of some of the dozen built proved the ruggedness of the type under very adverse conditions in the Pacific.

The first Douglas R3D-1, c/n 606, BuNo. 1901 for the US Navy crashed on take-off from Mines Field on 1 June 1940, on its initial test flight. The aircraft history card NAVAER-1925 (9-44) reveals that it was burned to complete destruction. All on board were killed, including Harry E. 'Bud' Bogen, pilot, William Benson, flight engineer, Walter M. Mulvoney, crew chief, and James Jewart, inspector. Cross-rigged controls were blamed for the accident.

This left the US Navy one short on their order. They did take on charge the VIP DC-5 owned by William Boeing, which became R3D-3 BuNo. 08005, and one report indicates it remained as a VIP aircraft with the navy for a short period, based on the Atlantic seaboard. It was later returned to El Segundo where it had Wright R-1820-60 engines of 1,200 hp installed, supposedly for a special assignment in the Aleutians. (Production aircraft for the US Navy and Marine Corps were normally powered by Wright R-1820-44 engines). This gave the transport a 25 per cent increase in power for high-altitude performance.

After the fatal crash, Contract No. C68537 was completed with six aeroplanes instead of seven. Douglas R3D-1 BuNo.

Douglas R3D-1 BuNo.1902 c/n 607 was accepted by the US Navy on 3 July 1940 being assigned to naval air station Anacostia, Maryland, remaining there until 1941. It was eventually struck off charge in January 1946. It is depicted at NAS Anacostia. (Douglas)

1902 c/n 607 was accepted by the US Navy on 3 July 1940, and on 6 July was assigned to NAS Anacostia, Maryland, remaining there until 28 July 1941, when it was transferred to NAS San Diego. It was briefly in custody for some unknown reason at Santa Monica, and on 25 October 1941 was transferred to NAS New York, where it remained until struck off charge on 31 January 1946.

Douglas R3D-1 BuNo. 1903 c/n 608 was accepted by the US Navy on 5 July 1940 and was also assigned to NAS Anacostia three days later. It was transferred to San Diego on 3 March 1941, and according to the aircraft history card remained there with various units such as AirPac HQ, to whom it was assigned from 10 May to 29 November 1943, finally being struck off charge on 31 January 1946. Another source indicates that BuNo. 1903 was sent to the Pacific in May 1943, and it is believed to have been used briefly by General MacArthur.

Seen parked at Lydd Airport, Israel, in March 1948, is the last DC-5 in service. It is VH-ARD of New Holland Airways charter service named Bali Clipper. *It ended its days at the Tel Aviv Aeronautical Technical School.* (H. Simon)

The first Douglas R3D-2, BuNo. 1904 c/n 609, was delivered to the US Marine Corps as a cargo aircraft on 10 September 1940, and assigned to VMJ-2 Squadron at NAS San Diego. On 5 March 1941 it crashed and suffered damage to the nose wheel. The damage is detailed on the aircraft history card: both protecting doors of nose wheel-well destroyed, lower edges of nose wheel well on both sides bent, three former ribs on each side of nose wheel-well bent. Both pitot tubes broken off. Nose wheel tyre and tube blown out. Side of nose wheel scraped and scratched.

By 31 March it was at NAS Pearl Harbor under repair. One source suggests that on 7 December 1941 it was in the A & R shop on Ford Island on the strength of VMJ-252 Squadron ex-VMJ-2, but although it was reported by the Commander-in-Chief Pacific as available on 23 December, its history card records that it was destroyed by fire on 7 December, which seems more likely. Yet another source indicates that it was on the strength of the C-in-C Pacific and based in Australia on 7 December 1941, and that it crashed on a remote island off the Australian coast after being hit by fire from a Japanese submarine. Whatever the truth of these reports may be, it was struck off charge on 31 January 1942.

Douglas R3D-2 BuNo. 1905 c/n 610 was delivered to the US Marine Corps on 14 September 1940 and assigned to VMJ-2

Squadron at NAS San Diego. It was transferred on 24 November 1941 to Commander, Air Battle Force, Pearl Harbor (ComAirBatFor). After a brief secondment to VMJ-252 at Ewa, Hawaii under Marine Air Group 2 (MAG-2), it went back to Pearl Harbor on 18 October 1942. On 2 November it was transferred to NAS Alameda, California, and south to the Marine Corps Air Detachment at San Diego on 29 April 1943. Records show it was transferred to AirPac at San Diego the following day. Still at this air station it went to the USMC Air Base Group 2 on 15 November and when this unit was transferred to El Toro, California in mid-1945, the R3D-2 was also re-assigned. On 31 October 1946 BuNo. 1905 was struck off charge.

Marine Utility Squadron 252 was commissioned at Ewa, Hawaii, on 15 July 1941, under the command of Major Perry K. Smith, USMC, and was a remnant of the oldest utility squadron in Marine Corps aviation. One of its earlier designations was VJ-2, and from the date of its commissioning until 7 December 1941, it functioned as a utility squadron. When the Japanese attacked Pearl Harbor the unit was stationed at Ewa and lost an undetermined amount of materiel, and all its aircraft except one Douglas R3D-2. At that time it was in fact primarily a transport squadron using the R3D-2 type aircraft, although it was still designated a utility squadron, using various types of aircraft including Sikorsky JRS-1, Douglas R3D-2, Vought SB2U Vindicator and Douglas SBD-1 Dauntless. The duties of the squadron included carrying personnel and materiel in the transports and towing targets for other units. The transport flights were mainly flown between Ewa, Hilo and Ford Island. Shortly after the attack on Pearl Harbor, the squadron received more transport aircraft and from that date it was constantly expanding its flights, both in numbers and in distances. The strength of VMJ-252 on 31 December 1941 was eleven officers and sixty-seven enlisted men.

On 22 February 1942, Major William A. Willis, USMC, assumed command, and on 12 April was relieved by Captain John S. Carter, USMC (Reserve). On 11 April 1942, VMJ-252 was assigned on permanent duty overseas. It established the first air transport service to outlying island air bases in the Pacific. The first transport service between Ewa and Midway was established in May 1942. Prior to and during the Battle of Midway this squadron transported personnel, ammunition and other vital materiels to forces for use during the historic battle. This flight was led by Colonel Claude A. Larkin, USMC, then Commanding Officer of Marine Air Group 21 (MAG-21).

On 22 September 1940, the Marine Corps accepted their penultimate Douglas R3D-2 BuNo. 1906 c/n 611 and two days later it was assigned to VMJ-1, later designated VMJ-152, based at Quantico, Virginia. It went to Air Base Group 2 at San Diego on 20 April 1942, to VMJ-153 also at San Diego on 15 June and back to Air Base Group 2 on 14 September. It transferred with the unit to El Toro in mid-1945 and was struck off charge on 31 October 1946.

The last R3D-2 BuNo. 1907 c/n 612 was accepted by the USMC on 22 October 1940 and assigned to VMJ-152 at Quantico on 25 October. It went to VMJ-153 at San Diego on 6 March 1942 and, like BuNo. 1906, served with MAG-2, being struck off charge on 31 December 1945.

John M. Elliott, a researcher with the Smithsonian Institution in 1973, had personal experience of the USMC R3D-2 transports: he was with Air Base Group 2, the unit responsible for preparing the F4U- Corsairs for delivery to the first operational Marine Corps squadron. The Douglas R3D-2 transport flew a round-robin flight to all Pacific west coast USMC air stations. John was at North Island, California, and two R3D-2s were under operational evaluation. They were flown each day with a given weight and Marine Corps personnel or sand bags were used to augment the freight load when necessary. The Marine Corps R3D-2s were used for paratroop training and the aircraft based with VMJ-1 at Quantico dropped USMC paratroopers over the Naval Air Station located at Lakehurst, New Jersey. Douglas R3D-2 BuNo. 1907 was last noted in the scrapyard at USMC El Toro on 27 May 1946. It was minus its engines.

Very little has previously been written on the Douglas DC-5 transport. This is perhaps understandable, as so few were built, yet it appeared to be a very advanced and well thought-out design in the period leading up to the Second World War. Few attempts have been made to catalogue the history of the type, and even some of the information released by the Douglas Aircraft Company is a little misleading. For example, one company-generated paper states that the reason the DC-5 was a failure was the high wing configuration and its resulting higher structural cost. However, the main reason that the DC-5 did not become a high production aircraft was the timing. It was designed not as a DC-3 replacement, but as a short-range feeder airliner. With the advent of the Second World War, there was little demand for a short-range aircraft, especially when high production rate tooling had not yet been fabricated. One source suspects that if the Douglas Aircraft Company had pressurised the designs and put that modified version into production, the Convair 240/340/440 may have experienced some real competition.

Douglas drawings reveal that as an alternative to the standard Wright Cyclone powered DC-5, the company also offered a version powered by four 600 hp Ranger SGV-770 twelve-cylinder inverted-vee air-cooled engines. Among proposed Douglas DC-5 developments was a 'DB-5' version which could be used either as a bomber, with forty-four 50-lb bombs, or as a military transport with thirty troops on canvas seats along the fuselage sides.

The demise of the Douglas DC-5 certainly did not mean the end of that particular configuration. It appeared in the post-war prototype of the Lockheed 'Saturn', the advertised but never built Boeing 417, and in several European aircraft manufacturer designs. The most notable of these was the Fokker F.27 'Friendship', one of the most widely-used turboprop airliners ever built.

However, it is always interesting to speculate on how the design of any good aeroplane affects that of others. For example, it is said that Boeing engineers developed the original design of the Fokker F.27 turboprop airliner and sold it to Fokker, from whom it was later acquired by Fairchild and appeared as the FH.227 turboprop airliner in the United States. Since the 1959 Fokker F.27 does resemble the 1939 Douglas DC-5 airliner that William Boeing owned, could it be surmised that the Boeing Airplane Company design engineers got some ideas from the Douglas DC-5? The answer, of course, is that the two aircraft are quite different in many aspects of design. But whatever its contribution to the high-wing, twin-engine design, the Douglas DC-5 just happened to be the right aeroplane built at the wrong time.

RIGHT: *Four DC-5 R-1820-G102A powered aircraft were ordered by KLM for use on its European routes and tentatively assigned registrations and names. Depicted is PH-AXB Bergeend c/n 426. Due to the German invasion of the Netherlands KLM diverted the airliners to its overseas operations.* (Douglas)

LEFT: *Another factory view depicting DC-5 VH-AXB which went to KLM in the West Indies in May 1940 re-registered PJ-AIZ Zonvogel operating from Curacao. It later went to KNILM in Java as PK-ADC and survived World War II in Australia.* (Douglas)

RIGHT: *This DC-6B seen as LN-SUK with Braathens was delivered as CF-MCL c/n 45506/1002 to Maritime Central on 9 July 1958. On 17 July 1958 sold to US Overseas as N400US and to Norway on 25 February 1964. Today this airliner is back in Canada as C-GIGY with Conair Aviation modified as a fire bomber. It was ex-OO-VGE.* (Braathens)

e first pressurised airliner to enter service with Delta was this DC-6 N1901M c/n 43139 livered on 1 October 1948. The legend on the fuselage proclaims The Airline of the South d it was named The Flying D. On 16 October 1968 it was sold to Aero Tech and stored at cson, Arizona, being cancelled on 9 July 1974. (Delta)

Northeast Sunliner DC-6B N6581C c/n 45217/773 delivered on 23 February 1957. The airline operated eighteen DC-6B airliners of which ten were purchased direct from Douglas, being ordered in March 1955. They operated on the Boston to Miami route via New York. In 1967 N6581C was sold to Carco Air Service. (Delta)

LEFT: *Douglas DC-7 N6322C c/n 44286/530 Mainliner Waipahu seen in flight over Hawaii. It was delivered to United on 3 December 1954 and on 31 December 1959 was traded back to Douglas. After two owners in California it went to Spain with TASSA as EC-BAF, registered on 4 June 1965. After the operator went out of business a year later, the airliner stood derelict at Palma, Majorca.* (United Air Lines)

LEFT: *This DC-7 N4781C c/n 44261/447 was delivered to Delta on 24 February 1954. It was involved in a landing accident at O'Hare Airport, Chicago, on 16 December 1961. It was dismantled on 30 April 1962. During the summer of 1964 it was in use as a restaurant, but by January 1967 had been moved to Sterling, Illinois.* (Delta)

RIGHT: *Cockpit photograph taken in June 1986 when many DC-3s participated in the large EXPO 86 DC-3 armada in Canada. The aircraft is Canadian Armed Forces C-47 '12959' c/n 26641 named* Pinnochio *from 402 Squadron and fitted with a pointed nose cone from a CF-104 Starfighter. This DC-3 is still flying today having been sold to an operator in the USA.* (Ed Long)

RIGHT: *Seen in World War II markings as a C-49H is DC-3-178 c/n 1918 built for American as NC17332* West Virginia *delivered 18 February 1937. Today it is operated by the Confederate Air Force, modified with panoramic windows and purchased by the CAF on 25 January 1982. It is seen over the Exxon Refinery at Baytown, Texas, in September 1987.* (Phil Makanna)

BELOW: *Seen parked at Brunswick Naval Air Station on 26 July 1992 is a unique DC-3 N130Q c/n 11761 fitted with World War II Edo floats built for the C-47C. This DC-3 was purchased on 9 December 1985 by HBF Inc., Greenville, Maine, and after the floats were restored and fitted to the DC-3, the combination was flown from a lake. The unit was advertised for sale during 1992 for $1,200,000.* (Ken Marshall)

LEFT: *This DC-3 N34 c/n 33359 was built as a TC-47B-35-DK 44-77027 and delivered on 26 May 1945 going to the US Navy as a R4D-7 BuNo.99856. It served in the United Kingdom with VR-24 Squadron during 1948. Two years later as N7091C it went to the US Navy Department, then in 1956 leased to the CAA as N34, later transferred to the FAA on 29 August 1966. It was restored to the US Department of Transportation – FAA – in August 1985 and painted in period livery and used for education display work.* (FAA)

LEFT: *In a unique flight over southern California, a DC-2 and a DC-3 are seen in flight together on 14 June 1990. The DC-2 was restored by the Douglas Historical Foundation and is one of two flyable of the type in the world. The DC-3 N514GA is operated from Van Nuys by Clay Lacy Aviation. The DC-2 is flown at least once a month carrying fourteen invited passengers.* (Harry Gann)

BELOW: *This DC-3 was delivered to the RNZAF in 1945 and served New Zealand National Airways as ZK-APK c/n 34227. It later became a top dressing aircraft with Fieldair. John Eames who owned a garage at Mangaweka bought the DC-3 for $4,500, spent a further $20,000 in cleaning and repainting it and having it mounted and used as a tea room and today the DC-3 is a tourist attraction.* (Charles Cooke)

Chapter Twelve
Douglas DC-6

When the Douglas Aircraft Company team designed its second type to bear the DC-4 designation, the decision was made to offer this transport initially without cabin pressurisation. However, the company intended to develop pressurisation for later installation. The appearance of the Boeing Stratoliner and the Lockheed Constellation, both constructed with pressurisation, reinforced the willingness to market pressurised versions of the DC-4 'Skymaster'. Wartime pressures demanded large quantities of aircraft rather than more comfortable ones, and so as we have seen, the Douglas transport was mass-produced as the unpressurised C-54 military transport.

One of the principal disadvantages for the Douglas Company in the immediate post-war period was the fact that TWA, as the primary sponsor of the original L-049 'Constellation', held an option on its initial post-war production. This was offset by the fact that the production L-049 was not to be sold to major United States airlines which were in direct competition with TWA. These carriers, specifically American Airlines and United, had to manage with converted Douglas C-54s for a year or more while TWA was operating the speedier and more comfortable pressurised 'Constellation'. The advantage for Douglas in this situation was not only that these two major trunk carriers placed early and relatively large orders for the successor to the DC-4, but that this greatly encouraged the pace of both its development and its production.

The Douglas Aircraft Company had been both far-seeing and fortunate in another circumstance. The gap between the dates of service introduction of the Lockheed 'Constellation' and the new Douglas Commercial – the DC-6 – would have been much longer and prospectively more damaging had it not been that an improved military version of the C-54 was already under construction at Santa Monica in 1945. The company had, from the earliest days of the definitive DC-4, every intention of providing pressurisation and other improvements, and although military requirements did not include such refinements for the C-54, it was ready to market the DC-4-1037 for cargo work, and did make pressurisation available on the successful DC-4-1009s it built post-war. It is interesting to record that the pressurisation system in the only other long-range land-plane transport available in 1942, the Boeing 307 'Stratoliner', had either been deactivated or removed when the US Army Air Corps took over the few aircraft. The system was never replaced when the 'Stratoliners' were declared as surplus and refurbished for the civil market.

Aware of the likelihood of future and strong competition from the Lockheed stable, the first example of which, as the military C-69 'Constellation', had flown in January 1943, the Douglas design team, led by Arthur Raymond and Ed Burton, proceeded, so far as wartime restrictions would allow, in preparing for an improved version of the DC-4/C-54 'Skymaster'. The company was fortunate in interesting the US War Department to the practical extent of ordering a prototype – one of three transports for the USAAF under a funding title 'Skymaster Improvement Program'. This prototype, based on the C-54E, the penultimate of the principal wartime variants, was designated the XC-112A with USAAF serial 45-873 c/n 36326. It was later re-designated YC-112A-DO.

Redesignated YC-112-DO, the prototype DC-6, is seen in military markings as 45-873 c/n 36326. Orders for the DC-6 had preceded the first flight of the XC-112 and the first of these commenced flight trials on 29 June 1946. Subsequent civil and military orders kept the production line open until the end of 1958. (Douglas)

The unmarked XC-112A-DO flying off the Malibu coastline, north of Santa Monica. This was a pressurised development of the C-54E funded by the US Government. It had a longer fuselage, large rectangular windows, and was powered by 2,100hp Pratt & Whitney R-2800-34 radials. John F. Martin flew the aircraft on its maiden flight on 15 February 1946. (Douglas)

The other two transports in the government-funded programme were the Allison V-1710-powered XC-114 and XC-116. The pressurised prototype XC-112A was conceived as a much improved aircraft, incorporating not only full cabin

United Air Lines DC-6 NC37526 c/n 43015 Mainliner Iowa *seen parked at Oakland, California, during September 1947 shortly after delivery. After a lease it was sold to Delta in December 1959. On 16 October 1968 it was sold to Aero Tech Inc. which became ARTKO. It was stored at Tucson, Arizona, and cancelled on 17 June 1976 as destroyed.* (William T. Larkins)

The XC-112A was civilianised in July 1959 registered N6166G and after several ownershps went to Mercer Enterprises Inc. as N901MA. Unfortunately it crashed on a golf course shortly after take-off from Hollywood-Burbank Airport, California, due to an explosion in one of the engines. (Harry Gann)

pressurisation, but also a fuselage 81 inches longer with large rectangular windows in place of the circular portholes of the 'Skymaster'. Power was from four Pratt & Whitney 2,100 hp R-2800-34 radial engines. An improved de-icing system, made necessary by higher operating altitudes, and better radio navigation equipment were incorporated, giving a substantial all-round enhancement of performance.

Test work on this prototype of the Douglas DC-6 commenced on 15 February 1946, when Douglas test pilot John F. Martin and crew took off from Santa Monica for the first of a series of successful flights culminating in its acceptance by the USAAF. It was used briefly by the USAAF prior to sale as N6166G to non-scheduled US airline Conner Air Lines. It was modified and approved by the FAA on 20 August 1956, and after many owners, including two in Ecuador, c/n 36326 was lost on 8 February 1976, whilst being operated by Mercer Airlines as N901MA. It crashed on a golf course shortly after take-off from Hollywood-Burbank Airport, California, due to an explosion in one of the engines.

Post-war curtailments of military transport orders eliminated the prospect of the USAAF ordering the C-112 in quantity, but at the same time this freed Douglas to proceed with the marketing of the previously thinly-disguised DC-6 commercial variant. Some fifteen months before the first flight of the XC-112A, Douglas had received an order for fifty DC-6s from American Airlines. The first flight of the XC-112A was made in the same month as TWA introduced the 'Constellation' into commercial service, emphasising the competition Douglas faced. The first of the true DC-6s did not fly until 29 June 1946, some four and a half months after the military XC-112A prototype. It was registered NX90701 initially with c/n 42854, entering commercial service with American Airlines on April 20 1947, as '*Flagship New York*'. Delivery had been made simultaneously on 24 November 1946 to both American and United, but as the type was still awaiting its FAA certificate of airworthiness, the two airlines had to use their DC-6s for crew training and route proving for five months. By the time American inaugurated a DC-6 service on the New York to

Chicago route on 27 April 1947, some twenty-two DC-6s had been delivered to these two airlines, and to Panagra. Over the highly competitive US transcontinental routes, American and United operated their DC-6s against the 'Constellations' of TWA. On 1 May 1947, United inaugurated the DC-6 on routes to Hawaii.

National Airlines, which had been granted rights as the second airline on the lucrative New York to Miami route, introduced its DC-6s in 1947, in fierce competition with the 'Constellations' of Eastern Air Lines. Braniff introduced DC-6s on the Chicago to Texas routes in 1947, replacing DC-3s. The remaining US airline operator of the type was Delta, who replaced its DC-4s with DC-6s on the Chicago to Miami route on 1 December 1948, enabling it to compete effectively with Eastern and its 'Constellations'. Before the Second World War, American Airlines had been heavily committed to the luxury transcontinental sleeper trade, and in 1947 it reintroduced this service, using DC-6s under the name 'Mercury'. However, the service did not prove very successful and was withdrawn in 1951.

On 1 July 1947 the US Air Force took delivery of the 29th DC-6 for use as a Presidential aircraft, designated VC-118-DO 46-505 c/n 42881. American Airlines had released a delivery slot. It was named The Independence *after the Missouri home town of President Truman as shown in the landing photograph. It was later donated to the National Air & Space Museum.* (Douglas)

Exports and Problems

The US Air Force took delivery of one production DC-6 originally intended for American airlines, which became the one and only C-118-DO. It was delivered on the first day of July 1947, as 46-505 c/n 42881 and became the presidential aircraft. Named '*Independence*', it replaced the C-54 '*Sacred Cow*'. This VIP DC-6 was the twenty-ninth production airliner and was named after President Harry S. Truman's home town in Missouri.

This Luftwaffe DC-6B c/n 44175 was initially built for Sabena as 00-CTM delivered in January 1954. As a DC-6A/B it went to the German Air Force (Luftwaffe) on 20 May 1965 becoming 'CA+024'. On 3 June 1969 it was delivered to Sterling Airways registered OY-STY. (APN)

The first European operator of the DC-6 was Sabena, who introduced them on its Brussels to New York service in August 1947, and on its Johannesburg service early in 1950. Although KLM had bought 'Constellations' for its North Atlantic services, it purchased six DC-6s, which were used to inaugurate a new Amsterdam to Tehran service on 21 April 1948; KLM also reopened the southern route to Curaçao in May 1949. The newly-formed Scandinavian Airlines System placed an order for seventeen DC-6s, but four were sold to British Commonwealth Pacific Airlines before completion on the production line. SAS used the DC-6s on its North Atlantic services, and the Copenhagen to London service. A South Atlantic service was started on 30 October 1948, and a service to Hong Kong in April 1951.

After the DC-6 had been in service for about six months, two in-flight fires led to its early grounding. The first involved a United DC-6 N37510 c/n 42875 which crashed in Bryce Canyon National Park, Utah, on 24 October 1947, with the loss of fifty-two passengers and crew. More fortunate was a DC-6 of American Airlines which, on 11 November, less than a month later, burst into flames but was successfully landed at Gallup, New Mexico.

The next day, all DC-6s were grounded, and painstaking and lengthy investigations of both accidents revealed that, under certain conditions, fuel could overflow from the tank vents straight into the intake of the cabin heater in the belly hold. Suitable modifications were devised, and the aircraft were flying again in March 1948, but understandably the intervening four months had been expensive ones for both Douglas and the airlines. Douglas, in addition, bore the cost of the modifications. Services were resumed on 21 March 1948, and the DC-6 and its derivatives were then operated without difficulty.

Philippine Air Lines introduced the DC-6 on its routes stretching from London to Manila and on to San Francisco on 29 May 1948. However mounting losses, rejections of various of its proposed routes and finally the crash of PI-C 294 c/n 42902 on 14 January 1949 at Ciampino Airport, Rome, led the airline to suspend all its long-haul international services in April 1954 and its DC-6s were sold.

British Commonwealth Pacific Airlines introduced DC-6s on the Auckland–Fiji–Canton–Honolulu–San Francisco route on 16 February 1949, but the aircraft passed to Tasman Empire Airways Ltd when BCPA was dissolved in March 1954, and were then employed on the trans-Tasman routes.

The Argentinian airline, Flota Aérea Mercante Argentina – FAMA – ordered six DC-6s in December 1946, and the first, LV-ADR c/n 43030 was delivered on 18 May 1948. It was not until long after FAMA had been nationalised in May 1949, becoming part of Aerolíneas Argentinas, that the DC-6s were introduced on the long-haul routes, serving New York from March 1950, and London from the following month. Mexicana took delivery of three DC-6s late in 1950.

The final airline to order the DC-6 was the Italian Linee Aeree Italiane – LAI – in January 1950, bringing the production total to 175, excluding the single XC-112A, but including the presidential C-118. Later, many other airlines acquired secondhand DC-6s, with a number being modified as freighters by installation of either C-54 sideways-opening cargo doors or DC-6A upwards-opening doors. Many of the secondhand aircraft found their way to Central and South America, particularly Argentina and Mexico.

In general, the DC-6s had long service lives with the trunk airlines, firstly on the long-haul services, and then, often with high-density seating configurations, on the shorter-haul and coach-class flights. Most European operators disposed of their DC-6s in the late 1950s and early 1960s, whilst in the United States many were operated by their original owners until the late 1960s. United sold many of its airliners to Mars Aviation in 1968, but with total airframe hours generally around 55,000 hours, it is not surprising that most of these ex-United aircraft were subsequently broken up for spare parts and scrap.

Mercer Airlines in California operated a fleet of seven secondhand DC-6s, while Aerolíneas Argentinas turned some of its fleet over to the Argentine Air Force, including c/n 43030/43032 and 43033. Although the original DC-6 was not as much in demand as the later DC-6A and DC-6Bs, the price of a DC-6 in reasonable condition in 1960 was around $500,000, compared with a factory price of around $600,000 in 1946. Naturally the price has dropped considerably with the passage of time, but the type is still in service and today two are on the list of aircraft used as tankers contracted in the United States to fight forest fires by the US Forest Service. These are N666SQ c/n 43004 ex-United N37515, and N90739 c/n 43044, which retains its original American Airlines registration.

Liftmaster

The Douglas DC-6A was, as the designation of this freighter version implies, the successor to the basic DC-6, but only one, the prototype N30006 c/n 42901, was completed, test-flown and delivered before the first of the passenger-carrying DC-6B version reached the airlines. It was registered to the Douglas Aircraft Company, making its first flight on 29 September 1949. It was, in fact, a DC-6 with c/n 42901, the last DC-6, c/n 43219

N90898, having been delivered to Delta on 4 January 1951. To take advantage of the increased power of the water- and methanol-injected R-2800 engine developed by Pratt & Whitney, the DC-6 fuselage was lengthened by 5ft and the gross weight increased by 10,000 lb, most of which was additional payload. Designated DC-6A, this version retained cabin pressurisation, had a reinforced cabin floor, no fuselage windows, and two upwards-opening freight doors – one forward and one aft of the wing on the port side. The electrical system, which had given trouble in the DC-6, was upgraded, the access for maintenance was improved and typical fuel capacity was increased from 4,260 to 5,525 gallons. Cargo capacity was 28,188 lb. The seventy-fourth and last DC-6A was delivered to the Brazilian carrier Loide Aéreo Nacional on 10 February 1959. Some DC-6As were subsequently converted to passenger use by removing the metal plugs normally fitted over the cabin windows, while others – designated DC-6C – were built with normal cabin windows to enable rapid conversion from cargo to passenger configurations and *vice versa*.

The US Navy designated the VIP staff version of the DC-6A as R6D-1Z and depicted parked at the Long Beach factory is BuNo.128424 c/n 43207 delivered initially on 7 September 1951, becoming a VIP aircraft during 1956. (Douglas)

The US Armed Forces used the DC-6A extensively, some sixty-five, designated R6D-1s, being delivered to the US Navy and 101 to the US Air Force as C-118As. Several R6Ds were used as VIP aircraft, but the majority of both the Navy R6D-s and USAF C-118s were assigned to the huge worldwide USAF Military Air Transport Service – MATS – serving on routes across both the Atlantic and the Pacific oceans until replaced. In 1958 MATS took over surviving US Navy transports and after the type was retired from ocean routes, they were re-assigned to shorter range duties which included medical evacuation – CASEVACS – and staff transport assignments.

Any detailed account of the civil operations of the DC-6A is rendered somewhat involved by the numerous lease arrangements, and by the sizeable number of sales and transfers before delivery. The first civil operator of the type was Slick Airways Inc. of San Francisco, to whom the prototype was delivered on 7 March 1951, registered N90806; the DC-6A was introduced into service by the company on 16 April. The first trunk carrier to order the DC-6A was American, who placed an order for six in October 1951. Although the Flying Tiger Line of Los Angeles ordered seven in December 1951, only one of these entered service with the airline, two going to Japan Air Lines for passenger use, and four on long-term lease to Northwest

Airlines of Minneapolis. However, orders continued to trickle in, firstly from the major airlines, with KLM ordering two, Pan American Airways three, Sabena two initially, United Airlines five with two more later. Various non-scheduled carriers, both in the United States and overseas, recognised the potential of the DC-6A and placed orders: Trans Caribbean Airways of New York ordered four, Overseas National Airways of Washington DC two, Great Lakes Airlines of Burbank, California, two, and Hunting Clan in the United Kingdom two. There were more to come.

American Airlines took delivery of their first aircraft, N90777 c/n 43840, in May 1953, and placed it on their long-haul freight routes. The first DC-6A to go into service with an overseas operator was PH-TGA c/n 44076, delivered on 18 July 1953 and put into service on the North Atlantic route in August. Airwork of the United Kingdom ordered two for its trans-Atlantic freight service, but the project was abandoned before the Douglas transports were delivered, and they were sold on the production line to Slick. Of the four sold to Trans Caribbean, one was sold to Air Liban of Beirut before delivery, and two of the remainder went to the US Weather Bureau. These were N6539C c/n 45227 and N6540C c/n 45368, fitted with special radar and heavily instrumentated; they were used in the bureau's hurricane research programme.

The differences between the civil and military versions – the first USAF C-118A 51-3818 c/n 43565 was delivered on 16 July 1952 – were relatively minor, apart from internal arrangements, the use of a military version of the engines designated R-2800-52W and, when operating as an all-cargo aircraft, a higher maximum take-off weight of 112,000 lb. Normal maximum accommodation was for seventy-six passengers, or sixty litters for wounded, and a crew of four or five depending on the mission requirement. Cargo capacity, including the two lower compartments, was 4,677 cubic feet. The twenty-five US Navy R6D-1s – BuNo. 128428 c/n 43401, delivered on 11 November 1951 – which were not later transferred to the USAF were re-designated C-118B in 1962. Under a US Department of Defense Directive dated 6 July 1962, the R6D- designation allocated to US Navy variants of the C-118 was standardised with those of the USAF variants. The last of the military versions C-118A 53-3305 c/n 44676 – was delivered on 10 January 1956, the type having served with Fleet Logistic Air Wings and Naval Air Transport squadrons with the US Navy, and with MATS units with the USAF. The last C-118A became the personal transport

The USAF and US Navy consolidated into one huge transport organisation with their Douglas transports during the 1950s. Depicted is R6D-1-DO BuNo.131616 of VR-6 Squadron is MATS ATLANTIC tail markings. This Liftmaster was broken up after serving at Alameda, California, in May 1983. Its c/n was 43719. (MAP)

Seen during 1977 is DC-6A c/n 44063 of the French Aeronavale '63' using radio callsigns 'F-YEPA'. It was built as CF-CUS for Canadian Pacific being delivered on 4 September 1953. It had several owners in French Equatorial Africa prior to going to the Aeronavale on 8 March 1974. (MAP)

The Royal New Zealand Air Force operated the DC-6. Depicted is NZ3631 c/n 43126 which went to 40 Squadron in 1961. It was sold in 1968 to Laos and as XW-PEH crashed near Tegal, Central Jona, on 1 February 1971 resulting in five fatalities and four injured. (MAP)

Excellent cockpit photograph of C-118A-DO 53-3243 c/n 44614 delivered to the USAF on 4 January 1955. Capacity of this Douglas military transport, known as the Liftmaster, was seventy-four troops or 27,000lb (12,247kg) of cargo. (Douglas)

This Douglas R6D-1-DO BuNo.131599 c/n 43702 also served with the USAF as C-118A-DO 51-17549 in 1958, returning to the US Navy in 1964. It served with VR-24 Squadron at Rota, Spain, and between 1971-73 was based at Keflavik, Iceland. It was scrapped at Alameda, California, in May 1971. (AP Photo Library)

The US Navy C-118 transports served the transport squadrons well until replaced by the Douglas C-9B Skytrain II twin-jet. Depicted is C-118B-D0 BuNo.131568 of VR-51 Squadron based at Glenview, Illinois. It is c/n 43671 delivered 19 September 1952 going to the USAF in 1958, but back with the Navy by 1969. (Douglas)

Seen at London (Heathrow) Airport during 1956 is R6D-1Z-DO VIP transport BuNo.128433 'RP' c/n 43517 of VR-1 Squadron and showing the early all-metal of US Navy transports. This transport later went to the US Marine Corps. (Tom Pharo)

ABOVE: *Seen over the Golden Gate Bridge at San Francisco is R6D-1 BuNo.128425 c/n 43208 delivered on 21 September 1951. It is seen in the livery of the Continental Division of MATS a joint US Navy and USAF organisation. The type was re-designated C-118B in November 1962.* (Douglas)

LEFT: *Excellent photograph depicting a US Air Force C-118A-DO 53-3245 c/n 44616 of the huge Military Air Transport Service. It was delivered on 13 January 1955. The US Air Force ordered 101 of these transports which were similar to the DC-6A but fitted out with military equipment and powered by four P & W 2,500hp R-2800-52W engines.* (Douglas)

The profile of the DC-6 is seen in this excellent plan photograph of a US Navy R6D-1 transport of the US Navy. Preceding the US Air Force order the Navy ordered 65 DC-6As equipped as logistic transports, or configured as VIP staff transports. Forty were transferred to the US Air Force in 1962. (Douglas)

of General Emmet O'Donnell, Commander-in-Chief of the Pacific Air Forces until at least May 1970.

Apart from the military versions, sales of the Douglas DC-6A initially went slowly, and some of the earliest deliveries, as already mentioned, went to airlines in Europe and Canada rather than the United States. In later years, the DC-6A was much in demand and aircraft changed hands frequently, especially among the US non-scheduled operators. Many were sold by the major airlines as they were replaced by freight versions of the new DC-7, and were rapidly snapped up in the selling market which existed at the time.

As the supply of original DC-6As dried up, numerous DC-6Bs were converted to freighters. The full conversion involved the installation of a cargo door and a reinforced cabin floor. In 1965, the Douglas Aircraft Company granted the Pacific Airmotive Corporation, the sole licence to convert DC-6Bs to DC-6As, and many conversions took place. Other conversions and partial conversions were carried out by airlines and other engineering firms. These carried a variety of designations such as DC-6AB, DC-6AC, DC-6A(C) and DC-6BF. Passenger facilities such as windows and air conditioning were often retained to allow convertible or combination operational patterns.

A number of military air arms worldwide were quick to recognise the potential of the type and purchased aircraft which had been converted to DC-6C standard. These included the air arms of Argentina, Belgium, Brazil, Chile, Ecuador, France, Italy, Panama, Portugal, West Germany and Yugoslavia. Others were used on US military charters for rapid transit of troops and military freight during NATO exercises in Europe, and during the many bush wars involving the US Armed Forces over the years.

It must be explained that the DC-6C was a version of the DC-6A so equipped that it could quickly be converted for passenger operations. Later aircraft of this nature carried the

suffix 'QC' on the designation. The true Douglas-built DC-6Cs were ordered in small numbers, principally by major carriers when it became clear that the life of the DC-6B as a first-line passenger airliner was limited. The large freight doors made it easy and relatively cheap to convert the aircraft to a freighter role, and this also substantially increased the resale value.

Two DC-6A conversions worthy of mention involved the aircraft N6813C c/n 44889 and N6815C c/n 45110, which were converted to fly television transmitters for the Midwest Program for Airborne Television Instruction, operated by Purdue University of Lafayette, Indiana. They had a retractable antenna which projected below the fuselage for transmission. They were both operated successfully for some years from 30 April 1960, finally being sold in 1969. Both aircraft had originally been ordered for Airwork in the United Kingdom, with c/n 44889 even being allocated the British registration G-AOFX, later cancelled.

During 1968 Sabena converted two DC-6Bs into swing-tail cargo aircraft. Operated by Kar Air in Finland as OH-KDA, c/n 45202 DC-6B was converted in mid-1968 and used in the Biafran operations in 1968/69. Spantax DC-6B EC-BBK c/n 44434 was delivered to the company on 19 August 1965 and also converted to swing-tail configuration. There was a hybrid DC-6, N710A c/n 45059, which had a DC-6A door in the front fuselage, certificated as a DC-6B, so really a DC-6A/B.

Any student of Douglas DC-6 and DC-7 series production can easily be confused, as throughout the series, production of the various types were interwoven with each other so the c/ns do not run in any consecutive order with type. In addition, the c/ns 45138 to 45141 were intended to be DC-6Bs N37586 to N37589, but these were completed as c/ns 45491 to 45949. During October 1961, DC-6B c/n 43747 was sold to the French government for use by the French Air Force as '43748' and radio call-sign 'FRAFB'; it was used as a VIP aircraft for the French Prime Minister. It crashed on 10 March 1968, on take-off from Reunion Island. At least one ex-USAF C-118A, 51-3828 c/n 43575, went to the National Aeronautics & Space Administration in 1965, as NASA-428 N428NA and was used by the Goddard Flight Space Center, located at Greenbelt, Maryland.

Pan American DC-6B N6518C c/n 43518 Clipper Liberty Bell *was delivered on 29 May 1952. In March 1960 it was leased to Capital and in October 1962 to Austral in Argentina as LV-PVS, later sold and registered LV-HRC. In 1971 it went to Inair Panama as HP-536 and scrapped at Panama City in February 1975.* (AP Photo Library)

Airline Service and the 'B' Model

Delta had ordered five Douglas DC-6 airliners in February 1948, and when it put them into service on the first day of December of the same year, it did so with style. The DC-6 was Delta's first pressurised type, and it was promoted as the fastest airliner of the day – the 300-Plus Deltaliners. It set new standards of comfort with the Skylounge in the rear of the cabin. And the 'Airline of the South' advertised boldly 'None Faster, None Finer to and thru' the South'. Competing successfully with Eastern's 'Constellations', Delta built up its fleet of DC-6s to eleven in the next decade.

At first, the DC-6s were crewed by two pilots plus two cabin crew, but shortly after they entered service, CAA regulations dictated that a flight engineer be added to the cockpit complement. Delta's DC-6s – the first, NC1901M c/n 43139, was christened, '*The Flying D*' – had seating for fifty passengers, in pairs on either side of the aisle, although there were an additional six seats in the Skylounge which were not for sale, but for the use of passengers during flight.

When, on 1 November 1946, Delta commenced service on the Chicago to Miami route, initially with DC-4s, it was the first non-stop service in this market. With the introduction of the DC-6 Delta were able to compete effectively with Eastern Air Lines, just one of their rivals.

On 1 January 1946, the entire United Air Lines fleet consisted of seventy-seven twin-engined Douglas DC-3s. When United put the pressurised Douglas DC-6 into service on 27 April, 1947, they were desperately trying to match the Lockheed L-049 'Constellations' which TWA had introduced on 1 March. Competition was on the increase, was broadly-based and it intensified both in the United States and overseas, where a healthy export market was open and vigorously pursued by both Lockheed and Douglas. Pan American purchased the improved Lockheed 749 Constellation on 17 June 1947, but it took the Douglas Aircraft Company four years to match it with the DC-6B, which entered service with United on 11 April 1951. Competition continued and Eastern Air Lines launched the Model 1049 'Constellation' or 'Super Constellation', in service on 17 December 1951. Douglas responded with the DC-7 on 29 November 1953, when American Airlines placed an order for twenty-five. On 1 April 1955 TWA introduced the L-1049G; Pan Am followed with the Douglas DC-7B on 13 June; and finally, on 1 June 1957, TWA introduced the Model 1649A 'Starliner', which took the Lockheed and Douglas rivalry to its ultimate conclusion before the Boeing 707 made its appearance and became involved in the battle.

There were bigger and better Douglas airliners produced from the Santa Monica stable during the 1950s, but none gained the respect and confidence-inspiring reputation of the Douglas DC-6B. The proof of this was to be found in the sales figures. Including the DC-6A cargo version, 362 Douglas DC-6Bs were built. This was twice as many as the 175 standard DC-6s and more than the combined production total of the DC-7, DC-7B and DC-7C. Western and Northeast chose the DC-6B, with more operators to follow.

Dimensionally identical to the DC-6A, the DC-6B was a passenger transport without the reinforced floor and main deck cargo doors. Initially, normal accommodation was provided for fifty-four passengers, but in high-density layout up to 102 passengers could be carried. Like the DC-6As, the DC-6Bs were powered by either 2,400 hp Double Wasp CB16s or 2,500 hp Double Wasp DB17s driving three-blade fully-reversible propellers. Produced in larger numbers than any other version in the Douglas DC-6 series, the DC-6B was first flown on 2 February 1951. The first production model – N37547 c/n 43257 – went to United on 27 April, having already received its certification and was named '*Mainliner Newark*'. By the time it was sold to Mars Aviation Inc. on 22 October 1968, it had accumulated 43,758 flying hours. The 704th and last aircraft in the DC-6 series, the 288th DC-6B, was delivered to JAT Jugoslovenski Aerotransport on 17 November 1958. This was YU-AFB c/n 45564. In 1966 this airliner was transferred to the Yugoslav government.

As mentioned earlier, after being taken out of service by the major air carriers, a substantial number of DC-6Bs were modified as freighters by the installation of cargo doors and reinforced doors. Other DC-6Bs were modified as air tankers for use against forest fires in the United States, Canada and France. The current US Forest Service listing of aircraft includes several DC-6Bs, examples being N888SQ c/n 43562 ex-United, N444SQ c/n 45320 ex-Northwest, N555SQ c/n 45137 ex-United, N111AN c/n 44087 ex-Swissair and N999SQ c/n 43274 ex-Swissair.

The Douglas DC-6B was without doubt the finest piston-engined airliner ever built, yet it was no faster than the DC-6 from which it was developed. Its success lay in its extremely low operating costs, which resulted in a lower seat-mile cost than any other comparable airliner. Almost all DC-6 customers, headed by American and United – bought the DC-6B. The first orders were placed late in 1949 at a unit price of $900,000. American was the first to put the type into service on its transcontinental routes on 29 April 1951, just preceding United. During July 1951 Swissair became both the first European and first Atlantic operator, to be followed by SAS, KLM, Sabena, Alitalia, Linee Aeree Italiane – LIA, Cie de Transport Aériens Intercontinentaux – TAI of Paris, Union Aéromaritime de Transports – UAT, also of Paris, Olympic of Greece and JAT of Jugoslavia. All these airlines purchased new DC-6Bs from Douglas between 1951 and 1958.

The DC-6B was heavily involved on the important North Atlantic route, to a much greater effect than its predecessor. Pan American, which had been using 'Constellations' and Boeing 'Stratocruisers', replaced the 'Connie' with DC-6Bs and put them into service on the 'Rainbow' economy flights – from New York to London on 1 May 1952, and to other European capitals shortly afterwards. In the United States Western, Northwest and Northeast were non-DC-6 trunk lines which acquired substantial fleets of the Douglas airliner. Northwest, with a fleet of thirteen, introduced them in June 1955, and Northeast with ten in January 1957. Even Eastern Air Lines, at this time almost exclusively Lockheed-equipped, operated seven on long-term lease.

When Western Air Lines acquired two trunk routes of more than regional range, it moved into a programme of fleet improvement consistent with its new aspirations as a trunk airline. Early in 1953 it put into service, on the west coast and California to Minneapolis routes, five Douglas DC-6Bs bought at a cost of $6 million. These proved to be so successful that Western's eventual fleet of DC-6Bs numbered thirty-one, purchased between late 1952 and 1957. The first was N91302 c/n 43822, delivered on 24 November 1952. Later Western was awarded the service from San Francisco to Denver, via Reno, Nevada, so having the distinction of offering a service to the two main gambling cities in the United States.

Along with the new DC-6B flagship came service improvements with Western. The passenger was given a positive welcome on boarding and the cuisine was excellent. Champagne was served on the Champagne and Fiesta flights, whilst in the morning, a Hunt breakfast was dispensed by a suitable attired flight attendant. Sound effects of a traditional English hunt, complete with 'tally-hos' and hunting horn calls, were produced from a tape recorder mounted on the serving cart, until this feature was, for some unaccountable reason, banned by the FAA.

Continued Success

The Douglas DC-6 series as a whole had a very remarkable longevity record. In 1978 there were over sixty DC-6Bs, some fifty DC-6A freighters and converted DC-6A/Bs in service, as well as ten of the original version plus numbers of the US Armed Forces C-118s in civilian use after being declared surplus to requirements.

With the crash of one of its de Havilland 'Comets' on its delivery flight from the United Kingdom, Canadian Pacific hastily put its three DC-6Bs on to its Pacific route services in April 1953, and placed orders for more. On 3 June 1955 these were used to inaugurate the long-sought-after Polar route from Vancouver to Amsterdam via Edmonton and Sondestrom fjord in Greenland. The large but compact SAS, whose DC-6B OY-KME c/n 43744 *'Arild Viking'* made the first commercial polar transatlantic crossing on its delivery flight on 18 November 1952, used DC-6Bs to open its Oslo to Thule to Anchorage to Shemya in the Aleutians to Tokyo service in May 1953. On 15/16 November 1954 SAS inaugurated its Copenhagen–Sondestrom–Winnipeg–Los Angeles route. However, a true-over-the-Pole service had to wait for the Douglas DC-7C.

Seen in SAS markings is DC-6B LN-LMO c/n 43745 Hjalmar Viking *delivered 4 December 1952. In February 1961 it was sold to REAL Brazil as PP-YSL. On 6 May 1970 it went to the Brazilian Air Force as '2414' and it crashed on 27 April 1971 the remains used as spares by the Paraguayan Air Force.* (SAS)

Other long-range routes operated by DC-6Bs were those of TAI, whose service from Paris to Saigon was extended to

Darwin and Noumea, New Caledonia, on 6 January 1956. Routes were extended to Auckland, New Zealand, on 4 January 1957, and then on 28 September 1958, through to Noumea to Bora Bora in the Society Islands, from where a flying-boat service continued the flight to Tahiti. In the Far East, Japan Air Lines put DC-6Bs, albeit converted DC-6As, on their Tokyo to San Francisco route in February 1954, and the DC-7C took over this route, transferred the workhorse DC-6Bs to the high-density domestic trunk routes from Tokyo to Osaka, Fukuoka and Sapporo. Civil Air Transport – CAT – of Taipei, Formosa, the last but one DC-6B customer, put its one and only aircraft of the type – B-1006 c/n 45550 – on its regional services to Hong Kong and other points during October 1958.

Other operators worthy of mention include Australian National Airways, later Ansett-ANA, which put the DC-6B into service during February 1955 to meet competition from Trans Australian Airline's Vickers Viscounts. Línea Aérea Nacional de Chile – LAN-Chile – of Santiago took delivery of its first aircraft in January 1955, and Ethiopian Air Lines commenced operations in April 1958. Secondhand DC-6Bs were operated by such notable scheduled airlines as Loftleidir, Icelandic Airlines of Reykjavik, who placed their first two on their below IATA fare North Atlantic service in July 1961. Further south Syrian Arab, which was formed from the Syrian section of United Arab Airlines commenced operations with the type in October 1961. UAT, and later UTA, seconded its DC-6Bs for periods with Air Afrique, whilst secondhand airliners from SAS were operated by both Icelandair and Thai International. United Arab Airlines – UAA – of Almaza purchased a number of DC-6Bs in the United States in 1964/65 for use on regional and domestic routes.

Maintenance being carried out on DC-6B 00-CTI of Sabena c/n 43830/352 delivered on 7 April 1953. It was leased to AVIACO in the summers of 1961-62. On 3 April 1963 sold as SE-CCZ to Transair as Uppsala *and went to the USA on 3 December 1965 as N998BC with the Boreas Corporation. It was back in Norway in June 1966 with Braathens as LN-SUI, being cancelled during 1969.* (Sabena)

In Europe, many charter operators such as Sterling, Transair Sweden, Societa Aerea Mediterranea – SAM – of Rome, Adria Aviapromet of Yugoslavia, Kar-Air of Finland, Cunard Eagle in the United Kingdom, Braathens of Oslo and Spantax of Madrid all used the DC-6B on inclusive tour work. This was seasonal operation and led to low utilisation. Almost every Central and South American airline became the possessor of a small fleet of the DC-6Bs. Others were operated in the Middle East by Iranair, Saudi Arabia and the already mentioned Syrian Arab Airlines of Damascus. During the hostilities in Biafra, Nigeria during

1968/69 a number of DC-6Bs, plus some DC-6As and DC-7s, were used in relief efforts, many under Icelandic registration.

A proposal to re-engine the DC-6 series with Rolls-Royce Dart turboprop engines was shelved, as was a nose-loading vehicle-ferry conversion similar to the ATL-98 Carvair, itself a conversion from the earlier Douglas DC-4.

The introduction into service of the Douglas DC-8 and the Boeing 707 during the late 1950s rapidly relegated the DC-6B to less important routes, and the appearance in the mid-1960s of large numbers of medium- and short-range jetliners finally forced its retirement from the fleets of the world's major carriers. Nonetheless, the low initial price of used DC-6Bs, together with their favourable operating costs and high reputation for reliability, ensured them a future. Many were modified as freighters or as passenger/cargo convertible aircraft and, over the years, underwent many changes of ownership. The DC-6Bs not only saw service with pure cargo airlines, charter operators and the airlines of developing nations, they were also acquired by many of the world's military air arms and a significant number are still in service.

The unmarked XC-112A-DO. The US Government funded this pressurised development of the C-54E. It had a longer fuselage, large rectangular windows, and was powered by 2,100hp Pratt & Whitney R-2800-34 radials. John F. Martin flew the aircraft on its maiden flight on 15 February 1946. (Douglas)

Chapter Thirteen
Douglas DC-7

It is not generally known that the first Douglas project to bear the label DC-7 was the civil version of the C-74 military Globemaster I of 1946. During the Second World War Douglas had studied the feasibility of adapting the C-74 as a long-range commercial transport for passenger use, and in late 1945 Pan American Airways had placed an order for twenty-six which were designated DC-7. However, Pan Am cancelled its order in 1947, as the transport was then found too large for existing traffic loads, and due to the reduction in the military C-74 contract – fifty were originally ordered, but only fourteen built – production costs had risen substantially.

Late in 1951, the Curtiss Wright R-3550 turbo-compound engine, developing 3,250 hp for take-off, became available. Using the new engine, Lockheed stretched their 'Constellation' to produce the 'Super Constellation', which TWA introduced into service as the L.1049A in September 1952. In the medium- and long-range markets the Douglas DC-4, DC-6 and DC-7 series plus the 'Constellation' series had a virtual monopoly. It should be said that the superiority of the Douglas and Lockheed four-engined airliners was partially the result of fierce competition between the two rivals. The DC-7, the last of the Douglas piston-engined transports was the product of this competition and represented the ultimate refinement of the basic DC-4/C-54 design.

In the Douglas stable, there was some hesitation about developing the DC-6B, mainly because the turboprop engine was under successful development. Lockheed had a four-engine turboprop design called the 'Electra' it was about to offer the airlines. But with great persuasion from a good friend of the Douglas Aircraft Company, Cyrus R. Smith, President of American Airlines, Douglas decided in January 1952 to go ahead and develop the DC-6B around the new Wright Cyclone R-3350 turbo-compound two-row radial engine. American Airlines immediately ordered twenty-five of the new DC-7s at $1,600,000 each – a total of $40 million.

In the design of these new engines, sponsored by the US Navy and first fitted to the Lockheed P2V- 'Neptune', a generally successful effort had been made to provide a power recovery system in which the exhaust efflux from six of the eighteen cylinders was used to drive three turbines, the energy from which was transmitted, via a fluid coupling, to the crankshaft. The result was increased power with reduced fuel consumption.

It is recorded that Donald Douglas, Arthur Raymond, Ed Burton and the rest of the Douglas design team were not very enthusiastic, and originally doubted whether a market existed for the DC-7; they were also concerned that its design and construction might drain profit away from the now well-established DC-6 production line. However, the American Airlines order provided the necessary impetus. The new fleet of DC-7s would supplement its already existing fleet of fifty DC-6s, six DC-6As and twenty-five DC-6Bs. With most of the development costs paid for by the American Airlines order, Douglas committed the new aircraft to production. In time, the company realised a substantial profit by selling a total of 338 DC-7s, DC-7Bs and DC-7Cs, which were produced at the Santa Monica factory on the same line as the DC-6As and DC-6Bs.

The increased power of the DC-7 allowed a further 40 inch stretch of the fuselage and brought the speed up to 360 mph. But more important was the range, which allowed, for the first time, sustained non-stop transcontinental operations. Other differences from the DC-6 series included four-bladed propellers, the use of titanium for added fire resistance in the engine nacelles, and the availability of the main landing gear to increase drag for rapid descents. Produced with remarkable rapidity, the Douglas DC-7 was first flown on 18 May 1953, and given its full passenger certification on 12 November. American Airlines had taken delivery of two aircraft for crew training prior to this date, and were able to introduce the new aircraft on a daily non-stop New York to Los Angeles service on 29 November 1953. The scheduled time was 8 hours eastbound and 8 hours 45 minutes westbound. TWA replied to this challenge with the L.1049G version of the 'Super Constellation', but not until 1 April 1955.

The DC-7 was sold exclusively to trunk carriers in the United States with American Airlines purchasing thirty-four (adding nine to their original order), Delta ten, National four and United fifty-seven. Boardman C. Reed, friend of the author, has indicated that during flights in Douglas DC-7s operated by both Delta and United Air Lines the name 'Cloudster' appeared on the door leading to the passenger cabin. Aircraft noted were Delta's N4872C c/n 44262 and N4879C c/n 44683, and N6307C c/n 44271 belonging to United. Despite extensive enquiries, no explanation for the name 'Cloudster' has been forthcoming.The total production figure was therefore 105. National introduced the DC-7 on the prosperous New York to Miami route on 15 December 1953, just after Eastern had introduced L.1049Cs. Delta put the DC-7 into service on their Chicago to Florida route on 1 April 1954. Unfortunately, the new Wright R-3350 turbo-compound engines were later to gain an unenviable reputation for poor reliability and noise; but they were powerful, deriving extra horsepower from an ingenius turbine mechanism that was driven by exhaust gases.

The cabin layout with Delta included an eight-seat Sky Room, and a five-seat Sky Lounge, in addition to two main cabins, giving a total capacity of sixty-nine passengers. The aircraft was furnished throughout to provide an air of affluence. Meal service and on-board amenities were intended to match: these even included a typewriter for workaholics and a shaver for last-minute arrivals. The inaugural flight involved three services on the Chicago to Miami route and, in keeping with a now well-established Delta tradition, they were named the '*Royal Biscayne*', the '*Royal Poinciana*' and the '*Owl Comet*', the last being an overnight 'red-eye' service. More 'Golden Crown' services were added during the next few months and on 1 April 1955 the '*Royal Caribe*' brought the new standard of excellence to the Caribbean as far as San Juan and Caracas, so claiming the first intercontinental DC-7 service.

Big Apple

Delta had greatly enlarged their operations in 1953 through a merger with Chicago & Southern Air Lines, so it was with great pride and confidence that the airline looked to the future. Wrangling over the expansion of routes went on for months, but on 20 January 1956 the Civil Aeronautics Board – CAB – announced its verdict, giving Delta permission to operate from Atlanta to New York using Newark. The airline could now serve New York, biggest commercial city of the western hemisphere, possibly of the world.

Douglas DC-6 'Daycoach' and DC-7 'Golden Crown' services started on 1 February 1956, with three daily services to the south, as far as Dallas-Fort Worth and New Orleans, all named services; as a bonus, they served the federal capital, Washington DC. On the first day of April 1956, additional services were added to Charlotte, Baltimore and Philadelphia, and direct services to the main southern destinations were soon augmented. On 15 May 1956, the New York terminus was transferred from Newark to Idlewild, later to be named John F. Kennedy International Airport, and in September Tampa became an additional destination in Florida.

During 1959 American sold its first twenty-five DC-7s to a firm called Galco in a package deal. This included the first DC-7, N301AA c/n 44122. American had several more DC-7s converted to DC-7F configuration, while most of the others were scrapped in 1964 and 1965. Many of the Galco aircraft were leased to Overseas National until that carrier experienced financial difficulties, and some found their way to Osterman in Sweden and Flying Enterprise in Denmark. The large United fleet was disposed of in small batches, with some being traded back to Douglas on a part-exchange deal for DC-8s, and some to Sud Aviation in France in exchange for Caravelle airliners. Many were sold for spares, while others went to aircraft brokers.

In terms of seat-mile costs, the DC-7 was more expensive to operate than the DC-6B and the resale market was very limited. Although, as mentioned earlier, the R-3350 engine was probably the most sophisticated piston engine ever produced, its reliability was not as good as the earlier R-2800. In particular, the new engine in the DC-7 was rather prone to catch fire. This unreliability understandably detracted from the appeal of the DC-7 on the secondhand market. The sixth American DC-7 N306AA, c/n 44127 '*Flagship New York*' went to the FAA via Galco in October 1961, registered N464; on 9 October it was delivered to the Royal Aircraft Establishment, Bedford, for installation and flight trials with the autoland system developed by the resident Blind Landing Experimental Unit – BLEU.

There were several accidents involving the DC-7. On 20 June 1961. DC-7 N312A c/n 44133 of Overseas National collided with a Constellation N5595A on the ground at Oakland, California. It was beyond economical repair. Another ex-Galco DC-7, N317A c/n 44138 leased to Overseas National, had undercarriage trouble on landing at Norfolk, Virginia on 26 September 1961, and hit an embankment. The nose section was later used to repair a DC-7C c/n 45215. On 16 December 1961, N4871C c/n 44261 of Delta was involved in a landing accident at O'Hare Airport, Chicago, and during the summer of 1964 was used as a restaurant. A United DC-7 N6311C c/n 44275 lost part of its fin and rudder in flight over Sacramento on 14 October 1962, but landed safely. An unusual use for a DC-7 occurred to N6315C c/n 44279 of United, which had been stored at San Francisco with parts used to repair N6311C. On 31 October 1963, the remains were donated to the US Coast Guard for

ditching training. It floated in San Francisco Bay until 1968, when it was retrieved and used in that city for fire training.

There were fatalities on 30 June 1956, when United DC-7 N6324C c/n 44288 collided in mid-air with a TWA L.1049A N6902C over the Grand Canyon in Arizona. A total of fifty-eight people on the DC-7 were killed. On 13 January 1963, a taxying Delta DC-7 N4875C c/n 44679 collided on the ground at Memphis, Tennessee, with a parked US Air Force Fairchild C-123 'Provider' 54-0589. One person was killed. The DC-7 was repaired. Another fatal accident occurred on 21 April 1958, when DC-7 N6328C c/n 45142 of United had a mid-air collision with a US Air Force North American F-100F-5-NA 'Super Sabre' at 21,000 ft whilst en route from Los Angeles to New York. The fatalities numbered forty-seven. United DC-7 N6339C c/n 45153 was in use for crew training at Denver from late 1965. On 18 May 1966, a tyre failed on landing; the aircraft was damaged, so was sold and later broken up.

The last DC-7 built was N6357C c/n 45490 for United, which in late 1964 was painted in full US Air Force – Military Air Transport Service – MATS – colours for a film. Three DC-7 transports are listed on the 1991 US Forest Service listing air tankers. All three were original ex-United airliners still carrying their original US registrations which are N6318C c/n 44282, N401US c/n 45145 and N6353C c/n 45486.

Douglas DC-7B

If any student of aviation history bothers to research deeply into the history of the Douglas Aircraft Company, he will quickly discover history repeating itself, in addition to many Douglas types being stretched from the original design. One must recall that it was Cyrus Smith of American Airlines who had talked Donald Douglas into redesigning and upgrading the DC-2 into the DST and the twenty-one-passenger DC-3. Now American Airlines were in trouble with the DC-6, which just could not keep pace with the much faster TWA model 749 'Constellations' on the non-stop New York–Chicago–Los Angeles route.

Smith outlined the problem to his friend Donald Douglas, and promised that if Douglas could deliver an updated airliner he would guarantee an order for a sufficient number to make the project worthwhile. Douglas started immediately on a design to fill the requirement. However, Donald Douglas was not completely happy with the commitment he was about to make. Intelligence reports within the aircraft industry informed him that Boeing in Seattle were almost ready to launch a four-engined jetliner, and that Lockheed at Burbank had a four-engined turboprop design called the 'Electra' which they were about to offer to the airlines.

Fortunately some of the Douglas team who had worked on the DC-1 and subsequent Douglas Commercial models were still in harness – these included Arthur Raymond, Ed Burton, Ivar Shogran and others. The Douglas team discussed a number of airframe-engine combinations and finally decided to fit new engines in a DC-6 to increase the range and payload. The result was the DC-7, the last of the propeller-driven piston-powered airliners in the unique Douglas Commercial family. It was a wise decision, as history has recorded.

The DC-7B, an aerodynamically-refined and prospectively longer-ranged version, featured an increase in gross weight. Most of the increased fuel tankage was obtained by extending the engine nacelles to form saddle tanks. Power came from four

3,250 hp R-3350-18DA-4 radials, the gross weight was 126,000 lb and the tankage in fuel up to 6,460 gallons. The DC-7Bs delivered to the US domestic trunk carriers and to Panagra were not fitted with the extra tanks, but this feature was incorporated into the airliners purchased by Pan American and South African Airways. The first flight of the DC-7B was made in October 1954, with N70D c/n 44435, later certificated and delivered to Delta on 10 December 1955 as N4881C and as a DC-7. Pan American introduced the DC-7B into service on 13 June 1955, on non-stop New York to London schedule.

On 13 June 1955 Pan American World Airways introduced the DC-7B into service on a non-stop New York to London (Heathrow) service. Depicted is DC-7B N777PA c/n 44865/578 Clipper Jupiter Rex delivered on 25 May 1955. After several owners after 1964 the airliner was scrapped at Miami during 1970. (PAA)

Many of the aircraft listed in registers as DC-7Bs should strictly be considered as hybrids – DC-7/DC-7Bs. The last twenty-four of American Airlines' order for fifty-eight DC-7s were described as DC-7Bs, but none had the extra fuel tankage, and some were not initially certificated for the increase in gross weight. An unexpected Douglas customer for the DC-7B was Eastern, who ordered fifty. One of these, N846D c/n 45452, crashed on 10 March 1958, before delivery from Santa Monica, and was not replaced.

Although the range of the DC-7B was not quite adequate for the North Atlantic, Pan American bought seven as an interim measure. South African Airways bought four and introduced them on the Springbok service to London on 21 April 1956, in competition with BOAC's Bristol 'Britannia' 102 airliners. Other DC-7Bs went to Panagra who ordered six and National four. A further eleven were ordered by Delta, to give a total of 112, including two aircraft, one already mentioned, which crashed before delivery and were never replaced. Almost all the DC-7Bs operated by Eastern, at least those that survived, were sold during 1965/66 to California Airmotive, and a large number of these were acquired by Transair of Malmo, Sweden.

In the mid-1950s the relationship between Collett Everman Woolman, the President and General Manager of Delta Air Lines, and Donald Wills Douglas Sr, Chairman of the Douglas Aircraft Company, reached a stage whereby any new Douglas airliner could automatically be assumed to have the Delta name on it, sooner or later. So, when the DC-7 was followed by the higher gross-weighted DC-7B, Delta responded by ordering eleven of them. Oddly, this was reduced to ten, as Delta had taken delivery of the first production model but, as mentioned earlier, this was certificated as a DC-7. Delta then had a total of twenty-one of the two DC-7 series, and promoted them as 'America's Fastest and Finest Airliner' after record-breaking 6½-hour transcontinental delivery flights.

Although the earlier DC-6s outlived the DC-7s by several months in Delta service, the DC-7 was chosen to introduce the 'Royal Service' standard of catering, introduced to Delta passengers on 22 September 1958, to improve the competitive impact of this trans-Atlantic airline against its more powerful rivals from the north. The 'Royal Service' was possibly unmatched by that of any other airline. An additional stewardess provided the flexibility to serve drinks separately from the meals, which featured a choice of main course and free champagne, accompanied by taped music – quite an innovation in those days. On the ground, baggage handling was re-organised and special airport agents were available to welcome the clientèle. It must be emphasised that this is a Delta Air Lines feature frequently observed today at terminals on the airline's large route network.

In March 1958, the Civil Aeronautics Board – CAB – made another important decision which affected Delta, adding new points to the route map. It enabled the Atlanta-based airline to consolidate many new non-stop routes from Chicago and Detroit direct to Florida, and also to establish Atlanta as an even more important hub than before. By the end of 1958, Delta had intensified its services throughout the system. The route map changed, bearing no resemblance to the predominantly east-west pattern of 1945, which was now difficult to identify in the web of intersecting trunk lines in a closely-woven network that embraced the Great Lakes, the Mississippi Valley, Texas, the

This DC-7B N802D c/n 44853/587 was delivered to Eastern Air Lines on 8 July 1955, being the second of a block of twelve. The majority were eventually sold to California Airmotive Corp. and placed in storage at Lancaster, California, during 1965. (Eastern)

Atlanta hub, Florida, and the Caribbean. Both the Douglas DC-6 and DC-7 series were heavily involved in these amazing Delta Air Lines developments.

As with most of the Douglas Commercial series of airliners, there are survivors still to be found active in many corners of the globe. In 1991 there are five DC-7Bs serving on US Forest Service contracts as aerial fire-bombers, all retaining their original registrations. These include two ex-Delta DC-7Bs, N4889C c/n 45353 and N4887C c/n 45351, two ex-Eastern, N838D c/n 45347 and N848D c/n 45454, and one Panagra, N51071 c/n 44701. One Pan American DC-7B, N774R c/n 44868, was sold to Global Presentation Inc. of Hartford, Connecticut, on 30 October 1963 and fitted out as a flying showcase; for a short period from May 1968 it was operated by the pop group Herman's Hermits. It is interesting to record that a DC-7B, N759Z, ex-American, was flown by a United Air Lines captain, Clay Lacy, accompanied by Allen E. Paulson, President of American Jet Industries, in the 1970 California Air Races held at Mojave under the sponsorship of Omni Aviation Managers Inc. The DC-7B c/n 45233 was named '*Super Snoopy*' and carried the race number 64.

There were accidents and incidents. On 29 October 1962 N51702 c/n 44702 of Panagra was involved in an accident at La Paz, Bolivia and written off. An Eastern DC-7B, N808D c/n 44859, was burnt out at Miami on 28 June 1957 after a ground collision with an Eastern Lockheed L.1049 N6212C. An ex-American Airlines airliner, N762Z c/n 44922, of Universal Airlines of Willow Run, Michigan, was making an approach to land at Philadelphia during a storm on 2 July 1968 when the undercarriage failed. It was written off and the remains sold. Another Eastern DC-7B, N815D c/n 45084, crashed on 30 November 1962, when the pilot missed the runway during an approach in bad weather at Idlewild, New York, killing twenty-five people. Outside the United States, an ex-Eastern DC-7B, SE-ERC c/n 45088 on lease to Turk Hava Yollari – THY – of Istanbul, was damaged on landing at Munich on 20 January 1958, when the nosewheel collapsed. It was beyond economic repair; the engines were removed and abandoned. HC-AIP c/n 45194 ex-Continental, of Area – Aerovias Ecuatorianas de Aviación of Quito, Ecuador – was written off during March 1966, when it taxied into a ditch at Miami, causing the main spar to break.

The Swedish Red Cross used the DC-7B for relief work in the bush fires of Africa in the late 1960s. An ex-American DC-7B, SE-ERP c/n 45401, went to the Red Cross early in 1969. On 5 June it was shot down over Eket, Biafra, by Nigerian Air Force fighters, and it crashed in flames killing the crew of four. Another ex-American airliner, SE-ERO c/n 45402, was also operated by the Swedish Red Cross, as was SE-ERR c/n 45404.

There were several instances of the DC-7B having undercarriage problems. On 21 August 1968 an ex-Eastern DC-7B, SE-ERK c/n 45451, was damaged by anti-aircraft fire over Nigeria whilst assisting in relief work in Biafra. It was operated by Transair of Sweden. A horrific accident on 8 February 1965 involved Eastern DC-7B N849D c/n 45456 when it crashed into the sea off Jones Beach, New York, only eleven minutes after take-off from Kennedy Airport. A total of eighty-four passengers and crew were killed, and the accident was attributed to the pilot losing control in a violent manoeuvre to avoid an air-to-air collision.

Some DC-7Bs and a few DC-7s were operated by numerous travel clubs which grew up in the United States as the airliner became surplus to the major airlines requirements. These clubs took advantage of the exceptionally cheap long-range aircraft made available, and the financial advantages afforded by this type of very low-overhead operation.

The Seven Seas

The DC-7C was developed by the Douglas Aircraft Company to meet the requirement of Pan American for an aircraft capable of scheduled non-stop trans-Atlantic services in either direction. The DC-7B could not fly non-stop westbound against average winds. The new DC-7C became the world's first truly long-range commercial transport, and so fully deserved its name 'Seven Seas', derived from its numeric designation within the Douglas Commercial series. To achieve the required range, the wing span was increased by 10 ft by adding sections between the fuselage and the inner nacelles. This modification not only enabled the total fuel load to be increased to 7,825 gallons, but also moved the engines further outboard to reduce noise and vibration in the passenger cabins, a very important consideration for long-distance flights. Furthermore, the fuselage length was further increased by 42 inches, making a total of 112 ft 3 in, as compared to only 93 ft 10 in for the original Douglas DC-4. Maximum gross take-off weight was increased to 143,000 lb and all DC-7Cs were powered by 3,400 hp R-3350-18EA-1 radials driving four-bladed propellers. It was this more powerful version of the R-3350 which was the impetus for Douglas producing the longer range version of the DC-7, one which would be capable of operating across the North Atlantic on the profitable London to New York route non-stop with a full load under all but the most adverse head winds. In the extra 5 ft wing sections the extra fuel tankage increased the still air range to over 5,600 miles. A taller fin and rudder were developed to cope with the extra power.

The DC-7C moved the balance on the North Atlantic still further towards Douglas aircraft. Pan American put the aircraft into service on the oceanic routes on 1 June 1956, but TWA were not able to introduce the Lockheed L.1649 'Starliner' on the ocean services until 1 July 1957. Although the DC-7 series in general had higher seat-mile costs than the DC-6B, this was less marked in the DC-7C, and was more than compensated for by other features. The Lockheed Starliner, on the other hand,

Today at least four ex-BOAC DC-7C airliners survive, two as fire bombers in the USA. Depicted is G-AOIA c/n 45111/727 of BOAC delivered on 23 October 1956. The fleet of ten were all named Seven Seas. The airliner was sold on 25 May 1964, being flown by several operators in the USA. (British Airways)

though having a greater range, was markedly less economic, and only Air France, Lufthansa and TWA bought it.

The first Douglas Seven Seas, N70C c/n 44872, first flew on 20 December 1955. It was sold via Pan American to Panair do Brasil as PP-PDO '*Bartolomeo Bueno da Silva*' on 12 June 1957. On 1 November 1961, whilst on a landing approach to Recife, Brazil, the DC-7C hit a hill, killing forty-nine people.

A total of 121 DC-7Cs were produced for thirteen airlines, including a new customer for the Douglas Aircraft Company – British Overseas Airways Corporation. To cover the hiatus caused by the long delay in production of Bristol 'Britannia' 312, BOAC purchased ten DC-7Cs. The other principal customers were Pan American, who ordered twenty-five, KLM with an order for fifteen, Scandinavian Airline System with fourteen, Northwest also with fourteen and Sabena with ten.

The scene at Copenhagen on 24 February 1957 for the inaugural flight of DC-7C LN-MOD Guttorm Viking *to Tokyo via Anchorage, Alaska. With c/n 44930/717 it was delivered to SAS on 25 September 1956 and was broken up at Kastrup Airport, Copenhagen, in April 1968.* (SAS)

Polar Route

The DC-7Cs carried the brunt of the North Atlantic traffic from 1956/7 until the introduction of the Boeing 707 and Douglas DC-8 in 1959/60. The 'Seven Seas' era also saw a marked expansion in airline activity over the North Pole routes, with SAS – commencing the first true 'over the pole' service on 24 February 1957, bringing Tokyo only 30 hours away from Copenhagen. The first SAS DC-7C was OY-KNA c/n 44926 '*Brage Viking*', delivered on 16 August 1956. Pan Am introduced the DC-7C on a Los Angeles–San Francisco–London service on 11 September 1957, preceding a similar service by TWA 'Starliners' by just three weeks. KLM introduced an Amsterdam–Anchorage–Tokyo–Biak service on 1 November 1958. Polar services were also introduced by Japan Air Lines, KLM and Pan American on its west coast routes from the United States to London. It must be stated that the DC-7C's main claim to fame was its ability on non-stop long-range commercial operations across the United States, over the

Atlantic and Pacific and over the North Pole. The great appeal of its services forced several foreign flag carriers to switch from 'Super Constellations' to the 'Seven Seas'. Alitalia, Sabena, SAS and Swissair, all Douglas DC-6B operators, also made the change.

With the arrival, unexpected popularity and rapid technical improvement of the new turbojets, the lifespan of the DC-7s was short by comparison with those of the DC-6 variants, which were more economical and often more reliable even in their old age. However, on the secondhand market, DC-7Cs were much more sought-after than DC-7s or DC-7Bs, although fewer were available initially. There were trade-ins, but some were scrapped fairly early, in spite of low hours on the airframe, even after their conversion to long-haul freighter and other supplementary roles. By March 1960, ten of the Pan American fleet of DC-7Cs had been converted by Lockheed Aircraft Services to an all-cargo layout, with strengthened floors, large freight doors and special handling systems. Many more conversions followed. During 1959/60 the Douglas Aircraft Company converted some twenty-five DC-7s, DC-7Bs and DC-7Cs for major US and foreign airlines, including two DC-7Cs each for BOAC, KLM, Alitalia and Japan Air Lines. Many others were partly converted by Douglas – doors and floors – and partly by the airlines themselves and some were designed as quick convertibles known as 'QCs'.

Among the unusual tasks applied to the DC-7s series were those converted for US Forest Service contracts as aerial fire fighters, fitted with external tanks able to carry up to 3,000 gallons of fire-retardant mixtures. The possibility of using the DC-7 for this role had been considered much earlier in its history, when the crew of the prototype jettisoned 1,300 gallons of water ballast at Palm Springs Airport, California, and discovered that it spread over an area 200 ft wide and a mile or so long. The Douglas Aircraft Company, seeing the potential, modified another DC-7 with special tanks and other equipment for demonstrations. However, at this time, a DC-7 was too expensive to be put to such seasonal and relatively limited use, and plans came to nothing. Later, when the type became surplus to airline requirements, it joined the fire-tanker fleets at attractive secondhand prices.

A look at the current (1991) listing of US Forest Service contract fire bombers reveals at least three DC-7Cs in service as aerial tankers in the United States. These are N90804, c/n 45116 ex-G-AOIF of BOAC; N97342 c/n 45215, ex-SE-CCF of SAS; and N90802 c/n 45112, another ex-BOAC DC-7C, G-AOIB. Three other DC-7Cs were heavily modified for flights by Union de Transports Aériens of Paris, in support of French nuclear test work in the Pacific. An ex-Swissair DC-7C, HB-IRK c/n 45061, became F-ZBCA and two ex-Cie de Transport Aériens Intercontinentaux DC-7Cs from the French independent carrier – F-BIAQ c/n 45367, which became F-ZBCB, and F-BIAR c/n 45446, which became F-ZBCC in April 1964 – were involved. One source indicates the French Air Force operated the aircraft. Later, in 1966, these same three aircraft were again modified and flown by UTA for the tracking and observation of satellite launching and re-entry, using special radar and other sophisticated equipment.

With a flight crew of six and a similar number of technicians, the DC-7Cs included rest facilities and accommodation for twenty passengers. They had a maximum endurance of approximately twenty hours at 240 knots and were operated from an air base in French Polynesia. To suit the new role, the aircraft were fitted with a large radome above the centre of the fuselage, with another radome beneath the forward fuselage, a Doppler radar beneath the rear fuselage, and additional direction-finding equipment on the port wing-tip.

Highly accurate clocks and timing equipment were installed in the fuselage while five visual observation stations were provided on each side of the fuselage, fore and aft of the wings, and one on top. The crew consisted of two pilots, a navigator, a radio operator and two flight engineers. Six technicians operated the special tracking and timing equipment. As a result of these many modifications, the small fleet had an empty weight of 37,334 lb and a maximum weight of 64,863 lb. The first flight of the modified DC-7C, which became designated DC-7 AMOR – Avion de Mésure d'Observation au Réceptacle – was made on 14 September 1966. They were initially test-flown by personnel from the Centre d'Essais en Vol – CEV – for the benefit of the Centre d'Etudes Spatiales – CES. Later the aircraft were operated by the Groupement Aérien Mixte GAM 85 from Tahiti-Hao in French Polynesia. They appeared in French Air Force markings using their Douglas c/ns as the fin serial as follows: 45061 coded 'CA', 45367 'CB' and 45446 'CC'.

The last aircraft in the DC-7C series to be delivered was PH-DSR c/n 45549, which was handed over to KLM on 10 December 1958. It was named '*Barents Zee*'/Barents Sea and was traded back to Douglas on 24 October 1962. It was later sold as N904ME and operated in the United States by various owners. For the record, the last Douglas Commercial propliner built, and the one with the highest c/n, was 45564, a DC-6B YU-AFB delivered to Jugoslovenski Aerotransport of Belgrade, Yugoslavia on 17 November 1958. In 1966 this airliner went to the Yugoslav government.

Many 'Seven Seas' had a fantastic history, being sold to a wide variety of operators in all corners of the globe, employed on an equally wide range of tasks. A good example is the fifth DC-7C, c/n 44875 ex-N733PA of American, which was converted to DC-7CF configuration during 1959, re-registered N7334 in 1965 and sold to Liberty Air Inc. on 21 May 1965. On 20 February 1966 it became G-ATOB with Trans World Leasing Ltd and was operated in the United Kingdom by Air Meridian, named '*Lady Thelma*'. It was sold in the USA in late 1967 and in January 1969 registered as VR-BCT with ARCO Bermuda, owned by Hank Wharton. On 26 July 1970 it made a belly-landing at Abidjan, on the Ivory Coast, and was written off.

Substantial fleets of DC-7 aircraft were acquired secondhand by such cargo operators as Riddle, renamed Airlift in 1964, and Saturn. Many were converted freighters and used on US military contracts around the globe in support of the US Armed Forces. One such DC-7CF was c/n 44926, ex-SAS N4059K, whose landing gear collapsed on 30 December 1966 on take-off from Saigon in South Vietnam; the aeroplane was destroyed by fire, but fortunately there were no fatalities. A DC-7CF of Universal, operating a US military cargo flight contract, crashed on final approach to Cherry Point USMC air station in North Carolina on 27 September 1968, again with no casualties. It was registered N7466 c/n 45090 and was ex-Pan American.

There is no doubt that in both passenger and cargo versions the DC-7C became like the DC-3 before it, the 'workhorse' of the airlines. The 'Seven Seas' had the same wingspan as the DC-4, some thirteen years her predecessor. But she was 8ft longer, had room for thirty more seats, was capable of carrying half as much again payload, twice as fast at altitudes well above 25,000 ft, with a maximum range of 5,000 miles. It was undoubtedly the most luxurious air transport of the day and very, very popular. With inboard engines farther out on the wing, the DC-7C was also the quietest propeller airliner. The pressurised cabin was commodious, bright and colourful with wall-to-wall carpeting, air conditioning and an on-board galley.

Despite all this splendour and its excellent performance qualities, the DC-7C, which went into service in 1956, was soon to have strong competition. The new Boeing jetliner was no longer a paper design, the prototype 707 having made its first flight on 15 July 1954, and it was soon to join the Douglas DC-6s and DC-7s in scheduled passenger service. Although early models of the 707 did not have the range of the DC-7s, it was nearly 100 mph faster. Within the United States the Lockheed turboprop 'Electra' was also flying, and for the first time, a foreign-built airliner, the British four-engine turbo-prop Vickers 'Viscount' was also serving the domestic routes, in the livery of Capital Airlines. The new jetliners were the harbingers of airliners of the future, and they had one advantage. Dependent as they were on the thrust available and on aerodynamic design, they seemingly had unlimited speed potential, whereas the propliner had limits when it entered high-speed ranges.

The Douglas Aircraft Company, before turning its attention to the design and development of a jet-powered transport – a must if the Douglas Commercial family was to continue – looked carefully at a proposed propeller-turbine-powered development of the DC-7C which was to have been procured either through production of new aircraft or through the modification of existing airframes. This would have been the DC-7D, powered by four 5,800 esph Rolls-Royce Tyne engines. However, the sudden emergence of the Boeing 707 and the pressure to develop the Douglas DC-8 jetliner rendered the proposed programme obsolete.

Without any doubt, the Douglas DC-6 and DC-7 series were the most successful peacetime piston-engined airliner series. A grand total of 1,042 were built, all at Santa Monica, and comprised one XC-112, 175 DC-6s, 74 civil DC-6As and DC-6Cs, 166 C-118As and R6D-1s, 288 DC-6Bs, 105 DC-7s, 112 DC-7Bs and 112 DC-7Cs. As a comparison the total production of the competitive Lockheed 'Constellation' to the 'Starliner' series was around 850.

Production of the DC-6/7 series continued from 1946 to 1958, almost exactly comparable with the life of the earlier DC-2/3 series, 1934 to 1946. Although the early troubles with the DC-6 added to costs to such an extent that Douglas did not break even until after 300 DC-6 series had been sold, more than this number were produced. Looking back, perhaps the most successful period for the Douglas company was the first two months of 1955, during which no less than seventeen airlines ordered 109 aircraft, comprising 49 DC-6Bs and 60 DC-7 series including 38 DC-7Cs, to bring the Douglas order-book backlog to a record 208 aircraft, worth some $350 million. It is interesting to note that the 1991 US Civil Register of aircraft records no less than 108 DC-4s, 164 DC-6s in the series and 63 DC-7 series all within the United States. Many more are today scattered around the globe, many revenue-earning and still paying tribute in their own way to the successful Douglas Commercial series. After all, the DC-6/7 series did pioneer many new airline routes for the new breed of jet airliners then on the horizon.

Chapter Fourteen
Survivors

Today, many fifty-year-old aircraft are preserved in museums around the world. One might expect that by now the oldest serving Douglas DC-2s and DC-3s would be museum-bound. This is not so.

At Long Beach, California, the Douglas Historical Foundation has carefully restored the seventy-seventh DC-2 built. On 25 April 1987, some fourteen years after it last flew, this DC-2, after careful restoration by Douglas retirees and foundation members, flew again. Now, every two weeks it is flown by FAA-qualified pilots along with fourteen guest passengers. It is a DC-2-118B c/n 1368, delivered as NC14296 to Pan American Airways on 16 March 1935.

In South Carolina resides another veteran DC-2, c/n 1404, a DC-2-142 NC39165 which went into service with the US Navy as R2D-1 BuNo. 9993. Today it is owned by Colgate Darden and despite being in storage will soon fly again. In November 1983 it was shipped to the Netherlands, appearing in KLM livery as PH-AJU for a special commemorative flight to Australia for the fiftieth anniversary of the 1934 air race.

Efforts are being made in the Netherlands and Australia to restore two more examples of the DC-2 to flying standard. The Dutch Dakota Association (DDA) in Schiphol, Amsterdam, has c/n 1288 DC-2-112 NC13738 of Eastern Air Lines, which went to the RAAF as A30-14 'VH-CRH'. The remains were shipped to Amsterdam a few years ago.

The oldest surviving DC-3 is an original DST-144 c/n 1499, the sixth built, delivered to American Airlines as NC16005 on 10 July 1936, as '*Flagship Tennessee*'. It survived the Second World War, serving as a C-49E 42-56092, then returned to American, reconfigured as a DC-3. During 1950 it was purchased by Ozark Airlines being re-registered N133D in 1957. In August 1968, it made its last passenger flight from O'Hare, Chicago, to Atlanta. Ozark sold its last DC-3s, including c/n 1499, to Aviation Academy in Griffin, Georgia. Bob McSwiggon bought the academy in 1972, this including the oldest flying DC-3. By 23 June 1989, c/n 1499 had accumulated 76,586 hours on the airframe. Despite problems with the Wright Cyclone engines, it is anticipated that, with support from spare parts available, this DC-3 will fly for a further five or even ten years.

At the ripe old age of fifty-two, a DC-3-277B c/n 2213, delivered as NC25673 to American Airlines as '*Flagship Big Springs*' on 8 May 1940, has been reborn. It has been completely restored and in like-new condition, it is now the flagship of the Continental Historical Society; and as N25673 it is in Continental Airline livery. It has amassed more than 72,000 flight hours and has flown in the colours of several US airlines. Between 1974 and 1988 it was part of a huge twelve DC-3 fleet operated by Provincetown-Boston Airlines and registered N130PB. Today N25673 is based at Hobby Airport, Houston, Texas.

Meanwhile the society is taking advantage of abundant in-house restoration talent by commencing work on yet another veteran DC-3, N18121, which with possibly 92,000 logged

This US Navy Super DC-3 spent most of its working life flying the airspace in Europe. It first flew on 23 December 1952 arriving in Europe in 1959. Between 1971 and 1973 it was based at NAF Mildenhall, Suffolk, and on retirement from service at Keflavik, Iceland, it was preserved as depicted outside the US Naval air facility. (Ken Ellis)

hours is believed to have more flight time than any other transport aircraft. As a DC-3-201, NC18121 c/n 1997, it was delivered to Eastern Air Lines on 28 October 1937. It returned to Eastern after serving as a C-49G between 1942 and 1944. After post-war service it was bought by Provincetown-Boston Airlines (PBA) on 24 January 1974, and registered N136PB. By 1982 it had flown no less than 85,544 hours.

The first formal recognition that the Douglas DC-3 had at last earned a permanent place in aviation history came in 1952 with the installation of an early Eastern Air Lines DC-3-201, NC18124 c/n 2000 delivered 7 December 1937. The transport had logged a total of 56,758 hours, flying 8½ million miles up to January 1952. It had spent the equivalent of 6½ years in the air. Going to the Smithsonian on 1 May 1953, it later went on display in the magnificent National Air & Space Museum in Washington DC on 1 July 1976, and remains on view today.

North Central Airlines DC-3-201B, NC21728 c/n 2144, was originally delivered to Eastern Air Lines on 19 August 1939, serving the Wisconsin Central before going to North Central Airlines on 16 December 1952. Over a thirteen-year period with Eastern it logged 51,398 hours before being sold for $35,000. Up to April 1965, it flew another 31,634 hours in scheduled airline service, and then logged a further 1,843 hours up to 1975 as a VIP aircraft for North Central.

During its long career it is estimated that N21728 had 136 engine changes, its landing gear replaced 550 times, and that it used over 25,000 sparking plugs to burn 8 million gallons of fuel. This DC-3 taxied more than 100,000 miles and carried 260 million passengers during its thirty-six years of service. It spent more than 9½ years in the air and covered 12 million miles – the

Beautifully restored to its original wartime livery, DC-4 N76AU ex-C-54 42-72442 c/n 10547 is for sale by Aero Union. It is named Santa Monica Maid. *This transport had a chequered career during World War II being delivered to the Royal Air Force in 1945 as KL977 and returned to the US Navy in 1946 as BuNo.91994.* (MAP)

equivalent of twenty-five trips to the moon and back. At 185 mph, each one-way moon trip would take roughly fifty-four days. In June 1975, N21728 was donated to the Henry Ford Museum at Dearborn, Michigan, where it is still on display.

Credit for the preservation and restoration of DC-3A-197 N16070 c/n 1910, the second oldest DC-3 surviving and flying, must go to Larry Ray of Tucson, Arizona. Today it has accumulated over 74,000 hours. Acquired by Larry Ray in November 1971, just forty-five years after it was manufactured at Santa Monica for United Air Lines, it was carefully restored, involving many hours of back-breaking work and the expenditure of many thousands of dollars. It was test flown in United Air Lines livery in November 1986. During 1990 it was auctioned at Santa Monica, being purchased by Evergreen International Airlines of McMinnville, Oregon.

This Pratt & Whitney Twin Wasp-powered DC-3A was the first of a small batch of four for United Air Lines with c/n 1910/1/2/3. Two of the four survive today, with c/n 1911 ex-NC16071 now registered EI-AYO and in storage with the Science Museum at Wroughton airfield, Swindon, Wiltshire, since 28 November 1978.

Today many of the older established airlines are searching for original DC-3s, preferably transports which served with them at one time, to be restored and brought back into service for promotional services. The retired chairman of Piedmont Airlines, Tom Davis, promoted the idea of a DC-3 in answer to many requests to demonstrate at air shows, dedication of airport and terminal buildings, employee functions, etc. Any airline finds it upsetting to its operational programme to divert an expensive airliner to a promotional activity. With 14,100 hours on the airframe the current Piedmont DC-3, registered N44V c/n 9914, was bought originally on 21 February 1948, having been built as a C-47A-40-DL.

Other US airlines currently reviving the DC-3 include Delta and American. The ideal candidate for the huge American Airlines museum project would naturally be the DST-217A N139D c/n 2165 delivered to American Airlines as NC21752 on 30 August 1939 as '*Flagship Memphis*'. The current owner, Lee Schaller, purchased two DC-3s, N139D and N74KW c/n 7317, in a bankruptcy sale at Las Vegas and had both airliners flown to Schellville, Sanoma, California. In late 1991 the author visited the owner and saw N139D, which is patiently awaiting restoration.

Seen by the author parked at Atlanta in November 1991 was DC-3 N86553 c/n 4715, which served with Delta Air Lines from 1946 to March 1963. It could be a prospective candidate for restoration and promotional use by Delta.

Due for its official opening late 1992 is the American Airlines C.R. Smith Museum, a projected 24,000 sq ft area in Chicago; it will feature historical and contemporary exhibits inspired by Cyrus Rowlett Smith, the 'father' of the airline, who passed away in 1989. The $8.7 million museum complex will include a hundred-seat large-screen theatre, the lobby of which will be modelled after an airport check-in area. A restored DC-3 in American Airlines livery, donated by Grey Eagles, will be displayed outside the museum.

Today over 200 Douglas DC-4 'Skymasters', over 200 Douglas DC-6 transports and over fifty Douglas DC-7s survive. They are employed on various tasks including crop-spraying, fire tankers, cargo transports, and are to be seen working in all corners of the globe. At least two ex-BOAC Douglas DC-7C airliners are employed on fire-bombing duties in the United States. The Douglas DC-4/C-54 is appearing preserved in US military air-base museums, whilst both the DC-4 and DC-6 are to be found preserved and in use as cafes and night clubs or as gate guardians.

At least three Russian-built Li-2 transports of TAROM – Transporturile Aeriene Romane of Bucharest have been preserved and used as cafes, these include YR-TAB, YR-TAF and YR-TAM. The airline was formed in 1954 and took over the Li-2 airliners operated by TARS – Transporturi Aerienne Romana – Sovietica Soc De. (MAP)

When Donald Wills Douglas Sr passed away on 1 February 1981, the chairman of the board of the McDonnell Douglas Corporation, Stanford McDonnell, wrote this epitaph, which summed up the effect one man had on the world:

He was one of the most famous pioneers of the early days of aviation. His design genius gave birth to the world-renowned DC or Douglas Commercial line, which revolutionised the airline business. Mr Douglas contributed mightily to the victory in World War Two. After the war, he led the way once again in building fleets for the airlines and in pioneering space flight. Our nation has lost a great leader, and a man with unparalleled vision.

Footnote: On 3 July 1993 American Airlines opened the C.R. Smith Museum in Dallas, Texas, with veteran DC-3-227B NC21798 c/n 2202 '*Flagship Knoxville*' as the centre piece. It had been completely refurbished which took twelve months, and was flown from Tulsa to Fort Worth/Dallas airport before continuing its journey by road. After 53 years service with many owners it had accumulated in excess of 50,000 flying hours.

As a fitting tribute to the aircraft and airlift personnel who delivered food to the beleagured city of Berlin in 1948, two Douglas workhorse transports are permanently on display at Tempelhof, Berlin. The C-54 Skymaster is 45-557 c/n 36010 and the C-47 Skytrain 45-951 c/n 34214 the latter ex-G-BLFL of Aces High, Duxford. (USAF)

Appendix
Technical Data

Type	DC-1	DC-2	DC-3	DC-3S	DC-3 Turbo	DC-4E
First flight	1 July 1933	11 May 1934	17 Dec 1935	23 June 1949	27 Aug 1949	7 June 1938
Wing span – ft/in	85 0	85 0	95 0	90 0	95 0	138 3
metres	25.91	25.91	28.96	27.43	28.96	42.14
Length – ft/in	60 0	62 0	64 6	67 9	67 9	97 7
metres	18.29	18.89	19.65	20.75	20.67	29.74
Height – ft/in	16 0	16 4	16 11	18 3	16 11	24 6
metres	4.88	4.97	5.16	5.56	5.16	7.48
Wing area – sq/ft	942	939	987	969	987	2,155
sq/metres	87.515	87.236	91.695	90.023	91.7	200.207
Max t/o weight – lb.	17,500	18,588	28,000	31,000	28,750	66,500
kg.	7,938	8,432	12,701	14,075	13,040	30,164
Max cruise speed – mph	190	185	170	251	240	200
km/hr	306	298	274	401	389	322
Max range – miles	1,000	1,000	1,025	2,500	1,000	2,200
km	1,609	1,609	1,650	4,025	1,850	3,540
Engines	Wright SGR-1820-F3	Various	P&W Twin Wasp SIC3G	Wright R-1820-80	Various	P & W R-2180-SIAI-G
hp	690		1,050	1,475		1,450
Number built	1	198	607	105	Still in production	1
In service	Nil	2	Yes	Yes		Nil

Type	DC-4	DC-4M	ATL-98	DC-5	DC-6	DC-7
First flight	14 Feb 1942	July 1946	21 June 1961	12 Feb 1939	15 Feb 1946	18 May 1953
Wing span – ft/in	117 6	117 6	117 6	78 0	117 6	117 6
metres	35.81	35.81	35.81	23.77	35.81	35.81
Length – ft/in	93 10	93 8	102 7	62 2	100 7	108 11
metres	28.60	28.54	31.27	18.96	30.66	33.2
Height – ft/in	27 6	27 6	29 10	19 10	29 1	28 7
metres	8.38	8.38	9.09	6.04	8.86	8.71
Wing area – sq/ft	1,460	1,460	1,462	824	1,463	1,463
sq/metres	135.639	135.639	135.825	76.55	135.918	135.918
Max t/o weight – lb.	73,000	82,300	72,500	20,000	97,200	122,200
kg.	33,113	37,331	32,885	9,072	44,089	55,429
Max cruise speed – mph	227	289	184	202	328	359
km/hr	365	465	296	325	528	578
Max range – miles	2,500		2,070	1,600	3,340	2,850
km	4,025		3,330	2,575	5,375	4,585
Engines	P & W R-200-3	Merlin 620	P & W R-2000-7M2	Wright Cyclone GR-1820-F62	P & W Double Wasp R-2800	Wright R-3350
hp	1,350	1,725	1,450	900	2,100	3,250
Number built	1,315		21	12	704	338
In service	Yes	Nil	2	Nil	Yes	Yes

Index

Page references in italics refer to illustration captions.